Some people seemed to get all the sunshine,

and some all shadow.

–LOUISA MAY ALCOTT, *Little Women*

Beverly DeAngelis
2020

Praise for *Shadows on the Porch*

Shadows on the Porch delivers a riveting expression of inconceivable events. Beverly De Angelis shares her innermost thoughts through her courageous journey of pain, hurt and shame, delving into the domain of living, loving and coping with mentally ill loved ones. Beverly paints a clear picture of how mental illness impacts lives, while imparting hope for those currently living the nightmare.

–LYNN MOON, mental health advocate and GriefShare facilitator

In *Shadows on the Porch*, Beverly De Angelis shares an extraordinary, personal account of the pain, guilt, and despair associated with living with family members who suffer from mental illness. It is a powerful story of love, hope, and survival. Its reading elicits a critical understanding of the disease and compassion for those afflicted.

–KATHIE POHL, mental health advocate and author of *Mentor—The First 200 Years*

Shadows

on the

Porch

Shadows

on the

Porch

A Cleveland memoir of survival
and three generations of mental illness

BEVERLY DE ANGELIS

Wednesday's Child Press

SHADOWS ON THE PORCH: A Cleveland memoir of survival and three generations of mental illness

Copyright © 2019 Beverly De Angelis

Photos copyright © 2019 Beverly De Angelis unless otherwise noted

ON THE FRONT COVER: The author at age three

ON THE BACK COVER: The author's childhood home on Frank Avenue in Cleveland, Ohio

The stories in this book reflect the author's recollection of events. Some names, locations, dates, and identifying characteristics have been changed to protect the privacy of those depicted. Dialogue has been re-created from memory.

Cover design, editing, and formatting by Janine Kuestner

Published by Wednesday's Child Press

Willoughby, Ohio, USA

Printed in the United States of America

FIRST EDITION

ISBN-13 978-0-578-54043-6

This book is dedicated to my five loving children.
It is also written in memory of my beautiful and
misunderstood mother, Angelina.

ACKNOWLEDGEMENTS

This book began simply as a way for me to share my life's story with my children. It would have remained as a small project without the invaluable influence of several people. To the following, I owe my sincere appreciation.

To Donna Peltz, for grammatical and editorial suggestions, for your commitment to my cause of bringing mental illness awareness to the public, and for the generous giving of your time to help me complete this project. You encouraged me to share my story with a wider audience and helped open my eyes to the possibility that my story could make a difference in the lives of other people. Our decades-long bond is deep, and was forged through shared trials and tribulations. Through our conversations, you have helped give me so much insight into myself. I am deeply grateful for your irreplaceable friendship. I'm so glad that we have proved the naysayers wrong!

To Linda McGraw, Ph.D., managing director of the Organization for Psychological Health, for helping me find some peace and light in the dark places of my journey. Without your purposeful counseling, I believe that I would not have examined my life and written this book.

To Rakesh Ranjan, M.D., for writing a powerful forward in praise of my work, contributing the valuable "lessons to be learned," and delving into my psychological conflict—the "Why?" that appears in the afterword. Thank you for your validation. I am privileged and honored. *Namaste.*

To Roger Sparhawk, M.D., for reading *Shadows on the Porch* and for writing the powerful and compelling summary that appears on the back cover. I am honored.

To Janine Kuestner, for editing, formatting, and redesigning this volume. You have been a breath of fresh air. You have the special ability to help me take a step back from my deeply personal writing and view it with fresh eyes. In the short time I have known you, you have endeared yourself to me.

To my dear friend Adrienne Lund, for listening to me read, chatting with me, day or night, and providing your whole-hearted support.

To Lynn Moon, for your friendship and captivating praise that appears inside the cover. You are my go-to source for information on Extended Housing, Inc. and never fail to brighten my day. Without you, I might actually have to check my email.

To Kathie Pohl, for offering the praise found inside the front cover, for your encouragement, and for helping to edit my book. I am forever grateful for your help and friendship, and I am in awe of how much you give of yourself to so many worthy causes.

To my readers and cheerleaders—Dennis Barstow, "Bebe" Crone, Gayle Cunningham, Jennie Femec, May Hill, Dorothy Jankowski, Erwin Jay, Robin Jay, Bob Oblocki, Judy Parmenter, Ed Peltz, Donna Ralston, Dave Roman, Amanda Swiggum, and Robbyn White—for providing feedback and encouragement.

To my dear friends and colleagues from the organizations I have served, for your kind words of encouragement.

To computer geniuses Bill Brumbough and Chris Winney, for technical support that made the production of this book possible.

To my final beta readers—Linda Evans, Georgianna Garry, Nancy Golinski, Sue Huff, Edwin and Patricia Koporc, Nancy Rispoli, Pauline Rittenhouse, Sheila Sirl, and Tari Trebotich—your corrections and encouragement were the final push I needed to cross the finish line.

To those contributors I may have forgotten to mention, my apologies.

To my loving family members, my parents, grandparents, aunts, uncles, cousins, husbands, children, and other loves, for providing me with lessons to learn and a purposeful life. Without you there would have been no story to tell. Because of you, my life has mattered. I will always love you.

FOREWORD

Shadows on the Porch is the story of a daughter, wife, and mother fated to battle the trials and tribulations of living and coping with loved ones afflicted with severe mental illness. Beverly De Angelis displays extraordinary courage and candor in depicting, with an unusual ease, the interlocking stories of immense emotional sufferings, shattered dreams, and intrigues of unimaginable proportions.

The poignancy of Beverly's story grips you from the first chapter and carries you through to the end. Her intuitive style and keen sense of observation provide us incisive insights into the inner, often-chaotic worlds of the severely mentally ill. These insights are useful to both the professionals involved in treating this population and lay people, including family members of the mentally ill.

Shadows on the Porch, so far as Beverly's story is concerned, affirms the adage "fact is better than fiction." I would add that fact is definitely more intriguing than fiction. Her story puts into focus the fear, shame, dejection, anger, horror, guilt, and self-pity that family members of the mentally compromised have to deal with daily.

Even though the storyline of *Shadows on the Porch* is mostly rooted in the '60s, the '70s, and the '80s, decades later, our society and culture continue to struggle with the same challenges of recognizing and treating mental illness. In this vein, her book is a stark reminder that we must continue our best efforts to overcome these challenges and obstacles. Our efforts to destigmatize mental illness need more vigor and determination.

In the end, this book tells a story of indomitable and indestructible human spirit. It's the story of a woman who overcame and survived indescribable suffering and loss while loving family members ailing from schizophrenia.

This courageous book is for everyone who cares about and wants to learn more about the impact of severe mental illness on families and our society.

–RAKESH RANJAN, M.D., president and CEO, Charak Center for Health and Wellness, executive medical director, Charak Clinical Research Center

CHILDHOOD

CAST OF CHARACTERS

THE DE ANGELIS FAMILY

Grandfather Mario – My paternal grandfather, the patriarch of the De Angelis family

Grandmother Maria Conti – My paternal grandmother

Baba Rose Novak – Mario's landlady and companion, and mother to Paul and Elsie

Carlos – My father

Uncle Dom (Dominic) – My father's younger brother, married to Aunt Elsie, Uncle Paul Novak's sister

Donna and Ted – My cousins, Uncle Dom and Auntie Elsie's children

Uncle Ted (Theodore) – My father's youngest brother

Jean – My father's younger sister

THE MARTINELLI FAMILY

Grandpa Vincenzo – My maternal grandfather, the patriarch of the Martinelli family

Adriana – Vincenzo's first wife and the mother of their four daughters

Grandma Caroline – Vincenzo's second wife

Aunt Beatrice – My mother's older sister

Angelina – My mother

Auntie Sue (Assunta) – My mother's younger sister

Auntie Julia – My mother's youngest sister, married to Uncle Paul Novak, Auntie Elsie's brother

Brad and Bobby – My cousins, Auntie Julia and Uncle Paul's children

1

SHADOWS ON THE PORCH

When I was four and a half years old, my mother tried to kill me.

My parents and I were living in the four rooms on the third floor of my grandfather's house on the East Side of Cleveland, Ohio. The house had been home to my grandfather and his family since 1913. It was in this house that he raised my mother and her sisters and withstood the Great Depression of the '30s.

When the '40s arrived, Grandpa Vincenzo converted the attic of the house into a rentable flat with a large kitchen, one bedroom, a bathroom, and a sitting room. Dark paint and dark wallpaper covered the walls. Each room had only one large, narrow window. Cross ventilation was never a consideration, nor was natural sunlight. Our accommodations were sparse and uncomfortable and since I had outgrown my crib, I slept on a large, hard, rough brown sofa.

It had been an unseasonably hot and humid day for early June. The penetrating rays of the sun had beaten down on the asphalt-shingled roof all day long, making the air inside the small six-by-eight sitting room stale and the temperature unbearable. An adjustable screen had been placed under the window sash in an attempt to let fresh air enter.

Bolted to the exterior of the house, in front of and beneath this window, was a fire escape. As the sun changed position in the sky, the railings from the horizontal steel platform cast rectangular shadows on the wood siding and walls in the room.

It was approaching midnight when loud noises jolted me from my sleep.

I sat up and rubbed my eyes. The familiar daytime shadows were gone. The dim light from the streetlamp below created eerie images on the brown, flowered wallpaper.

I made my way down the hall to the kitchen. *What is happening?* Although I was afraid, my curiosity prevailed and I continued. With each step I took, the noises became louder and louder.

Once I could see Mommy, I immediately stopped. She was slamming doors, smashing dishes, and dumping drawers and the contents of cupboards onto the floor. *What is she doing?*

Suddenly, she looked up and caught me watching her. Her sullen stare frightened me. I couldn't move. *She looks so different.*

Mommy's long, black curly hair was pinned behind her head. Perspiration dripped from her forehead and ran down her face. The outside corners of her eyebrows and bow-shaped lips were contracted in anger. Lunging toward me, she seized my arm and dragged me across the floor into the kitchen. Her hands felt cold and clammy.

"Ouch! You're hurting me! Daddy, help me!" But he wasn't home to hear my cries.

"This will teach you." Slap…slap. Again and again. My ears rang and my face hurt.

She dragged me to the sink. Tears spilled down my cheeks as she began shaking me like a rag doll. My head hit a cupboard door. Blood oozed from the wound.

I tried to grab Mommy's arm. She tightened her grip on my shoulder. With her free hand, she held my long hair, and yanked it several times, forcing my neck and head back.

An open bottle of laundry bleach sat on the countertop. She reached for it and began pouring the nasty liquid over my mouth screaming, "Drink it!"

2

I knew better. Bleach was poison.

Terrified, I shut my eyes and mouth with all my might. *Help me!* The last thing I recall is that my nose, mouth, chin, and neck felt like they were on fire.

I woke up in Grandma Caroline's arms, aching and black and blue, but alive. The warmth of Grandma Caroline's arms and the gentle to-and-fro motion of the large rocker eventually restored my sense of calm.

Grandpa Vincenzo had heard the loud disturbance from his bedroom on the first floor. The ruckus woke him from a sound sleep. He knew that his son-in-law was working late and he had no reason to believe that his sweet, loving daughter, Angelina, was responsible for the noises that he heard. He feared someone had broken in and called the police.

The policemen arrived and removed me from my mother's grasp. They carried me downstairs to my grandparents' suite and took Mommy to the police station, then to the hospital.

After my physical bruises healed, one nagging question remained: *Why did my mommy change?*

Her rage was totally baffling and confusing to me. *I must have made her angry. Mommy doesn't love me anymore.*

Before that night, she had never given me reason to doubt that she loved me. Mommy would smile at the mere glimpse of me, calling, "Beverly Ann, come here." I would run into her open arms. She would kiss my forehead, my cheeks, my nose, and sometimes even my arms. She would never scold me.

She would patiently instruct me, saying, "Beverly, take care of your toys. Put them away. That's why you have a toy box."

"Beverly, throw the candy wrapper in the trash basket."

From the time I'd awake in the morning, Mommy and I had a routine. After washing my face, arms, and hands in the bathroom, we would move to the kitchen and she would brush my hair.

I'd squirm and pull away from her as she worked through the tangles and knots. "Ow!" But Mommy found a clever way to make

3

me stay still. She would place a chair in front of the window that faced the backyard. I could see a tall, leafy buckeye tree with conical clusters of white flowers on branches that extended to the sky. Occasionally, a flock of red-winged blackbirds would fly past the window. Sparrows would often casually perch on the branches closest to the window. I delighted in watching the playful, carefree way the birds fluttered from branch to branch as they sang their joyful song. Mommy still pulled my hair when she brushed, but I didn't care. These engaging little birds would capture my attention.

If the birds didn't appear, Mommy pretended to discover bright copper coins hidden within my tangled hair.

"Pennies!" What a delightful surprise. I would save my precious treasure in an empty coffee can.

Before noon, Mommy would have dressed me in a white ruffled pinafore that she had washed, starched, and ironed the day before. She would polish my white sandals and secure them to my feet. I was ready to go.

In the morning, I would watch her spread yummy peanut butter and grape jelly on thin slices of toasted Italian bread. She would quarter each sandwich.

"Beverly, how many pieces do we have to eat?"

"Eight, Mommy."

Hand in hand, Mommy and I would walk down the two, twelve-step staircases and exit through the backdoor. Swinging our arms, we would stroll down Frank Avenue, past St. Mary's Catholic Church, and across the boulevard to Wade Park. Our destination was the Cleveland Museum of Art.

The scenery would change dramatically once we were across Euclid Avenue—no buildings or homes, no streets to cross, no cars or buses—just lush grass, beautiful trees, a lagoon, and brightly colored flowers. It was a heavenly place to escape to from the confinement of our four dismal rooms.

When I became tired, we would sit on one of the park benches in front of the Wade Park Lagoon. Here we would eat our lunch and watch the white swans float effortlessly upon the crystal-clear water, mirroring the clouds above us adrift in the sky.

We would enter the stately granite and marble building by way of

The Cleveland Museum of Art, 1940. Negative 19242F, Cleveland Museum of Art Archives.
Frequent childhood visits to the Cleveland Museum of Art had a lasting impact on my life. I still have a great appreciation for art and beauty. I go there to escape the outer world, and it remains a haven for me.

the domed entrance. We would idle about the Armor Court and move leisurely along into the courtyard, a beautiful room inside the museum where leafy plants lived and trees grew. It housed a pond filled with live water lilies, Greek and Roman statues, and a fountain. We would sit on a marble bench admiring the beauty before us, listening to the gurgling sounds of the water as it jetted from the fountain.

My favorite statue in the museum was the Turtle Baby—a bronze replica of a whimsical nude child holding two turtles, one in each hand. I would take one look at naked toddler and extend my hands and arms in awe, wide-eyed and smiling with delight. Then I would cover my eyes, shaking my head as the giggles would bubble out, saying, "You're a naughty child. Shame on you!"

The museum guard would smile, give me a stern look, and place his index figure to his lips. "*Sh.*"

Before we would leave the museum, I would grab Mommy by the hand, and pull her along with me to the wishing well. I would stand on my tiptoes to peer over the edge at my reflection in the mirror at the bottom. Those pretty pennies my mother gave me made the most satisfying, "Ker-plunk!" sound as I would toss them, one by one, into the water and watched them flip and spin on the way down.

This was the before—a time of peace and contentment. A time when Mommy was good, loving, and *normal*. Now would always be the after, and Mommy had been changed forever. Mommy had schizophrenia.

My mother's breakdown dominated the conversation around the dinner table, but only when my father wasn't around. Any time it came up, I wanted to run and hide. It hurt to hear it over and over again. I sometimes thought that if I could just hide long enough, she would change back.

It was during those dinner table conversations that I heard Grandpa Vincenzo speak about the questions the neighbors would ask him. They would come over while he was cutting the hedges or raking the lawn, saying, "I saw the police at your house. What happened? Why did Angelina leave with the police?"

Grandpa Vincenzo, like everyone else, had been shocked by his daughter's bizarre behavior, asking Grandma Caroline, "Why did my daughter act so *pazzo*, crazy? How could a *figlia mia*, daughter of mine, act like that?"

Auntie Sue, my mother's younger sister, was living with my grandparents at that time and she wasn't afraid to share her disbelief at her sister's change.

"Angelina has everything: beauty, talent, love, and a darling daughter. Why did this happen to her? She must have done something wrong to deserve this!"

It was difficult for Sue to follow in the footsteps of Angelina. Family and friends were constantly comparing the two Martinelli girls. People pointed out the sisters' similarities: the perfect hairline, a widow's peak, the dark black hair, and deep-set brown eyes. They were much more alike in appearance than their other two sisters.

Everyone agreed that Angelina was the most beautiful of all the sisters. In fact, she had been voted "Most Beautiful Italian-American Girl in Cleveland." Sue heard others rave about Angelina's beauty all the time: a heart-shaped face, huge brown eyes, bow-shaped upper lip, an exquisitely chiseled upturned nose, and volumes of curly black hair. No one ever acknowledged Sue's good looks: long wavy hair, an oval face, and pinup girl figure with shapely legs like a ballerina.

What distressed Sue the most about their differences was Angelina's perfectly shaped lips. Whereas Angelina had a bow-shaped upper lip, Sue's thin upper lip had a small birth defect that made it appear pinched together.

Sue wasn't entirely sad about Angelina's breakdown. It turned out that her "perfect" sister wasn't so perfect after all.

Two weeks after Mommy had been admitted to the hospital, she begged my father to bring me along with him when he went to visit. When Daddy told me that Mommy wanted me to come, hope sprang into my heart. *She wants to see me. Mommy loves me. Everything's going to be okay again!*

The following Sunday, Daddy and I set out for City Hospital on Scranton Road in Cleveland. As Daddy's car entered the hospital grounds, thirteen dark red, brick buildings surrounded us. I felt lost in this brick and mortar forest.

The psychiatric unit in the rear of the complex was the tallest, most austere, and foreboding looking-building. It had gothic pillars and the wings of the building seemed to close in on us as we approached.

I looked up and felt smaller than ever. I took a deep breath. *I mustn't tell Daddy how afraid I feel or he won't let me see Mommy.* I was desperate and determined to see her.

Squeezing Daddy's hand for protection, I bit my lip and held back my tears. We walked inside. The interior of the building was even more frightening than the exterior. Poor lighting and strange sounds and smells made the inside dark and scary.

The elevator took us to the seventh floor where our path was blocked by a large thick metal door with a small window. Daddy rang a bell. A woman on the other side of the door looked at us through the small pane of glass. *Click.* As the door swung open, I heard faint cries. *Someone's hurt.* I took hold of Daddy's arm.

The hallway, like the previous one, was narrow and dimly lit. The female attendant led us down the hall, which was lined with doors, each with its own small window.

Midway down the hall, the cries became louder. *That sounds like Mommy.* The attendant stopped and removed a keychain from the pocket of her uniform.

The moment I saw my mother, I understood the reason for her cries—leather restraints tied her wrists to the black, iron bedframe, forcing her arms above her head. Her kimono-covered body twisted and turned as she violently flung her torso and legs about the mattress.

Why is she being punished? Mommy reminded me of the neighbor's puppy. A few weeks before it had been chained outside for wetting the carpet. It had cried incessantly as it fought to free itself.

Mommy panted and gasped for air. Then, in a staccato-like speech pattern, pausing between words to catch her breath, she shouted to my father, "YOU...youuu...son...ofa...BITCH! Get me out of here!" A tirade of gibberish and obscenities followed her demand.

Daddy's face reddened. Beads of perspiration formed on his forehead. He ran his hands through his wavy black hair and then balled his hands into tight fists. He looked as if he was preparing for a prizefight, but quickly regained his composure.

A sullen and disapproving look came across his handsome face, and then his large, deep-set brown eyes told another story: one of sadness and loss.

I began sobbing. *Mommy is as upset today as she was that night in the kitchen. Why is she tied up? Is she mad at me? What did I do?* At the sight of my distress, Daddy quickly lifted me up into his arms and we left.

I could not understand that my mother's behavior was not my fault. I felt that, somehow, I was to blame. The undeserved guilt I felt became a negative part of my thinking that remained with me for years.

I wasn't the only one impacted by that incident. Even though he

8

had heard about my mother's breakdown, this was my father's first personal encounter with the degree to which mental illness can change someone's personality. Seeing his beautiful, kind, loving wife suddenly transform into a violent being must have disturbed him. Nothing could have adequately prepared him for what he had witnessed and what was to come.

Back then, the mental healthcare "Rule Book" was being rewritten daily through a process of trial and error. The hospital staff clearly had made a mistake. Someone should have advised my father against bringing such a young child into the facility, or at least checked on my mother's condition before letting us into her room.

After that awful day, the hospital staff members and my father recognized that seeing my mother behave violently caused me stress and anguish. From that day forward, the staff did not permit me to visit.

On Sundays, Daddy would leave me in the care of my grandparents and visit Mommy. I hated being left behind, knowing that I was missing another chance to see her. I would cling to his legs as he tried to leave, crying, "Daddy, Daddy, pleeease take me with you! I want to see Mommy!"

I imagine that my pleas took a toll on him, for Daddy finally devised a plan: I could observe my mother from a distance. I would wait outside the building, next to Daddy's car. We had to park outside the twelve-foot tall chain link fence, which was topped with barbed wire. Alone and frightened, I stood waiting with no hand to hold! Meanwhile, Daddy went inside and up to Mommy's room. He had obtained permission to take my mother out to the seventh-floor porch.

I had to assume the shadowy figures moving their hands in speech were Daddy and Mommy. It was hard to see them. I had to look through the fence, across the courtyard, and through the mesh of the screened-in porch.

Though they were unrecognizable, I waved back and threw kisses to Mommy. All too soon, Mommy's shadow disappeared from sight. After two weeks, my visits from afar were stopped, as my mother was restricted to the ward. There had been another change in her behavior.

9

I overheard my father explaining Mommy's condition to Grandpa Vincenzo, "Angelina looks like a statue. She appears to be frozen in place. She refuses to move for long periods of time. She doesn't want to eat or sleep. The doctors call her condition a catatonic state." I remember hearing my father talk about shock treatments but didn't understand what that meant.

Following the treatments, Daddy questioned her about her violent outbursts, but she had lost all memory of her behavior. The shock treatments helped bring her back in touch with her environment, but it would take time for her to be capable of resuming all of her homemaking duties.

August arrived and Mommy was permitted to return home. The discharge papers indicated her condition as "improved," but she was a quiet, withdrawn, and confused woman, hardly ready for the task at hand—taking care of a child.

In preparation for his daughter's homecoming, Grandpa Vincenzo had moved all our belongings from the third floor to the second floor of his house. That way, he could easily hear what was happening directly above him. He would need to look in on us daily because my father was working long hours.

All too soon, my mother's behavior again changed. She became a nocturnal creature, sleeping throughout the day. At night, she tried to do a few household chores and drank cup after cup of coffee as she chain-smoked cigarettes. Something was wrong.

I could hear Daddy pleading with Mommy, saying, "Angelina, you need your sleep. Your daughter needs your help in the morning. Come to bed. Something is definitely wrong. Why can't you sleep at night? You worry me!"

His once-smiling face now bore a perpetual scowl.

Worrying was not new behavior for Daddy. He had been a worried man before my mother's breakdown. I remember hearing him say to Mommy, "I may have to quit working for my dad. We have no savings, and I don't know what will happen to you if I get drafted." Now his wife's mental state only served to intensify his fears of an uncertain tomorrow for him and his family. In fact, the very future of the "crazy" world in which he lived was uncertain. The United States was preparing for war.

In 1940, Germany conquered France. The United States braced for involvement in the war by passing legislation that required all men ages eighteen to forty-four to register for the draft. Each draft board assigned numbers to the registrants in its district, and then a lottery was held to rank the registrants. A blindfolded Secretary of War reached into a bowl and pulled capsules containing each unlucky number.

Daddy was twenty-five years old. He registered for the draft but maintained his civilian status. His younger unmarried brothers immediately enlisted in the Armed Forces. Dominic joined the United States Army. Ted, the youngest, enlisted in the United States Marines.

Then, after a chain of events in Europe and Japan's attack on Pearl Harbor on December 7, 1941, Americans had no other choice than to enter World War II. Four days later, the United States declared war on Japan, Germany, and Italy.

More men were needed to fight the war, but in 1945 there was a decline in volunteers. My father had managed to remain a civilian, but he feared it would be just a matter of time before his number would be up!

There was one possible loophole: men in certain occupations deemed essential to the war effort were excused so they could continue to do their work at home. Knowing this prompted my father to quit his job at the Central Wholesale Grocery, his father's imported food business, and seek factory work. He took a position with Alcoa, the largest aluminum producer in the U.S.A., hoping it would enable him to receive a deferment.

Personal circumstances, like my father's, carried no weight whatsoever with Uncle Sam. And although aluminum was essential to the war effort, the statistical analysis and timekeeping position Daddy held was not. There would be no exception for him.

In the first week of August 1945, just after Mommy came home, my father was inducted into the United States Army. What would become of his wife and child? He had heavy responsibilities on the home front; his mentally ill wife and young daughter needed care.

Before his departure for San Antonio, Texas, Daddy told me, "Beverly, I have to go away for a while and serve my country. You'll be okay. You're a big girl now. You can take care of yourself and Mommy. If you need anything, you can go to Grandpa and Grandma for help."

Daddy never brought his impending departure up again, and when it actually happened, it was swift—now you see him, now you don't. It was as if a magician had waved his wand, and poof— Daddy disappeared! He left in the middle of the night, without saying goodbye.

The next morning, I opened my parents' bedroom door to see an empty bed with disheveled covers. I continued on to the kitchen, where I saw Mommy drinking coffee. I asked her, "Where's Daddy?"

She stared off into space, a blank look on her face. I had to repeat my question before she finally answered, "He's gone." That was all she said.

I ran back into my room and picked up my rag doll, choking back my tears. I squeezed it tight, imagining I was instead hugging Daddy. I looked through my window, wishing I was the little sparrow perched upon the ugly fire escape so that I could fly away and find my daddy, and whispered a soft, "Goodbye."

At the time of Daddy's departure, Mommy's mental health was very tenuous. Before he left, Daddy also made an attempt to prepare her for his departure.

"Do you understand that I am going to be inducted into the United States Army?"

"Yes."

"Will you co-operate and take care of your child?"

"Yes."

However, in his absence, she continued with her erratic upside-down schedule.

All Mommy wanted to do was sleep. She never gave me directions or asked me if I was hungry. I made my own meals. My breakfast was Kellogg's Corn Flakes covered with milk. Marmalade jelly bread was lunch. At times, all I had to eat was burnt toast covered with peanut butter.

12

Being resourceful and clever, I observed that when my grandfather, one floor below, could hear me coughing excessively, he would soon appear at our door to investigate. "What's wrong?" It was then that I would tell him, "Grandpa, I'm hungry!"

Within minutes, Grandpa Vincenzo would return with a dinner plate of leftovers for me and Mommy. After a few trial runs, I had both Grandpa Vincenzo and Grandma Caroline trained. In fact, by standing on top of a heating vent, I made sure they could hear my cue better. A behavioral psychologist could have taken lessons from me!

In September, Grandpa Vincenzo enrolled me in the kindergarten class at Observation School on East Boulevard. Although he escorted me to school the first day, I was left in my mother's hands from then on. Despite being an exceptionally self-sufficient child, I needed someone to help me choose my clothing and perhaps help me with buttons and zippers.

On my third day of kindergarten, Grandma Caroline was looking out the window when I left for school. She saw me wearing uncoordinated play clothes, mismatched socks, and worn-out shoes with paper-patched soles. She called Grandpa Vincenzo to the window, saying, "Vincenzo, *vieni qui*, come here!"

That September morning, after seeing an unkempt child go out the door, all alone, en route to the highly trafficked boulevard, Grandpa Vincenzo came out to get me. He took hold of my hand and we returned upstairs.

Entering the bedroom, Grandpa Vincenzo called out to my mother, "*Come stai*, how are you? *Ottieni fino*, get up!" No answer. He called out again and again, with no response.

Until then, my grandfather hadn't known that Mommy always slept until noon. Finally, he understood why I looked like a ragamuffin—I had dressed myself. Now, Grandpa Vincenzo taught me how to lay out my clothing the night before school.

Grandpa Vincenzo also helped in another way. With no school buses to transport us, everyone walked to school. I had been able to get there on my own by being resourceful—I had followed the older children. Coming to my rescue, Grandpa Vincenzo walked me to school until I was able to memorize the route for myself.

Winter came, with sub-freezing temperatures, high winds, and lots of snow. Instead of wearing leggings and boots in the snow, I went out barelegged and in street shoes. The zippers on the side of my boots had gotten stuck, and Mommy wasn't aware enough to help me.

I had a wool hat and gloves, but they were often lost beneath the cushions of the sofa. And when I could hear the wind swirling around the house I didn't put a sweater over my cotton dress to keep me warm. This improper dress, along with my diet of cereal, peanut butter, jelly, and toast, made me susceptible to colds and weakened my immune system.

One Monday morning. Grandpa Vincenzo was watching the clock, waiting for me to leave for school. When I didn't appear, he investigated.

The hall door was open. Walking into the kitchen, Grandpa Vincenzo was greeted by an overflowing wastebasket, a sink full of dirty dishes, and a coffee-stained countertop. There was his daughter, Angelina, dressed in a dirty muumuu, sitting on a chair with a blank look on her beautiful face. Her tobacco-stained fingers held a tiny cigarette butt. Her hair looked wild, curls going every which way.

"Angelina, where's *la bambina,* the child?" She made no eye contact. Her voice was low pitched and unrecognizable, as she answered questions asked by voices only she could hear.

I was too sick to get up and ask for help. Grandpa Vincenzo found me, still in pajamas, lying on my bed, the couch, with a raging temperature. He returned to the first floor to call the doctor.

The doctor my grandfather called diagnosed me with pneumonia and placed a large heating pad on my torso to make me sweat the poisons from my body. According to my grandparents, I looked so ill they questioned whether or not I'd survive. When I did, they proclaimed my recovery to be a miracle. My sheer determination had prevailed!

My serious illness illustrated to Grandpa Vincenzo just how disconnected from reality his daughter was. She lacked the presence of mind to recognize that I was a feverish, incoherent child. She didn't even know that I was there, a sign that she was physically present,

14

but mentally void and unable to care for my needs. No matter what anyone said or did, Mommy sat and stared into space, refusing to move or eat. She had become a person incapable of properly caring for herself, let alone anyone else.

My near-death experience finally forced Grandpa Vincenzo to make arrangements for Mommy's return to the hospital, leaving me solely in the care of my grandparents. While I loved Grandma Caroline, she could never replace my mother. And though I loved Grandpa Vincenzo with my whole heart and soul, he could not replace my father. They had their own routine: Grandpa Vincenzo worked, Grandma Caroline cleaned and cooked, and on occasion, they listened to "Amos and Andy" or "The Shadow" on the radio. It didn't include trips to the museum or play time. I had a few books and my rag doll, Raggedy Ann. Time dragged.

Being separated from my parents was painful. I was just too young and reasoning the "why" was beyond my comprehension. Without my parents, my world moved at a snail's pace. In the final year of the War, an unexpected turn of world events occurred, and once more, my life would change.

Before my father was drafted, Germany had surrendered, ending the war in Europe. The war in the Pacific continued, in spite of the Allies' demands for the unconditional surrender of the Japanese.

In an effort to end the war, the Allied Forces made preparations for the invasion of the Japanese mainland. Later in July, the Allied Manhattan Project successfully detonated an atomic bomb in New Mexico. Our new president, Harry Truman, called for Japan's surrender, threatening devastating air strikes.

On August 6, 1945, the U.S. dropped the world's first atomic bomb on the Japanese city of Hiroshima. Three days later, another A-bomb was dropped on Nagasaki. The devastating power of the bombs destroyed both cities, killing approximately 120,000 people.

Japan quickly surrendered, ending the war. This saved the lives of thousands of American soldiers and prevented the deployment of several thousand more men to foreign soil.

My father was one of the fortunate. Although he had been unable to avoid being drafted, he had been stationed in San Antonio, Texas, and narrowly escaped being deployed. Instead, he was able to stay in the States, and received an honorable discharge.

During the thirteen months of Daddy's absence, my Mommy had remained hospitalized, and our flat on the second-floor had been rented to strangers. I had been living with my grandparents and my mother's sister, Assunta. When I was very young, I couldn't pronounce *Assunta,* so I called her Aunt Soondy, and later, Auntie Sue.

In my mother's absence, I had become greatly attached to Auntie Sue, though she worked day and night. As a little girl, I didn't understand why she didn't stay at home to help Grandma Caroline clean, bake, and sew; or that, like many women, my auntie was part of the at-home war effort.

My Auntie Sue was employed by TRW, a manufacturer of aircraft engine parts. TRW was the eighth-largest military contractor at that time. I remember hearing her proudly proclaim, "I can operate two turret lathes concurrently for two eight-hour shifts."

In September of 1946, we were anxiously anticipating my father's arrival. One Saturday, Grandpa Vincenzo gave Auntie Sue money to purchase new clothes for me. We rode the streetcar to Euclid Avenue in downtown Cleveland.

Auntie Sue held my hand tightly. The sidewalk in front of the Terminal Tower Building was crowded with so many people: young, old, big, and tall. We were engulfed in a sea of pedestrians as we crossed the street to the May Company department store. The smell of roasted coffee and nuts from the nearby factories permeated the downtown air.

The outfit Auntie Sue picked out for me was like something Shirley Temple wore in the movies. It matched an army uniform: a bomber jacket, a T-shirt, a full short skirt, and patent leather shoes.

The night before Daddy's return, Auntie washed and brushed my long hair, just like Mommy used to do. Before I went to bed, she wrapped strands of my straight hair around thin strips of materials. When she took them out in the morning, my hair was filled with curls. Between my new curls and clothing, Auntie Sue turned "Raggedy Ann" into a fashionable little girl.

Auntie Sue took me to the Terminal Tower. It was an amazing building with fifty-two floors. Auntie opened the heavy brass-plated door and we entered the brightly lit lobby. I was awed by the high, arched ceilings and glossy marble floors.

Daddy's train arrived at Cleveland Union Terminal at noon. When Daddy saw me, he smiled from ear to ear, and dropped his duffel bag as we ran into each other's arms. He scooped me up, hugging me tightly to his chest. I squeezed back with all my strength! For now, all was right in my little corner of the world. "Welcome home, Daddy!"

When Daddy returned to Cleveland, he didn't stay with me at Grandpa's. He roomed with his brother Dominic, who had also returned from the service.

During an evening meal hosted by Grandpa, Daddy made an announcement to all of us. "When Angelina's released from the hospital, I believe a different environment will be a healthy change for her. I've found a house I'd like to buy. Just wait until you see it. It's beautiful. And, best of all, the rentals make enough to pay the mortgage each month.

"Papa, please don't feel that I'm unappreciative of your offer to live on the second floor, but moving back here, after what happened...I just can't do it. I want to let go of the past. Having those memories return...No! I can't."

Daddy's dream house was a three-family brick and stone home on Edgerton Road, in University Heights, Ohio. The lot was 150 feet wide and 175 feet deep. The house and lot were surrounded by evergreens, Japanese maple trees, flowering pink and white dogwood trees, forsythia bushes, pansies, bluebells, and more greenery.

The flats on the first two floors were identical. They had five rooms with a wood-burning fireplace in the living room and a large screened porch off the master bedroom. The third-floor flat was unique: it had knotty pine walls, built-in drawers, a book-case, and storage units. The antique, early American furniture and appliances were included in the sale.

Daddy and I drove to our soon-to-be new home on a rainy spring morning. He pulled onto the long driveway and parked in front of the three-car garage. As I climbed out of the car, Daddy took hold of my hand. He walked me from the cement drive to the plush wet backyard grass.

To protect my shoes, he directed me to step onto a stone path through the garden. The walkway passed under a white trellis blanketed in climbing rose vines. In the center of this garden was a birdbath. Rain drops splashed upon the water in the dish. We were surrounded by tulips, hyacinths, and daffodils.

Daddy took deep breaths through his nose. "Beverly, breathe through your nose, like this." I copied him. The air, lightly scented by the perfume from the flowers, awakened our senses. We laughed as tiny droplets of rain fell on our faces. With the exception of the Cleveland Museum of Art, I had never seen a more peaceful and beautiful place.

"Daddy, I love it here! Is this really ours?"

My mother's breakdown had taught me that nothing in life is permanent. I had already been uprooted several times in my young life. At that moment, I was so very hopeful that at last there was a place for us where we would live "happily forever after."

Shortly after the real estate transaction had closed, doctors at Cleveland Psychiatric Hospital gave permission for my mother's release. My father stood extra tall, smiling from ear to ear, as he gave her a tour of her new surroundings. My mother remained silent, but the corners of her mouth were turned up. Her eyes had a slight stare—a sadness.

We took the second floor flat for our home and when the first-floor tenants moved, Mommy convinced her parents to move into the empty suite. Everyone was hopeful that the shadowy past could be left behind.

I was enrolled in the first grade at Canterbury Elementary School. On the first day of school, I happily discovered that a neighbor who lived four houses away was my classmate. Everything was *right*

18

with me—my parents were together, our home was beautiful, and I had new friends.

All too soon, Mommy began staying up late, the radio softly playing in the kitchen as she smoked and drank coffee. She cooked and cleaned but said very little to me. Outside of her doing the domestic chores, I was basically self-sufficient. The honeymoon effect of a new environment wore off quickly for my mom.

One particular day in September, I returned home from school, entered the side vestibule, and swiftly climbed up the back stairs. When I reached the first landing, I heard my mother's voice. One moment it sounded low and husky, like a growl. The next, it was high-pitched chatter, like a monkey. In between her repeated animalistic, jungle-like utterances, there were outbursts of cackling laughter, shrill screams, and garbled, deep guttural sounds.

I stopped abruptly, took hold of the banister, and, without turning around, descended backwards, two steps at a time. *No! Not again.* Once I reached the ground floor, I turned around, and rushed to seek refuge in Grandpa's flat.

My grandparents were at the kitchen table discussing my mother's behavior. Grandpa Vincenzo had gone upstairs, attempting to calm her down. She had refused to acknowledge Grandpa Vincenzo and carried on her conversation with someone only she could see or hear.

After I arrived home, her rage escalated. In between her utterances, we heard her franticly pounding against the doors and toppling furniture. Then, a distinct smashing noise told us that she had broken the front bay window. Pieces of glass plummeted onto the shrubs and ground.

The next-door neighbors and several strangers had gathered on the sidewalk in front of our home. When a new person joined the group and asked what the problem was, someone would point their finger at the house. Concern emanated from their faces because the tranquility of their quiet suburbia had been violated.

Grandpa Vincenzo, Grandma Caroline, and I watched them from the first-floor suite. We hoped that they couldn't see us through the bay window. Grandma Caroline and I were sitting on the couch. Grandpa Vincenzo was seated at his desk, his back to the window. He was dialing the phone. After a long silence, he placed the receiver down, and said, *"Dio Mio!* My God! Where's Carlo?"

Grandpa Vincenzo turned and looked out at the crowd. A University Heights police car was now parked across the street. He became red-faced, and angrily said, *"La polizia,* the police. *Che diavolo sta succedendo?* What the hell is going on? *Chi chiama la polizia?* Who called the police?"

Two policemen got out of the car and walked up the driveway. We heard the vestibule door open and their footsteps as they climbed the stairs. CRASH! Loud thumping and shuffling noises could be heard from above us, and then my mother began screaming.

The next time I saw her, she was being escorted down the driveway. She was handcuffed, her hands pulled behind her back. On each side of her, an officer held onto an arm. They appeared to be lifting her off the ground as she struggled to free herself. Then they shoved her into the squad car. My mother's fate was in the hands of the law.

As the police car drove away, I began sobbing. I prayed. *Dear God, please don't let them hurt her!* I wanted to protect her, but I couldn't. I felt utterly helpless and hopeless. I was ashamed of my mother's behavior, but I didn't know how to stop her.

I looked at my grandparents. Grandpa Vincenzo shrugged his shoulders. Tears were running down his cheeks. Grandma Caroline had a calm, almost stoical reaction to the unfortunate outcome.

The neighbors remained clustered together until the cruiser disappeared from sight. Then, one by one, they returned to their homes.

Why would they treat Mommy like someone to stare at? Don't our neighbors know anything about illness? She's ill. Even I know that!

My grandparents said a few words to each other in Italian. From what I could make out, they didn't understand why the policemen hadn't knocked on our door before driving off with my mother.

Grandma Caroline kept insisting that Grandpa Vincenzo should have gone outside to talk to them. Grandpa Vincenzo kept saying, "I couldn't stop them. What could I do or say? *Sono arrabbiato!* I'm angry! *Volevo sputare su di loro.* I wanted to spit on them. *Volevo dare un pugno a qualcuno nel naso.* I wanted to punch someone in the nose."

I didn't quite understand everything that happened, but I did know I felt like I had been shaken like a rag doll once more. Grandma Caroline's body was trembling as she sat next to me. Grandpa Vincenzo walked back and forth across the living room, balling his hands together and mumbling in Italian. An hour had passed before Grandma Caroline and I got up from the couch. Now we knew what catatonic meant.

At last, Daddy's car pulled onto the driveway. He started up the stairs to our flat. Grandpa Vincenzo called out, *"Vieni qui!* Carlo, come here! We need to talk."

Daddy's face flushed as he entered the kitchen. Grandpa Vincenzo pointed to a chair. "Sit down, son. Join us."

Once Daddy was seated at the table, Grandpa Vincenzo went to the upper cabinet over the sink and removed a bottle of vermouth from the shelf. He poured two shots, one for my father and one for himself, and sat down. "You're going to need this."

He proceeded to explain what had happened. My father's face paled and his eyes dropped as he gulped down the sweet licorice-flavored white wine. Daddy shook his head in disbelief, then got up and rushed to the police station.

The University Heights police had come to our house on behalf of a neighbor, who had called to report a disturbance next-door. When the patrolmen had investigated the situation, they heard the disturbance my mother was causing and went directly to the second-floor to find its source. They found my mother breaking and damaging things, just as the neighbor had reported.

The policemen had been in a quandary. They concurred that the woman certainly was acting abnormally, but were hesitant to arrest a woman who was misbehaving in the privacy of her own home. Nevertheless, her behavior had escalated to a point that she was guilty of disturbing the peace, so they decided to arrest her. In her present state of mind, she was incapable of telling them anything about her diagnosis, which might have helped her situation. My mother was locked in a cell.

This was how my father found her. When he came home, I heard him say, "One look at Angelina and my heart ached for her. My cultured, beautiful wife behind bars. Papa, I didn't know what to feel or say, but I remained calm and explained that she was ill—schizophrenic.

"The captain understood and apologized for the patrolmen not recognizing a psychiatric problem. They drove your daughter and me to the hospital and waited until she was admitted, so they could drive me back to the station."

My father looked tired. His tension showed: crinkled brow, a frown, and rounded shoulders. He said, "When will this stop? What's happened to our dreams? Will the life Angelina and I planned together ever come about? God knows, I've tried."

2

The Way They Were

Family and friends affectionately labeled my parents the "loving couple." Their bond was visible to everyone who saw them together. Their faces glowed when their eyes and hands interlocked. When they sat near each other, their bodies settled close together. Whenever my mother sat next to him, she would place her hand on my father's thigh, affectionately caressing his leg. Their looks complemented each other. They were a beautiful pair, like the silver screen stars Vivien Leigh and Clark Gable.

Throughout my childhood, I overheard the adults in my life discuss my parents' romance. I wanted to know more than the bits and pieces I had overheard during many dinners, so, as a teen, I asked Grandpa Vincenzo about them.

I learned that they were not neighbors, nor did they meet at school or work. Both of my grandfathers played a role in their chance meeting.

Grandpa Vincenzo's neighborhood had no stores where he could purchase fresh produce or the foods from his beloved homeland, Italy. If he wanted to purchase those items, he had to shop downtown.

Grandpa Vincenzo, in his fifties.

Early every Saturday morning, Grandpa Vincenzo would equip himself with handled bags made of cloth and paper, and walk from Frank to Euclid Avenue to board a streetcar to Public Square. Once at the Square he had to do more walking. His first stop was the Central Wholesale Grocery to purchase foods imported from Italy: cheeses, meats, oils, pastas, wine, and his daughter's favorite nougat candy. The store was owned by Mario De Angelis.

In Grandpa's words, "I knew your grandfather, Mario, long before your parents met. We talked a lot when I shopped at his store. The man knew how to make money.

"I had been his customer for over a year before he told me, 'We deliver large orders.' *Va bene.* That's fine. I took advantage of the service.

"The first time the groceries were delivered to our home, your Auntie Sue answered the door. She was the only one home at the time of the delivery, so she was the first to meet the driver. A cream-colored van with black lettering — The Central Wholesale Grocery — was parked in front. The driver had come to the front door. Sue knew that I wouldn't approve of having the delivery boy enter the house through the living room, so she instructed the driver to pull his van onto the drive and park next to the back door.

"I had built a wine cellar and cold storage locker under the porch in the basement. To keep it secure from our tenants, I had a padlock

24

on the door. The key hung on a hook in the kitchen.

"From then on, every time there was a delivery, Sue raced to the key rack and opened the back door before anyone else, including me.

"One day, I happened to come home just as Sue was escorting a young man down the steps. He was tall, dark, and good-looking, with lots of wavy hair, and deep-set brown eyes.

"Sue bobbed up and down while tossing her long dark hair from side to side. She turned to look at him as she opened the locker. From the look on her face, I knew she liked him.

"When I returned to the grocery store, I asked Mario, "Who's the handsome delivery boy? 'My son, Carlo. He's the oldest.'

"I told Sue about my conversation with Mario De Angelis. But I didn't surprise her. She knew much more than his name. Carlo was twenty years old and an eligible bachelor. She had been waiting for him to ask her out on a date. But he never did.

"The day your parents first met, Sue and Carlo were standing in front of the entrance to the first-floor suite, saying goodbye. Angelina opened the back door and walked into the hall, took one look at them, and quickly walked between them and disappeared from sight.

"Ah, once your father set eyes on Angelina, it was love at first sight. He said, 'Never have I ever seen a woman so beautiful.' He believed her to be the most beautiful girl in the world.

"The next time Carlo came to the house with a delivery, he told Sue how he felt. Auntie Sue reluctantly arranged for them to meet. Sue said to me, 'Papa it's pointless, I can't compete.'

"Carlo wasn't the only one who found Angelina beautiful. After she finished high school, nearly two hundred young Italian-American women entered a beauty contest. She won the contest.

"For her talent, your mother sang a portion of an operetta she had performed in high school. A gentleman who worked for The New York Metropolitan Opera was in the audience. He liked her soprano voice and looks. He went backstage and asked her to come to New York for an audition. An official offer letter was delivered to the house.

"After she met your father, the audition and possible singing career were never mentioned again. She wanted to get married. I liked your father and reasoned that he was a good catch for her. He was Italian, he had a job, and his father was my friend and a respected businessman in the Italian community.

"On Christmas Eve, December 24, 1939, they visited briefly with your father's family and arrived at our house about eight for dinner. I should have suspected something when your mother left with him after one o'clock in the morning. But it was Christmas, and they left in the van. How could I have known their plans? I went to bed thinking, 'She'll be right back. What's wrong with a few kisses? It's a holiday.'

"Later, your mother told me that they drove in circles for hours, looking for a justice of the peace. They finally found one in Ripley, New York.

"Grandma Caroline and I wanted them to have a church wedding, but they never asked us for our opinion. They had their own ideas. I'm not the best Catholic and I'm not superstitious, but I would have liked my daughter's marriage blessed by the church.

"But it was too late. They eloped. I kept telling myself, 'It's a good marriage.' In my heart I still believe that. I've got you, after all.

"Despite my initial doubts, I thought the marriage had to be made in heaven. Why, their names belong together! Her new name was beautiful — *Angelina De Angelis.* Angel of the Angels!

"After the wedding, your parents rented a two-room efficiency with an inner-door bed on the corner of East 55th Street and Woodland Avenue. I didn't like the neighborhood. They lived above the bank. Your father wanted to be close to the Central Wholesale Grocery. He left at six in the morning. He had too damn many deliveries. He'd come home after midnight. His father's a hard man...money, money, money!

"When your mama was pregnant with you she said, 'Look at me, Papa. I'm fat. What man wants a fat woman for a wife? I see how Carlo looks at pretty, shapely woman lately, and how they look back at him.'

26

Angelina and Carlo, beautiful together, but emotionally detached, at Carlo's fortieth birthday.

"Your mother thought your father was a god, but she was alone too much. She had too much time to think. You get *pazzo*, crazy, when you think too much!

"Every day there were questions. 'Papa, do you think someone else has caught his eye? Is he being untrue to me?' Then she'd change her mind. 'No, he can't be. He loves me. I've never found lipstick on his shirt. He's working.'

"Jealousy is awful. It makes people kill. Angelina was jealous. She was a beauty queen. Men considered her a goddess. But still she asked, 'How could Carlo look at another woman?' What did I know? Nothing.

"And then you were born and your mother stopped questioning me about your father. But it was like she had been bitten by a snake and never got rid of the poison."

3

BETWIXT

My mother had been in the hospital for several weeks. The psychiatrist had spent considerable time discussing her mental disorder with my father. Nevertheless, the doctor had failed to answer his most urgent questions: "How long will it take to stabilize my wife this time? When can she come home? We have a six-year-old daughter who needs her mother."

My father wanted and needed answers. The doctor's reply was a plausible—but certainly not definitive—response. "Your wife could be hospitalized indefinitely." Father had to make his decisions immediately.

What would become of his daughter? How could he manage as a single parent? He had to work, and his workday habitually extended long past his daughter's bedtime—often after midnight. He literally lacked the time needed to run a household and care for a child, especially a little girl. He concluded that it would be best if I lived in a more supervised setting, with regular meals and a woman's guidance.

First, my father approached my mother's side of the family. This made the most sense, since they had helped care for me after my mother's first breakdown. "Papa, what shall I do? I can't work and take care of *Bevelina*. Can you let her live with you?"

It took a lot of courage for my father to even ask. He knew getting a "yes" would be a long shot. Grandma couldn't handle an active child like me. He had heard her scold me a number of times for running on the back staircase. She had shown him that she couldn't tolerate noise at her advanced age.

Grandpa Vincenzo slumped in his chair, tears filled his eyes, and he sadly shook his head, saying, "No. Caroline's not able to cook and clean like before. She has too many problems."

In 1920, Grandpa, recently widowed, had brought Caroline over from Italy and married her. Soon after, Grandma Caroline fell, and broke her hip. She had undergone an operation to repair the hip that had instead left her crippled. She had been left with one leg shorter than the other, causing her to limp. Ever since then, she used a cane for balance. Now that she was fifty-six years old, she had become frail and arthritic, and stood with her back rounded.

Grandma Caroline smiled and said, "Carlo, my son, children are for the young."

My father blushed. "I understand why it's 'no.' I can't tell how long Angelina will be hospitalized. I wouldn't want you to commit to a promise you couldn't keep."

The very best my grandparents could do was to care for me until Daddy could make other arrangements. Auntie Sue wasn't available either, since she worked.

Although I knew Grandma Caroline and Grandpa Vincenzo loved me, I was too young to understand the challenges of aging, and I took their, "No," personally. I was hurt! *Why don't they want me to live with them?*

Backed into a corner, my father had no other choice but to ask his family for help. He approached his brother, Dominic, first. How Dominic got the other three adults in the house to agree to letting me live with them, I'll never know. But thankfully, they all did accept me!

The day Daddy told me I would be moving, he sat me on his lap, and affectionately stroked my hair. "Beverly, tomorrow I'm taking you to the West Side. You've been there with me many times. It's

30

Baba Rose's house. Grandfather Mario, Uncle Dominic, Auntie Elise and Cousin Donna all live there, too. We've eaten dinner there. It's the house with the big backyard."

I pouted, bit my lower lip, and the tears came. "Yes, I know. Yes, I know everyone. Do you mean the big, brown house?"

Uncle Dominic was shorter and stockier than my father, with broad shoulders. He had been a star football player in high school. His face always had a boyish grin, and though he never said very much, he always had a hug or a pat on the head for me.

Auntie Elsie's large, brown eyes lit up when she talked. Her round face was enhanced by clear skin, naturally rosy cheeks, and a pleasant smile. She gave her short, brown hair some texture with regular perms. She was fairly tall for the time, five feet five, with a sturdy frame.

Auntie Elsie and Uncle Dominic's daughter, Donna, was my playmate. As for Grandfather Mario, I had had little interaction with him. And I knew that Baba Rose was Auntie Elsie's mother.

My memories of the brown house were mostly of long, formal family dinners. I would have much rather spent time in the back-yard feeding the chickens.

I also remembered meeting my paternal grandmother, Maria, at my future home—a strange and confusing event for a six-year-old child. It occurred shortly after my father's discharge from the Army.

I hadn't even known Grandmother Maria existed. Nor had I known about the breach in her relationship with Grandfather Mario, or that the two had never been married, despite having four children together.

When I had walked in the door with my father, an unfamiliar woman was seated at the kitchen table. My father announced, "This is your grandmother." She may have hugged me or commented on my size or dress, but I don't remember any affectionate exchange. I just felt awkward, and blushed.

With the exception of my younger cousin, Donna, Grandmother Maria was the only person in the room. My father said, "Take Donna and go outside and play." In those days, dismissing children from the room was typical behavior for adults. The mantra was "children are to be seen and not heard."

Donna and I skipped out of the house. To entertain ourselves, we decided to dance up and down the wooden porch steps, as if we were doing a Shirley Temple routine. The open staircase was hazardous and the steps creaked and bounced as we stomped. The loud noises had to have been heard by the adults, but Daddy and Grandmother Maria were too absorbed in their own affairs to realize that we were misbehaving and could get hurt, especially Donna, for she followed my every move in spite of her limp and leg brace. When her brace pinged as it hit the wood, she giggled with glee.

Donna's right leg had been twisted and deformed from a birth defect. Since infancy, she had worn a series of braces on her leg as it grew, to strengthen and straighten it. The entire right side of her body had been affected. Even her ability to hold things in her right hand and to control the movements of her right arm was limited.

Through the closed storm door, we could hear Grandmother Maria's angry sharp and piercing voice. My father could also be heard loud and clear. They were having a bitter argument. The words *money* and *insurance* had been repeated several times, but these words meant nothing to me. Later, I learned that the disagreement was over Uncle Ted's G.I. combat insurance, after he was killed while fighting with the 1st Marine Division in the battle of Peleliu.

Finally, my father called Donna and me into the house. His face was beet red. Grandmother Maria's face was also flushed. They could not disguise the truth that they had had a heated argument. There were no parting hugs or pleasantries between the adults as we prepared to leave.

My father gathered up my sweater and books, but before we could exit the house, Grandmother Maria approached me. She gave me a quick hug and fastened a pretty gold necklace with a heart-shaped locket around my neck. While holding me at arm's length, she momentarily stared at me.

As I was about to walk out the door, I turned to blow Grandmother Maria a kiss. My father quickly took hold of me and lifted me up into his arms. The door slammed behind us!

The locket from my Grandmother Maria can be seen just on the edge of this photo.

Now I had another new address; another change. My new neighborhood on the west side of Cleveland, unlike the one around my grandparents' house on Frank Avenue, was mostly made up of lower-middle-class German- and Slavic-speaking people. My new house was a large, single-family Colonial with brown, shingle siding, and a front porch. The lot was deep. Part of the yard had been fenced off for a sizeable garden of lettuce, corn, tomatoes, cabbage, beets, and garlic. Beyond the garden were two huge chicken coops enclosed in wire-fencing. No free-range chickens in there. These birds were egg-producers.

33

Since the early 1900s, my new home on West 46th Street had been a boarding house. The most recent owner, Rose Novak, supported herself and her two children following her bitter divorce by providing rooms and meals to strangers in her home, and cleaning several office buildings in the evening, twice a week.

One evening, Rose was scrubbing the floor in a chiropractor's office. The chiropractor needed someone to help him lift his good-looking patient off a table. The patient was Mario De Angelis, my father's father, the owner of the Central Wholesale Grocery.

She took hold of Mario's right shoulder and arm while the doctor held his left side. Together, they lifted the five-foot-eight, muscular man up to a sitting position. The phone rang, leaving Rose at Mario's side. She helped him stand and continued to hold onto him until he no longer needed assistance. Meanwhile, they engaged in a cordial conversation.

Rose, a slightly stocky, strong woman with a full, round face and a large mole on her left cheek, was always on the lookout for roomers. She said she owned two houses on West 46th Street. She lived in the larger five-bedroom Colonial with her children. "My tenants are moving soon. Do you know anyone in need of a room?" Mario didn't answer her question, but he did say he would like to call on her. She gave him her address.

Mario was impressed with what he saw: the clean home, garden, and chicken coops. Within a week, Mario moved in with his three teenage sons, Carlo, Dominic, and Theodore.

Rose's two children, Elsie and Paul, were also teenagers. Elsie, attractive and bosomy, quit school at the age of sixteen to help with the housekeeping. Roomers were a lot of work.

This chance meeting between Rose and Mario resulted in the union of the families in 1941, when my Uncle Dominic married Rose's daughter, Elsie.

When I moved in with the Novak-De Angelis family, it was very clear that Rose's household was Grandfather Mario's domain. He was the King. Never mind that it was Rose's castle—royalty ruled. Rose looked upon Grandfather Mario's every wish as her command.

In spite of his good looks, Mario's demeanor made him a man who was easier to dislike than like. He demanded attention with his royal stance, aristocratic speech, and military manners. He was a veteran of the Ethiopian War, during which Italy unsuccessfully attempted to annex Ethiopia.

When I looked into my grandfather's deep brown eyes, I could see that his brain was cunningly calculating his next thought and move. Each word he spoke was enunciated precisely as he spoke in deep, throaty tones.

Grandfather Mario had a favorite chair in the living room. There he would sit, licking his Cuban cigars and blowing large, thick rings of smoke into the air. A spittoon sat in the corner of the room for his occasional use. I'd watch him out of the corner of my eye as I frolicked around the small, drab living room with Donna.

My grandfather smoking and spitting appalled me! The cloud of smoke seemed to hang in the air of the living room, irritating my nose. I always felt like I was on the brink of a sneeze when I was in the room. It seemed as if the only time Grandfather Mario extinguished his cigar was when dinner was served. While I found his use of the spittoon obnoxious, he did present himself well in many ways. He was impeccably groomed and dressed in the finest business attire each day. He wore Italian-made suits, imported shoes, and white, starched shirts with silk neckties.

My relationship with Grandfather Mario was the direct opposite of the loving closeness I felt with Grandpa Vincenzo. He never showed me any affection—no kisses, no hugs, and no gentle touches. He didn't care about me.

My grandfather, Mario De Angelis, was the son of a wealthy landowner. The *De* prefix connects his family to the royal dynasty of Napoleon. It's no wonder that he had to be in charge. It was my grandfather who decided "what, where, and when" dinner was served.

From Monday through Saturday, everyone in the household—except Grandfather Mario—was served their dinner in the kitchen. He usually ate his meals alone in the dining room, but Sunday was different. That day, the entire household dined with him. Sundays were always a special occasion.

As housekeeper, cooking was Rose Novak's chore. She was Czech by birth, descending from peasant stock. Basic, simple-to-cook meals had been served at her table until my aristocratic grandfather and his sons became her roomers. Then, Mario's culture had to prevail. His food had to be Italian.

Rose, who we affectionately called Baba, obliged, and my grandfather gave her instructions on how to cook his native cuisine. His grocery store supplied the costly ingredients essential to classic Italian cooking. She was an outstanding student, mastering the art. Her food tasted authentic.

On Sundays, all of Baba's activities revolved around the multi-course dinner she served at two in the afternoon. Prepping for the meal began early in the morning. From the upstairs bedroom, I could hear her shouting orders to Auntie Elsie, and I could smell the earthy fragrance of vegetables sautéing in virgin olive oil. The smells and sounds coming from Baba's kitchen were unforgettable.

When the scent of freshly baked bread permeated the air in the upstairs bedrooms, Donna and I knew that it was time for our breakfast. It consisted of the most delectable slices of warm bread, butter, and jam served with steamed milk and just a taste of coffee.

We would scurry down the stairs to the kitchen. Baba stood by the stove, cooking. Her short hair was brushed away from her face, exposing tiny droplets of perspiration on her brow. A large, white apron covered her paisley-patterned dress. Auntie Elsie stood nearby. At her mother's command, she fetched cooking utensils, pots and pans, herbs, vegetables, meats, cheeses, and uncooked pasta.

After breakfast, Donna and I would place the silverware and non-breakables on the dining room table. The banquet-sized table could comfortably seat twelve. The tabletop was impeccably dressed with starched and ironed white linen and colorful porcelain china.

Each place setting included bread, salad, and dinner plates. Sparkling cut glass goblets for water were placed directly above the knife with the stemware for wine set to the right.

The wine also came from Grandfather Mario's store. It was Chianti, an Italian import, bottled, and then packed in straw baskets for shipping. This was served to both the adults and—diluted with water—children.

Dinner was a succession of five small courses. The first course consisted of soup or *antipasto*, appetizer—an assortment of marinated vegetables, meats, cheeses, and olives. The second course was some form of pasta, usually long, thin spaghetti noodles that—if eaten properly—were twirled around one's fork. Platters of roasted veal, pork, beef, chicken, or fish were next. After the meat was served, the salad and fresh fruit were placed on the table. Occasionally, gelato concluded our meal.

After dinner, Grandfather Mario lingered at the table, slowly sipping anisette, reveling in the elegant, sumptuous Sunday meal. Donna and I found the two-hour meals fatiguing. We began to twist and turn in our tall ladder-back, black mahogany chairs after the first course! Nevertheless, I must acknowledge that those meals were memorable and definitely left me feeling stuffed.

Every Sunday after dinner, Donna and I received a weekly allowance from Grandfather Mario. He would sit smoking his cigar in his special chair, the large, comfortable, brown one that matched the sofa. After requesting that we come and sit down on the floor before him, he would pull a large wad of bills from his pants pocket. He gave Donna a five-dollar bill each week, while I received only a dollar.

I knew five was more. *Am I not good enough to receive five dollars?* To me, his inequity meant I wasn't as good as Donna—I wasn't liked or loved as much.

As a child, I could not understand my grandfather's rationale. In retrospect, I now grasp that Donna was not only his granddaughter, but also Rose's because of my Uncle Dominic's marriage to her daughter. Perhaps to remain in Rose's favor, Grandfather Mario felt compelled to dote on Donna.

It was easier to accept the inequity of my allowance from Grandfather Mario than the all-too-rare visits from my father. It felt like he had abandoned me.

Each Sunday, I had high hopes of seeing him. From week to week, my disappointment mounted. He appeared once a month, if I was lucky.

When he showed up, I'd ask about my mother. "Can we visit Mommy?"

"Not now, another time."

My mother was on an emotional rollercoaster. With her rapidly changing emotions, even my father stayed away. Daddy had a legitimate reason to keep me away, too. The doctors hadn't removed the restriction placed on my visits since I had witnessed my mother in leather restraints. But I missed both my mother and father.

To help cope with the separation from my parents, I discovered a new diversion. After school, I often made trips to the five and dime store, F.W. Woolworth and Company, to shop for candy or trinkets with my allowance. Shopping helped me cope with the love I needed but was unable to receive from my parents. This was how I nurtured myself. Unfortunately, I find that I still continue this pattern as an adult, even though I know well that monetary gifts are always an inadequate substitute for love.

Another escape for me from the darkness in my life was the time I spent in the living room, seated at the large French walnut Majestic player piano. Auntie Elsie taught me how to insert a perforated roll of paper and pump the pedals so that music would emerge. No ability or talent was needed to play the instrument. Simple, yes!

Once the adults in the house granted me permission, I would sit on the bench, rhythmically peddling the footrest and scaling my fingers over the cool ivory keys. I pictured myself in a beautiful gown, imagining that I was an acclaimed concert pianist.

My fantasy brought me happy moments and planted the seeds of desire in me to become a musician. While other girls may have dreamt of becoming a circus performer or ballerina, I pictured a piano-playing Beverly – beautiful, perfect, and loved by her audiences.

One year passed and Uncle Dominic finally saved enough money to move his family to their own home. He purchased a run-down, drafty Colonial with a large front porch on Almira Avenue near West 82nd Street, just south of Denison Avenue. In spite of the need for me to move again, and the condition of the newly purchased house, I was happy to move with my aunt, uncle, and cousin. I felt very uncomfortable with Rose and my grandfather.

There was one person I would miss by moving away from West 46th Street. That person was Julia, my mother's youngest sister. Auntie Julia looked nothing like Mommy. She had dark black hair, sharp features, and black eyes.

Julia had married Paul Novak, Rose's son. Uncle Paul had enlisted in the United States Navy. For Paul, the Navy was a career. His home base was Chanute Field, Illinois. Julia remained in Ohio. Julia and Paul had two boys, Brad and Bobby, who were my playmates. They lived in the house next door, also owned by Rose Novak.

Unlike Auntie Elsie, who was always under her mother's thumb, Auntie Julia had lots of time to play games with Donna, her boys, and me. On hot summer days, we would play in a small canvas pool in her back yard. When restricted to the indoors, she drew pictures for us and taught us how to color them. Occasionally, she played with paper dolls like a seven-year-old. Spending time with Auntie Julia and my cousins taught me how to play.

My aunt could sew like a professional seamstress. On Halloween, she made a ballerina costume for me. On Valentine's Day, she helped me make a Valentine box for my classroom. The time she spent with me on play and crafts made me a happy child.

I bonded with Auntie Julia because she did for me what my mother couldn't. She spent time with me and gave me praise and affection. She showed me a mother's love during a time that I felt unlovable. But despite how dear Auntie Julia was to me, the attention I received from her was not a powerful enough incentive for me to continue living with Baba and Grandfather Mario.

The move to Uncle Dominic's new home took place in the middle of the school year. Even though I was only eight years old, one of the adults in the family suggested that it would be better for me not to transfer to a new school, but to ride the trolley car to and from my current school, Clark Road Elementary. I was thrilled by this suggestion, because there was no way I wanted to change schools. To remain enrolled at Clark, I was willing to endure discomforts and inconvenience.

Not only would I have a fifteen-minute ride each way, but my school did not have a cafeteria. This hadn't been a problem when I was living with Baba and Grandfather Mario, a ten-minute walk from the school. The only way I could eat lunch at home now was another trolley car ride back and forth.

We had an hour for lunch. My ride to and from home took thirty minutes, and there was a bit of a walk from the bus stop to the house. That left me only fifteen minutes to eat. Jelly doughnuts and milk were the daily luncheon special. Time was important; not nutrition.

What mattered was that the adults were beginning to consider my feelings. I would not have to attend a new school and begin again.

The move was good for my aunt and uncle. They enjoyed their new life. The family next-door befriended us. The adults played poker and gin rummy for quarters. On Saturdays, they attended the horse races. My aunt and uncle were happier in their new home and fun to be around. Having their own home gave them a newfound freedom.

The neighbors owned a cottage on the Vermillion River. During the summer, Uncle Dom and a very pregnant Auntie Elsie would load Donna and me into the backseat of their old Chevy. The trunk was packed with a picnic basket full of food and treats. We spent the hot, humid days swimming or sitting on the banks of the Vermillion River. Believe it or not, I could swim across the river! It may have been at the narrowest point, but I was very proud of my accomplishment. Life had a degree of normalcy. I still longed for my parents, but life was good for now.

4

CARLO'S CHILDHOOD

As an adult, I learned that I was not alone in having a turbulent childhood, as I shared that trait with my father. His parents, Mario De Angelis and Maria Conti, parted ways when he was barely a teenager. Following their split, Maria moved several states away. The physical separation between parent and child, and the challenges Carlo faced as the child of a broken home, caused deep personal hurt to my father.

The time I met Grandmother Maria at Grandfather Mario and Baba Rose's house was the first and last time I remember seeing her. By the time I reached the age of understanding, I was able to reason that the mother-son relationship had been simmering long before the incident I had observed. That day had simply brought it to the boiling point.

Grandmother Maria was almost a complete mystery to me, and unbeknownst to me, this would be the last time I would ever see her. As the years passed without a visit from Grandmother Maria, I wondered what had happened to her. *Why doesn't she come to see us anymore? Has she died?*

After my father's death, Uncle Dominic's son, my cousin, Ted, told me that Grandmother Maria had kept on visiting his family through the years. But the name *Maria* and the word *mother* had been deleted from my father's vocabulary just like her presence had been blocked from my life. If anyone questioned Carlo about his mother, he became evasive and changed the subject. At most, he would say, "We have our differences."

Despite the apparent inability of Mario to show his devoted oldest son any acceptance or affection, Carlo was a respectful and dutiful son to his father. Almost every Sunday until Mario's death, my father would spend time with him. But not once in Mario's lifetime did he tell Carlo, "I love you." Even on his death bed, Mario remained cold, austere, and devoid of feeling.

His parents did not share a common background, although they were both born in Italy. Maria's family was working class and lived in a big city while Mario's father was an aristocrat who owned a large villa on several acres of land in a small town and had servants.

Maria, a divorced teen, and Mario, a worldly, older man of position and wealth, were brought together by circumstance and their mutual attraction and passion. But Mario had too much pride to introduce a girl who was so beneath him in status to his parents. And marrying her because she was carrying a child? That would have been totally unacceptable to his family. She became pregnant so soon after they met. The ink on her divorce papers had barely dried. Carlo's mother would never become Mrs. De Angelis and Maria's past cast a shadow on Carlo's birth and ultimately his whole life.

My father was born in Newark, New Jersey, in 1915, a little more than nine months after Maria and Mario met. Whether due to the timing, or just an inability to accept responsibility for his actions, Mario seemed to harbor resentment towards his firstborn. Mario wouldn't even allow Maria to name their first son after him, as was the convention at the time. After my father's death, I was surprised to learn that not only was my father not named after Mario, but Carlo wasn't even his given name. His birth certificate revealed his legal name to be Albert Edward De Angelis. Albert was the name of

Mario's older brother and may have been the closest Maria could come to claiming Mario's first name. From the pictures in my scrapbook, anyone can see that Carlo was a handsome boy, with lots of black hair, and his father's dark brown eyes. There was no denying my father's DNA; he was the mirror image of Grandfather Mario.

Until I was well into adulthood, I knew very little about my father's youth or my paternal grandparents. Occasionally, facts about our relatives would nonchalantly slip out in Dad's conversations. Over the years, I was able to piece together several stories about his childhood.

Young Carlo was constantly tripping over his feet or accidentally breaking things. After all, his feet grew faster than the rest of his body. Maria criticized his awkwardness, uttering profanity as she reprimanded him. He felt verbally abused. When she was home, her younger children needed her more. Consequently, he felt unloved and ignored. She just wasn't there for him when he needed her. My father's perception of her was that of a distant and unloving mother.

Before Maria began her nursing education, she asked her mother, Fran, to live with them to help care for the household. Great-Grandma Fran was a tiny, frail woman. Doing the laundry for a family of seven was an exhausting job. Buckets and tubs of water, a washboard, soap, and strong arms were needed to complete the task.

When Carlo was in his eighties and living with me, he watched me preparing to transport our week's wash to the utility room, filling a granny cart with detergents and soiled laundry. His face glowed, his features softened, and a boyish smile transformed his face into that of a youth. I could envision him as a timid little boy. His eyes started to tear. His voice trembled and became a whisper. Choking back sobs, he shared his love for his grandmother, as he told me the following story.

The basement of the old frame tenement house was dark, damp, and cold, even on steamy summer days. The dim lighting made it difficult for his grandmother's old, weary eyes to see the soiled spots.

Great-Grandma Fran, needing help, recruited Carlo. He willingly

43

assisted by carrying soiled clothing, fetching water, lifting the heavy wash buckets, and finding the dirty spots on the clothing. The clean smell of naphtha soap would permeate the air, as Great-Grandma Fran rhythmically slapped and scrubbed towels and garments over the washboard's surface in time as they sang together and recited Italian verses. Grateful for his help, Great-Grandma Fran gave Carlo all the love and attention he craved, but never received from his mother.

Throughout my father's childhood, he witnessed in his parents' relationship a growing intolerance of each other. They were both hard-headed. Neither knew how to give in. They would scream and curse at each other in Italian. Rather than resolving their issues, Maria decided to slip away.

When my father was about thirteen and his brothers were approaching their teens, they came home from school one day to discover that their mother, sister, and grandmother had left.

My father's stories about his adolescence without a mother could have filled the pages of a Charles Dickens' novel. Although the boys were knocked around from the day their mother walked out of their lives, or perhaps because of it, their bond was strong. Being the oldest son, Carlo had almost a fatherly love for his brothers.

One beautiful summer day, Mario asked Carlo to take himself and his brothers to the barbershop. Haircut—what young boy wants a haircut? Carlo said to his brothers, "I can cut your hair better than the barber. Just let me give you a haircut. Then we can use the money for a day at Euclid Beach."

Euclid Beach Park on the southern shores of Lake Erie was a favorite entertainment site for Clevelanders. An arcade, roller-coasters, a Ferris wheel, and other thrills provided a day of fun and popcorn and custard treats to eat. Carlo, Dominic, and Ted were fun-loving and thrill-seeking, just like their peers. But a day at the park was hard to come by, as they had no allowance to save for amusement.

Before the boys left home, Carlo proceeded to cut his brothers' hair, and Dominic attempted to help Carlo cut his own hair. The scissors were dull. Needless to say, they looked like they had been the victims of a blind barber, but they thought Mario would never notice!

44

On the way home, Carlo was beginning to worry about facing his father as he studied his handiwork. There was no symmetry, no layers, only chopped and uneven pieces of hair all over their heads—including Carlo's.

When the boys arrived home, Mario took one quick look at his sons and unbuckled his belt. Carlo knew what was coming and cowered as far away from his father as he could get. Red-faced and shaking, Mario went into a rage and demanded "the truth." Carlo had no choice but to tell what he had done as Mario was swinging his belt across his bottom. His brothers were luckier, as Mario felt Carlo, as the oldest, was responsible for the indiscretion.

Maria's swift departure had left the boys devastated. Mario was left with complete custody of his three sons. He was overwhelmed with their care and placed his sons in St. Joseph's Orphanage on Woodland Avenue. My father made sure they stuck together when they were sent off. They stayed there for almost a year until Mario found a caregiver for the boys.

The caregiver was a woman named Mrs. Leary who lived on the poor side of town. Unfortunately, she drank too much and gambled with all the money Mario gave her for the boys' food and lodging. Often going hungry, the boys sometimes wouldn't even return to their beds at night. It was my father who made sure they were safe and street-smart when they were roaming the neighborhood and sleeping under bridges.

For entertainment, Carlo and his brothers roamed the shanty areas under the bridges in the area we now call the Flats in Cleveland. This area was frequented by panhandlers and beggars. The boys would watch them hop the trains or see them jump off the train. Most of the tramps would cling to the curved grab rails of the caboose car.

Carlo, being a bright, resourceful and thrill-seeking youngster thought he could use the train as a means of free travel around the city. He hopped a train on Miles Avenue and rode it into downtown Cleveland.

He successfully navigated the train ride for several months. Then one day as he jumped off, he lost his balance when landing and rolled down the hillside breaking his left femur.

This incident led to an operation which resulted in his spending two months in City Hospital and nearly a year following that to totally heal from his injury.

Mario was very angry with Carlo for what he called his *stupidity* and showed him no sympathy. Thankfully, he had no lasting injuries from the accident.

Carlo worked at his father's grocery store throughout his adolescence and for much of his adult life. As long as he was attending school, Mario refused to pay Carlo, so he had to sell newspapers in front of the Standard Drug Store on the corner of Miles Avenue to have spending money.

Carlo was assigned two responsibilities at his father's grocery store: to stock the basement with perishables and make deliveries. According to my father, he taught himself how to drive the store's pickup truck when he was thirteen years old.

One story my father would often repeat was about carrying a fifty-pound bag of coffee beans. While he was hurrying down the stairs to the basement, the fragile fabric bag tore open. The beans spilled out, marking his trail behind him. Mario was sitting at his desk with his feet propped up, cigar hanging out of his mouth, the basement steps in full view. Observing Carlo's carelessness, he lashed out at him, saying, "*Stupido figlio,* stupid son, Marcoffee." From that point on, every time Mario disapproved of Carlo's behavior, he would angrily holler out, "*Stupido* Marcoffee!"

His father's use of the nickname troubled Carlo. Even at eighty years old, it was clear he still was hurt by it. He always felt like his father was especially hard on him.

A year after they moved in with Mrs. Leary, Mario found a companion who invited the boys to live with them. Carlo, Dominic, and Ted moved into her large front-porch colonial on the south side of Cleveland, and finally had a home with their father. The new woman in his life insisted that Mario's three sons receive religious instructions at the neighborhood church, Holy Name Catholic Church. The boys attended South High School where Dominic was a star football player.

Although living with their father and his companion provided stability for the boys, this arrangement still failed because once again, their father's romantic relationship went astray. They all moved to a rooming house—the house with Baba Rose, Paul, and Elsie.

The young man who met Angelina Martinelli was ready for a loving marriage. He wanted his own home and a happy family. These were the things that had been missing from his life. Although Carlos won Angelina's heart, his dreams would never come to fruition. The specter of mental illness cast a shadow over both their lives, and robbed them both of what might have been.

5

The History of Maria and Mario

The fractured relationships my father had with his parents I suspect are a legacy of their own childhood. As a shadow follows you, so does one's past. Maria and Mario each bore a legacy of emotional and psychological baggage when they met, otherwise their story might have been different.

Grandmother Maria was born in Vallata, Italy in 1898. She was the youngest of twelve children. The entire family immigrated to the United States when she was four. Their home was an over-crowded tenement house in Newark, New Jersey. They were poor, uneducated, working-class citizens. Their life was hard.

Grandfather Mario was born in Guardia Lombardi, Italy in 1877. He was the youngest of three sons born to aristocrats. His parents owned a villa and acres of land with lush gardens, fruit trees, and grape arbors.

Maria became a woman by the age of twelve and at fourteen years old, married her childhood sweetheart, the Italian boy who lived next door. A year later, she gave birth to a baby girl she named Jennifer. Just before her first birthday, the baby contracted double pneumonia, then whooping cough, and died. The loss of their only child in infancy caused irreparable damage to their relationship and the couple separated. Maria returned to her parents' home.

As a child, Mario was educated by Catholic monks who taught him the English language. As an Italian soldier, he fought in the battle to annex Ethiopia to Italy. Later, following his brother's lead, he immigrated to the United States. Having wealth, servants, and a good life living in Guardia Lombardi, Mario's parents chose to remain in their homeland.

In 1914, Mario also could be found in Newark, managing the grocery store he had owned for several years. Maria shopped for her parents at his store. They met soon after she moved back into the tenements with her parents.

I can just imagine the scenario. The first time sixteen-year-old Maria opened the door to Mario's store, he must have been immediately drawn to her beauty. The auburn hair, blue-gray eyes, and translucent skin immediately caught his attention.

Two decades her senior, Mario carried himself with an air of confidence that was complimented by his deep-set, dark eyes, olive skin, and stature. He was quite good-looking. Their attraction was mutual.

Maria was shy and nervous as she glanced up at the proprietor. While counting out her change, Mario's fingertips gently brushed Maria's palm, sending a current through their whole bodies with each touch. Their eyes locked and they stood, frozen in place for a moment. Then, they suddenly became embarrassed by their public display, and jerked their hands back. Maria quickly turned away to gather her bags then glanced up at Mario again. Her cheeks flushed as she saw him looking right back at her, a smile on his face.

During each trip to the store, the lonely and grieving Maria would attempt to make small talk with Mario, telling him about the death of her daughter and separation from her husband. By opening up to him about her losses, she revealed her vulnerability and need for affection. Mario, the mature worldly man, used this knowledge to his advantage.

Maria quickly acquiesced to the advances of a man much older, wealthier, and wiser. Everything seemed rosy until the teenager approached Mario with news of her unexpected pregnancy. She

50

quickly learned that he wouldn't marry her, but he did give her the money to file for a divorce from her first husband.

The everlasting-marriage-type of love that Maria, a naïve youngster, surely imagined and hoped for with her older suiter was never in the cards for them. Her humble roots prevented it. Mario was too ashamed of her social status and past to ever introduce her to his aristocratic parents. Her youthful hopes didn't have a chance.

Yet the unanticipated pregnancy tethered the May-December couple to each other for thirteen years. Sometime after Carlo was born, Mario welcomed Maria and their son into his home. Over the next five years, three additional children were born to the couple: Dominic, Theodore, and Jean. After the birth of each child, Maria begged Mario to marry her. But for Carlo's father, marrying a woman wasn't a necessity; Maria's pleas fell on deaf ears.

In 1920, shortly after the birth of their daughter, Maria, impressed by the midwife who assisted her, expressed to Mario a desire to become a midwife.

Mario readily agreed to arrange and pay for her schooling. After all, the job would elevate her status. Midwives were influential and well-respected in the community. In addition to helping women birth babies, they had the power to investigate crimes of incest and rape.

Maria wasn't the least bit concerned about image. Midwife was a profession that she could imagine herself doing, even with her humble background. She also liked the fact that midwifery was quite lucrative and would provide her some economic independence.

Caring for a home and four children is a twenty-four-hours-a-day, seven-days-a-week job. Before Maria could begin her studies, she asked her mother, my great-grandma Fran, to live with them to cook, clean, and care for the children.

Maria completed her education with honors. Her services were in high demand and she was constantly working. She made lots of money as a midwife and secretly saved every penny. The shy, naïve young girl, had become a worldly, headstrong, independent woman.

While Maria was busy with her career, Mario spent the majority of his time at his grocery store. What little free time he had he spent gambling. Every Friday night he played cards with the good old boys. Every Sunday, he could be found at the race track, betting on the ponies.

For a couple with less income, gambling might have caused a serious rift, but Mario had sufficient luck and a large enough bank account to keep his pastime from dividing them. His gambling was not a problem, but their relationship had begun to sour. Mario and Maria had become very much alike and constantly tested each other's will. In spite of the bickering and growing intolerance between them, they remained a couple and the family unit moved to Cleveland.

It took at least a year for Mario to establish his own business, the Central Wholesale Grocery. In the interim, Mario took a position as a foreman for Richman Brothers' clothing factory on East 55th Street.

Mario's older brother, Felix, a successful New York importer, had suggested moving to the growing metropolis. Of course, Mario hadn't consulted with Maria before selling his grocery store in Newark and deciding to move his family to Cleveland. Once she heard the words, "We're moving," another battle between them began.

Maria resented being uprooted and failed to understand the great business opportunity the move presented. And Mario saw Maria as shrewish and difficult. "This is my house. I make the decisions. Not, you!"

Then, one day, Mario returned home and found that Maria had packed her things and left, taking their daughter, Jean, and Great-Grandma Fran back to Newark.

I don't know much about Maria's life after she moved back to New Jersey. From business records, I discovered that Maria owned two sandwich and coffee shops at Coney Island. She was always close to her daughter, Jean, and her family. Beyond that, her life is largely a mystery to me.

I will never have the opportunity to understand Mario and Maria's challenges and hurts. I have been left with many questions. I've particularly wondered about what made Mario tick. Were his parents unaffectionate? Did he lose his connection to his spiritual being? Did his Catholic schooling or military training make him devoid of feeling? Or was he taught to shut off his feeling? After all, revealing ones' feelings can be considered a sign of weakness or irrationality.

Did he ever love anyone? Did he give his heart in his youth, and it left him emotionally unavailable for a lifetime? What about our grandmother? Did he love her? Maybe, as they say, "in his fashion." Unfortunately, the reason for his cold, austere manners will never be uncovered.

So many questions about my grandparents will forever be left unanswered. Since writing their story, I've sat back and pondered their lives. There is so much I admire in each of my grandparents. Mario was very hard-working and had terrific business acumen. Maria was strong and independent and had an entrepreneurial spirit in an age when that made her a rarity among women. But even though I am proud to see such traits in my ancestors, I also believe that emotional baggage leaves a legacy of more baggage.

I've held up and examined my life, trying to identify the qualities I've inherited from Mario and Maria. I find myself left with more questions. How much of them is within me? Do I see myself in them? Have they molded my character in some way? Are any portions of their personalities within me?

How much of my story was written before I was even born?

6

HOPEFUL HOMECOMING

Here we go, once more.

My mother had improved. She would be released from the State hospital. I was anticipating my fifth move.

During the past year, Grandpa Vincenzo had purchased the three-family home on Edgerton from my father. Before the transaction closed, I heard my father say, "I want no part of the stuffy, nosey, finger-pointing neighbors. I'll never go back there." He now had the funds to purchase a new house, and one day he surprised me.

Father smiled and sighed. "Beverly, I bought a new house. I feel good there. You'll love it. There's a wood-burning fireplace in the living room, a large bay window in the dining room, and on the second floor, a huge knotty pine dormer with built-in drawers and a walk-in cedar closet. The upstairs can be your bedroom."

While happy about the thought of being united with my parents, I was scared stiff! Moving back to the east side of Cleveland was going to be very difficult for me—new school, new friends, new routine, and, undoubtedly, unforeseeable difficulties.

Please, let this be my last move. Please, please, dear God!

The day the house on Eastway Road in South Euclid, became my home, I was happy. I was pleasantly surprise to find that it was everything Father said it would be.

From the outside, the large, white, frame-and-stone bungalow resembled an English cottage in the "Better Homes and Garden" magazine. Large oak and maple trees lined each side of the street, and each house had its own unique architecture. This upper-middle class neighborhood was built in the '40s and zoned for single-family occupancy.

The interior was cozy, and the furniture was in place. I immediately recognized the Duncan Phyfe dining room set and two fireside chairs—antiques from the Edgerton home. Daddy had also purchased new furnishing, including quality pieces from the J. L. Goodman Company in Cleveland.

The tasteful way it was decorated elicited a feeling of warmth, comfort, and security: soft pillows on the sofa, a conversational seating arrangement in front of the fireplace, and candlesticks on the mantel. If a beautiful environment could maintain my mother's sanity, this home was it!

And that it did. When she returned home she cooked meals! When I woke up on Sunday mornings, I could smell chicken or beef roasting in the oven. Sunday dinners were served in the dining room, where we could see our plush lawn and a black dwarf maple tree and brightly colored flowers.

There was a large mirror over the buffet in the dining room. The person who sat at the head of the table could see their image reflected in it. My parents would playfully banter about who would take the seat of honor. Carlo would say, "Angelina, it's my turn."

"No, Carlo, it's mine."

I'd sit at the table, blushing, while trying to withhold my giggles. I hadn't seen my parents this happy in a long time. They were smiling, talking, and jesting with each other.

Sunday dinners were usually preceded by a brief vocal recital. It would begin with an "Ahhh," from my father. He had no professional training, but God had gifted him with the lyrical voice and vocal range of a tenor.

My mother harmonized with him, singing, "Ahhh...sweet mystery," in her melodic soprano. This was their favorite duet, "Ah, Sweet Mystery of Life," the hit recording sung by Jeannette MacDonald and Nelson Eddy.

I thought my parents were egotistical and vain, but justifiably so, because they had perfect features—they were beautiful! Little did I know that mirrors were used as tools to authenticate a performer's facial expressions, but my mother knew this from her experience as a starlet in high school operettas.

Following their performance, my father would pour Chianti into the cut-glass goblets, adding water to mine, and we'd toast. "*Cento l'anno!* May you live a hundred years!"

Seeing them happy, made me happy. *Everything will be all right.*

As happy as my life was in this new house with my parents, I missed having my cousins and Auntie Julia as playmates. I would fill my time with solitary pursuits, like bouncing a ball to myself against the outside of the chimney or playing hopscotch. I remember sitting outside on our stone steps, playing jacks. I tossed the six-pointed, little metal stars on the ground, bounced a ball, and looked around. *Isn't there anyone my age living on this street?*

One day during the summer before my eleventh birthday, I was playing hopscotch by myself. That's when I met the eleven-year-old girl who lived next-door. I took one glance at her short, curly, strawberry-blonde hair and the way it framed her pretty, rosy-cheeked freckled face and felt insecure. Girls who looked like Margaret Zerbes were featured on the cover of "American Girl."

She asked if she could "have a turn at it."

"Yes! Yes," I responded.

When exchanging names, she requested, "Call me Marty. It's short for Margaret. I swim at the Cumberland pool every day. Can you get permission to join me?"

Marty was the first girl in the neighborhood to befriend me, and from the moment we met, I began to make comparisons between us.

Despite being close in age, Marty and I were so different. I was olive-skinned with dark hair. Marty was fair-haired and fair-skinned. When it came to swimming, I couldn't dive off of the high board. I stuck to belly-slams off of the side of the pool. Marty could swim like Esther Williams. I hated wearing a bathing suit because of how self-conscious it made me feel. Marty was confident and comfortable in her tightfitting one-piece suit.

Mrs. Zerbes was a Girl Scout leader and Marty proudly exhibited many badges on her uniform. My mother couldn't socialize with the neighbors let alone become a role model for a group of giggly adolescents. I'd watch the girls gather at Marty's house for meetings and long to join the group but was too shy to ask. *I'll never be accepted.*

Marty had a religious upbringing and attended Catholic school. I didn't know if I had ever been baptized. To me, my new friend had everything—loving parents, a stable home life, talent, personality, and beauty

Although I valued my friendship with Marty, especially since I had no other playmates, spending so much time with someone who seemed to have every advantage in life played on my insecurities.

People had been comparing me to my mother since I was a baby. I, too, had learned to compare myself to her. Wanting to be like my former beauty queen mother meant that I set a goal to be beautiful. Throughout my childhood and adolescence, I used a critical eye to evaluate my progress towards that goal. I had yet to learn that we mortals are not in charge of God-given gifts. My unattainable quest for perfection had begun.

When I looked at Marty, I saw everything I wanted and thought I could never have. Yes, I was envious of Marty!

When September came, Miss Popularity and I saw less of each other. My father had just enrolled me in a new school for the fifth time in six years! I was frightened, insecure, and timid. *Will I make friends at this new school?*

The curriculum at Taylor Elementary was far more advanced than that at my former school. This also added to my worries. Coming from the Cleveland School District, I found the lessons difficult, especially spelling. Even at my previous school, it was not my forte! Auntie Elsie had spent a lot of time quizzing me on my spelling homework. How well I remember her saying, "Repeat after me, E-L-E-P-H-A-N-T." The word *elephant* completely eluded me. I just couldn't grasp the *ph* sound.

My teacher, Mrs. Gimbel, was a sweet, gray-haired lady who recognized my need for greater self-confidence. With her encouragement, I volunteered as a school crossing guard.

Dutiful and dedicated, I would be at my post no matter the weather. Soon I was promoted to captain. No one could have worn her badge more proudly. To me, it was a great sixth-grade accomplishment.

Over time, my pride in my captain's badge wore off and with it my new-found confidence. I couldn't risk bringing friends home, nor could I be forthright about the reason why. My mother's illness had to be kept a secret. *How can my friends understand that she is ill, if the neighbors couldn't? I can't let them get to know me.* Aesop coined the phrase, "Familiarity breeds contempt." From my young perspective, it assuredly would. I couldn't afford to let my classmates know that my mother was ill. Shame is learned early in life. Yes, I was ashamed of her past and fearful that she would do something to embarrass me.

In lieu of spending my time with my contemporaries, my Saturdays were spent in the company of my mother's parents. Their home was about two miles away—a short bike ride or brisk walk.

After Grandpa Vincenzo had purchased the Edgerton Road home from my father, he did extensive remodeling to the common areas of the basement and shared hallways. The painted ceiling and walls in the back hall were now covered with white ceramic tile. He'd say, "Easy to clean and long lasting." It was, but for other people it was not appealing; it was too antiseptic and sterile. "Cleanliness is close to godliness," remained his retort.

The house came furnished with electric appliances. The Roper gas range from the Frank Avenue house initially sat unused in the basement, but Grandma Caroline preferred to cook with gas. She eventually convinced Grandpa Vincenzo to run a gas line from the furnace to the range. He placed the basement's six washtubs, back to back, three feet in front of the range. By placing a wooden tabletop across the tubs, Grandma now had an area to prep food. She did all her cooking in this make-shift kitchen.

Grandpa Vincenzo also cut out a portion of the cement block foundation and removed the soil from beneath the back porch to build a wine and fruit cellar. He installed a bathroom with a stall shower, and made a spacious room for entertaining that was used for recreation as well as large family dinners. All of these amenities were for his use; not the tenants. Grandpa Vincenzo had designed the basement to compliment his lifestyle. To an Italian, that means eating fine food, drinking homemade wine, and enjoying a meal with family and friends.

On Saturday mornings, I dusted the furniture in my grandparents' five-and-a-half-room flat, for which Grandma would pay me a dollar. Their exquisite mahogany dining room table seated twelve. The intricately carved table legs and their supports needed special care. Equipped with Old English Furniture Polish and a clean cloth, I sat under the table and began wiping down the legs. *I don't know why Grandma has me do this. There's no dust!*

With the long, white tablecloth spilling over the sides, the table became a hideaway just for me. I'd sit and think about what the future would bring, daydreaming about living happily ever after.

When I heard Grandma Caroline approach, I'd quickly put the lemon-scented polish on the cloth and act like I'd never stopped rubbing the wood, but she knew what I was doing. She had caught me goofing off.

When the dusting was complete, my next job was ironing hand-kerchiefs, rags, and sheets. Grandpa Vincenzo had installed a fold-out ironing board in the wall of the laundry room/kitchen in the basement. As lunchtime approached, I would hear a hissing sound from the black cast-iron pan as Grandma placed thin slices of round steak into hot olive oil. She would stand and watch the juice run from the meat until it was ready to turn. In a matter of minutes, the steak would be finished, and we would carry the prepared food upstairs to dine.

I'd crunch on homegrown cucumbers, tomatoes, and greens mixed with olive oil, vinegar, and herbs; salad dressing that only Grandma could make. I'd savor the juicy steak and sop up the drippings from the meat with chunks of Italian bread. It was fun to wipe my plate clean and it tasted good, too. How I wished that every day could be a Saturday!

Some of my happiest memories from the years after my mother's first breakdown were associated with food and my grandparents. Never mind that they were unable to let me live with them. I had no hard feelings towards them, because they continued to be there for me, and provided a positive influence.

Sadly, my mother didn't instill me with homemaking skills. Even now, Mom didn't make her bed every morning or pick up her soiled clothes. She did the laundry every few weeks, but left the ironing undone. Lucky for me, my father chose to live close to his in-laws, and Grandma taught me some of the skills my mother couldn't.

By June of 1952, my parents and I had been living together for at least twelve months without another episode, but I was becoming increasingly aware of how my mother's illness had changed her. She never left the house. *We never go for walks.* She didn't shop for groceries or clothing. *Dad does it.* Although she was more likely to prepare dinner, I was left to fend for myself for most other meals. *I can take care of myself, do dishes, dust, wash clothes, and iron the best I can.*

One morning, I woke up and rolled over to read the time on my alarm clock. *7:15 am. It's almost time to leave.* School would be closing for summer vacation in two weeks. I pulled the shade and it snapped upward, letting the bright sunshine flood my room. *Not a cloud in the sky.* I pulled up the window and felt the breeze. *Gosh, it's beautiful!*

I called out, "Mom, I'm leaving." No response. She had been sleeping later recently, so I checked her bedroom. The bed was empty. I found her in the kitchen. A month ago, there would have been a glass of freshly squeezed orange juice waiting for me. Today was different.

"Mom, I'm leaving." No response.

My mother picked up her coffee cup, took a sip, looked up, and stared at someone. That someone wasn't me. She looked right through me and began speaking indecipherable words in a strange voice.

She doesn't recognize that I'm here. NO! Not again!

On this clear day, a heavy cloud of despair hung over my head. Perhaps I should stay home.

You're mistaken. She's fine. Go to school.

When the last bell rang to signal the end of the school day, I immediately got out of my chair and pushed my way through my classmates. My mind raced as I walked home, ruminating on what I might find when I got there. As I turned onto my street, my pace quickened. I had to get home fast. With my eyes partly closed against the blinding sunlight, I scanned the sidewalk and houses until our front yard came into focus. *You must be mistaken. That's not our house.*

It's no wonder I didn't recognize our dream home. The small cypress trees, box ferns, and the perfectly shaped Japanese maple had vanished. All that remained was a mishmash of stumps, small branches, leaves, and crushed flowers. *Who could have done this...for what reason? There must have been some mistake!*

I followed a trail of leaves and tree branches from the lawn to the closed side door. Entering our house, I saw that the foliage had been brought inside.

As I stood on the landing above the basement stairs, I saw our living room sofa lying halfway down the steps. My stomach churned and my head felt like it was about to explode. *Oh, my God! What has happened?! Where did she get the strength to do this?!*

I suddenly had to clear my throat. Every muscle in my body tensed as I realized that smoke was filling my nostrils. I began coughing as the acrid stench of sulfur permeated the air.

I followed the path of branches and greenery through the kitchen and took a step into the dining room. I could see that the wreckage continued past the center hall and into the living room.

From where I stood, I could see a woman with a deranged look in her eyes sitting on the hearth, smudges of soot on her face, and dirt and grime on her hands, arms, legs, and torn clothing. *This is my mother?!*

She had the cover from a box of matches in one hand and a wooden matchstick in the other. She repeatedly struck the match against the side of the cover. The force of her erratic movements snapped the match in half. She cursed and threw the broken pieces into the air. Sweat ran down her forehead and her face turned beet red.

My mother had stuffed the fireplace with paper and tree limbs. The paper had burned, but the twigs, maple limbs, and moist pine had refused to ignite, filling the room with a cloud of smoke.

She was too preoccupied to look up and see me. It was obvious that she had gone mad again.

I had to get away. On my way out, I opened the kitchen window. Then I fled from the house.

I needed help, but who could help?

The fire department...?

No. Anyway, she'll run out of matches soon.

The police...?

No! They'll take her to jail.

Help! Who will help me?

Daddy!

But when will he come home?

Fearful of talking to the wrong person, I concluded that my father was the only one who could help. I paced up and down the driveway and back and forth on the sidewalk. *God, please don't let the neighbors see me.*

Keeping watch from this vantage point was my only logical option. From here, I could see if Mommy left our house, and I could see my father as soon as he returned home.

An hour passed. I paced. My mouth became dry, my stomach tied in knots, and my bladder was ready to burst. But I kept pacing.

Mommy, please, please, don't come outside!

After what felt like an eternity, my father arrived home. When he got out of the car, I didn't have to say a word. His face said it all. He knew.

Searching for Mom, we discovered that she had abandoned her plans for starting a fire. We found her lying in bed looking around at the four walls. Her agitation had dissipated and miraculously, she was manageable. Dad easily persuaded her to get into the car. Once again, our destination was Cleveland State Hospital. I knew what to expect. My mother would be admitted.

Tears running down my face, I witnessed my mother being placed in a straightjacket before the attendants forcibly removed her from the nurses' station.

My tears turned to sobs. My father appeared emotionless. Together we walked down the long corridor. A uniformed male attendant unlocked the steel door with its small barred window to let us out. The door clanged as it closed and the click-clack of the security lock echoed behind us. It was all surreal, like a bad dream.

Returning home without my mother filled me with anxiety. *Now what? I'll be all alone.* Despite my mother's lack of connection with me and reality, her presence in our home had provided me with a sense of security. My father was usually out of the house until the wee hours of the morning. At least my mother had been there.

Somehow, I managed to cook for myself and for my father, when he was around. I washed clothes and ironed a bit. We had withstood the embarrassment of the shrub incident, though continuing to live in that house was extremely difficult. Judgmental, disapproving eyes were forever watching us. I knew that the neighbors were keeping tabs on my father. I saw the neighbors across the street looking out of the window as his car pulled onto our drive. The lady next door would raise her shades, coincidentally of course, when I played outside. I was keenly aware that my family was the embarrassment of the neighborhood.

This time, amazingly, Mom's hospital stay was short—a little over a month. The next ten months passed without an incident.

The following June arrived with its warm breezes and sunny blue skies. For most people, June is a happy month, one to celebrate with weddings, graduations, and the completion of the school year. Yet for me, June seemed to be a vixen and a jinx! I must admit, I felt vexed.

One particular June day, the sun shone brightly, the sky was azure blue, and I could feel a gentle breeze against my back as I walked home from school. The semester would be ending in a few days, and we had been dismissed early.

Strange. I had reached the sidewalk in front of our home. A car was parked in front. *No one ever parks in the street, unless it's a visitor. We never have visitors. Why is that shiny red Buick parked here?* An odd feeling came over me, but I ignored it.

The side door was open and the house was quiet. "Mom," I called. No one answered. *She's probably sleeping.*

I took a magazine from the kitchen table with the intention of going out onto the back screened-in porch to read. Passing the closed bathroom door, I heard voices. *Is that my mother talking?*

Pressing my ear against the door, I clearly heard my mother and a man laughing as water ran into the tub. I knew that there was something wrong with this scene.

Approaching my teens, my understanding of relating, dating, and mating was formed by what society had taught me. My mother lived in a world of delusions and never approached the topic of puberty or the fact that I would soon have a menstrual cycle. Most of my information on dating etiquette came from Archie and Veronica's relationship in the "Archie" comic strip and my sex education came from the romance magazines I read. I had learned enough to know that a married woman could get into trouble being alone in her home with a man who wasn't her husband, especially in the bathroom with the door closed.

Overcome with fear, I dropped the magazine and fled from the house. Instinctively, I looked back at the license plate and began repeating its letters and numbers. I had to memorize them.

I also had to think about what had just transpired. I knew it wasn't right. I headed to the corner drug store soda fountain on Cedar Road.

Be careful about what you do or say. You're in a real dilemma! Do you think your mother was having sex with that man?

I don't know.

Then why were they in the bathroom?

I don't know. Should I tell my father?

You'd better. What if that man returns?

Over and over I posed these questions to myself. For an hour, I sat sipping my soda, until it was obvious from the dirty looks the soda jerk kept shooting my way that he wanted me to leave.

When I returned home, the car was gone. I waited outside.

An hour dragged by. At last, my father's car pulled onto our driveway.

My heart pounding, I ran to Daddy and hugged him fiercely. Trembling, without thinking of the consequences, I blurted out the entire sequence of events.

Immediately, my father's face reddened and contorted into an angry grimace. He clenched his teeth, like a boxer biting down on his mouth guard. *God, I'm sorry I said anything!*

I watched helplessly as he ran into the house. Trailing a safe distance behind, I saw him pull my mother from the chair where she was now sitting. "You whore! What the hell were you doing, bitch?" Then he slapped her face with his open hand. He held her with one hand and balled the other into a fist, punching her in the ribcage. When he threw her back towards the chair, she fell onto the floor, and he kicked her in the side. "Oh, God! Daddy, stop!" He looked at me and stopped.

He froze like a deer in headlights. His eyes widened and his face seemed to turn gray as the color drained from his face. He knew he had used excessive force. Now that he had awoken to the reality of what he had just done, he backed away from Mom in shame.

The way he had used my mother like a punching bag frightened me. And the way he swore and called her names caused a stabbing pain in my chest. *He doesn't love her anymore.*

Now I worried about *his* behavior. *He's a mean man.*

Tears streaked my mother's red face. Raising her hands to her face, she bit her lips and sobbed. Her contusions were swelling and turning blue.

Dad helped her into a chair. I washed the blood from her face and applied petroleum jelly to her wounds. Then I sponged her beautiful face with a cool, wet cloth to reduce the swelling. She never commented on what happened that day, nor did she ever explain her behavior.

Now that my father had become rational once more, he asked me for the letters and numbers on the license plate. I remembered them correctly. He gave this information to the police department. With their assistance, he learned the man was a door-to-door salesman. His intent to sell a product was probably legitimate, but I knew that closed doors don't hide innocent motives.

Even though the extent of my involvement had just been discovery and reporting, my remorse was overwhelming! I felt directly responsible for my mother's beating. How I wished I had never mentioned the stranger's presence! But it was too late. The damage had been done, and I remained soaked in guilt for telling.

The magic of my father's relationship with by mother had been poisoned by her promiscuous conduct. The way he physically punished her after the episode with the salesman was proof of his humiliation and hurt. She had stomped on his manhood.

After that incident, my father was home even less than before. He seldom had anything to say to my mother. Her bruises healed but she never received psychiatric assistance. All remained quiet, because my mother never left the confines of our house. And then, before I knew it, it was June all over again!

Another year had gone by. It was time again to welcome the warming rays of the sun, and time to change your wardrobe. For me, that meant blouses and billowy cotton skirts, or pedal pushers, shorts, and T-shirts—extra-large ones that left my shape a mystery.

Like many young girls who would soon turn thirteen years old, I was struggling with my imperfect self-image because of my lack of cleavage. The boys at school definitely paid more attention to the girls who had developed earlier. *Here I am looking like a stick of spaghetti. Will anyone ever notice me?*

Then there was my beautiful, shapely mother who turned heads when she walked down the street, no matter what she wore. From the time I was old enough to comprehend the words, "Are you going to grow up as pretty as your mother?" I understood that I was presented with a goal—to be as pretty as Mom. I wished I could look like her.

To me, my mother's features were perfect: she had been endowed with a heart-shaped face, huge brown eyes, and an exquisitely chiseled, turned-up nose. She also had a widow's peak, volumes of black curly hair, and a voluptuous body. People said she looked just like Vivien Leigh in her role as Scarlett O'Hara in the movie "Gone with the Wind."

I thought I looked nothing like my mother. What I saw in the mirror was a square face, blue-green eyes, a small nose, an undefined hairline, and straight hair. I thought I would be stuck forever with my flat chest, protruding tummy, and a gangly string bean arms and legs. I was too young to understand that most adolescent girls go through an awkward stage, but I was certainly in mine.

I desperately needed reassurance that the changes my body was going through were normal. But there was no one in my life to nurture me and give me that reassurance. In my mind, I could never attain my mother's beauty; I would always remain imperfect.

At that age, I had a strong sense of what was considered appropriate for women my mother's age: white gloves, stockings, loafers, and shirtdresses were in style. Other mothers wore plain clothing, without much skin showing. That certainly didn't describe the outfit my mother chose one warm spring day.

She boldly walked out of our back door wearing shorts and a black, mesh see-through bra. I repeatedly shouted at her, "Come back. Please, come back here!" Defiantly, she continued walking.

Why is she doing this?! She's shameless. I'm so embarrassed. I wanted to run and hide as my humiliation merged with anger.

Never had I felt such fury! I felt out of control as I followed her. My voice became hoarse from shouting. "Come back home!" My words seemed to make her walk faster.

When it became clear that shouting wouldn't work, I began begging. "Please, come back home!"

Tears began running down my face. *It's no use! She won't listen. I'll be the laughingstock of the neighborhood!*

I squinted in the sunlight as I watched my mother make a right turn onto Fenwick Avenue. This was not good. Fenwick would take her to a busy main street. Looking like a hussy would get her in trouble. She would be highly visible to the multitude of shoppers who frequented the Cedar Center shopping district. If she entered any of the shops, restaurants, boutiques, or grocery stores, with her breasts exposed like that, someone would certainly approach her or call the police. This was not proper attire at a beach let alone a shopping mall.

My mother had placed herself in harm's way by venturing outside of our home dressed so provocatively. She was asking for trouble. The potential was there for her to be beaten by my father, incarcerated, or raped. The possible consequences from her actions terrified me! *What will happen to her now?!*

Feeling despondent and filled with anguish by my mother's excruciatingly embarrassing behavior, I returned home. I didn't know what else to do. But I did know for sure that I wasn't about to tell my father anything. Remembering my father's rage over the previous episode, I decided to keep my big mouth shut! *If I tell him, he'll hurt her. I can't betray my mother again!*

When my father returned and asked about my mother, I replied, "She went out." No response. He paced back and forth like a caged tiger and badgered me with questions. I merely responded by shaking my head or replying, "I don't know." Our wait began.

The silence was finally broken when the police came to the door with Mom. My father took one look at her and shook his head in disbelief. I expected him to react with anger. Instead, he bit his lip and let them in.

I looked at my mother as she slumped in her chair. She had bruises on her face, arms, and legs. Her lower lip was bleeding. Two of her long fingernails were broken. Her bra and shorts were snagged and torn. She appeared to have been in a fight. When we asked her what had occurred, she was incoherent. The police told us what they had concluded had happened.

The South Euclid police were making their customary rounds when they saw that the rear screen door to a Chinese restaurant's kitchen had been flung open and failed to close. This was highly unusual. They had decided to investigate. They found my mother in the rear storage area sitting among the boxes, talking to herself. Perhaps someone grabbed her in the parking lot, dragged her into their car, and molested her. Upon freeing herself, she may have sought sanctuary in the restaurant's kitchen.

According to the dishwasher and two cooks, they were about to call the police, but the evening dinner rush had kept them from doing so. "She came here looking like this. We didn't touch her!" Their story could have been true. It was their word against hers and my mother couldn't even tell anyone what had happened.

My father assumed that she had been raped. "Now this—she's been violated!" Whether or not she had been, we'll never know.

My mother's very promiscuous attire deeply disturbed Dad. Her behavior shattered his ego and angered him. As her husband, he felt that both this incident and the encounter with the salesman were unforgivable! He wanted to be free of her and free of shame.

He was a conflicted man, torn between hate and pity. Being able to separate the illness from the person was impossible for him. If he had any feeling left for her, perhaps it was sympathy.

My shame over her behavior was overwhelming, perhaps much more so than my father's. I knew her public display was indecent. *Who saw her dressed that way? Will anyone question me about her roaming the street, half-exposed? And if they do, how will I explain it?* Her provocative dress repulsed me. *Why doesn't she dress and act like other mothers?* No matter what, she was my mother and I loved her. I chose to forgive and forget.

Although I envied my mother's beauty, her bizarre actions assured me that I wanted to behave nothing like her. I hated her when she was out of control! *She embarrasses me to death.* At the same time, I had to acknowledge that she was my mother. For this reason alone, I loved her. At that age, I didn't understand that a person may hate another's behavior but not the person herself.

No one could explain to me why my mother was different. I would dream about having a normal, reassuring mother. I had to learn how to surrender my ideas of how she should be. She was incapable of being a role model for me. Schizophrenia robbed my mother of her senses, and robbed me of having a mother.

Once again, a muddled and confused woman had to be taken to the hospital. Seeing her institutionalized again reopened wounds that had only begun to heal. Fear of the unknown, insecurity, and loss washed over me again, but I found it easier to accept this time. Life is a wise teacher. I was beginning to accept that some things were out of my control. *What can I do to change things?*

Nothing!

I could face a home life without my mother, as long as I could cling to the hope that my father would return home at night. But even that wasn't certain.

Mother's uncontrollable shameful behavior embarrassed us socially and hurt us emotionally. My father's way of coping with his shame seemed to be not to deal with it, but to try to escape from it. As much as I dreaded it, I knew that we would be moving again soon.

7

THE "HELPFUL" KRAVITZ FAMILY

The Kravitz family, Mr., Mrs., and three children, lived down the street in a small, white-frame, two-story Colonial. I had befriended their oldest daughter shortly after moving into the neighborhood.

Mrs. Lillian Kravitz, a first-generation Italian, possessed a classic oval face, large deep-set brown eyes, and a Grecian profile. She must have been a beauty in her youth, but now looked worn-out. She had dark circles around her eyes and deep indentations framed her red, brightly painted lips. Her raven black hair was streaked with strands of gray and pulled tightly behind her head and rolled into a bun. She was carrying an extra fifty pounds on her five-foot-one frame. She looked older than her thirty-eight years, making her appear a more suitable match for her husband.

Mr. Herman Kravitz, a Polish Jew, sold scrap iron for a living. He had a large bulbous nose that was always red. I realized later his nose's appearance was a result of alcoholism. He was fifteen years older than Lillian. His face had been wrinkled with age and by constant exposure to the outdoors. His large boney hands were chapped and red from hauling discarded metal or machinery year-round.

Lillian and Herman were an unlikely pair, and their union produced beautiful children. Sonny, the oldest, was a senior at Heights High School. He was not a scholar or athlete, but he was good-looking. He looked like his mother.

Sonny wore his shiny dark black hair in a ducktail cut, a style of the '50s. He monopolized the bathroom for what seemed like hours, standing in front of the bathroom mirror, trying to comb his black hair back into a perfect V. When he wasn't combing his hair, he was out of the house chasing girls.

Their oldest daughter, Beth, was my friend. She was a dark-haired, dark-eyed beauty who also resembled her mother facially, having the same oval face and high cheekbones. With her pale-white skin, she appeared anemic. Perhaps her pallor was due to her loss of a kidney when she was twelve. Now, approaching sixteen years old, she was fatigued and ill most of the time. Being that I was only thirteen at the time, having a friend who would be a high school freshman next year was a privilege. I really couldn't understand why I was her best friend. I had reasoned that Beth chose to spend time with me over her younger sister because the girl was just too much competition.

The couple's youngest child, Lois, had long, wavy, strawberry-blonde hair and a pretty face with a turned-up nose. The gene pool can be a fascinating trickster! *Who does she resemble?*

Ballet lessons from the age of five had toned and matured Lois' figure: petite, with well-developed breasts, long shapely legs, and firm, rounded buttocks. She was twelve years old and seeking television stardom.

On Saturdays, Lois took weekly singing and dancing lessons in downtown Cleveland. The studio sponsored a weekly talent show on Channel 5 television. The talented students were featured regularly on the show. Mrs. Kravitz, Beth, and I, would go to the TV 5 broadcasting studio to watch her perform.

On one occasion when we were at the dance studio waiting for Lois to finish rehearsing for the Sunday show, Beth and I observed the modeling class. There was a brightly lit stage, with a ten-foot walkway. A tall, slim, attractive blonde appeared from behind the curtain. She stood tall, her back straight, and chest out. She strolled down the runway, swinging her legs from her hips, and stopped and removed her jacket with grace. Placing the garment over her left arm, she turned and disappeared behind the curtain. "Bravo! Perfect," exclaimed her instructor as she applauded her. The instructor was the exercise queen on TV 5. Modeling looked so easy. "Yes! We can do it." Beth and I enrolled in an eight-week class.

Modeling was more difficult than it looked. There were pivots and turns, like a dancer. It was easy to get twisted up, like a pretzel. *Do you turn on the left foot or the right? God, I'm not sure. I'm so awkward.* Beth lacked grace too.

We whispered and giggled, every time one of us made a wrong turn on the runway. Modeling proved to be a challenge, but we completed the class and received a certificate for charm and poise.

Because of my friendship with Beth, my afterschool hours were filled with new enjoyable activities and my Sundays were exciting. I felt special and important being present at the actual filming of talent show at the TV 5 broadcasting studio. These diversions were good.

The pain from the hard reality of what was going on at home was hard to endure. For weeks, I had observed people pointing fingers at our house when they drove by or had the neighbors ask me prying questions that I couldn't and didn't want to answer. What a relief it was not to have Mrs. Kravitz embarrass me by bringing up my mom.

Our home sold. Dad had to make new living arrangements for us. He explained that living with him was not possible, and that he was looking for a suitable place for me to live. He saw my eyes become teary, and said, "It's only temporary."

Dad knew the Kravitzes. After all, he was the one who gave me permission to join them on their exciting adventures. When Lillian heard that I would be moving, my father and I were invited to dinner. The Kravitzes volunteered to take me in—for a fee, of course.

I was a seventh grader in junior high. It was mid-semester. Completing the school year where I was presently enrolled made sense. I was totally on board, "Dad…please let me stay with them!" With my enthusiastic acceptance, he agreed of course. All too soon, I would learn that my friends had concealed their issues well.

The scrap iron business wasn't providing enough income for the family. Money was a constant source of friction between the couple. Lillian was a compulsive shopper. She constantly overspent the household budget, purchasing the latest-style clothing for her children and costumes for Lois.

"God damn it. Lillian, you bitch! I can't keep up with these fucking bills!" blasted Herman. He was pouring beer into a glass. "Son-of-a-bitch." The beer spilled on to the table. Lillian cringed and bit her tongue.

Most of the arguments between Lillian and Herman occurred when he was drinking. Their home life was definitely not what I had anticipated. Nor were my accommodations.

I knew I couldn't have my own room. The house only had three bedrooms. Beth, Lois, and I shared a room. It was small and crowded with two dressers and twin beds. The thirty inches between Beth's bed and the wall were mine. To make a bed for me, they placed couch pillows on the floor and covered them with a sheet. These arrangements were okay with me. I had slept on a couch before. This was a minor discomfort compared to sharing one bathroom with five other individuals, especially if one's timid about one's body functions.

I had to awake at 4:30 a.m., an hour before anyone else, in order to have enough time in the bathroom. Otherwise, someone was always knocking on the door with an urgent need. If I didn't get up early enough, those interruptions would result in a tummy ache. *You can't inconvenience anyone in the family. You must get up early.*

One morning when I went into the bathroom, an eight-inch by ten-inch framed picture sat on the commode lid. *Strange!* I looked closer. It was a photo of Sonny's girlfriend. *Why is this here?*

Later I found out Mr. Kravitz had put it there. It wasn't a joke. He didn't like the girl. This is how he expressed his disapproval. Sonny, and everyone else in the house, got the message about how his father felt about his girlfriend. I was disappointed in Mr. Kravitz's gauche behavior and shocked that an adult could act that way. I felt sorry for Sonny, for I, too, had experienced insensitivity.

The Kravitz children fought constantly, but, being an only child, I never understood sibling rivalry or fighting. Now that I was living with them, I soon found myself held responsible for things I did not do. I became their scapegoat.

If Sonny's comb turned up missing—who did it? Well, most likely it was Mr. Kravitz, but Sonny would exclaim, "Beverly did it!" This incident occurred almost daily with his obsessions with his hair.

No matter what happened, it was Beverly's fault! Being the scapegoat didn't feel good. I wanted to fight back, but I didn't know where I would go if they threw me out. To keep from arguing, I would meander around the neighborhood or sip sodas at the corner drug store until dusk. I would sit at the counter for hours, lost in my thoughts. I'd be brought back to reality when the "soda jerk" would jest, "Don't you have a home little girl?" I'd smile at him and look away, blinking back tears. I'm sure he meant it as a friendly jibe, but it was a constant reminder of the home I didn't have.

How I longed for a bedroom of my own, with a closet filled with pretty clothes. Instead, here I was living with the Kravitzes, my clothing kept in two large brown paper bags. My wardrobe consisted of white shirts, blue jeans, undershirts, and panties. They grew stiff with dirt before they ever encountered soap and water. Lillian seldom asked for my dirty laundry and I was too shy to take the liberty of placing my soiled clothing with the family's.

I had begun feeling resentful, unkempt, and unloved. *Beth and her family can't be my friends. They don't give a damn!* My opinion of them had changed.

My only friend in this big unwelcoming world was Murphy. We met at the soda fountain. He sat two stools away from me. *How can he stand that messy mop of hair flopping over his forehead?* He turned to look at me asking, "Is something wrong?" He had a broad smile and freckles. I didn't want to tell him what I was thinking, so I said, "Do you live nearby?

He brushed his red hair off of his brow, and said, "Yep. A few streets away."

I responded, "It was getting dark, I'd better leave, "Nice meeting you…"

He responded, "My name's Murphy. I own the motor bike out front. How about a ride."

"Yes. Yes," I said.

After school, I would ride on the back of his bike as we cruised the adjacent streets until dusk. This chubby, sixteen-year-old, Irish boy became my confidant, and I was his, as much as we were both able. There was only so much we were able to open up to each other about because of how taboo the subjects of our home lives were. I was able to gather that his mother had just filed for divorce. But just as I was hesitant to speak about my mother's problems, I suspect he felt the same. I could only tell him about the Kravitzes.

We were companions until I moved away from the Kravitzes' house. I wish I could have met him as an adult, so I could have heard the rest of his story. I would love to know how his life played out. Although we were only friends for a few months, his companionship was a crucial lifeline during that tough time. We were clean-cut kids seeking asylum from dysfunction. This was also the first time I had ever really connected emotionally with a boy. We filled a need in each other's lives. We could have gone bad, or experimented with sex, but we didn't!

The Kravitzes never questioned me about my whereabouts or why I returned to their home so late. They were indifferent to my behavior. They simply didn't care, and I was miserable.

What's the lesson? My experience of living with the Kravitz family opened my eyes to the fact that other families were perhaps every bit as dysfunctional as my own—we just had different problems.

8

GETTING TO BE BEVERLY

I needed my stay with the Kravitz family to end soon. If I'm forced to stay here longer, I'll just run away. I'll take my two shopping bags and go!

But, Beverly, where to?

I don't know.

You'd better tell your dad how you feel.

It had been five months since I had seen or heard from my father. I felt abandoned. In the distant past he had been an adoring father, but now I wasn't sure how he felt about me. I had begun to question his love for me. *If he doesn't love Mom anymore, how can he love me?* Seeing his dark side had made me fear and distrust him. *He's a mean man.*

When Dad finally came for a visit, he parked his car in front of the Kravitz house. I had been sitting on the lawn next to the driveway, eagerly awaiting his arrival, and hopped into the passenger seat before he had a chance to open his door. All my pent-up emotions had to be released. Between my tears, the words rushed out. "Daddy, please. Please help me! They hate me. Everything is my fault."

I recounted the events of the past months, and then exclaimed, "I can't go back there! Take me home with you!" *Foolish girl, what home? I don't even know where he lives.*

But being true to the father I had known, he came to my rescue. He asked his brother and his sister-in-law for help, and then asked me if I could live with them. *Yes! Thank God for Auntie Elsie and Uncle Dominic!* I would be happy to live with them in their new home. My move in date would coincide with the last day of school.

The month of June and the end of the school semester couldn't arrive too soon, especially for me. The final countdown began. As each day passed, I crossed it off of the calendar in the back of my notebook: June 1, 2, 3, 4, 5, 6. Then, on day seven, my classmates and I assembled in the auditorium for a brief speech.

To end his speech, the principal spoke the joyous words, "School's out for summer!" Without hesitation, the elated audience stood, and we responded with loud enthusiasm, shouting out, "Hurrah!" Then the entire student body exited into the hallway, pulling me along with them.

Separating myself from the crowd, I waved at friends and said my goodbyes to a few of my favorite people. "Goodbye, Mrs. Cohen. I'll miss you. Goodbye, Marybelle. I'll try to call you." I had no time for more conversation. My father was waiting outside.

I pushed through the door to exit the building and caught a glimpse of it closing over my shoulder as I ran down the steps. *Goodbye, Roosevelt Junior High School. Goodbye, Cleveland Heights.* Scurrying to my father's Chevy, I climbed into the front seat and leaned over to give him an appreciative hug.

Dad pointed to the back seat, "I've already stopped at the house. Lillian gave me your things." There sat my meager belongings. There was no going back.

Thank God! I settled back in my seat and smiled from ear to ear. Before nightfall, I would be living on the west side of town.

For once, moving was my choice. I can't believe it! At long last! Kravitz family—goodbye and good riddance!

Having lived with my aunt and uncle in the past, I knew that I'd be treated like a valued member of the household. After all, we were family. This would become a chapter of self-discovery, self-worth, and new companions.

Auntie Elsie, Uncle Dominic, and my cousins, Donna and Ted, were waiting at the door when we pulled up to the house and greeted me with open arms. *They're happy to see me!*

I looked back at my father for reassurance that I had made the right decision. As I caught a smile teasing up the corners of his mouth, my eyes flooded with tears. He had restored my trust. He was still the Daddy whose shoulder I had cuddled my head against as a toddler. He was still the Daddy whose return home meant hugs and praise for his little girl. *He still loves me.*

My emotions were mixed: joy, for my wish had been granted, and sadness, for my father would be leaving without me. Hugging and kissing my father goodbye, I felt hopeful that this change would be a good one.

The house was compact with five small downstairs rooms: an eat-in kitchen, living room, two bedrooms, and full bath. Donna and I shared the space under the large dormer over the garage which had been converted to a big airy bedroom.

We also shared the big, black, cast-iron bed covered with a fluffy goose down comforter made by Baba Rose Novak. Though I still felt uncomfortable sharing a room and a bed, even with family, I nevertheless was grateful that I didn't have to sleep on the floor anymore.

The summer passed quickly. In 1955, I was one of approximately two thousand students enrolled at Parma Senior High School. Never had I attended a school with so many students. Not knowing any of my classmates undermined my confidence. I felt scared, insecure, and out of place. Because I transferred from an affluent neighborhood, teachers and students alike expected me to be scholarly and rich. On more than one occasion I heard students whispering things like, "You know those Heights kids—they excel in academics, athletics, and music. Their parents have lots of money for tutors, lessons, or whatever they need to succeed."

What a stretch! Money? Tutors? That's not me. What if I don't measure up to their expectations? My new classmates know nothing about the real me and I'll make sure they never will.

I would never tell them about my frequent moves from the east side of town to the west and then back again. They would never hear from me about what it was like to cope with dysfunctional living arrangements and a revolving door of new schools, new teachers, new studies, and new friends. Nor would I lament that much of my brain power was spent on coping, not studying. *Let them try to concentrate and focus when their mother's in the kitchen loudly talking to herself or you can't go home to study, because it's not YOUR home.* And, most certainly, I could never tell them the reason for all these changes in my life was because my mother had schizophrenia.

And how could I tell them about the constant chatter in my head? My thoughts were consumed with a battle between my resilient inner child and my personal self-defeating demon, negativity.

I'll never be a scholar!

That's not true.

What's the use? Why try? Nobody cares!

Your father cares! Auntie Elsie cares. Your teachers care.

Nobody cares about me!

My mind's civil war depleted my energy and made learning and studying more difficult. When my grades were good, they were only the result of repetitious study. To achieve anything better than a B, I had to put in a lot of hard work.

My whole life felt like a struggle. The many obstacles that were placed in my path were not by my design, but were thrust on me by my destiny as the daughter of a woman with schizophrenia. From the age of four and a half, I had learned to put up emotional walls to protect myself from unpredictable forces of destruction and change. I needed friends to help me learn to have fun again.

I found someone to hang out with during the second week of school. Helen Stafanski, at five feet eleven, was the tallest girl at Parma Senior High and had been given the nickname, "Skyscraper." Her small frame and lack of curves only served to emphasize her stature. She was self-conscious about her height, so whenever the boys came around, she rounded her shoulders to appear shorter. Her face was attractive and framed in tight blonde ringlets, but no one noticed because her height overshadowed all of her good features.

Just like me, she had entered the classroom unaccompanied, sat in

80

a seat at the back of the room, and spoken to no one. As history class ended and fifty teens rushed for the door, we were shoved next to each other. This gave me the nerve to ask her directions to my next class.

Helen, like me, was excessively shy and in need of friendship. After several days of spending time together between classes, we discovered that Helen lived just a couple of blocks west of me and decided to walk to school together.

The next day, I stood on the corner of West 54th and Pershing, waiting for her. She approached and we exchanged greetings. As we started on our walk, I was completely taken aback by Helen's first question. "Bev, what's your nationality?"

"Italian. Why do you ask?"

Helen laughed. "Beverly, I should have known you were Italian. Your long black hair gives you away." *Do I look that ethnic? Some people peg me as Irish with my green eyes.*

I didn't question her ethnicity. I thought her last name was the giveaway. *I've been stereotyped because of hair color. Well, then, she has to be Polish; after all, she's blonde!*

The next day, Helen asked another probing question. "Are you Catholic?"

"…Yes." My response was affirmative, yet technically, it was incorrect. *Why elaborate now?* Although I had been told I was a Catholic and felt like I was a Catholic, I do not recall ever attending regular Mass as a child. I didn't think my parents had baptized me. In the eyes of the Church, I was not a Catholic.

However, like many other Italian families, many of our traditions were centered on the Church. Grandma Caroline, in particular, held on to the religious traditions from her upbringing. Her bedroom mirror was covered with prayer cards. A rosary hung from the lamp beside her bed and another one was tucked into her change purse. Before traveling anywhere in a car, she kissed the rosary and made the sign of the cross, but she never attended regular Mass, either.

The fondest memory I have of being in a church was during the Feast of the Assumption when I was eight or nine years old. Grandma Caroline handed me a quarter for the donation box and asked me to light a vigil candle for my mother while she waited outside, leaning on her cane. She somehow made me understand with her broken English that lighting the candle represented a promise to pray for a specific request.

As I walked into the vestibule, I was in awe of the beauty that surrounded me. Sunlight streamed through the stained-glass windows, casting the floor and walls in beautiful shades of rich reds, deep purples, and brilliant blues. Majestic wooden chairs graced the altar behind a hand-carved mahogany railing. The splendor of the church's interior brought back memories of my happy childhood trips to the Cleveland Museum of Art.

Helen's voice snapped me out of my reminiscing. "My sister and I attend Mass at St. Francis De Sales Church on Sunday. Dorothy drives. If you'd like to come with us, we'll pick you up at 8:30."

My instincts told me that having a religious foundation was healthy and normal. In my mind, religion and happiness went hand in hand. Any time my mother's mental illness distressed me, I would find my way to the nearest church to light a candle and pray with my whole heart and soul for her sanity! Like a child wishing on a shooting star, I hoped that embracing religion would miraculously return my mother to normalcy.

Of course, I answered Helen in the affirmative. Saying "no" to a friend was impossible for me, even though I had reservations. I was full of fears that I'd make a fool of myself.

Upon entering the church that Sunday, I started to get anxious. *Just follow the crowd.* The bells chimed, incense and candles burned, and the choir began to sing. The parishioners stood; I stood. *Phew, this is easy!*

Feeling proud of myself, I continued moving in unison with the worshipers while standing, kneeling, and making the sign of the cross. *I'm doing well!*

The Our Father and Hail Mary prayers were familiar from spending time with Grandma Caroline as she listened to the rosary on the radio. I mumbled or lip-synched my way through the unfamiliar prayers. How my friends didn't catch on to my ineptness, I'll never know.

All was well until it was time for communion. *What shall I do? Surely I'll blunder this and they'll see what a fraud I am!* The faithful stood, exited their pews, and formed a double line up the center aisle of the church.

I can't do this. It will be sacrilegious to receive the host. I haven't made my First Communion.

I stayed put. *Everyone is staring at me!* Helen and her sister made their way to the altar, along with everyone else in the church—so it seemed—to receive the Communion host. As for me, I just sat there, my face burning, too embarrassed and self-absorbed to realize that there were other people who also remained seated. The sacrament was completed and the benediction given. *Thank goodness, I made it through!* I was grateful that we made our drive home in silence. I wasn't prepared to answer any questions about why I hadn't taken Communion.

This episode prompted me to ask my father if I had been baptized. His answer was vague. "Your mother's best friend, Carmella, was chosen to be your godmother, but I don't remember if you were ever baptized. Your mother destroyed family pictures and records during one of her breakdowns. You might check with the church."

My father was referring to Saint Mary's Catholic Church, which was within walking distance of my childhood home on Frank Avenue. I called the rectory of the church and quickly established that there was no record of my baptism.

After overcoming my pride and confiding my dilemma to my friends, we made plans for me to officially join the Catholic Church. Helen's sister, who was in her early twenties, offered to be my godmother or sponsor. Dorothy was most definitely my religious role model. Because of her commitment to her faith, I believed her to be an infinitely good person. I wanted to be like her.

For three months, six of us attended weekly Catechism classes and memorized prayers to recite aloud. There was homework and studying. At the completion of the course, we would be baptized and then make our First Communion.

The morning of my baptism, while grooming and gazing in the mirror, my thoughts drifted to another time and place. I was sitting on the front steps of the dream home on Eastway Road, playing jacks. My next-door neighbor and playmate, Marty Zerbes, was getting into the backseat of her father's car. The family was on their way to church. Marty looked like a mini bride in a white organza dress. I now knew that her sheer white veil symbolized purity.

You missed out. No white dress for you or white veil cascading from a tiara made of white daisies and lace. Remember how you envied her. How badly you wanted to play grownup and dress like a bride!

She made her first confession that day. Did Marty truly understand Catholic doctrine, absolution, penance, and contrition? Did she understand the commitment she was making to the Catholic Church that day? She probably didn't. She was too young, but I'm older and I know.

My baptism and Holy Communion were held after Mass without pomp and circumstance or fancy clothing—just the priest and Dorothy. *Finally! Growing up feels so good!* I had just taken another step on my own that enabled me to be accepted by my friends. There was so much more that I wanted to learn.

9

LEARNING TO PLAY

Enrolling in a new school meant a fresh start and new opportunities. Parma Senior High School offered me the chance to make my childhood musical aspirations come true. The decision I was about to make, to play an instrument, introduced me to people who would affect the course of my life forever.

My school counselor said my aptitude tests showed musical ability. "Do you have any interest in learning to play a musical instrument?"

Without hesitating, I responded, "Yes, the piano."

There was a long pause. *Yes, it is my dream. But how can I practice without a piano?*

"I don't have a piano, but possibly a woodwind instrument will do. Maybe a flute?"

Suddenly visualizing myself as the "Pied Piper," I practically giggled out loud. What was I thinking? I'm a silly girl.

But the flute's lightweight and easy to carry. That's it.

"Yes …a flute."

"Good. You can rent a reconditioned instrument. Just have one of your parents sign this permission slip. You'll need money for a deposit, and one month's rent in advance." Auntie Elsie readily signed the consent form and funded my new venture.

My first assignment was learning to make whistling sounds with a Coca-Cola bottle. Auntie was forced to listen to the piercing, shrill sounds for an hour per day, five days a week.

After two weeks, much to the relief of Auntie Elsie and our neighbors, I advanced from the Coke bottle to an Armstrong flute, but the high-pitched, breathy sounds continued. It was then that Auntie arranged for private lessons. By the end of the winter semester, I had improved so much that my teacher encouraged me to audition for the school orchestra and marching band.

To try out, one played a solo for the director. He was a tall, good-looking, talented, passionate musician who could play an assortment of instruments, including the flute. His wife just happened to be my instructor.

I shook like a leaf on a windy day as he placed the sheet music on the stand. He had selected excerpts from a John Phillip Souza march and Ravel's Bolero. Somehow, despite my nerves, I managed to complete the selected music. Although I was excited when I learned that I had succeeded, it was no surprise to me that my ability only merited a fourth-chair assignment…the last chair.

I attended my first orchestra rehearsal. The room was brightly lit and five rows of chairs were placed in a semicircle. The flute section was in the center of the first row right under the director's nose. Seated three chairs away from me practicing scales on a flute was Joyce Serraglio, a strikingly beautiful girl I had met at tryouts. She looked like an artist's model with a perfect oval face, classic features, long blonde hair, green eyes, and a slender figure. *Here we go, another femme fatale like Marty Zerbes.*

Joyce and I had hit it off from our very first meeting. Surprisingly, the fact that she was my competition, the first-chair flutist and a beauty, didn't keep me from bonding with her. I managed to harness the envy that had reared its ugly head when I met Marty.

Our camaraderie was initially due to our mutual paternal ethnicity—Italian. She told me that her father, Angelo, was from Sicily, the island at the foot of Italy's boot.

86

She must be kidding. Her father's name is Angelo?! "I don't believe it! Say his name again."

"My father's name is Angelo, Angelo Serraglio."

Is this an omen of some sort?

"My last name is De Angelis. My great-grandfather was named Angelo De Angelis."

Now that we had established that her father and my grandfather had the same first name, we looked for other similarities between our family members, especially our fathers. Both men were strict, protective, and mysterious men who kept secrets about their private lives. After all, I didn't even know where my father lived, and Joyce's father left home each evening after she went to bed. She, too, often wondered about her father's whereabouts.

After discovering the similarities between our fathers, our youthful imaginations conjured up pictures of them connected in some way to the Mafia. Each conversation we had about them always ended in giggles. That's what fourteen-year-old girls do, isn't it?

Joyce and I studied and hung out together whenever the opportunity allowed, which wasn't often, since her father seldom gave his permission for her to socialize after school. Despite his hesitance to let Joyce spend time outside of the house, he readily approved of my occasional visits to their home.

Like Joyce, her mother was beautiful. She was an Austrian/German beauty, tiny and petite with a large, exaggerated, beehive hairdo. Joyce had a younger brother, Paul, who resembled her father—a tall, good-looking, olive-skinned, muscular Sicilian.

Angelo Serraglio was a heavy equipment operator. Spreaders, backhoes, and steam shovels were the tools of his trade. He had built their home, a stone and brick ranch on a three-acre lot located on Pleasant Valley Road, an undeveloped section of Parma.

By the time I met Joyce, five years had passed since the family's move-in date. A roughly built construction shed still remained at the end of the long gravel drive. It was actually a bit of an eyesore—a misfit—when compared to the dwelling next to it.

One school day afternoon, as our school bus pulled away from the drive, Joyce and I began our walk to her side door when she abruptly stopped. "Wait." Changing directions, she turned and I followed her across the drive. We stopped in front of the door to the shed beside her house. *What could she possibly want me to see in here?*

Joyce opened the door. I inhaled dust. Stowed away in this most unlikely place was a small grand piano. "It's a beauty!" *Never mind that the instrument's finish is scarred.* We sat upon the bench and began attempting to play.

Never mind the dirt, dust, or October dampness. Never mind that two of its yellowed ivory keys do not produce sound, or that it's out of tune and the bench wobbles. Once again, another revelation, another likeness: she, too, had dreamt of becoming a pianist and she, too, had become a flutist.

Joyce and I studied, spent time together, and shared intimate secrets. In our minds, we acted and thought alike, and we were even the exact same height. Our classmates called us "the Bobbsey twins." We affectionately called each other *Twinnie,* a nickname that remains in use to this day. Even as new friends, we could complete each other's sentences—that's sisterhood!

I had to fortify myself with determination and pay no attention to school gossip. *Ignore their comments. Ignore their stares. After all, I've been through this before.* Resiliency and thick skin helped me remain

Although I remained an only child my whole life, I have had one friend who might as well have been a sibling, given how long our friendship has lasted. Three words best describe my chosen sister: *beautiful, perfect,* and *determined.* Her physical beauty was combined with a keen mind and a thirst for knowledge. She was driven to be number one in whatever she set out to do. In addition, she possessed a loving, giving heart. One couldn't be blessed with more.

10

PUPPY LOVE

I had joined the orchestra and marching band in the middle of the school year. Marching band required rehearsals after school during which we practiced our formations on the field. Joyce would always have to hurry to catch the last school bus to get home after practice. Helen and I would part ways earlier in the school day. I was on my own after practice, and I dreaded the walk home.

After a month of rehearsals, I was growing accustomed to walking home alone in the cold. On my way home one day, I found myself walking behind a group of kids. Too shy to just join them, I had to either pick up my pace to walk ahead of them, or slow down and stay behind. Introducing myself to unfamiliar classmates was an impossible task. As I slowed my pace, I could hear footsteps approaching from behind. I turned to see who it was. *That's Dennis Richards.* He was the brown-haired, boyish looking, five-foot-eight saxophone player. *Shall I'll say, "Hello," or just let him pass me?*

"Hi, Denny." I was barely audible.

His face lit up. He knew who I was. To my surprise, he adjusted his pace to walk beside me. We talked continuously until we reached my street. We were practically neighbors, since he lived only two blocks north of me. Each time he accompanied me home, we'd linger longer and longer on the corner.

One brisk January day, it was too cold to stand on the corner and talk, so Denny accompanied me to my side door inside the garage. He turned his head slightly to the side. Instinctively, I moved closer. When he closed his eyes, my heart went pitter-pat. *He's going to kiss me!* Then the flood-light in the garage went on and the door to the house swung open. Like two fawns caught in a car's headlights, we jumped apart

My younger cousin Donna was standing in the doorway. Her face was beet-red, she was breathing heavily, and she looked totally frazzled. *Did I do something wrong?*

Donna wasn't the least bit concerned about me or the fact that I was with a young man.

"I was feeding Tweety and he got out! You gotta help me!"

Denny and I looked up to see Donna's feathered friend perched on the kitchen curtain rod, defiantly looking at us. She quickly slammed the door.

The door reopened to reveal Donna, holding Auntie's large hairnet in her left hand. The bird was frantically circling the kitchen. As it flew towards the door, Donna threw the hairnet into the air. Tweety became tangled in the net and fell to the floor. Flapping his wings, he freed himself and the game of catch-me-if-you-can continued in the kitchen. White, green, and yellow pin feathers flew about in the kitchen, hall, and garage.

I yelled, "Close the door. Tweety will get out. Then we'll never catch him. I'll help you in a minute." She banged the door shut.

Denny closed his eyes once more, and leaned over to kiss me. Our lips were an eighth of an inch apart when the door swung open again. This time Donna held a flyswatter in her hand. She gave me a stern gaze and said, "When are you coming in here?!" and closed the door.

Donna's beside herself. I'd better go inside. Anyhow, she'll just continue annoying us until Tweety is in his cage.

The magical spell was broken. Disappointed, I turned away from Denny, and said, "I'll see you."

Of course, I caught the bird, but the next week there was no one to escort me home after practice. Our potentially sweet friendship had ended abruptly.

And then there was Johnny. He was quite the catch: six-foot-tall, with a muscular body, brown eyes, and wavy black hair. The girls agreed he was the best-looking guy in the school. When he played his horn solo in Chet Baker's rendition of "My Funny Valentine," the girls were mesmerized. His combination of good looks and musical talent charmed all the gals, including me. *Too bad he only has eyes for his girlfriend, the clarinet player.* The fact that he was unavailable didn't matter, because no one else caught my eye.

There was a guy who paid attention to me in the only way he knew how—by behaving like the class clown. He sat behind me in eighth period study hall, but my secret crush on Johnny meant that I never paid attention to him. Shy and serious, I kept to myself, studying. Day after day, he would tap me on the shoulder and ask, "Can I borrow a pencil?

Ignoring him didn't work, because then he would ask, "Do you have an eraser?" He was a real pain!

The school year would end in a week and it was a hot and humid 85 degrees outside. There was no air-conditioning in the school, and the windows were open. The guy behind me must have been extremely bored or uncomfortable because he became even more of a nuisance. It started with the same old pencil routine.

What?! He must have had a pencil earlier in the day. How could he make it to eighth period without one?!

Turning to look at him, I shook my head no. I found myself staring into large brown eyes. *Thin oval face, blond hair, and a brush haircut…*

I think I've seen him before. Where? When?

I had my English final the next day, so I turned back to focus on my studies. I did my best to ignore him again, but when the pest wasn't slouching in his desk to stretch his long legs in the open aisle, he was putting his feet on the back-support bar and rhythmically tapping or pushing my desk, moving it to and fro.

Can't the teacher see what he's doing? Obviously not. With seventy-five students, she can't keep an eye on everyone.

My feet felt sweaty, especially my right foot. My toenail had snagged my cotton socks and my big toe hurt. I took off my right penny loafer and started wiggling my toes. *Gosh, that feels good.* I tucked my shoeless foot beneath me and tried to concentrate.

The dismissal bell would ring in ten minutes. My sock-clad foot began searching for its shoe. *Where is it?*

I looked under the desk and in the aisles. *No shoe! What will I do?* My face burned as I twisted and squirmed. *God, I hope the teacher doesn't notice. What will I say?*

An image of a clown flashed across my mind. *I know who's responsible.* Tears filled my eyes, my lips pursed together, and I turned the corners of my mouth down to keep myself from screaming. I turned to look at him. *You did it! You trouble maker!*

He took one look at my face and he knew what I was thinking.

He jumped up, took four steps, and the metal pull bar clanked as he opened the emergency exit. He stepped outside of the building.

When he returned, he handed me my loafer. He had thrown it out of the open window!

Taking my shoe, I smiled as the teacher called out, "Mr. Kowalski, report to detention!" *He deserves it!*

The following day during band practice, I looked up from the sheet music and spotted a familiar pair of eyes looking at me. *That's him! He plays the clarinet?!*

At the end of practice, he waited for me outside the classroom. I had to look up at him. My five-foot-seven-inch stance was dwarfed by his six-foot-three-inch one. I felt small by comparison, which didn't happen too often with other boys.

I looked into his large deep set dark-brown eyes. They were captivating and sorrowful, like a Beagle puppy.

He said, "I hope you can forgive me for yesterday."

He's apologized. I like him.

Looking up, I gave him a wide-eyed innocent look, and asked, "Are you on the basketball team?" He had the look, willowy and agile; with long legs and long arms. He could reach up and dunk the ball into the hoop, *voila*! A basket. How simple.

Smiling, he replied, "No, I've never tried out for the team. I wanted to, but I can't find the time. I work three evenings a week and a half day on Saturday to pay for my clarinet lessons.

"Several of the varsity guys are in my gym class; they say I play a mean game. They've nicknamed me 'Rail.'"

The name fits him. He's very tall and very thin.

He gave me an ear-to-ear grin and said, "By the way, my name's Chet…Kowalski."

"I'm Beverly De Angelis."

For the next three days, there were no more shenanigans in study hall. We waved and smiled at each other in halls. I had forgiven him for embarrassing me. I sensed that someday we would be much more than acquaintances, but our new friendship was put on hold until the fall semester.

11

THAT'S LIFE! REAL LIFE!

It was June, and school was out for the summer. This was the beginning of my second year of living with my uncle and his family. During the previous year, my life had been good; normal. The relatively uneventful year had given me a chance to heal, to build friendships, and to trust my father once more. Then the unexpected happened!

Donna and I were awakened late one evening by a loud thumping noise and my Auntie Elsie's frantic calls. We both hurried down the stairs from our second-floor bedroom to see why she was so distraught.

Auntie was standing on the landing between the kitchen and the garage, pounding her fists against the locked door to the basement steps. Between her sobs, she begged, "Dominic! Open the door! Please! Dominic! Please!" But there was no response.

The next-door neighbor overheard my aunt's pleas from his backyard. He took the liberty of entering our open garage where he could see my aunt. He asked, "Elsie, can I help?"

She blurted out, "Please call the police. Dominic wants to kill himself. God only knows what's triggered this. He has a gun. Hurry. Please!"

The police station was located a few blocks south of Pershing Avenue and within minutes of the neighbor's departure, a patrolman arrived at the house.

Auntie exclaimed, "He's threatening to blow out his brains. You must get him to unlock the door. Break the door down if you have to! He has a gun!"

The responding officer was persuasive. Without calling for backup, he convinced Uncle Dominic to relent and open the door.

Meanwhile, Donna and I wanted to remain out of sight, and fled up our bedroom steps, stopping below the landing. Donna slipped her arm through mine and held on tightly as we peered down the stairs. From there, we could see into the living room and eavesdrop on the adults below.

My aunt and uncle entered the living room and sat on the sofa. The officer followed and sat across from them. *Where's the gun?*

The man who sat on the couch was not the Uncle Dominic whom I had seen earlier. His round face looked red and bloated. His dark-brown eyes seemed to bulge like those of the actor, Peter Lorre. Perspiration was dripping from his forehead and his hair. Even his clothing was drenched with sweat. *My God, what has happened to him?*

The patrolman pulled a small pad out of his shirt pocket and began questioning my aunt and uncle. "Is there any friction between the two of you? Any domestic issues? Any financial problems?" They responded "no" in unison. There was a long-drawn-out silence, and he left. However, I was puzzled by what the officer didn't say or do.

Why didn't he ask about his gun? Where is it? Uncle Dom was empty handed when he entered the living room. Even I knew that he hid souvenirs from World War II in the basement ceiling—a Luger pistol, a bayonet, and a helmet.

And why didn't he take my uncle to the police station or the hospital? If my mother had behaved that way, that's exactly what the policeman would have done.

And I had another question. *Why would Uncle Dominic want to kill himself?*

96

In the year I had lived there, Uncle Dominic worked every day, returned home on time, and watched television, mostly sports. He drank an occasional beer, but he never swore or argued like Mr. Kravitz. And he always kissed Auntie goodbye. My unresolved questions lingered in my thoughts. *Here we go again.*

The next day, Auntie Elsie went about her business just as she had done for years, maintaining her routine, containing her worries, and saying nothing. No explanations for Uncle Dom's behavior were given. In fact, no one said a word about it.

That evening, Donna and I sat down on the living room floor with Auntie Elsie to play games—checkers, Monopoly, or Parcheesi—just as we had done for countless days and months earlier. I got the feeling that they were so embarrassed that they couldn't face bringing up what had happened with Uncle Dom.

But I knew that I would have to tell my father what had happened. I had learned from my time at the Kravitz house that denying a problem didn't make things better.

The following day, when my father and I were returning from a visit with my mother, I broached the sensitive subject. I needed clarity and after recounting the event, I asked my father for answers.

My father responded, "Do you mean, has he been suicidal? No! I'm not aware of any other incidents."

"Daddy, did Uncle Dom snap like Mommy?"

"Do you mean, is he schizophrenic, like your mother?"

"Yes."

"Beverly, it's not the same." There was a long pause.

"But since returning from the War, he has changed."

His eyes remained focused on the road ahead. Several minutes passed, before he turned to look at me. My father's eyes had lit up.

"That's it. That's the problem. Dominic can't talk about Normandy. Elsie's told me that he has nightmares. Some nights, he wakes up screaming, covered in sweat. He's had a hard time. Any time I ask him about it, he shuts me down. But a lot of people had a hard time after the War."

I had heard about the invasion of Normandy, but I had been a small child when it had happened. In my teenage world, it was remote, like scenes from a movie. I had no real understanding of the devastation my uncle had survived.

Somehow, someway, Dominic had been fortunate. But he had been there, wading through the rough, dark, waist-high water of the Seine, trying to make it to the shore. Many of his fellow soldiers and friends had been blown into unidentifiable pieces before reaching land. Those who escaped death were literally bathed in the blood of their companions.

Uncle Dom had seen the bloodbath with his own eyes. There was no escaping the sight or smell of death for death had surrounded him on all sides. How could he forget memories like that? Impossible!

My father's only exposure to battle was through the news media. He viewed the War from a sheltered distance via photos, broadcasts, and newsreels. Having never experienced the War on a first-hand basis, he could only imagine the trauma his brother had suffered.

"Dad, where's the gun?"

"Ever since Dom brought the gun home, he's stored it in the unfinished basement ceiling, between the studs and joists. I'll find out. Stop worrying, everything will be all right."

There was another pause. "By the way, the doctor said your mother will return home soon." This news on top of my uncle's incident was just too overwhelming for me to ask any more questions. Our conversation left me feeling confused.

I'll never understand him; how can he take the whereabouts of the gun so lightly?! What if Dominic tries again?

Then he nonchalantly changes the subject: "By the way." And his new topic is like an unexploded bomb—Mother's coming home.

Thoughts flashed in and out of my brain, like the changing fragments of glass in a kaleidoscope. *When will this happen? Will I have any say in where I live after she comes home? How long will it be before she has another breakdown?* There was always the likelihood that my mother would experience a schizophrenic episode. *It always happens; we just never know when.*

The mere thought of having to move again made me sick to my

stomach. *Does Mom coming home mean that I'll have to move? Where does Dad even live? Would moving back with him and Mom mean I would have to start all over again at a new school? Just when I feel like I've gotten things together, another change comes along. Every time I find out I have to move I can feel my heart thumping in my chest. This is just too much!!!*

In spite of Uncle's recent breakdown, perhaps living with him and his family is the better option for me. After all, Auntie Elsie is a positive influence on me, and I love her!

My recent conversation with my father left me with nagging thoughts about my uncle's need for hospitalization. *Auntie Elsie has to know that Uncle Dom has mental issues. They sleep in the same bed. She has to know his nightmares aren't normal. How could she not know?*

My other worry was that possibly their marriage was in trouble. Events in my short lifetime had taught me that, in spite of their love, mental illness could break the bond between a husband and wife. And if that happened, they definitely didn't need me living with them.

My fears about Uncle Dom's mental health and his marriage to Auntie Elsie were never realized. Growing up in the same house had bonded Elsie and Dominic. Their love was long and enduring; she was there for him, "in sickness and in health, 'til death do us part."

All too soon, my apprehension about my uncle's behavior was replaced with concern for the welfare of my naïve and overly affectionate cousin. Donna craved affection and attention from everyone. When she said, "Goodbye" to you, her "Goodbye" became a long, drawn-out procedure. She would coil her arms around your neck. Then, while steadfastly clinging to you, she would smother you with kisses until you were breathless and begging for your freedom. Your pleas for release fell on deaf ears. There was no getting away from her, once she had you in a bear hug! Auntie Elsie would have to literally peel her off you.

No matter how annoying Donna's childlike behavior was, in my mind, she was my "little sis" and I, her "big sister." I put up with her. Like younger sisters, she could be a pest. Age-wise, we were contemporaries since our birthdays were separated by only two years. But before she was even born, Donna's brain sustained trauma that affected her learning ability and meant that she would never mature the same way I did.

When my Auntie Elsie was three months pregnant with Donna, her appendix burst. My aunt's life and the life of her baby were in jeopardy! Doctors performed an operation, miraculously saving both their lives. Sadly, the tiny fetus' brain was damaged by the procedure.

Once Donna was born, her injuries became apparent. Her cerebral palsy meant that she lacked muscular control on the right side of her body. Epilepsy—reoccurring seizures—also afflicted Donna. There was no predictability as to where or when she would experience an attack. She would begin by gagging and seeing flashing lights.

Thankfully, most of the time, giving Donna a glass of water would stop the onset of the seizures, but, on occasion, her spasms would appear and then intensify. Her arms, legs, and body seemed to move involuntarily. As she lost her balance, she would fall onto the floor and thrash about while choking on her saliva. Watching her undergo such an episode was unnerving, and being alone with her when this happened was my worst nightmare, another challenge I learned I could survive.

Donna's hands are moving funny. Her eyes are fluttering. Beverly, turn her on her side. Now she's biting her tongue. I see blood. Oh God, I'm frightened! Call for help! Thankfully, emergency services always arrived on time.

Already severely handicapped with cerebral palsy and epilepsy, each illness being a challenge itself, Donna also faced psychological and social burdens as a result of her immaturity and learning disability. Before closing school for summer vacation, the Parma City Schools' guidance counselors recommended that Donna transfer to a school that could accommodate her needs. The new school offered a six-week summer class which she took.

Donna rode to school in a small jitney that pulled right up in front of our driveway to pick up and drop her off. As she boarded the bus one morning, I noticed for the first time that her tight clothing revealed a mature and voluptuous body. *But she's only twelve years old.* She began waving "Goodbye" and throwing kisses. *She's just a kid!*

Donna was the first passenger on the bus in the morning and the last one off at the end of the day. For five weeks, the driver maintained the given schedule. Then, on the sixth and final week of school, the drop-off time became very irregular.

Auntie Elsie and I asked ourselves, "Why was the bus delayed? Was traffic the cause? Were there delays in loading the wheelchairs on the bus?"

On the last day of school, Auntie Elsie kept looking at the clock. "Damn it. She's late again!"

Donna returned home with disheveled hair and clothing. *What had happened?* Her face was puffy and red. She kept rubbing her inner thighs and complaining of pain. Auntie Elsie took one look at her daughter and immediately took her into the bathroom. She drew her a warm bath, and dissolved several cups of Epsom salt in the water. Once Donna was undressed and soaking in the tub, Auntie Elsie pulled the door almost shut and joined me on the living room couch.

"Auntie Elsie, how did she hurt herself? Did she fall?" Now I was the naïve one. Looking at my aunt and seeing her horrified expression, I knew: the driver had molested her.

My aunt looked back at me and screamed, "No! That bastard!"

We hugged each other for several moments, and then Auntie Elsie pulled away. Her face seemed more lined than usual, her brow crinkled.

"You just can't tell Uncle Dom. No matter what, he can't know. Swear to me, you'll forget what happened! The first thing he'll do is get that damn Luger and find the driver and shoot him. If it made sense, I'd shoot him for what he did to Donna, but why spend a life in prison?"

Donna said nothing to us. Nor did she say anything to anyone, because she truly didn't understand what had happened to her or its implications.

Without saying a word to my uncle, my aunt filed a complaint with the school. The driver may have been disciplined. If this incident had occurred today, the school bus driver would have been arrested, convicted in a court of law, and served time in prison for being a pedophile. But we never knew if there had been any consequences and the subject was dropped.

Knowing that someone had violated Donna hurt me. I realized that things could change in a split second—that was all it took for someone's life to go astray. *How could someone take advantage of her like that?!*

She needed a big sister! The very way Donna said her goodbyes to everyone made her vulnerable to unsolicited advances. She viewed all hugs and kisses as affection, regardless of the source. Being young, developmentally delayed, and totally naïve about sex, while possessing a voluptuous, mature body was not a good mix. Donna was left open and defenseless to perverted, lecherous men.

Sharing a home with my Uncle Dominic's family revealed to me the challenges that others encounter during their lifetime. In many ways, my uncle's mental health struggles and the afflictions and the experiences Donna faced were, to me, more frightening and challenging than living with a schizophrenic.

God! It's difficult growing up and learning how tough life can be. But growing up also meant that I had more of a say in the decisions that affected my life. My mother was coming home, and I wanted to be the one to decide if that meant I would move back with my parents and possibly start over at a new school, or stay with my aunt and uncle and my friends at Parma Senior High.

During the months leading up to my mother's return, new construction on the corner of West 54th and Orchard Avenue captured my attention on my walk to and from school. First, I saw the builders dig and pour the foundation. Shortly thereafter, the wood frame was erected. After the hip roof was in place, I found myself on the corner, caught up in my thoughts.

Moving out of the area would be devastating. But it would be wonderful to live there! It's only a stone's throw from Auntie Elsie and Uncle Dom's house, and I could stay at my school! Soon, my every thought and prayer fixated on living there, and I couldn't help but bring it up the next time I saw my father.

"Dad, did you notice the house they're building?" No answer. *Why doesn't he answer me? Dare I tell him how I feel? Can't he see that it's the perfect place for us? God, he's unapproachable! Better say no more.*

102

My father's silence dashed my hopes of moving into the new house. Unbeknownst to me, he had also been eyeing the new construction, and had been eagerly waiting for someone to put up a For Sale sign. He also liked the location and the added sense of security of having his brother's family close at hand.

Perhaps my father kept quiet when I brought up the house to keep me from getting my hopes up. He couldn't afford to take on the debt of purchasing the house himself. The expense of providing care for my mentally ill mother for more than a decade had drained his cash reserves. I suspect he felt that my grandfather should have bought the house for my family out of either gratitude or obligation. But this was a tricky matter.

Prior to my mother's most recent hospitalization, my father had filed for divorce, and in turn, Grandpa Vincenzo had filed an injunction on my mother's behalf. The law protected her, for her mental illness rendered her incapable of handling her own affairs. My father withdrew his divorce action and the couple remained married. Carlo's relationship with Grandpa Vincenzo remained strained but amicable, as long as Carlo managed my mother's care.

After my father filed for divorce, however, Grandpa Vincenzo never fully trusted him again. To protect my mother and me, Grandpa Vincenzo purchased the home himself. At a later date, he transferred ownership of the house to me. This meant that my father would have no authority to sell the property; consequently, he would have no financial gain.

Although I was thrilled to learn that the new house would be my new home, Auntie Elsie's honesty also meant that I found out all about what had gone on between my parents and grandfather over the previous year. My excitement was tempered with doubt and insecurity. *Does this mean that Dad really doesn't love Mom anymore? How long will he stay with us? No wonder he's gone all the time!*

In August, the transition to our new home was complete. My mother really wasn't mentally together, but the doctors felt she could function at home, and they released her. My father and I had absolutely no input in their decision.

Our family's new living arrangements required quite an adjustment. Although my mother still wasn't capable of managing a household, our family was reunited, and in my mind, that's all that mattered. And anyway, now I could handle the household chores.

Over the past year, Auntie Elsie had shown me how to cook, bake, and sew. She nearly turned me into a *Heloise,* the cleaning guru. There were no *Modern Romance* magazines to read. I now read *Good Housekeeping.* If Mom couldn't take care of our house, I could.

I had my own room with a new bedroom set and a phone to use. *What more could I ask for?* Yes, I was happy! Silently singing to myself, I would waltz in and out of each room. *All I've ever wanted was to return to my own home! Finally, a room to myself with my own closet! Lilacs and birds singing outside my windows! Isn't life lovely!*

While I was elated with my new surroundings, my father appeared troubled. I surmised that he had concerns regarding my mother, his work, or finances. Actually, it was none of those. The truth came out while I was eavesdropping on my father's conversations with Grandpa Vincenzo. During a visit to my grandfather's home, I learned Uncle Dominic was the origin of my father's worries.

My father must have known that his brother was either unstable or had some sort of problem after his suicide attempt. Yet he chose the path of noninterference and swept the incident from his mind. He forgot about it! In fact, shortly after the incident, he refused to acknowledge that something was wrong even when he noticed a change in Dom's work ethic.

Upon re-entering civilian life, my father and Uncle Dominic had resumed working for their father at the Central Wholesale Grocery Store. The brothers shared the management responsibilities of opening and closing the store, tallying the daily sales, and dropping off the nightly deposits at Cleveland Trust Bank.

In the past, Dominic never missed a day of work as he feared his father's disapproval. Now, he would miss two or more days a week, and excuse himself for hours at a time to supposedly run errands.

When their father, Mario, retired, he had handed over his authority and duties to his sons. Now, he chose to relax and enjoy life while receiving an income from his profitable enterprise.

Being an intelligent and shrewd man, every three months Mario performed a quarterly audit. One day, he discovered something was very wrong. The register tapes did not match the deposits. Numbers don't lie. In addition, he also noted that several invoices from suppliers were past due.

Grandfather Mario questioned my father about the sales receipts and unpaid bills, accusing Carlo of mismanaging the business and alluded to the possibility that he had been embezzling funds. Dumbfounded, Carlo replied, "What the hell's going on?!" He was damn mad, because he knew that Dominic must have been to blame. He gave no explanation to Mario, and slammed the door behind him as he left.

The next morning, Carlo found himself alone with Dominic. Dom owed his brother an explanation for his behavior and the financial discrepancies. Red-faced, his tone authoritative and stern, Carlo bombarded his brother with questions. "You son of a bitch! What have you done?!" When he eventually broke down and confessed, Dom had quite a story to tell.

After befriending the neighborhood bookmaker, Dominic had soon begun placing bets on horseracing and other sports. This accounted for the bookie's frequent drop-ins at the grocery store.

In an attempt to break his losing streak, Dom tried to make up for his loses by betting on also-rans, the long shots that failed to win, place, or show in a race. The horses didn't perform as he predicted. His personal coffers were soon empty so he simply used the money earmarked for deposit. After all, it would be a temporary loan, and he would replace the money just as soon as he won.

Dominic lost over $10,000. He should have explained his predicament to his brother long before this point, but he didn't know how to. He feared his father's wrath. Now, the bookmaker was pressuring him for payment. He was caught in a no-win situation.

The bookie's henchmen were now looking for Dominic. One day, he saw them coming and ran and hid in the basement. Carlo understood the threat that was implied by the bulge in the expensive jackets that the two well-dressed men wore. He had no idea that they were there looking for his brother, and simply helped them complete their strange purchase of a bag of pumpkin seeds.

My father couldn't understand why Dominic didn't tell him about his troubles the day the henchmen showed up at the store.

"Dom, you idiot! Why didn't you tell me those goons were here because of you?! Don't you know that owing a bookie $10,000 is a death sentence?!" Dad was afraid that one day he would find his brother lying in the street with a bullet in his head or beaten to a pulp. The bookie would be unrelenting. There could be dire consequences! Dominic knew this, too. No wonder he disappeared when the bookie's henchmen had arrived!

Once he came to terms with the alternative, Dominic's indiscretions were no longer an issue for Carlo. He had already lost his youngest brother, Ted, in World War II. That had been an uncontrollable circumstance, but Dom's situation was different. He could do something about that.

Carlo always felt protective of his younger brothers. My father stayed true to the role of big brother, looking out for Dom in any way he could. In return, Dominic had supported my father when he needed help, welcoming me into his home. Dom was an imperfect human being who needed help. Somehow, someway, Carlo would raise the money for the debt.

He asked his father-in-law for the loan. The gambling debt was paid.

How could Carlo continue working with his brother? He couldn't keep an eye on him and manage the business at the same time. After Dominic's run-in with the bookie, it was best for him to find employment in a different neighborhood, away from such unsavory characters and temptations. Without a family member at his side, Carlo lost all interest in running the business.

In everyone's best interest, Mario agreed to sell the Central Wholesale Grocery. For our family, it marked the end of an era.

12

THE CENTRAL WHOLESALE GROCERY STORE

Mario's favorite brother, Felix, was a confirmed bachelor who lived in New York City. As a practicing attorney, he was experienced in writing contracts and well versed in the rules regarding importing goods from Italy. In fact, he had become an established importer two years before Mario opened his store in New Jersey.

Felix became aware of how saturated the food industry in the New Jersey area was with Italian grocers. He had read about the industrial growth in Cleveland and the influx of Italians to the city and advised Mario to move. Like others before him, he told his younger brother, "Go West." In 1920, Mario moved his family to the City of Cleveland.

Until Mario could open a new store, he took a position as a supervisor at Richman Brothers Company's clothing factory. Although manufacturing was completely out of his realm of expertise, he did take great pleasure in wearing expensive, handmade suits.

After ten months, he opened the Central Wholesale Grocery Store on East 4th Street and Ontario Street near the Central Market.

He sold a large variety of food imported from Italy packaged in cases, barrels, boxes, and burlap sacks. His products included prosciutto, cheeses, beans, olive oil, tomato sauces, spaghetti, candies, and so much more.

The business was soon thriving. Lady Luck favored Mario, for he chose the perfect time to open an Italian wholesale establishment in area. A market analyst couldn't have predicted it better. The Italian immigrants who flocked to Cleveland had clustered together in several sections of the city and the Central Wholesale Grocery was conveniently located within their reach.

There were other factors that contributed to the store's success. Grandfather Mario understood the importance of networking. He had his dinners, relaxed, and gambled with wealthy Italian businessmen at the Matrice Club and the Sons of Italy. Mario met people who could help him and he found ways to help them. He understood the phrase, "one hand washes the other."

Another decided business asset was having strong young sons for free labor. From an early age, Carlo and his brothers worked for their father. After school, the boys waited on customers, swept the floor, washed windows, carried boxes, barrels, and bags of food to and from trucks, and stocked and restocked the shelves with goods. The boys did all of this without pay until they graduated from school.

The store played a significant role in uniting the two sides of my family. Grandpa Vincenzo discovered the Central Wholesale Grocery Store purely by chance while shopping nearby at the Central Market. Had the store been located elsewhere, he might not have met Mario De Angelis, and my parents might not have met.

My grandparents had dealings beyond that of buyer and seller of foods. A business relationship between the men developed due to the Central Wholesale Grocery Store.

Upon Grandpa Vincenzo's death, I found a large, dusty, black cardboard box, filled with canceled promissory notes—over one hundred—stowed away in the basement. The stacks of notes were neatly organized and rubber-banded together. One stack of notes was from Vincenzo to Central National Bank. The other was from Vincenzo to Mario. It was apparent that Mario had the larger fortune. Like the bank, he was the lender. Thousands of dollars had passed between them.

By the time Uncle Dom had his run-in with the bookie, Mario was an old man. There's a time and a season for everything in one's life. It was time for him to retire. His sons wanted to go their own way. Mario sold his store.

Under its new ownership, the building that had housed the Central Wholesale Grocery Store endured until 1988, when it was torn down to make way for urban renewal. This multi-billion-dollar venture was nicknamed *The Gateway Project*. The Central Market, as well as all the businesses on adjacent streets, was razed to accommodate the revitalization of downtown Cleveland. Progressive Field now covers the site where the Central Wholesale Grocery Store once stood.

Mario's grocery store enabled the Italian immigrants to preserve their native cuisine and their tradition of elegant dining, an integral part of their culture. It is evident to me that Mario was instrumental in establishing the love and appreciation for Italian food in the Greater Cleveland area which remains to this day. I am proud of all that he accomplished for himself and the City of Cleveland. I regret that, following the sale of the store and the demolition of its building, lost records eventually erased the name De Angelis and the Central Wholesale Grocery Store from the annals of Cleveland's history.

13

SEPTEMBER 1955—BACK TO SCHOOL

The dramatic summer events and move to the Orchard Avenue home had suppressed my thoughts about friends and school. The first day of school, while walking to homeroom, my eyes kept searching for familiar faces: Joyce, Helen, and Chet…yes, Chet, that chap from study hall.

It wasn't until seventh period—during orchestra practice and tryouts—that I was reunited with Joy. She was assigned again to first chair. She had probably practiced all summer. *I hear a little bit of envy in my tone.* And the understudy, of course, was "Twinnie," Beverly.

The bell rang. It was time to change classes. Now the music room was reserved for band practice. Along with a majority of the orchestra members, I remained seated while a few newcomers filed into the room. To my disappointment, there was no tall, blond, male clarinet player. *Why haven't I seen him?* Additionally, my performance of "Across the Field" had failed to earn me first-chair. *What a letdown.*

Meanwhile, football season had commenced and in preparation for the half-time show, marching band's practice sessions were held on the playing field. These daily rehearsals were a "must-show" for all band members.

Parma's marching band sounded and looked good thanks to Mr. Drew, our director. As the band marched in cadence with the rat-a-tat-tat of the drums, he would walk up and down the field shouting, "Right foot! Left foot! Step on the yard line." With the boom of the base drum, the left foot of each marcher had to touch the yard line in unison.

Whoops, I missed it! I even added a skip to catch up with my fellow bandsmen. Again, I missed the yard line. I reached the five-yard line and was about to make a pivot turn when, "Ouch!" the director stepped on my right foot. Other marchers were also out of sync and shared my fate of bruised toes. Some of us simply couldn't walk and chew gum at the same time without practice.

Coordinating one's steps with others takes practice. Once your steps are in sync, you must maintain your rhythm, stay in tune, and remember the music all at the same time. It's difficult. It takes talent…and lots and lots of practice!

It was the second week of school before I thought I caught a glimpse of Chet. He was making a turn at the end of a row. His clarinet swayed with his movements. Being a bit near-sighted, I wasn't sure at first glance. *I think it's him. Did he notice me?*

Still a bit shy, I observed Chet from afar for a week or two. I learned there was much more to him than being a class clown. He played first chair clarinet and tenor saxophone, which was considered a big deal when I was in high school.

After one of our practice sessions, Chet finally came up to me. We had the opportunity to talk and exchanged phone numbers.

Our friendship did a fast-forward with the help of Ohio Bell. We spent endless hours on the phone talking about school, band, orchestra, friends, and parents. Somehow, I managed to tell Chet about moving all over creation because of my mother's illness and lengthy hospital stays. When he asked me why she was ill, my straight-forward answer surprised even me.

"She's mentally ill. She lives in her own little world and constantly talks to herself."

His response was kind. "That's tough! I'd like to meet her sometime. Tell me about your father."

"He wouldn't approve of me talking to you, especially about our home life. He's very secretive and never home."

No boy since Murphy, my one friend during my stay with the Kravitz family, had ever spent so much time talking to me. Chet really cared about my feelings. Our conversations were not one-sided. Chet had a genuine interest in my well-being.

I couldn't help but compare my life with Chet's. He had moved too, but only once. Before moving to Parma, he lived in the Tremont area, a few miles south of downtown Cleveland.

The Kowalski family had lived on the corner of Professor and Literary Road above a grocery store. *That reminds me of my old neighborhood on Frank Avenue.* He had attended Tremont Elementary School and often played at Lincoln Park.

Coincidentally, the home that the Kowalski family had purchased in Parma was on Lincoln Avenue. He lived with his parents, John and Stella, his brother, Ted, and his black Labrador, Snyder.

A dinner invitation was extended to me by Chet, with his parents' approval, of course, and I gratefully went. I must have made a good impression, because from that day on, I had an open invitation and soon found myself joining them four times a week. *They like me!* His family was everything my family wasn't, or so I thought.

Stella's cooking is great, though her menus never vary. Still, who needs variety? Not me, when it's a home-cooked meal! Most decidedly, I was a grateful dinner guest. As George Bernard Shaw said, "There is no love sincerer than the love of food."

On Mondays, there were delectable mini-hamburger loaves and cucumbers soaked in vinegar. For Tuesdays, during summer, fall, winter, or spring, it was *le carte de jour*—soup, with boiled chicken or beef. Then on Wednesdays, it was leftover soup and burgers. On Thursdays, the menu was pork chops, pan-fried with onions and served with mashed potatoes and gravy. Friday's dish was fish, baked or fried. Since Saturday was a grocery shopping day, the selection had to be simple to make. We had boiled hot dogs and canned baked beans. Sundays were the greatest culinary treat: a variety of meats—chicken, beef, or pork—with vegetables, and freshly baked bread. Stella basically cooked meat and potatoes daily.

113

In contrast, my mother never cooked at all. Our meal of the day was canned food, store-bought pizza, or cereal. Here again, perhaps selfishly on my part, I desired a home-cooked meal. At times, I felt extremely resentful of having to cook or clean in order to have some semblance of family life.

My comparison of my and Chet's contrasting households continued to occupy my thoughts. Chet's mother, Stella, had a regular routine for her weekly chores. Her discipline reminded me of Grandma Caroline. She washed clothes on Monday, ironed on Tuesday, and cleaned on Thursday and Friday. Saturday was for shopping, and Sunday, naturally, was for church and relaxation.

There was no schedule at the De Angelis household. All too soon, my mother's mental health had drastically deteriorated. Chores got done only when I had the time to do them. How I wished it could have been my mother, not me, who cleaned.

The happiness I felt in moving to a new home and having my own room had dissipated. Housework and laundry had become my afterschool chores. Between homework and cleaning, I felt like I was drowning in responsibilities. My little pity parties began. I envisioned myself as Cinderella, scrubbing the floor, while longing for fun and recreation like my classmates. *Prince Charming, Prince Charming, wherefore art thou Prince Charming?*

Now let's look at our fathers. Chet's father, John, a core maker for Fanner Manufacturing, left for work at 6:00 a.m. and returned home each day at 4:30 p.m. You could set your watch by him.

On the other hand, my father had no apparent schedule. Each morning he left for work after my departure for school. No one knew when he left the house, because my mother would sleep until early afternoon, and if she happened to be awake, she was in a world of her own.

There was no family togetherness during our meals. Mom and I ate alone each day, because when my father wouldn't return home until two or three in the morning. *Where does he eat his meals? He does provide our groceries every week. Why doesn't he spend any time with us? Where is he? He's neglecting us!*

Soon our inviting new home's sunny environment changed. The Venetian blinds throughout the main living area were tightly drawn shut, day and night. The fresh new smell that had lingered in the air had now been replaced by foul cigarette smoke. Our home had become an isolation chamber for my dear mother. No one entered the house; no visitors, no friends, and no family members, just my father and me.

Day in and day out, my mother sat on a step-stool which was placed next to the G.E. electric range, chain-smoking and uttering unidentifiable garble while gesturing. Her hands and tobacco-stained fingers moved as if she were performing a pantomime or signing for the deaf. Mom's unkempt hair and clothing were covered with the ashes that dropped from her lit cigarette. She was such a sad, woeful sight. Trying to communicate with her was almost impossible, since she heard nothing except her own incessant, rapid chatter.

"Mom, would you like something to eat?" No response.

"Mom, are you hungry?" Again, I would receive no response from her. *I'm sure she eats but what and when—who knows? She doesn't appear to know that I even exist! Can't she see or hear me? She's oblivious to my existence. Why is she troubled like this? God only knows!*

After a day at school, returning home to these conditions often caused more hurt than I could endure; consequently, I would leave the house to seek a brief respite across the street at Uncle Dominic's house. Auntie Elsie would be there to greet me, and there would be cookies and milk on the kitchen table.

Chet and his family also welcomed me into their home and provided me with meals and an escape from the dark shroud of mental illness. To me, fulfilling those needs equated to love. The Kowalskis were good people; kind, modest, religious, and generous.

While the Kowalski family attended church on Sunday, I remained home. This was the only day I spent any time with my father. The Venetian blinds in the living room were open, for a change, allowing the sunlight to fill the room. Dad would sit in the living room reading the *Plain Dealer* and occasionally glancing at the television set. I would sit across from him doing my nails. Mom, like a canary, would sit on her perch, the little stool next to the stove, in a darkened kitchen talking to the wall. Was this family togetherness? No.

The connection and shared joy from being together was missing. At most, it was a contrived semblance of family life. I wanted more—a *normal* family.

Is it wrong to want more? How wonderful it would be if my parents and I could attend church and return home to dine together like Chet's family? What is there not to like about the Kowalski family? Nothing!

To me, wanting my family to be like them was good! This is what I wanted: daily nutritious meals that were prepared by my mother, to live in a clean home that *I* didn't have to clean, to attend church on Sundays, and to have a father who came home and remained home all night. Instead, our family charade continued, and I was totally incapable of expressing my dissatisfaction to my father.

Because of my youth, I truly failed to understand my father. He seldom revealed his inner-most thoughts to anyone, especially me. But he repeatedly said, "Angelina *was* the most beautiful girl I had ever seen and I loved her with all my whole heart and soul." Yet now, there was no tenderness between them. He appeared cold and aloof towards her.

Once they married, Dad promised to provide her with a home, forever. Both of them understood abandonment, for Mom had lost her mother when she was four and a half years old and Dad lived in an orphanage at thirteen, when his mother returned to New Jersey. By chance, they had lived at the same orphanage, St. Joseph's, on Woodland Avenue, in Cleveland.

When my mother became afflicted with mental illness and her behavior became bizarre, Dad kept his marriage vows until he felt their union had been violated. With his failed attempt at divorce, he had no other choice but to accept that my mother was his responsibility forever.

Time did eventually heal his hostile feelings. He felt she was a pitiful soul, worthy of compassion. He understood that she wasn't responsible for her behavior, and as long as she wasn't destructive, it was much better and kinder for her to live at home. Nevertheless, the fact that he was never home equated, in my young mind, to abandonment for both my mother and me. I knew he had conflicted feelings towards my mother, which was something I was just beginning to understand. To maintain his mental health, he, too, had to escape. Seeing the deterioration of my mother's mind and beauty was just too much for him to bear on a daily basis.

Little did my father know, at times it was also too much for me to bear! I, too, had found an escape—Chet and his family. The Kowalski family appeared to be perfect, but I discovered later that I was looking at them through rose-colored glasses, as they too had problems, as we all do!

Only later did I learn that when drinking, Chet's father, John, became mean and argumentative and often physically abused his mother. Chet, who was larger and stronger than his father, witnessed his mother's abuse. Not wanting to hurt John, he would pick him up by the waist and plunk him into the waste basket!

If I had known earlier about John's behavior, would it have changed anything? Most likely not! Dad's adamant objections and insulting remarks about the young man only succeeded in catapulting me and the relationship forward!

Dad decided not to like Chet even before meeting him. *Poor Polish boy!* I didn't want my father to hate him, but he already did. My father had a preconceived opinion about all young men who weren't Italian. "Only an Italian boy would be good enough for my daughter."

Perhaps an Italian boy wouldn't have been acceptable either. It was my belief that my father didn't want me to like anyone, or date, because he needed me home to cook and clean. In fact, for that very reason, I never uttered a syllable about my newly found friend to him, but somehow, he gained information about my friendship with Chet. Perhaps he eavesdropped on my phone calls. Or maybe Auntie Elsie, my confidant, mentioned him.

The day my father met Chet, he had gone to the garage and found that the front tire on his car was flat. He was impeccably groomed and dressed in his most expensive Italian suit for an evening out. He called the Cleveland Automobile Club for help. He returned to his car to wait.

A half-hour had passed when my father returned inside to get a glass of water. He mumbled to himself, "There's no excuse for this!"

He was stressed. He returned to the car.

Then, a half-hour later, Dad barged through the breezeway door into our home office to use the phone. I was talking on it. He shouted at me, "Get off the damn phone!"

Without saying "goodbye," I disconnected and handed the phone to my father.

The auto club's switchboard operator expressed regrets for the delay, but was unable to give him a definitive arrival time due to a high volume of calls. She stated, "Perhaps within an hour." My father slammed the receiver down in disgust.

With the best of intentions, I called Chet and asked him to come over to change my father's tire. *By helping, Chet will gain my father's approval. He'll show him that he's a good guy. Then, my father will approve of our friendship. Maybe this will soften his opinion of Chet.*

Heavens, no! Never in a million years! The minute Chet walked into view, my father's brow furrowed. His eyes narrowed as they seemed to turn black and his gaze bore right through Chet. Instead of being polite and expressing gratitude for a favor received, there was no "Thank you" involved. My father remained arrogant and condescending, that dark look never leaving his face. He offered Chet two dollars, all in change.

Chet refused to take the money. He would have refused any amount—after all, he was doing a good deed for his friend's father. He wanted appreciation, but sadly, he found rejection instead. From that day on, our friendship was strictly forbidden!

Since Dad slipped in and out of our house like a shadow in the night, he was unable to enforce his dating ban. Chet and I continued to meet on the sly, often at the risk of getting caught. On occasion, we would meet at my house after school to play ping pong and share a pizza with Mom.

My mother liked Chet and often came out of her shell in his presence. She would stop talking to herself and actually hold a half-way decent conversation. Miraculously, she never said a word to my father about the visits.

I continued to have dinner at Chet's house, especially on Mondays. I couldn't pass up a hamburger dinner. Washing dishes with his mother and walking the dog with him felt good. *How nice it is! You're happy! Pinch yourself.*

Learning to deceive my father was easy. After all, he taught me well. Wanting to go to church with Chet's family on Sunday

118

prompted me to fib to Dad. "Helen's sister is driving us to church." *God will forgive me, because I'm going to church!* It was often nerve-racking sitting in the breezeway, waiting for Chet's brother's car to appear.

The Kowalski family attended the Polish National Catholic Church on Broadway Avenue. The musical tones of the chimes rang out, beckoning our attendance to the mass, and followed us into the church.

Each Sunday, we seated ourselves in the second pew, on the left-hand side of the sanctuary. My eyes were immediately drawn to the simple wooden crucifix that hung above the red carpeted altar, and the monsignor, dressed in ceremonial red and golden robes. And there, sitting with him were the Kowalski brothers, Ted and Chet. As altar boys, they would bring the water, wine, and host to the monsignor as he performed the mass.

The smell of incense, along with the play of light against the stained-glass windows, the lyric chants of the celebrant, and the sweet, melodious sounds of choir had a profound effect on me. The mass was recited and the hymns were sung in their native tongue, Polish. Though the words were foreign to me, I felt God's presence.

When Chet didn't serve mass, he sat next to me. One day he reached for my hand. Shyly, I held on, fearing that his parents would not approve. If they noticed, nothing was said. Young love is sweet and innocent. There is an irreplaceable delight experienced from the euphoric state of first love.

Over the next few months, home life remained unchanged, but the world around me had; everything was in Technicolor! Hurt, abandonment, and lack of love disappeared. Someone cared!

December arrived with its winter darkness and blustery cold days. Soon it would be Christmas which—for me—wasn't the happiest of occasions. My earliest memory of the holiday was a sad and disappointing one: no special dinners, no tree, no presents, and no Mommy. She was hospitalized that year.

That Christmas morning, our Christmas tree and the baby doll that Santa had promised to bring me never appeared. My father told me that they were stolen off the truck while he was out making deliveries on Christmas Eve. All that I got that year was a Christmas stocking with goodies.

In the years that followed, unless the day was spent with my grandparents, Christmas was just like any other day, but *this* one would be special.

Stella Kowalski had been baking Polish treats all week. A small, modestly decorated spruce tree sat in the front window. The family would gather together for a dinner of cheese, potato, and prune pierogis before attending midnight mass, and I would be joining them!

As soon as my father left home, my plan was to have Chet's brother or a cab transport me to the Kowalski house. Nothing would deter me from getting there. I would even walk in the ankle-deep snow, if walking became my only means of transportation.

My concern was leaving my mother home alone on a holiday! *What difference does it make if I leave? I'm invisible to her. Why should I feel guilty? Besides, where's my father? He's not home. So what if he finds out that I am gone? Then what? I'll just deal with the consequences, if and when I get caught.*

It became easy for me to continue my defiant behavior because of my father's lifestyle. His long and late hours away from home kept my "little secrets" protected. Apparently, my father was totally unaware of the continuation of my friendship with Chet. As long as I arrived home before Dad returned, our game would continue.

But, sooner or later, one of us would have our secrets exposed.

Meanwhile, things were about to change. My sixteenth birthday was soon approaching, and this meant a driving permit was in my future. To avoid the fee a driving school would charge, my father volunteered his services and his car for my training.

As he began my first lesson, he told me to make a left turn off Pearl Road onto Biddulph Road. I did, except the car jumped over the curb and went towards the iron gates of the West Park Cemetery.

My father had taught himself to drive as a teen and he felt teaching me would be easy. It wasn't! He lacked patience and gave up on me after that first lesson. I guess he was frightened and concerned that his car would be damaged.

120

After that, the job of teaching Beverly to drive was turned over to driving school and, on occasion, to Chet—another truth never revealed to Dad. As Sir Walter Scott so eloquently wrote, "Oh what a tangled web we weave, when first we practice to deceive!"

By now, Chet himself was a licensed driver, and he often had the use of his brother's Chevy, the family's only car. In those days, there were no dividers between the seats and seat belts were optional. This allowed me to slide across the seat and sit right next to him. It was from this passenger seat that I mastered one of my first driving challenges: shifting gears. As Chet put his foot on the clutch to shift, I operated the hand controls. As an added benefit, it allowed me to snuggle close to him. *Nice!*

After passing my driving test, I felt confident that I could drive any car without a problem. One afternoon, I found the family car parked in the garage with the keys in the ignition. *I'll be back before Dad returns.*

Don't you dare do what you're thinking!

I can do it! I can drive to Grandpa's house. Why ride two buses to University Heights?

With the sale of Grandfather Mario's store, my father was now selling real estate for R. A. Gall. He had use of a company car and he habitually wouldn't return home until early evening. *Dad won't be home for hours. He'll never know.*

My better judgment told me not to go. But, being newly licensed and wanting to test my skill, this opportunity to drive to Grandpa Vincenzo's house was just too much temptation for me. My hands shook as I turned on the ignition and backed the car onto West 54th Street.

Being alone and driving across town about twenty miles for the first time without an incident was great! I approached the house and immediately thought that I should park in front.

No. Pull into the driveway and park in front of Grandpa's garage. The tenants need access to their garages.

All was well, the visit was good, and then it was time to leave. Now the car had to be driven backwards eighty feet to reach the street. *Why hadn't I thought about that before?*

The drive was long and narrow. For several minutes, I jockeyed the car backward and forward to align the wheels. My face burned from the frustration. *There's no one to help me.* Finally, the wheels were correctly positioned to move the car straight back. *Good!*

Stop!! If I continued, the car's left fender would have hit the tall stately oak that grew on Grandpa's tree lawn. I pulled forward, realigned the wheels, and stepped on the accelerator as I backed up, straight across the street. Bang!

What I hadn't seen was the oak tree next to the neighbors' drive on the other side of the street. It was difficult to hold back my tears while surveying the damage. The tree had only lost a bit of bark, but my entire car bumper had sprung loose. *What now?*

As usual, Grandpa Vincenzo had a solution. One of his tenants owned an auto-body shop on Carnegie Avenue, the route I used to return to the west side of town. He fixed the bumper while I waited, but there was a snafu.

When I returned home after seven that evening, Dad was already there! *Dummy! I'd better tell the truth!*

Since the car was taken without my father's permission, this meant disciplinary action. My penalty was no driving for two months. While Dad felt disgruntled, Grandpa Vincenzo was elated. After all, Beverly can drive!

Following my driving ban, Grandpa Vincenzo negotiated a win-win-win deal for me, my father, and him. He would give my father eight hundred dollars to purchase a reliable used car for me to drive. My father could profit if he found a good car for less money, and I, of course, would have transportation. The only stipulation was that I would have to chauffeur Grandpa Vincenzo on Saturdays.

My dear grandfather would ride two buses to get to the Central Market. This made for a long and tiring day. Since the freshest and best foods were sold at the market located in downtown Cleveland, that was where Grandpa Vincenzo shopped.

From the time I was a toddler, whenever possible, Grandpa Vincenzo would take me along on his shopping trips. He knew, without asking me, that I would agree to his deal.

Dad found a bargain—a flaming-red, two-door, 1952 Starlight Studebaker! Cosmetically, the car had seen better days, but the engine still hummed.

From my perspective, there were only benefits for me from the agreement: transportation, pocket money for gas, an enjoyable day shopping, fresh produce for our meals, and—best of all—I could pick up Chet.

Chet had desperately hoped to have purchased a car by now, but working only a part-time job, paying for his music lessons, and contributing to the Kowalski household expenses made saving difficult. He walked or rode the bus and occasionally got to drive his brother's car. But soon all this would change—Ted had been drafted into the United States Army and his car had to be sold.

Now that the family lacked access to a car, it just seemed logical for me to drive to Chet's house. *Forget Miss Manners and that social etiquette stuff!*

After arriving at Chet's home, he would drive my car, especially when we attended church with his parents. Thankfully, we never had an accident. Being sixteen, thoughts about insurance and liability never entered my mind. Instead, paying for gas was my concern, so I took a part-time job as a cashier at Federal's Department Store.

Though Chet and I both worked, we found time to be together. On those days, we could be found exchanging kisses in the park or in front of the fence that surrounded the Cleveland Airport. Occasionally, we could even be found smooching behind Harry Swartz Haberdashery where Chet worked. Risky, yes, but I was just a teenager in love.

We liked to take rides to North Royalton, Hinckley, and Medina County. The little red Commander coupe would motor south on State Routes 3, 42, or 94 with windows down, my long hair blowing in the wind, and the radio playing our favorite songs. We were free and happy—a teen's dream! We were living the good life.

Those brief moments and fleeting hours together allowed each of us to escape the responsibilities and the sadness in our lives. For Chet, it was his escape from the lack of opportunity and money. In his dreams, he owned rolling acres of fertile land, farm animals, riding horses, and a century-old farm house. Perhaps then he would be good enough, in my father's eyes, to marry his daughter.

For me, our time together was an escape from my abnormal life of seeing my slovenly dressed, psychotic mother sitting alone babbling to herself as she made weird hand gestures. *God, she is sad and wretched!* A vision of her was indelibly etched on my brain, never to be forgotten. Chet had given me something else to think about—his love and our future.

Though cherishing my time spent with Chet, I began to question what the future held for us. *Are we too young to be in love? Can our love endure separation?*

All too soon, the future was upon us; Chet was graduating. Parma Senior High School held graduation exercises at The Public Auditorium in downtown Cleveland in order to accommodate its large classes. The high school orchestra played the music for the event, and, like professional musicians, we occupied the orchestra pit. The auditorium was packed with families and friends.

As the procession of graduates walked on stage, the orchestra played "Pomp and Circumstance." Then the conductor, Mr. Drew, pointed at me. Yes, me! I would play the flute solo for the processional. Tears filled my eyes. Reading the sheet music would have been impossible, but thankfully, I had memorized my part.

As the program ended, holding back my tears was difficult. Contemplating the end of high school and becoming an adult created turmoil in my heart and renewed my fear of change. As the choir sang, I was wrapped up in my thoughts. *Now what?*

Though Chet was intelligent, he had not applied himself to his studies and would not attend college. He loved to work with his hands. Mechanical work and farming attracted him. After graduation, his only choice was to get a job.

American Greetings Corporation assessed his mechanical aptitude and hired him as an electrical machine repair trainee. He received accolades for his rapid advancement and his successful completion of the course. Unfortunately for Chet, fate intervened and cut short his apprentice training.

In 1958, Chet was drafted into the United States Army. After his basic training, he was stationed at Fort Knox, Kentucky.

For the first six months of his Army life, we wrote to each other almost daily. How I missed him! On occasion, Chet would get a weekend pass and return home to visit with his family and—more importantly—me.

Now that Chet was in the service and I had graduated from high school, I decided to continue my education. My decision was made easy. With my father's encouragement and Grandpa Vincenzo's financial backing, I chose to enroll in a liberal arts school in Berea, Ohio, which was a twenty-minute drive from my home in Parma. My first-quarter schedule consisted of fifteen credit hours of college requirements and an elective.

The guidance counselor had suggested that I consider an elective that would develop my creativity. As I read through the prospectus looking for a creative elective, I noticed a course titled Portrait Painting. *No outside assignments! That's for me.*

My class was a heterogeneous group of students. There were freshmen, sophomores, juniors, and seniors. Talent levels ranged from the ridiculous to the sublime. Then there was me, the high-cheekboned, cute, inartistic freshman whom the teacher chose to be one of the models. I felt very uncomfortable with thirty pairs of eyes studying my features, until I looked into a pair of dreamy, brown eyes.

Our gazes connected. *Nice!* His eyes held my attention until it was time to take a break. *Thank goodness!* I stretched and rose from my chair. *Dare I look at the paintings?*

The easels were placed throughout the room, which gave each artist a different angle. The first painting looked like a caricature, without the slightest resemblance to me. How the artist portrayed me made me want to cry. *Could that look like me? NO WAY!*

Some of the images made containing my laughter difficult. Then there were the few portraits that were realistic, and finally there was the one where I looked exceptionally beautiful. The art teacher applauded every brush stroke made by the artist, for he had photographically duplicated my high cheekbones by capturing every contour, plane, and hollow of my face.

The student was Robert Braun. Bob was a bright, young, good-looking, serious artist who was wholeheartedly involved in his studies. He painted in oils, pastels, watercolors, and sketched in pencil, pen, or charcoal. Other art mediums attracted him: clay,

Beverly, artist and model.

plaster molds, and woodblocks. Since his youth, he had attended classes at the Cleveland Art Institute.

Most recently, he had taken private classes from Grant Renard, a famed Cleveland watercolorist. Landscapes and seascapes were Bob's forte. Art was his major and teaching was his minor. If artistic fame bypassed him, teaching would sustain him. The portrait class was an elective for him, also.

Bob fell in love with me at first sight. *I think it is my cheekbones.* His attention charmed and captivated me to the point that remaining loyal to Chet became more and more difficult. *The mailbox is empty again.* Soon I was enamored with the prospect of a new suitor and although I never wrote Chet a "Dear John" letter, I took his lack of attention to mean that he had moved on...and so did I.

I was Bob's favorite art subject. After class, he would appear at my back door with his clay and sculpting tools and transform my father's office into an art studio. We would listen to 45 rpm records as he sculpted a bust of my head and shoulders. *I do like him, a lot.*

126

Most of the time, my mother sat in the kitchen smoking her cigarettes, gesturing and talking to herself. At times, Bob and I could hear her harsh and raspy guttural voice speaking bizarre jibber-jabber above the music. There was no way to avoid my mother, because she was always there.

He must know that something is wrong with her. Why did I ever let him come here? What was I thinking?

Occasionally, my mother would fleetingly walk past the open archway on her way to her bedroom. *God, please don't let Bob see her.* She was an embarrassment. Her hair was never combed, her clothing was disheveled, and her fingernails were a frightful sight, excessively long and stained with nicotine! I had to admit it: I was ashamed of her.

Yes. Yes...I am ashamed of my mother. What if Bob sees her? Can I make an excuse for her appearance?

Fabricating an excuse for my mother's appearance and behavior was impossible. Every explanation that came to my mind failed to ring true. Her slovenly look, cackling laughter, and weird gesturing were part of her illness. How could I explain it any other way? The answer eluded me.

Early on in life, not wanting to be judged unfavorably by what my mother did or didn't do, I discovered it was best to hide the existence of her illness from people. When my mother ventured outside our home, I saw how strangers looked at her—their whispers, laughter, and lack of understanding hurt and angered me. This woman whom society scorned and labeled *insane* was my mother and *I* loved her, even though she often embarrassed me.

To protect myself from further hurt and humiliation, I had misrepresented my life. School days taught me this. While my classmates were excitedly anticipating their parents' attendance at a school function, there I was, spinning a tale to justify my parents' absence.

For example, there was the time I told Mr. Drew that my parents couldn't attend the band concert because they were out of town. To me, a false—but plausible—excuse was easier to tell than the truth. It definitely stopped my teacher from questioning me further, avoided embarrassment, and ended the conversation.

What's wrong with wanting to create the illusion of a happy, normal home life? It's better than saying to people that my mother's "crazy" and that my father's never home. Somehow, I must try to make Bob understand why I've been deceptive.

All too often, once my mother's illness was uncovered, I became a leper, shunned by my companions. How would Bob react to the truth? I feared a negative reaction. *I can't cope with losing him.* Yet I knew even then that dishonesty never benefits a true friendship. The truth always makes itself known.

Tell Bob the truth; what choice do I have? Tell him about the illness, the schizophrenia!

After days of deliberating, finally I built up the courage to discuss my mother's illness with Bob. Feeling embarrassed and uncomfortable, I blurted the words out of my mouth. "She's schizophrenic!"

After giving him a brief explanation, I was still feeling flustered and as uncomfortable as if I had just fitted myself into my own straightjacket. *Can Bob ever understand my mother's illness? Will the shame attached to her behavior reflect back on me?* Feeling that I had to be defensive worried me.

Unlike my mother, Bob's mother had all her faculties. She was *normal*. She was known and respected in the community. Bob, being an only child, was very close to her. He would confide in her. *What will she think?*

On my first visit to the Braun home, after my candid conversation with Bob, it was apparent to me that Bob had divulged my woes to his mother. She asked me an unending barrage of questions: "When did your mother have her first breakdown? How many has she had? Was she ever violent?"

My replies were brief and vague. These were the types of questions that I had spent my entire life avoiding.

Chet's mom never ever quizzed me. Mrs. Braun made it very clear that she considered my mother's illness a hardship for me to bear. I had a strong feeling that his mother was no longer a fan of my relationship with her son.

On the other hand, my father approved of Bob, even though he wasn't Italian. He was second-generation German, Catholic, college-educated, and a future art teacher with potential for fame. Bob's

128

father and uncle worked for NASA, the space program, and his mother was on the Parma School Board. *Great credentials for a future son-in-law!*

Dad probably met Bob less than ten times during the year we dated and fell in love. Why? Because his schedule didn't permit any interaction with anyone, not even his family, because of the hours he kept. *Where was he all day? Where was he after midnight? At work? I don't think so!* Growing older and wiser, I began to question his fidelity to my mother.

Obviously, Mrs. Braun did not or could not dissuade Bob from dating me, because he invited me to his fraternity's formal dance. Now, I needed a dress. Rose's Bridal Shop, in downtown Cleveland, was considered the "in" place to purchase formal attire.

The day I drove to the bridal shop was a beautiful spring day in May. On my way there, everything was right-side-up in my world. While parking the car behind the bridal shop on Ontario Street, my heart raced with excitement. *I'm purchasing my first formal gown!*

The shop was splendid with the elegant mannequins dressed in bridal attire. There were racks of bridal wear. The sales associate had customers, a wedding party, which left me on my own.

When I found the size six racks and began looking at the selection, I was approached by the saleswoman. She was about my height, tall and elegant. She was dressed in the latest high fashion with expensive jewelry, a perfect pageboy hairdo, and a dramatic voice. I was in awe of her sophistication. She could have been an actress.

The lady led me to the fitting room, "My name is Mary. I'll assist you." She hung my selections and unfastened their zippers and hooks while I watched. "I'll check on you later."

I had tried on several dresses without glancing at the price tags. *This one is perfect.* First, I checked my wallet. *I have forty dollars.* Then, I checked the tag. *Fifty-five dollars?!*

Mary knocked on the dressing room door. "Can I help you with anything?"

"No." While feeling embarrassed for having insufficient funds with me, I explained my dilemma.

"When is the special occasion?"

"June."

"You need not fret; we have a layaway policy. You can put a small amount down and make payments."

In completing the transaction, she took my down payment of thirty dollars and requested my personal information. As she wrote down my last name, she stopped abruptly, and looked at me strangely before continuing, "Your address?"

"5408 Orchard Avenue, Parma, Ohio."

"Phone number?"

"Tuxedo: 884-8473."

Mary left the room to complete the transaction. When she returned with my receipt, she had tissues in hand, tears in her eyes, and could barely say, "Thank you." *Could she be crying? Perhaps she has an allergy.*

Not waiting to find out more, I swiftly gathered up my things and left the store. My father returned home early that day. As soon as he walked through the door, he turned to me and sternly demanded, "Why were you shopping downtown today?" *Who told him? I didn't tell anyone. It had to have been the saleslady. He knows that I was in the bridal shop!*

After I explained that I had purchased a dress to attend a formal dinner dance with Bob, Dad's harsh abrupt manner changed.

The dress, a white gown with several layers of white organza, could be worn as a wedding dress. That thought had never entered my mind until now. Though my father never verbalized it, I knew what he thought: I'd been secretly shopping for a wedding dress, and Chet Kowalski was the groom-to-be.

The next day, my father returned home carrying a large white box fastened with white satin ribbon. It contained my dress. Dad said he had paid the balance owed.

The combination of the saleswoman's odd reaction to learning my identity and my father's purchase of the dress sent my mind spinning. The bridal shop was located one block north of my grandfather's store where my father used to work. *That must be how he knew Mary. They must be friends. But why was she so emotional?* I continued to think about the incident and its implications.

Mary's attractive, but not beautiful like my mother. She has elegance and class, while my mother's illness has stolen her charms. Perhaps she is a good conversationalist and companion, but my mother lives in a world of solitary confinement.

My first thoughts were an expression of my girlish innocence and tolerant nature. *My father should be allowed a friendship outside of his marriage; everyone is entitled to pursue happiness. Why shouldn't he be able to escape from the harsh realities of his life?*

After my mother flaunted her wares publicly, and the Chinese restaurant incident, my father looked at her with shame and pity. Perhaps a new relationship healed his wounded self-worth or he came to the realization that she was a victim of her disease.

But this Mary, is she responsible for my father's absences from home? Is she to blame for his late nights? The thought of her destroying our home life angered me. *How dare he neglect us for her?! Did she bait him with sex? Or is he in love with her?*

I couldn't dismiss the thought that my father had deep-seated romantic desires for someone other than my mother. It hurt too much!

I love my mother. He was supposed to love her, too. How could he do this to her? And to me? I felt offended. This all came as a tremendous shock to me, a shock my teenage mind could not think about without feeling rage for my father's behavior. I had to put it out of my mind—and I did—or I would have snapped!

I had spent years making excuses for my mother, defending her behavior. After all, she was ill and she could not help it. Someone had to come to her defense; someone had to protect her. That someone was me. Naturally, I was defensive because I loved her. What more was there to do?

Would all this have happened if my mother was normal? Probably not. It doesn't matter how badly I want it, she'll never be normal.

What if my father was able to choose a wife who would enable him to live a normal life?

As much as the maturing part of my nature tried to be okay with my father's choice, I just couldn't accept it! *Isn't fidelity the moral way?*

In the end, I simply decided that how my father chose to live his life was his own business, not mine. I loved both my parents. I chose not to pry into his life. To the day my father died, I never questioned him about Mary.

The excitement and anticipation of attending the Alpha Sigma Pi dinner dance had been lost in the emotional turmoil of attempting to reconcile my father's apparent indiscretion. The beautiful gown elicited feelings of hurt and anger. I shoved the pretty box under my bed. It remained there until the day of the formal. That morning, I placed it on a hanger and draped it over my closet door.

While I was completing my morning chores, a strange phenomenon occurred. I felt a sudden burst of happiness and began to hum a waltz. *One, two, three; one, two, three.* Like a ballerina, I pirouetted around each room. Reaching my bedroom, I held the gown in front of my blue jeans as I danced in front of the large, round dressing table mirror. As I readied myself for the dance, I was unable to keep a smile off my face. *I look so pretty. I feel happy. How lovely!*

The dance was held at the Alcazar Hotel, a beautiful, exotic-looking, five-story building in Cleveland Heights. Everything about the evening seemed too good to be true! My happiness reigned. It was my first formal dance. I had never attended a prom. The only disappointment was that I had no proud parents at home to appreciate how Bob and I looked and no one to take our picture.

Bob was especially handsome in his black tuxedo. He was my Prince Charming and I was his Cinderella. My white, floor-length strapless creation had a formfitting bodice, cinched waist, and layers of organza flowing over a silk skirt. The frock was accessorized with a long, black silk ribbon to wrap around my waist and tie in a bow. It accented my small, twenty-three-inch waistline. A baby cymbidium orchid corsage—my first—adorned my left arm.

I couldn't have felt more beautiful as we danced together. He held me close as we glided across the dance floor. With each turn his thighs seemed to brush mine as we moved as one. I felt secure and loved. I wanted to dance all night!

Before the evening drew to a close, Bob escorted me outside into the botanical courtyard. We sat on a bench next to a large fountain. He ran his fingers through my long, silky hair. He traced my profile, gently running his finger from my hairline down the bridge of my nose, and then across my cheekbones. Then he looked intently into

132

my eyes and withdrew from his jacket pocket a small, heart-shaped, blue satin box. Bob presented me with the most beautiful diamond ring I had ever seen! "Beverly, I love you. Will you marry me?" *Yes! Yes!* My heart went pitter-pat at the sight of the princess-cut, two-carat ring and the thought of marrying him. *Pinch yourself! You're in love!* The excitement, the setting, the euphoria of it all swept me off my feet.

I didn't want the evening to end or to come back to reality, even after Bob dropped me off at home and I found myself alone in my bedroom. *How can I think about sleep? No, no, no, no sleep for me.* I felt too giddy to even think about sleep. Nor even sit down, for that matter.

Then the reality hit. *How can I introduce my mother to the Braun family? What will they think if I only introduce them to my father and grandparents? How can I plan a wedding around this abnormal situation?*

God, please make my mother well! I repeated this phrase at least one hundred times a day. *Dear God, please hear my plea!* My desire was a hopeless dream. Even God couldn't fix my mother! The doctors had already tried countless times.

Bob's parents asked that we wait a year before making wedding plans. After their request, I was left with the persistent, nagging feeling that they most assuredly did not want our wedding to take place. Waiting would allow Bob more time to see the obstacles he would face having a mentally ill mother-in-law.

In the end, it wasn't Bob who broke our engagement; I did. After too many sleepless nights, I returned the ring. The fraternity pin that he gave me when we first started dating remains in my jewelry box to this day. Bob never asked me for it. I often wondered why. Perhaps it was his way of saying, "Remember me."

After breaking off our engagement, my letter-writing campaign to Chet resumed and somehow our love was rekindled. We made plans to marry before his discharge from the Army. As always, Grandpa Vincenzo was my confidant. Trusting him completely, I secretly shared my wedding plans with him.

Grandpa Vincenzo didn't exactly approve of my intentions. He had hoped that I would follow family tradition and marry my third cousin, Etallo Martinelli, who was about to emigrate from Italy. I adamantly pooh-poohed his idea. *Never!*

"This type of marriage may be acceptable in Italy, but not in America! Grandpa, what are you thinking?"

Perhaps the real reason for his disapproval was that he viewed my relationship with Chet as a youthful infatuation. He also knew that Chet's background didn't measure up to my father's standards. Grandpa Vincenzo repeatedly said to me, "You're young and confused about matters of the heart and marriage."

Grandpa Vincenzo knew Bob. He knew that he came from a good family, was bright, and had an exciting future. He though I wasn't being sensible and asked me, "Is something wrong with Bob? *Bambino*, tell me. You're trading gold for iron!" *Perhaps I do need a shrink!*

I could not release myself from my bond to Chet. No, I wasn't being logical, but is love logical?

Deep down, I was conflicted about my attachments. I rationalized that my new relationship with Bob had only come about because of Chet's absence. In this situation, absence had not made my heart grow fonder. And I decided that infatuation, not love, had prompted me to make the commitment to Bob. I convinced myself that Bob, ever a mama's boy, would do his best to please her, and, sure enough, he ended up marrying his cute, blonde, piano-playing, next-door neighbor.

WIFE AND MOTHER

Cast of Characters

THE KOWALSKI FAMILY
Stella and John– My in-laws, Chet's parents
Chet– My first husband, father to Ted, Steve, and Martin
Ted and Lee– Chet's older brother and sister-in-law

THE LAZAR FAMILY
Rose – My mother-in-law, Allan's mother
Allan- My second husband, father to Michelle and Michael
Ronald and Ray – Allan's older brothers

14

MARRIED LADY

I never told Chet about my whirlwind romance with Bob, even after we became engaged. I hadn't outright lied to him, but I felt guilty about not being completely open with him. I also felt guilty for breaking things off with Bob, and felt like I had led him on. My habit of ruminating over my guilt was beginning to take up too much of my mental energy.

I mustn't think about Bob. He can handle rejection. I mustn't think about why I've decided to marry Chet. I'm not getting married because I'm on the rebound…

While Chet was finishing his tour of duty, I decided to concentrate on my academic studies. With the advice of my guidance counselor, I changed my college major to teaching. Then I enrolled in night classes to attain my goal — a temporary teaching certificate.

After completing my student teaching, I received my certification and applied for a position within the Parma School District. Many fully accredited teaching applicants had the same idea, leaving no room for that school to hire anyone like me with only temporary certification.

Fortunately, I did receive a bid from the Medina County Schools. They hired me to teach health and social studies to the fourth, fifth, and sixth grades. My new employer assigned me to Kidder Elementary School in Brunswick. Now that I had successfully found direction, career-wise, it was time to make plans to move away from home.

As usual, I shared my plans with Grandpa Vincenzo. He always backed me, in spite of any doubts he may have had, which was so unlike my father. He knew how much I wanted to leave home. He also knew my relationship with my father was strained and that all my plans to leave home had to be kept secret.

In support of my move and anticipating my marriage to Chet, Grandpa Vincenzo purchased a new house on Ridge Road in Parma. He thought that I needed to be close to my mother, because she needed me.

Our lovely three-bedroom ranch was everything a young couple could desire. The sandstone wood-burning fireplace in the living room would provide warmth and ambiance on cold winter nights. The large dining area had a pass-through opening to the kitchen. Double sliding glass doors formed the outer wall of the dining room. The backyard was more than 150 feet deep and lined with pine, maple, and oak trees.

The home was not purchased free and clear; it had a mortgage. After our marriage, Chet and I would assume the mortgage payment. It would have been a wonderful beginning for newlyweds, except for the fact that returning veterans, like Chet, had flooded the job market. How would we pay for a new home? Of course, Grandpa Vincenzo had the answer. Chet would work for him. He would teach Chet every facet of home remodeling.

By January, all our wedding arrangements were complete: the rings were purchased, a short white cocktail dress and veil were paid for, the date was set at the Polish National Church, and our reception would be held at Pisano's Restaurant and Lounge Bar.

Grandpa Vincenzo and Grandma Caroline would host the small reception. Auntie Sue would be the photographer. Chet's brother Ted would be his best man, and his wife, Leona, would be my matron of honor. Wedding attendance was by verbal invitation only.

140

Long before my wedding date, I wanted to break the news to my father. An opportune time never occurred. Perhaps my father's erratic schedule was a factor, but much of the delay was caused by my fears. *I can't talk to him. He never approved of Chet!* The phrase, "He'll never approve," kept ringing in my ears.

Finally, one week before my marriage, I knew that I had to talk to him. How could I ever maintain an acceptable relationship with my father if he learned of our marriage *after* the fact? How I dreaded his disapproval! *What can I say to him?*

It was Sunday morning, and my father and I were sitting in the living room. He was reading his paper and I was manicuring my nails. Before speaking, I looked around the room and studied each object, wanting to imprint their images forever on my mind.

I'm really going to do it…tell him that I'm leaving. The realization that I was going to leave home was overwhelming. Choking with emotion, I began.

"Daddy, I love you with my whole heart and soul. I know you need me to help you run the house." In the back of my mind, I always felt like he needed me to be his housekeeper.

"Please don't be angry with me! I plan to marry Chet next Saturday. Please come to the church and reception. Grandpa Vincenzo has helped me with the arrangements."

As I spoke to him, I felt as if food were stuck in my throat with every word I said. Finally, I had broken the news.

Instantly, Father's eyes grew black, his face flushed red, and his entire body shook. This was the same look that I had known so well ever since Chet had entered my life.

I flinched, expecting to be slapped. The slap never came.

Displaying rigid self-control, Father spoke through clenched teeth. "Beverly, you can forget me. You can forget about your mother. If you get married Saturday, never ever return to this house again! Do you understand?" *Yes, I most certainly do understand!*

My father's manner of speech and venomous tone expressed hatred and rage. *Why, Daddy, why?* A slap on the face would have been far easier to deal with than the mental anguish his words induced. His adamant disapproval of my decision hurt.

141

I love you Daddy. I'm so sorry it's come down to this! I never wanted to have to choose between you and Chet. My father had vowed never to talk to me again. I left home with an ache in my heart that would take years to repair. Moving on was bittersweet.

My father was true to his word; neither he nor my mother was present on my wedding day. After I recited my vows, their absence hit me like a punch in the gut, robbing me of the joy I should have felt. There were tears of pain and loss in my eyes as I descended the steps of the church.

There was no honeymoon for Chet and me. We had furnished the new house on Ridge Road, and so we spent our wedding night there. I had waited so long to tell my father about our wedding that I had left most of my belongings behind at my parents' home. Being frightened and very cowardly, it took me over a week after the wedding to build up the courage to return there. Not wanting a confrontation with my father, I chose to go at midday. By then, he was usually gone.

Good, he's gone. The door to the garage and breezeway was open, as usual. I entered the office, and stood still before calling out to my mother. "Mom, it's me."

No answer. *What did I expect?* The scent of cigarette smoke permeated the air. *Nothing has changed.* Yet feelings of uneasiness and melancholy came over me.

Sunlight glared through the office window. My eyes scanned the room. *Something is missing, but what? There's the desk, the companion chair, the adjoining bookcases, and the phone. Everything seems to be here.*

Then, while focusing my attention on the walls, my gaze became fixated on the bare space above the desk, where a painting once hung. In place of the picture were tell-tale demarcation lines formed in the surrounding faded paint. *My portrait—it's gone!*

The painting had been done by a street-artist on a visit I had taken to Miami, Florida, with my friend Helen and her family. I was sixteen at the time. The composition, color, and resemblance were amazingly good, and even my father had liked it. *Perhaps it's in the closet.*

Opening the closet door brought another disappointment. It was empty: no picture, no portable record player and records, absolutely nothing of mine could be found.

Then I opened my bedroom door. Someone had removed everything that I had on display from sight.

The most dramatic change made in the room was the choice of bedding on the twin beds. The week before, very soft, feminine comforters, decorated with abstract bright yellow tulips with green leaves and stems, had covered the beds. Antique white dust ruffles had covered the box springs and bedframe.

My former bedding had been replaced by heavy brown masculine blankets and beige sheets. Men's slippers could be seen beneath one of the beds. *It's his room now.* I couldn't bring myself to think of him as my father.

I sat down on the dressing table stool and looked at the large round mirror. The pictures I had artistically placed upon it were gone. Looking at my reflection and biting my lip, I was determined to hold back my tears. *You're such a sad sack!*

I know I left jewelry on this dressing table: my class ring, a silver ring, a charm bracelet, an Indian necklace, and my watch. The Chanel No. 5 perfume is missing too.

There were two drawers on each side of the dresser. One at a time, I pulled them open. To my chagrin, they were both empty. *Oh, well! I'll look in the dresser.*

In less than a minute, I had inspected the contents of the dresser without results. The only place in the room that I hadn't looked was the closet. When I opened the door, I expected to see my summer clothes hanging there. Instead, my father's clothing was neatly hung in their place. *Perhaps he's boxed my belongings and placed them in the basement*

The basement stairs were located off the kitchen. There, sitting in the kitchen on the straight-back step-stool, sat my mother, blowing thick rings of cigarette smoke from her nostrils. *Nothing's changed.*

Mom smiled as I quickly kissed her on the cheek and continued on my way past her to the basement. *Nothing!* It was a futile search.

Disappointed again, I returned upstairs feeling anxious and annoyed. *Perhaps my mother knows something.*

Her conversation was very coherent. She had missed me the past week and asked me to continue seeing her. *What a surprise!* I didn't think she would have noticed my absence.

She said Dad had burned my portrait, books, papers, and pictures in the large rubbish barrel in the back yard. The clothing had been donated to Goodwill Industries. Mom's description of my father's fury was somewhat humorous, coming from her. "First, he ransacked your bedroom, dumping and throwing things like a thief. Then he smashed the glass covering your painting and broke the frame into bits and pieces—just like a crazy man!"

She was right. Upon leaving, I checked the garage and found ashes in the empty barrel.

Now I could see the situation with clarity; my father had cast me off. He had disowned me. His words kept ringing in my ears. "You can forget about me. You can forget about your mother!" I couldn't do that, especially now that she had asked me to visit.

What could I do? At that point in time, nothing could be done to change my father's opinion. *I must adjust. I will do what needs to be done. I will visit her when he's not here. I'll see my mother on the sly!*

Knowing that my father was embittered and dissatisfied with me still hurt, and his disapproving voice kept ringing in my ears. Part of me longed for his approval, but there was no way I could be who he thought I should be.

A place I often found solace, despite the falling out with my father, was at school. Depending on the weather, my drive to my teaching job in Brunswick took approximately sixty minutes. The ride was most enjoyable once I traveled outside the city limits. There were no stoplights, just open roads and hilly terrain. It was a very scenic trip with an array of farm animals, barns, and greenery.

Along with the other teachers, I arrived at school between seven and eight in the morning. The six school buses began pulling into the circular dirt-and-stone drive at approximately eight thirty. I would smile with delight when a stray dog would race alongside the bus as it drove into the driveway. The scene was reminiscent of a "Lassie" movie.

The quiet interval between my arrival and that of the students was my own time. It was my time to plan, to dream, to kick-back, and to gaze out the window until the arrival of the children. They look so happy.

But are they? Did I ever feel that way?

144

I don't think I did. I tried to remember feeling joyful as a child but it was difficult.

My students were restless, eager-to-learn fifth and sixth graders who genuinely liked me. It was a joy to have them as students.

The fresh-faced, rosy-cheeked little girls often said I was beautiful and they wanted to be just like me. The boys thought me pretty, and they would shyly turn away if I paid them extra attention. *What a morale booster!*

Teaching school was easy for me to do and I enjoyed it, but being Mrs. Chet Kowalski was hard work. Somewhere along my journey, I had begun to demand perfection in myself and everything I did. My marriage needs to be perfect.

Who has a perfect marriage? Definitely not my parents!

Then where do I look for a good example?

It's not the least bit surprising to me now that I chose a television sitcom to emulate. Where else but in the make-believe world of entertainment would one find an abstract ideal of how married life should be? There you find beautiful people in resplendent surroundings, living a good life, free of unhappiness and strife.

To me, June Cleaver, of the *Leave It to Beaver* series, was the model wife and mother. She was perfect in every way: the ever-beautiful, perfectly dressed, always smiling, loving and dutiful wife. She vacuumed and cleaned while wearing a party dress and pearls.

Her Mr. Cleaver was the model husband and father. He, too, was perfect in every way. He was the ruggedly handsome, finely dressed, always happy, loving and attentive husband and father. He held a white-collar job, dressed in business attire, and worked five days a week.

Carrying the perfection premise further, the Cleavers were suburbanites who lived in a large, white-frame Colonial surrounded by a white picket fence. And let's not forget that parked in their driveway was a 1960-model station wagon. This is what women of the '60s grew up wanting, myself included. But the typecast marriage of June and Ward would be impossible for most couples to achieve, even if everything in their lives was perfect. As a new bride, I didn't understand that I would need to change some of my patterns if I wanted to have anything resembling that ideal marriage.

Even though I was now a grown, married woman, I nevertheless kept the promises I had made to my grandfather as a teenager. Remember the win-win-win deal: a car in exchange for transportation. As in the past, my Saturdays were spent shopping with my grandfather at the Central Market in downtown Cleveland while Chet found himself home alone. *Shouldn't I be at home with him? Would a perfect wife leave for the day?*

From early childhood, my life and activities had always revolved around my grandfather. He was my rock, my pillar, and my protector. He appeared to have a solution for each and every one of my problems. Following his advice was natural and right for me. When he devised a blueprint for my future, I gladly followed, but for Chet, the same bond and confidence weren't there.

Prior to my marriage, Grandpa Vincenzo had his attorney prepare a prenuptial agreement for me and Chet. It was because of this prenuptial agreement that Chet found out that I had agreed to help Grandpa Vincenzo by allowing him to transfer ownership of some of his real estate to me.

My grandfather was a bit of a real estate tycoon in his day. At one point, he had acquired ownership of more than seventy homes. Managing his real estate was his full-time job. The rentals provided him with income, and he was able to keep his maintenance costs down because he had the skills to repair his own property. He was a master at buying a fixer-upper, repairing it, and selling it for a profit. He "flipped" homes before the word *flipping* became synonymous with real estate transactions.

The real estate story that I enjoyed the most was about when Grandpa Vincenzo purchased a piece of Cleveland's history—a mini-mansion built in the 1800s. The home was one of many purchased by the city and then auctioned off. Imagine Grandpa's excitement when he was the successful bidder! His find had been part of "Millionaires' Row" on Euclid Avenue in downtown Cleveland. In the second half of the 19th century and in the early 20th century, Euclid Avenue was home to some 250 mansions.

The catch was that the homes, including Grandpa's new find, had to be moved after they were purchased to make way for an expanding business district. An elaborate pulley system and horses transported it from the center of town to property he already owned—a large, sloping lot already containing one home with two hundred feet of vacant frontage on East 105th Street near Quebec and Wood Hill Road. Grandpa and several laborers used a horse and plow to dig a basement for the new house.

Sadly, in order for Grandpa Vincenzo's purchase to be profitable, the stately interior had to be gutted to convert the mansion into a tenement house with sleeping quarters and cooking privileges. The beautiful crystal lighting fixtures, brass brackets from gas lights, and Italian marble windowsills and fireplace mantels—the grandeur of "days gone by"—were removed. During the Depression and Second World War this home was a real money-maker.

A year before our marriage, Grandpa Vincenzo had found himself in a bit of legal trouble. He was facing a lawsuit for hitting one of his laborers.

Grandpa Vincenzo had never discussed the event with me, but I later learned that the incident had arisen over the laborer's attitude and work ethics. For Grandpa Vincenzo, the man's poor workmanship was unacceptable. A reprimand became a verbal confrontation; tempers flared and the two men became combative. Grandpa Vincenzo picked up a shovel and hit the man on his head.

On the advice of Grandpa Vincenzo's attorney, to avoid loss in the event he was found liable in the suit, his real property and mortgages had been divided among Grandma Caroline, Auntie Sue, and me. I could only imagine the fee the lawyer charged for all that paper work. *Nice return on your advice, counselor!* As it turned out, the plaintiff sustained no injuries and the case was settled before ever going to court. Regardless, a number of properties remained in my name.

By signing our prenuptial agreement, Chet would relinquish his dower rights of ownership to the property that Grandpa Vincenzo had signed over to me. When asked, Chet freely signed the agreement. After all, my grandfather was the rightful—if not legal—owner of the property, and Chet was too full of love for me to consider the possible future consequences for his finances. But Chet vehemently opposed my participation in these property transfers. "Beverly, now legally, you're the responsible one, not your grandfather, but the transfers are on paper only. It's a sham. You know he will maintain all his previous interest and control. Can't you see? You're being used." I knew I was being used, but because it had helped my grandfather, I was on board.

Grandpa's mini-empire had grown to the point that he needed someone to help maintain his investments. Plus, being a wise man, he knew that he needed to prepare for his nearing retirement. Chet thought that my grandfather was too controlling, and repeatedly said, "He'll never relinquish his hold on the property or turn the management over to anyone else." Even with these reservations, Chet went to work for Grandpa.

Learning the trades was an opportunity that had always appealed to Chet; otherwise, working for my grandfather would have been a very unlikely happening. Chet agreed to an apprenticeship.

Around the same time, Grandpa Vincenzo employed my cousin, Luigi Martinelli. Both men would learn every skill needed for the building industry: carpentry, plumbing, electrical, masonry, roofing, and whatever else it took to build a home. Grandpa Vincenzo was their instructor and would work with them on a daily basis.

The one snafu to this situation was that Grandpa Vincenzo and Luigi didn't drive. That left Chet with the extra assignment of chauffeuring his co-workers. This necessitated leaving our home in Parma at five every morning to pick up his passengers in University Heights, at my grandfather's home.

Luigi used public transportation—two buses from Collinwood—to get there. But often his arrival was delayed. This caused another snafu and created an annoyance for whom? The driver. Once Luigi finally arrived, the three men would ride together another thirty minutes before reaching the job site.

During that time, Grandpa Vincenzo and Luigi would converse in Italian. They meant no harm by using their native tongue, nor did they realize they were being rude. Luigi had just arrived in the States and could barely speak English. *My husband is rightly offended, but what can I say or do about it? Nothing!*

The unlikely crew—the elder mentor, the immigrant, and the Polish-American—generally began work at seven in the morning. They would break for a twenty-minute lunch and then continue working until dark. Their working conditions were mostly poor, since they often remodeled older or ramshackle homes. At times, the work was pure backbreaking labor, but, nevertheless, the younger men were learning the trades.

When the workday ended, Chet once again put on his chauffer's cap and drove his fellow workers back to Grandpa's. Once there, a coffee break was had by all at the insistence of Vincenzo. And, once again, the conversation reverted back to Italian.

The mini repast should have been inviting. The sweet, robust aroma of perked coffee could be detected throughout the hall long before entering the kitchen. Grandma Caroline's ten-cup glass percolator sat on the gas range, filled to the top, waiting to be served. Italian bread, cheese, and thin slices of prosciutto sat on the table. While the food was appealing, the timing was not. The younger men were in a hurry to get back to their homes.

For Chet, this was a long day and felt like too much togetherness. Because he was an apprentice, Grandpa Vincenzo spent his entire day monitoring his every move. The driving, coupled with being under constant supervision—or surveillance, as it felt to Chet— stressed him greatly.

Chet began to come back home later and later each workday and abruptly stopped complaining to me about on-the-job problems.

Damn it! It's after eight, and our dinner's cold. What's happening? He's changed.

Smelling the alcohol on his breath, I asked Chet, "Did you stop for a drink?" I received the silent treatment, but soon discovered that his new routine now included an after-work stop at the local pub, The Coral Reef.

Why has he changed? Or had he already changed before our marriage? He was away for two years. Chet never used to frequent bars, but Army guys like their booze. It's those booze-drinking Army guys who taught him how to drink!

The more I thought about Chet's recent behavior, the more insight I gained. Army life hadn't helped his predisposition to a drinking problem, and Chet had a formidable mentor—his father, John— whose behavior set quite an example for his son. Quiet, dependable John—his routine was so precise that you could set your watch by following him. *Don't tell me that he's going to behave just like his father!*

I was aware that John stopped each evening after work at his local pub, The Lincoln Inn. He was a habitual drinker. How could I have understood the significance of his nightly stops when I was only sixteen and just a high school student? Now, however, college psych courses and maturity had educated me about the problems created by drinking.

Chet's uncanny resemblance to his father frightened me. *No! He'll never be like John.* His father was a problem drinker for he became angry when drunk. The alcohol turned him into an abusive husband.

Could his father's behavior foretell Chet's future?

No! Chet could never be that way. He's good, decent, intelligent, and loving.

While dismissing those negative thoughts from my mind day after day, I still had to acknowledge changes in Chet's mannerisms. Yes, he was changing. The man I used to love never had expressed anger. To him, being angry was foreign behavior. *Now he's different; even minor irritants trip him out. Yes, now he is an angry man!*

Early in our marriage, Chet never, ever cursed in my presence. It was taboo. It was a no-no. Now it had become commonplace. Wanting Chet's approval above all else, I became his verbal whipping girl. And I tolerated it.

In my mind, Chet was acting out against me because of the predicament in which he found himself: miserable at work but loving me and not wanting to hurt my relationship with my grandfather. I knew, beyond any doubt, that he did not want to work for Vincenzo Martinelli. He had consented to please me.

I kept remembering driving through the countryside, in my little red Studebaker, making future plans with Chet...his longing to work outdoors, till the land, and own farm animals. He had wanted to be a gentleman farmer, with me as his wife. That had been my dream, too. *What had happened to our dreams?* We had shared mutual aspirations. *How had our lives gotten so out of control? I don't know.*

What I did know was that Chet did not want to be controlled by money or his wife's family. Yet he had stopped voicing his irritations. Instead of sharing his feelings with me, he stuffed his agitation and anger within himself, using

150

booze to numb his pain. We used to talk to each other but now, instead of talking, Chet drenched his throat with liquor and beer to loosen the strings of commitment that choked him.

How did I get into this no-win situation? I always want and need Grandpa's approval, and for now, we must depend on his financial help. If I champion Chet's wishes, I will certainly upset Grandpa. On the other hand, if I encourage Chet to make the best of his situation and keep going along with Grandpa, I will upset Chet. I must remain silent! In today's terms, my behavior and our relationship are described as co-dependency. The co-dependent wants to be a good person, wants to be liked, and pleases everybody but themselves.

The sad realization of what was happening to my marriage was beginning to form in my mind. Our life together was out of control—all that time, alcohol was in control of Chet.

For months, the bar continued to be Chet's enticing mistress. And where was I? At home, possibly pregnant and most certainly alone.

15

AND BABY MAKES THREE

It was the week before Thanksgiving vacation. Several students in our school were home with the mumps; two of them were from my fifth-grade homeroom.

Throughout the day, thirty students took turns sneezing and coughing. Little virus droplets contaminated the confined air in our classroom.

Never having had mumps as a child, I had no immunity. My present exposure placed me at a great risk of contracting the disease.

Hmm…the incubation period is anywhere from sixteen to eighteen days from exposure. The medical books say a child is contagious for two days before symptoms appear and for nine days when symptoms are present. Julie's been out four days. Marc left school on Tuesday. I wonder how long…

Glancing at the desk calendar, I was startled by a realization: *I'm late for my monthly cycle! And a possible mumps infection could increase my risk of miscarriage or having an imperfect child.*

Uncertain if I was actually pregnant—but worried that I could be—I decided my wisest course of action was to make an appointment at the Cleveland Clinic.

The Clinic doctor advised me to get an injection of gamma globulin, a blood derivative product that helps strengthen the immune system. That way, my body would be more resistant to the contamination so prevalent around me. I took the shot for all the right reasons; yet later in my life, the fact that I had done so came back to haunt me.

In January 1961, the doctors confirmed that we were expecting a child in August. Chet and I were overjoyed but a bit scared. The thrill of my anticipated motherhood was unbelievable! *Soon I'll have a tiny person for me to love—always love. My very own baby. Our child, Chet's and mine! How wonderful!*

Each week, I took the time to visit my mother on the sly. Remember my promise? I continued to be a dutiful daughter.

Mom loved her cigarettes. On each visit, she requested that I bring her some. I did so, knowing full well that they were not good for her, and that Dad would disapprove.

While driving to see her, my mind raced. *Shall I tell her? No, I need to wait. How do I tell my father? I've had no contact with him since my wedding day. Damn it, I miss him!* Admitting that to myself, I knew how desperately I wanted to re-establish my relationship with him in spite of how he had hurt me!

As was customary, I walked through the attached garage, continued through the breezeway, and entered the house. "Mom, I'm home." I found her sitting on her usual seat, the step-stool, in the kitchen. Kissing her on the cheek, I handed her a carton of Pall Mall cigarettes.

There was no conversation between us, just short sweet salutations. "Thank you," and "You're welcome."

With my delivery made, I left for home and again began to ruminate over my misfortune—the broken relationship with my father. *Will a grandchild mend our differences? I'd like to tell both of them the news, but I certainly don't know how to begin a conversation with my father. Probably, I can't. For now, I'd better forget about reestablishing a relationship with him. Tomorrow is another day.*

For now, without workplace protections for expectant mothers, my biggest concern was that when the school board discovered that I was pregnant, they might force me to stop teaching. My contract will be jeopardized if I can't

154

work through June. With a baby on the way, we definitely need the extra income.

Finding the "right time" to tell our principal about my pregnancy is most important. Timing is critical. If I wait too long, I could lose credibility. Still, I'm only six weeks along, so for now, mum's the word.

Hiding my morning sickness was more than a challenge—it was a debilitating impossibility. A wave of nausea swept over me, more than once, just before the end of homeroom. Students and co-workers must have seen me rushing to the restroom as the bell rang.

Once I was safely inside the stall, I would vomit until green bile appeared. Even though I constantly flushed the "potty," there was no way to mask the sounds. Anyone else inside the restroom could hear me and would draw her own conclusion.

The students observed that I now had a new ritual on returning to my classroom. I snacked on saltine crackers and ginger ale, gave them a smile, and then resumed my teaching. Feeling fine was good, but remaining secretive was better.

How do you hide a "baby-bump?" Cleverly!

I purchased four-inch-wide pieces of elastic to increase the waist-line of my skirts and wore extra-long blouses and sweaters to cover my tummy and hips. My hope was to put off my transition into maternity clothes until the end of May. I knew there would be no hope of hiding a pregnancy in June.

By the beginning of April, camouflaging my predominant tummy was beginning to be an impossible task. My supervisors needed to be told about my delicate condition. My mid-August due date was rapidly approaching. I was surprised that when I relayed my news, it was accepted graciously. *I was worried for no reason!*

After my homeroom class was made aware of my pregnancy, the students, with the help of their parents, surprised me with a baby shower on the last day of school. Thus, my teaching career came to an end with a celebration. Teary-eyed and grateful, I left with my gifts and returned home to concentrate on being a wife and preparing to become a mother.

Although living with Chet was not all dramatic and bad, we did quarrel every day over simple things like the dinner menu. My attempts to find the humor in the situation prevented any serious confrontation.

Chet's preferences were basic: meat and potatoes. This was how he was raised. My palate craved a Mediterranean diet: salad, spaghetti, and fresh fruit. *Give me lots of pasta!*

With diametrically opposed taste buds, arguments over meals were commonplace in our household. *My God, it's just one meal! What's all the fuss about? I wish he didn't care what I made for dinner!*

One morning, Chet requested roast chicken and potatoes for our evening meal. For some reason, I forgot to defrost the chicken that day. Perhaps I really didn't want to eat meat and potatoes again! Perhaps the ever-pleasing Beverly was tired of his demands?

For whatever reason, I decided to make pasta with marinara sauce for dinner, in lieu of the *epic* chicken. I could never have predicted the comic farce that would ensue from my decision.

That evening, Chet came in through the side door. Before we'd even exchanged greetings, he walked into the kitchen, and with one glance, took in the bubbling sauce on the stove and the pasta in the strainer in the sink. He smirked at me, went to the refrigerator, and opened the freezer section. He took out the frozen chicken, and then opened the window over the sink. Without giving me a second look, he unceremoniously tossed the frozen bird into our backyard.

Once he completed his mission, I peeked out the window. Our neighbors, the O'Connors, were in their yard. What must they think?

What a senseless thing for him to do! "You're acting like a hillbilly. Guess you don't give a damn about what the neighbors think of us!" *When I received no response from him, I started to sulk while I brought out our pasta dinner.*

After seating himself at the dinner table, Chet twisted a forkful of spaghetti around on his plate, took one bite, swallowed, and abruptly stopped eating. Then he strutted to the wastebasket, opened the lid, and dumped both his plate and its contents. "That's where this belongs!" He left the room.

"You spoiled brat! You're wasting food!"

In actuality, my real concern was not about Chet's wastefulness, but about what the neighbors would think. Remember, Beverly's co-dependent. For me, ruminating was a constant happening. Just like a needle stuck in the groove of a vinyl record, the scene began replaying, repeating and repeating itself.

But this time, my review was from a different perspective—from outside our home. Imagine that suddenly, a frozen chicken comes flying out of your neighbor's kitchen window. It flies high into the air, glides straight as an arrow for thirty feet, then falls and rolls to a stop. Most certainly, witnessing this would be an unexpected event. *Surprise!* And even if you surmised that the *"wind"* behind the wingless soaring bird was an angry man, there was a childlike silliness about the incident. After all, how often do you see a frozen chicken flying through the air?

Once more, I thought about our neighbors and their perception of the frozen, featherless, wingless flying pullet. I said aloud, "So what?" *How silly!* As my anger gave way to a feeling of mischievousness, I began to giggle. The kid in me surfaced! *I'll get back at you! Tamper with my dinners, will you?! Let's see how you fare in the morning. Yours will be a baconless breakfast.*

Opening the refrigerator, I removed the bacon from the meat compartment and went into the half-bath off the kitchen in search of a place to hide his favorite breakfast meat.

The mirrored medicine cabinet was directly in my line of vision. *He'll never look there! Now who's the wasteful childish one?* The bacon would surely spoil overnight without refrigeration; however, acting responsibly never entered my mind. Getting even was more fun!

Morning arrived. Chet knew, all too well, that he had recently purchased bacon. Even before he entered the kitchen he asked. "No bacon and eggs this morning?" His olfactory senses were right on target.

"Sorry, we don't have any."

"You gotta be kidding!" Then he opened the refrigerator door and began searching every nook and cranny.

"Guess you're right. I could have sworn I saw bacon in the meat compartment yesterday." He shook his head in disbelief.

There was no brouhaha over the bacon. Chet left for work like a disappointed little boy. As he went out the door, I giggled like a school girl. *Got you, this time!*

That evening, I confessed. *I hope he forgives me!* Now it was Chet's turn to laugh—and he did. The truth of the matter was that we had both acted as spoiled, wasteful brats. Unfortunately, in the weeks and months following our chicken and bacon episodes, our childish bickering escalated to abusive language, combativeness, and unmanaged conflict.

Saturday, problematic, busy Saturday, why do you vex me?

Because, Beverly, you can't have a happy husband if you continue doing what you're doing: leaving home at the break of dawn, shopping, and running errands for your grandparents the entire day. Upon your return in the early evening, of course you find an angry, unhappy, and quarrelsome husband.

Saturday used to be the day that I anticipated most; the happiest day of the week. I remember that darling child I once was—the exuberantly happy little girl who held on tightly to her grandfather's hand as they walked the aisles of the Central Market. I felt protected and loved.

Saturday shopping with Grandpa Vincenzo had become a tradition. It was, in my mind, an unwritten law, especially following my teenage agreement. *I must continue to respect Grandpa's wishes.* There seemed to be no solution to the problem, so I continued to behave as in the past.

Doing things for my grandparents continued to be my Saturday priority, yet I had to find a way to appease Chet. To do this, he requested that the local beverage store be placed on my itinerary each week. And as a dutiful wife, I began to enable his alcoholism by purchasing a fifth of Kessler's liquor and a case of Stroh's beer. A shot with a beer was the workingman's drink. It was called the Boilermaker, and it did just that: it brought him to the boiling point!

Arguing with Chet each Saturday had become expected. *He'll never grow to approve of my Saturday trips to the east side of town. So be it!*

One day, I went to the basement to restock the extra refrigerator with newly purchased fresh fruits and vegetables. As I passed the landing to the basement, I saw a sorry reminder: a case of empty bottles. *I forgot to purchase his booze. I'm going to be in trouble!*

Chet appeared above me on the landing. His red face and glazed-over bloodshot eyes revealed his agitation. It was obvious that

158

trouble was brewing. As I climbed the stairs, Chet picked up the case and hurled it at me.

My baby!

Wrapping my arms around my pregnant belly, I instinctively ducked to protect my unborn child. When I looked up, Chet had disappeared from view and I saw broken glass on every step. The few bottles that hadn't broken were strewn about the landing and upper stairs. *Thank God, his aim is bad.*

Unharmed, I climbed upstairs. Crying frantically, I ran into the bedroom, locked the door, and didn't open it until the next morning. All was silent throughout the night, as Chet slept off his drunkenness on the couch.

Welcoming the morning sunlight, Chet cleaned his mess from the previous night. The hideous Mr. Hyde was gone. Chet had transformed himself into Mr. Congeniality, repeatedly trying to hug me.

In spite of Chet's attempts to apologize over the next two days, I remained hurt and angry. I wanted to lash out at him for his violent outburst. Instead, he received the silent treatment from me.

He really needs help! Acting as a true co-dependent, the gallant martyr, me, chose to endure the pain and forgive him. However, my psyche was hurt—too hurt to forget the pain.

This incident reinforced one of my growing concerns; that perhaps Chet wasn't ready for fatherhood. *He must feel trapped. We never discussed parenting. Perhaps, for Chet, a child is just a taut string, tying him to a marriage and the family relationships he clearly does not want.* Once more, my co-dependent thinking emerged. *Everything he did happened because of something I had done. I trapped him.*

August 11, 1961 was a hot, humid summer day. Before my pregnancy, the dog days of summer had always appealed to me. *Beverly never perspires. She never sweats. Why, she's as cool as a cucumber.* The word *perspiration* wasn't in my vocabulary.

Now, however, my body constantly felt hot, sticky, and in need of a shower. *You've gained twenty pounds—all because of the baby.* There was no denying my pregnancy. The baby was due very soon, but not for at least a few more days. At my advanced stage, even loose maternity clothing had difficulty covering my belly.

My beautifully flat tummy had expanded. The baby had positioned itself low under my breast bone. This placed tremendous pressure on my pelvis causing me to walk bowlegged. Oh, how my poor legs ached from carrying the extra weight!

Today required me to be on my feet the entire day. Chet and I were entertaining a special couple this evening—his brother and sister-in-law, Ted and Lee. There was much to do: shopping, cleaning, and cooking. Because of my physical condition, I needed help, especially with the cleaning. In fact, in my mind, it was a necessity! Remember, I was trying to be Mrs. June Cleaver.

With our budget strained from purchasing all the necessities for a first-born, I thought Chet would surely object to hiring a cleaning lady. Hiring someone, no matter who it was, had to be kept a secret.

Grandpa Vincenzo had hired a woman named Lilly to clean for my mother after I moved from Auntie Elsie and Uncle Dom's house to the new house on Orchard Avenue. I knew and trusted Lilly implicitly. She came into my life at a time when my newest hopes and dreams were being crushed and rescued me from the about-face my life had taken. Although I had longed for a fresh new start when we moved, before long, everything was moving backwards, or, as an astrologer would say, my life was in retrograde.

Within six months, our newly constructed house had lost its shine and freshness. Stale cigarette smoke from my mother's incessant smoking had permeated the air.

The bright, cheery, yellow kitchen walls had taken on a brownish stain. The Formica countertops had been defaced with cigarette burns.

It's happening again, and there's no way I can stop her from being overtaken by her madness. How soon will she return to the hospital?

While setbacks were not new to me, the constant recurrence of events had intensified my sensitivity to changes. I was terribly unhappy. That was such a sad state of mind for a teen.

These were my circumstances and mindset that first day Lilly came to work. The first thing she said was, "We need light and fresh air before we start." Following her lead, we walked through the house, letting up the shades and opening the windows.

Immediately, sunlight illuminated our tasks and the outside air refreshed the rooms. The pungent smell of cigarette smoke was now replaced with the pure clean scents of Murphy's Oil Soap, vinegar, and ammonia.

For a short time, Lilly's visits were a once-a-month occurrence. The changes her presence brought may have been temporary, but they were good because they gave me something to look forward to.

Cooking with her gave a new dimension to our house. It became a home. I'd plan ahead and purchase all the groceries needed to cook her specialties: Southern fried chicken, potato salad, cabbage, corn bread, and pumpkin pie.

Chatting with Lilly as we cut up veggies or rolled out pie dough was reminiscent of time I had spent with Auntie Elsie. Much like my aunt, Lilly gave me the attention my mother was incapable of giving.

"Let me look at you, girl. You're as pretty as a speckled pup!"

Lilly carried my picture in her wallet. "Let me show you a picture of my play-daughter," she would tell her friends. In essence, she was my play-momma. Our affection was mutual.

This history was the very reason I wanted Lilly around to help me with my chores on August 11th. She couldn't be replaced, especially now! *For God sakes, I'm pregnant! I need her help!*

Chet knew that Grandpa had hired Lilly in the past to help with the heavy cleaning at my parents' home. But from his comments, I knew only too well that he would disapprove of my decision to bring her into our home to work. She was excessively heavy and she was black. His objection to her size never concerned me. She accomplished more work in a day than her skinny sisters.

Was Chet prejudiced? NO! He would be concerned with safety, ours and hers. Several incidents of vandalism had been reported when blacks tried to move to the West Side. In the early '60s, Parma's population still remained 99 percent white, a portion of which maintained anti-black sentiment.

All the years Lilly worked for my parents in the '50s, I never heard her express concern for her safety. She rode two buses from the projects on East 55th near Woodland Avenue to our house in Parma. During that time, she remained safe.

Would anyone object to Lilly's working here? Most likely, yes. Dissidents always express their objections, but the fact remained that no one had verbally abused or hurt her. Our immediate neighborhood never experienced any racial conflicts. She was safe and so were we.

According to my reasoning, it just didn't make any sense to try to talk to Chet about Lilly. It would be a moot subject. He could never feel what I felt or even begin to understand why I cared for her or preferred her help, so rather than try to convince him, I decided to deceive him.

The day Lilly came to my rescue, the R.T.A. bus pulled into the turnoff in front of the Sohio gas station on the corner of Ridgewood Drive and Ridge Road at exactly 8:00 a.m.

"Lilly, I'm over here."

Lilly's large body rocked to and fro as she walked over to my 1959 black Ford convertible. "Hey there, girly, should you be driving? Gal, your belly is touching the steering wheel."

I looked down. *Yes, it is!* Amused by the way my baby bump stuck out in front of me, I giggled to myself as I drove home. But I had a one-track mind: we had work to do!

The four o'clock hour arrived quickly, and while feeling a bit spent from the cooking and cleaning projects, working with Lilly made the tasks enjoyable. We laughed at each other as we collapsed on the cushioned living room chairs, and surveyed our accomplishments with pride. *Gosh, I've missed her!*

My cozy abode sparkled. The bright sunshine illuminated the newly cleaned windows, polished, dust-free furnishings, and vacuumed floors. *This should certainly pass Chet's inspection!*

Taking in a deep breath, my nostrils filled with the sweet, spicy aroma from the three freshly baked pumpkin pies that were cooling on the countertop. The main course—two savory stuffed capons surrounded with celery, carrots, onions, and potatoes—I would place in the oven upon my return from the bus stop.

Looking at the clock, I came to the realization that we hadn't stopped a minute too soon. It was four fifteen. *We'd better get moving. The Cleveland-bound bus will arrive at four thirty.*

162

Lilly and I were a comical, large-bellied pair as we attempted to rush out the door and maneuver ourselves into my car. *Better watch my speed.*

The bus was slowing down to a stop as I pulled my car into the gas station without a minute to spare. Frantically, I waved at the driver. "Wait! Please wait for her!"

The bus driver acknowledged my request. Then he waved his hand beckoning Lilly to hurry. With each step she took, he waved faster, as if by waving he could speed her up.

Lilly stopped after each step she took, appearing to gasp for air. *The heat is affecting her.* Her movements were deliberate and clumsy.

God, he's impatient! Lilly's getting old. Poor woman!

Finally, she reached the bus stairwell and grabbed onto the side rails. She lumbered up the stairs, paid her fare, and at long last seated herself. *Thank you, God! Phew! My secret is safe; Chet will never know that I had help today!*

On arriving home, I kicked off my shoes, sat in my favorite chair and consciously reviewed my unwritten checklist. *The roast, I must start the roast.* I set the oven thermostat to 350 degrees.

Placing the uncovered roaster into the oven, I got to work. *Toss the salad, open the applesauce, and place the whipped cream on the top shelf where you can find it, and slice one of the pies. Why not taste the pie? See that broken piece? It's just a tiny sliver. Hmm…, delicious! Have another teeny-weeny piece; it won't hurt you.*

Damn it, look what you've done. One entire pie dish was empty! *Pies are not the healthiest snacks.*

My insatiable craving turned into remorse. Feeling guilty, I washed the dish and promptly returned it to the cupboard. *Phew! Another secret is successfully hidden.*

Our evening was also a success: the food tasted delicious. It also looked delectable, and Lee and Ted were enjoyable conversational-ists. Lee helped with the cleanup, and when they left at about nine in the evening, I immediately headed for the shower.

My tummy hurts.

What did you expect after eating a whole pie? Check your belly button.

It hurts, too. Looking at my inverted belly button, it appeared stretched to the max.

After showering, I joined Chet in the living room and sat on the floor to watch TV. *Pop!* A loud popping sound emerged from my body. I had no idea as to what was happening. I had felt pelvic pressure throughout the day, but dismissed the aches and pains.

Could I be in labor?

No! It's too soon.

Even though it was eleven in the evening, Chet called the doctor's office. Doctor Mayer explained that my water had broken. He unequivocally said, "Go directly to the hospital."

Doctor Mayer had received his training while serving in the United States Army, and most military-trained doctors believed that in most circumstances, natural childbirth was the best method. He would administer ether on an only-if-necessary basis. It was also my desire to deliver my child naturally.

Chet and I arrived at Southwest Community Hospital, on the corner of Bagley and Front Street in Berea before midnight. After two hours of back-breaking labor, our nine-pound, twenty-two-inch baby boy arrived at 1:10 a.m., on August 12, 1961.

Our little creature's first cries were loud and clear. I always considered them more like a roar, since he was born under the sun sign of Leo, the lion. Chet was sitting just outside the birthing room when our son was born. The nurse wrapped our red-faced, bawling newborn son in a towel, walked outside the delivery room, placed the baby in his arms, and proceeded to show him the rippling muscles on his son's body. "Here's your future fullback!"

If she returned to show me the baby, I do not remember, for my exceptionally rapid labor and intense contractions had left me spent and exhausted.

Upon opening my eyes, the scene before me seemed surreal and dreamlike in my drowsy condition. Someone had to have wheeled the gurney holding my sleeping body out of the delivery room, and placed it in front of a large, elongated, hallway window. Lightning zigzagged across the black sky. Buckets of rain streamed down the window pane. Forceful, swirling winds caused the nearby trees to dance as if they were being controlled by a puppeteer. The hardwoods swayed from side to side, dropping their green foliage and small branches.

164

In the distance, I could hear the explosive, frightening sounds of thunder, but my exhaustion was so complete that I had no concern for the weather conditions. The next morning's news revealed that this had been no ordinary cloudburst; a tornado had been sighted not far from Berea.

My next day began at 6:00 a.m. when the nurse entered the room with my baby sleeping in her arms. Hesitating before reaching out to hold him, I blurted out to the nurse, "I've never held a baby! He's so small; I could hurt him." In fact, at nine pounds, our son was considered a large baby.

"Just make sure you support his head with your hand or arm until he can hold it up on his own." She proceeded to demonstrate how to hold him. "Babies are quite resilient."

Once the little man was safely in my arms, nothing else in this world compared to the serenity and peace I felt. All the pain and stress of my delivery disappeared. The warmth of his little body cradled in my arms, the sweet smell of his skin, his silky hair, his little nose, his wide-open eyes, and his chubby cheeks mesmerized me. Holding his teeny hands and tracing each teeny finger with mine was amazing!

Every four hours the nurse brought him to me. He would stare into my eyes and grin as he instinctively drank his formula, stopping every few minutes to look up at me with what seemed like wonder in his eyes, letting the yellow-colored liquid trickle down his chin. In between his feedings, I would watch television in the sitting-room or linger in front of the nursery window to look at my darling baby boy.

My hospital room was a five-bed ward. In the bed next to mine was a fifty-year-old, first-time mommy. After twenty-five years of marriage, she had finally conceived a child. The couple was ecstatic with joy. Her husband lavished her with gifts on a daily basis. Their long wait made their son's birth an exceptionally momentous event. Gift-bearing family and friends also visited her daily.

All the attention she was receiving made me a bit jealous, especially since Chet arrived at my bedside empty-handed. *Flowers would have been nice. Even a candy bar would have pleased me.*

The "nifty fifty-year-old" received a daily goody bag from her hubby filled with chocolates and other sundries. Her favorite treat was Planters Jumbo Block peanut candy. Each day, immediately after lunch, you could hear the rustling of paper bags followed by her joyous munching, crunching, and lip-smacking. Guess what? The entire ward now craved peanut brittle.

Chet visited the hospital every evening. He said he wasn't working during the day. *What was he was doing?* His answer was vague. He said he was busy completing the nursery. *How long could it take to paint a room and assemble a crib?*

My thoughts drifted off. Four days after our son's birth, Chet and I were presented with his birth registration papers. We officially named our baby Ted Vincent Kowalski, to honor Chet's older brother and my grandfather.

I wonder what my father's doing today. He should be pleased we named our son Ted, like his youngest brother. Grandpa will be pleased with Ted's middle name.

I would have liked to make our son's first name Vincent, after Grandpa Vincenzo, but I didn't dare suggest that to Chet. He would never have approved. It was easy for me to agree to Chet's request for Ted to be the first name because I loved its meaning: *Gift from God.*

The day of our discharge, though I felt apprehensive about caring for an infant, the excitement of bringing my little one home overwhelmed my apprehension. *Home,* what a sweet word!

Ted had been circumcised the day before and, like a good mommy, I read and reread our homecare instructions. Taking care of myself was natural and understood, but caring for the baby was entirely different. Being a first-time mommy, I had concerns.

Deeming myself a modern woman, my baby would be bottle-fed. Bottle-feeding an infant presented a new set of difficulties: preparing bottles and mixing formula. In actuality, the sterilization process and preparing formula had been simplified, and having Madame Curie at your side was not a necessity.

But there was that circumcision wound. Just looking at it, I felt squeamish. It appeared so very sore, raw, and beet red. How could I change the dressing when I feared hurting my little son?

They must think I'm a nurse. Good God, I can't even diaper or bathe my child. I'd repeatedly told the nurses that five days ago was the first time I had ever held a baby. *Someone, please show me what to do.*

All of these tasks were new and foreign to me. The past five days had given me expertise in holding, feeding, and burping a baby, but nothing else. Caring for my baby at home, on my own, was a different and scary prospect. *What if...What if...?* I worried constantly. After expressing my distress to Grandpa Vincenzo, he came to my rescue, and hired a nurse, who arrived the afternoon of our release. She would stay in our home twenty-four hours a day, for ten days. According to Grandpa, she was highly recommended by the agency he had called.

"They said, 'She's a very capable registered nurse who will take care of the baby's needs and make light meals for you.'" *Now, I'll manage.*

Nevertheless, I continued to worry, because on the day of Ted's birth, so much of our baby preparations had been left undone; even the crib had yet to be assembled.

"You're home." Smiling, I looked around his room. *This explained why Chet was so busy and couldn't find time to visit me during the day.* I kissed my sleeping infant and placed him in his crib.

The room was freshly painted, not in the traditional blue for a boy, but in a cheerful, sunny yellow. Pale yellow curtains covered the windows. Nursery rhymes and story-book animals were illustrated on the surrounding border. The colors yellow, apple-green, and taupe were carried through the room in crib blankets and toys. Miniature animals hung from the large mobile attached to the side of the fully assembled crib. A fluffy white rug lay in front of a wicker rocker and end table. The nursery was befitting our little king of the jungle!

Chet took hold of my hand and led me to our bedroom. My eyes filled with tears of gratitude. Ted's room wasn't the only one Chet had changed. He had been hard at work on our room, as well. This room had been transformed into a flowering field of Parisian lavender. Varying hues of lavender were found on the walls, new bedspread, and sheets.

Draped across the bed was a beautiful lavender nightgown. The yoke was embroidered with tiny roses intertwined with a purple ribbon. This room was befitting a queen. *He must really love me!*

Hugging and kissing my husband, I cried tears of joy. *We'll make this marriage work! Chet will be a good father. Now he has a reason to give up drinking. Things will change. He'll change.* This is what I truly believed.

With prescriptions to fill and formula to purchase, Chet left for the pharmacy. Once the car pulled out of the drive, I returned to the nursery. Our son was sleeping soundly in his crib.

My euphoric state of happiness totally relaxed me. Feeling safe and sleepy, I lay down on the living room sofa to wait for Chet's return. Soon I fell into a deep sleep. Being a warm, August day, the front door had been left open.

Suddenly, I intuitively felt someone's presence in the room. I opened my eyes and jumped up from my prone position. There was my neighbor, Mae O'Connor—one of the witnesses of the flying pullet incident—standing before me, rocking Ted in her arms. She had come over to see the new baby, and had heard his cries as she approached our door. *Oh God! Was Ted crying that loudly?!* I hadn't heard his cries. Mae had ignored me, for her concern was the baby. She went directly to the nursery, and discovered the reason for his cries; Ted needed a diaper change.

Mae had raised five teens, and her presence made me feel secure. While she gave me instructions on preparing formula, the nurse Grandpa Vincenzo hired arrived in her pristine white uniform. From the looks of her, she was ready for retirement. *She must be sixty-five years old.* She had gray hair, a face etched by time, and a thin, petite, fragile frame.

Setting down her overnight bag, the nurse introduced herself to us. "Please, call me *Mrs. Myers.*" *Hah, a very formal English woman.*

I worried endlessly about how Chet would tolerate outside help, especially since I couldn't hide her, as I had Lilly. But Mrs. Myers' quiet, prim manner made her presence in our home acceptable to Chet, and she was a great help to me. Fortunately, her ten-day stay ended just before she wore out her welcome. *My, how bossy can one get?!*

Ted was three weeks old when we took him to Holy Trinity Church for his baptism on the third of September. Lee and Ted

Kowalski were his proud godparents.

Having a baby in the house appeared to change Chet. He stopped his mind-altering drinking while at home. On occasion, I could still smell alcohol on his breath when I would give him a kiss to greet his return home. He would catch the look of disappointment in my eyes and weakly claim, "I only had one..." In my habitual denial, I deeply wanted it to be true, so I believed him.

Now, Chet no longer criticized anything I did, even events involving my grandfather. If my Saturday shopping sojourns still made him angry, he controlled his temper. In my mind, he had transformed himself into a "normal" drinker, but "normal" is something that doesn't exist for an alcoholic.

To my way of thinking, the remainder of 1961 was blissful.

16

GOODBYE TO TICKING CLOCKS

In January 1962, Chet's father, John Kowalski, retired as a core maker for Fanner Manufacturing. His retirement was short lived. A week later, he was rushed to the hospital. The physicians acted as quickly as they could, but it was too late.

No one suspected that John's years of violent coughing spells were symptomatic of a fatal disease. Everyone reasoned that the bouts were natural consequences due to cigarette smoking. They probably were, as an autopsy revealed that he had had lung cancer, and it was the untreated cancer that brought him down.

At that time, there was little public awareness regarding the signs of cancer. Nor did the public understand the consequences of smoking. In fact, smoking was fashionable. Every movie displayed glamorous people with their cigarettes in hand.

Stella, Chet's mother, was devastated by the death of her husband. She had been a homemaker her entire married life. Like most women of her generation, she was completely dependent on her husband. He was responsible for making all their major decisions and for supporting her financially. Stella and John had immigrated to the United States together. They established themselves in

Cleveland, making their home in an apartment above a grocery store in the Tremont area, the city's Polish district. They were a poor and hard-working couple.

John never bought a car. He rode the bus to work. The couple scrimped and saved to afford a new home on Lincoln Avenue in Parma. Their world consisted of each other, their sons and daughters-in-law, a new grandson, Snyder—their chubby black Labrador, their home, and their church, the Polish National Catholic Church. *How will Stella manage without him?*

Stella and John had met in their homeland—war-torn Poland. Stella was twenty-eight years old when they married. By American standards, she married late in life. John was thirty-eight years old.

No doubt, residing in a land unsettled by war had much to do with the shaping of their similar personalities. They both were quiet, serious, and introverted. Deep lines etched their faces, prematurely aging them. Smiling was not part of their personas. Yet their facial expressions were pleasant and kind. This is where their resemblance ended, for they were a most unlikely looking couple— diametric opposites.

Stella had a full round face with large brown eyes, an upturned nose, and blonde hair. She was short—five feet tall—and large-boned. She was an unremarkably plain woman who was defined by her disabilities. She stuttered as she spoke. Her hands and arms trembled. She would stand with her head down and her back rounded and hunched. When she walked, she took long steps and dragged her rigid left leg behind her.

I suspected that Stella's gait and mannerisms were indications that she either had Parkinson's disease or suffered a stroke, but we never discussed the possibility of these medical conditions. Except for childbirth, Stella never consulted a doctor. For her, taking medicine was a "no-no." But she did believe in her magic elixir! This dietary supplement used for iron deficiency just happened to have 12 percent alcohol content, comparable to that of some wine. Unsurprisingly, it proved to have a tranquilizing effect on her.

Although her health was never a topic of conversation, Stella did share with me that she believed that the nerves in her young body were shattered from living in constant fear of bodily harm. In her childhood, she had been exposed to human suffering, loss of life, hunger, disease, violence, and constant fear. For days at a time, Stella's family would evacuate their large farm house for the confines of an underground shelter that was hidden beneath their home. The entrance was cleverly concealed beneath the front porch with shrubs, sticks, and rocks. She felt entombed in the dirt and darkness. She clung to her mother and sisters as they pressed their ears to the door of the hideaway, waiting for the silencing of the sounds of danger: gunfire, men talking, or the click-clack made by the propellers of the reconnaissance planes. Lacking food and sanitary conditions, her family's survival was a miracle.

To my knowledge, John never ever told his sons or anyone else anything about his relatives that remained in Poland. We found no written records regarding his birth or family. Without a paper trail, the following information about my father-in-law has been drawn from my observations and suppositions of the man.

To me, he was a dear and quiet little man. John appeared to be healthy. He had a thin oval face, baby-blue eyes, straight nose, and light brown hair. He stood erect and straight-backed, at five feet five. Though five inches taller than Stella, his thin, fine-boned, wiry body made him appear much shorter next to her sturdy frame.

Although I suspected that John had trained as a core maker in his native Poland, his poor grasp of spoken English made it hard for him to explain upon his arrival to America that he was a skilled tradesman; therefore, his naturalization papers listed his previous employment as a laborer.

Making cores or molds in the production of metal casting requires much more of a worker than the simple handling or lifting of material characteristic of a laborer's job. It requires an intelligent person to make measurements, arrange things in order, and follow a pattern.

When he arrived in Cleveland, he began his employment at Fanner Manufacturing. He never missed a day of work. His routine never varied. Most individuals would find his existence boring from its rhythmic repetition. You could set your clock by his schedule.

John left home at 6:00 a.m. and walked to the corner bus stop. After his work day, he stepped off the bus at 5:00 p.m. and entered the corner bar, the Lincoln Inn. He drank two or more shots of Kessler's whiskey with two or more Strohs' beers. Then he walked home, opening the front door at precisely 6:00 p.m., just in time for dinner. His daily activities never changed during the week. There was a sad, lonesome simplicity to his life.

Most likely, John's death from cancer resulted from cigarette smoking and working in a foundry. The dirt, debris, and toxic fumes—perhaps including lead—were absorbed by his lungs five days a week or more. For twenty-five years, John had unknowingly compromised his health in the process of earning a living.

As John's life turned out, he enjoyed only one week of retirement—one week of his choice to spend a quiet afternoon at home or do nothing—before he died. He had just cashed his last paycheck from Fanners. His pension benefits would have begun the following month, but his employer made no provisions for a surviving spouse.

Had he survived, John would have received his first full month's Social Security check in February. Stella would have been supported by those funds, but—because of the unfortunate timing of John's death—there was only a one-week check due her. It was uncertain not only if she would receive widow benefits, but also if she could manage financially on whatever that amount might be.

All that was left to show from his years of sweat and toil was a glass-domed, polished-brass, German torsion pendulum clock. The base was engraved, "To John Kowalski, In Appreciation for Twenty-five Years of Service!" The clock was commonly called an "anniversary" clock, or four hundred-day clock, because it could run for a year on a single winding.

The night John died, Chet and I invited Stella to spend the night with us in our spare bedroom. Meanwhile, Ted and Lee made the funeral arrangements at A.J. Tomon & Sons Funeral Home, on Pearl Road in Brooklyn. Calling hours were in the afternoon and evening. The grieving brothers greeted the visitors who filled the room. I was surprised by the number of mourners, and their almost-exclusive use of Polish left me feeling like an outsider.

Throughout the first viewing, Stella remained seated by John's side. She sat, stone-faced and expressionless, as she kept watch over

174

her husband's body. Any attempts to comfort or console her were soon abandoned once it became clear that she was oblivious to anything other than her lost love, her eyes locked on John's face. It was as though a canopy of depression shrouded her as she refused to leave her post at the casket. She sat there, motionless, without a single tear.

After six hours, Stella finally rose. As she began to stand, her body trembled like a leaf, and she would have collapsed back into her seat, but her two sons rushed to her side to support her. Chet and Ted, one on either side, held tightly to her as she shuffled towards the side of the casket. She bent forward to give her husband one final kiss. Standing back up, she nodded her head, a bewildered look on her face. Still unable or unwilling to speak, Stella pointed to the door. Her normally stout frame seemed to have diminished, and she was dwarfed by her two sons as the three of them slowly exited the room. Overwhelmed by the empathy I felt for Stella and sadness at her loss, my eyes filled with tears. As I looked away and wiped my eyes, I glanced around the room and noticed that the tableau had had a similar effect on the remaining small groups of mourners.

The day of John's burial, we gathered at the funeral home. The procession was short, and we soon turned south on West 54th Street. Crossing Theota Avenue, I looked past a few houses on my left and spied the black, wrought-iron fence that marked the boundary of the Polish National Catholic Cemetery. *What a strange place to have a cemetery! How odd it would be to have these permanent residents as your next-door neighbors!*

The maple trees that lined the road stood in stark relief against the pale gray January sky. As the car pulled through the wrought-iron gate, a gust of wind took hold of few lonely leaves and unsuccessfully tried to rip them from their branches. Although the car's heater was doing its job, I pulled my winter coat tighter around myself as a chill ran down my spine.

As we gathered by the gravesite, I clung tight to Chet's arm. This was the first time I'd witnessed a burial. Seeing the piles of dirt and mud beside the gaping brown gash in the earth forced me to recognize the finality of death. I don't remember much of the burial ceremony, but as we departed, my heart felt heavy. Without John in our lives, there would surely be change to come.

Chet and I both felt that Stella needed our emotional support. Sending her home to fend for herself would not be good for her. We moved her bedroom furniture and a few personal belongings into our spare room: our home became her home.

Stella's house on Lincoln Avenue was sold in April, along with most of her furnishings. We stored the remainder of her belongings in our basement.

As one chapter ended, another began.

17

BABY DRAMA

Meal preparation had always seemed like a chore to me. Now that Stella was living with us, I hoped that she could help with the cooking. I thought perhaps she would prepare one of Chet's favorite meals, like a pork roast, or perhaps she would treat us to her apple and rice casserole. As it turned out, meal preparation, household chores, and the physical care of my son were still my jobs.

What Grandmama Stella did do was to give Ted her undivided attention. Watching her hug, kiss, and play with him, when—for lack of time—I couldn't, began to irritate me. *My God, you're jealous!*

Ted learned very quickly that he could get his grandmama to remove him from the confines of a crib or playpen by screaming, crying, and shaking the railings. These were times when I became angry with my mother-in-law. *Let him be!* Though I never verbalized my thoughts, she knew how I felt.

Nevertheless, she would remove my teary-eyed, drooling child from his playpen whenever she saw fit to do so, even without my permission. A smirk would sometimes cross her face when she caught my eye as she picked up her crying grandson. She apparent-ly thought it was unnecessary to consider what I, his mother, thought on the matter. At his slightest whimper, Grandmama would come to his rescue.

As a new mother, without any guidance from my own mother, I had purchased and read through several books by childrearing experts. I was determined to do my best to follow their sage advice. By not setting limits for the little one, they claimed that I would create a mini monster. Letting my child cry himself to sleep was okay with me.

Stella, on the other hand, felt a child should not cry. If he cried, something was wrong, and she needed to fix it. My mother-in-law's behavior was well-intended, yet her constant interference in my mothering left me with growing feelings of resentment. I was learning very quickly that no home is big enough for two women to live together harmoniously! Meanwhile, Chet was encountering his own challenges while working with my grandfather.

Grandpa Vincenzo had just purchased a single-family dwelling in the Collinwood area. Grandpa Vincenzo planned to remodel the home and convert it into a two-family dwelling. Unlike some of his previous remodeling projects, this would require major structural, plumbing, and electrical work.

For years, my grandfather had managed to repair and remodel his properties without permits or the use of a licensed contractor. Inspectors were lenient and looked the other way when the owner of the property did the work, especially when the workmanship was to code, as Grandpa Vincenzo's was. But, in this instance, the magnitude of the project meant that the building inspectors would require a licensed contractor to oversee the job.

Grandpa Vincenzo was as skilled, if not more so, than any of the tradesmen who had licenses. Yet he lacked one necessary credential: a high school diploma. Otherwise, he would have applied for the license himself. Instead, he asked Chet to obtain a contractor's license, but he adamantly refused. Chet knew that although he would be the contractor on paper, my grandfather's intent was to remain in control of the project. Once more, Chet couldn't get past the doubts he had about my grandfather's integrity.

What now? I decided to apply for the license myself! I could not and would not say, "No," to my grandfather. Though in my mind, the fact that I, who knew very little about construction, could become licensed was a bit bizarre, since there was no test, just a large fee.

After many trips downtown to my attorney's office and the Building Department, located in Cleveland's City Hall, I, Beverly Kowalski became a licensed building contractor, operating under the name of Kowalski Construction. *Beverly, the building contractor. Ha! As if!* I was now in charge, but the reality was that I was Vincenzo's puppet and fall guy.

Chet was not happy about the arrangement; nevertheless, he resigned himself to what had transpired and continued working for Grandpa.

But there was a change in Chet. He no longer carried a lunch, and ate his food away from the worksite. If Grandpa Vincenzo was having any trouble with my husband's work ethic, he kept his thoughts to himself. My cousin hinted to me that Chet took long off-site lunches, but his warning didn't register.

Otherwise, Chet appeared to be behaving himself. If he stopped at the Coral Reef Tavern after work, he left early enough to have dinner on time. Stella's presence in our house meant that he would do anything to keep the peace. Life was good.

Our son Ted was now ten months old, and we were expecting our second child in less than four months. Once again, Doctor Mayer would be my obstetrician. This pregnancy was different; there were no worries about hiding my morning sickness or wearing maternity clothes too soon. I was a rosy-cheeked, healthy, happy expectant mom.

When the month of August arrived, Stella decided that she could live independently. She wanted her privacy. Chet and I found a lovely one-bedroom garden apartment for rent, approximately one mile west of our home. Stella's move didn't change our home situation very much. Most of her days were still spent visiting with me and playing with Ted. I picked her up in the morning and Chet would take her home after dinner.

In anticipation of the new baby, Chet and I reviewed the completed items on our to-do list: another crib had been purchased and placed in Ted's room, the bedroom Stella vacated now had a fresh coat of paint, Ted's hand-me-downs had been washed and neatly stacked in a drawer, and even the formula was put away. We had taken care of every item.

It was September 29th; my baby was seven days late. *I could give birth any day or any moment. Please, let it be today.*

Running my hands over my watermelon-shaped stomach, I traced the outline of the little person within it. While my tummy was stretched to its limits, the rest of my body remained thin. As with Ted, my bellybutton felt like it would burst open. Passing the full-length bedroom mirror, I giggled while watching myself walk.

What a silly looking walk! You're swaying from side to side, waddling like a duckling. Carrying this extra weight has made you bowlegged! I believe it's a boy—another boy!

I have much to do today. First, I'll ask Mae if she can watch Ted.

Check!

My hair's a mess. Call the beauty shop for an appointment.

Check!

Shower.

Check! It's now 11:00 a.m. Drive to Mario's Beauty Shop. The shop's just five minutes away.

Two doors down from Mario's was a bakery. Just before entering the beauty shop, I stopped, took a deep breath, and inhaled the heavenly sweet smells that escaped into the air from the shop's exhaust vent. That was a big mistake! I quickly retraced my steps, went inside, and purchased a dozen doughnuts.

While having my hair shampooed, I made sure that the bag of sweet treats, along with my purse, remained firmly in my grasp. *Don't worry, they're safe.* It wasn't until I sat down under the hairdryer that I placed the sack of doughnuts on the table next to me. Breathing in the sweet scent, I started salivating. *I'll just have one.*

After four bites, it disappeared. *Willpower, you must have willpower! Stop!*

Stopping at one delectable doughnut proved impossible. While sitting under the dryer, I ate all twelve of them. *Oh my God! I sat under the dryer for forty minutes. That means I devoured each doughnut in less than four minutes.*

Now, a nauseated and bloated Beverly had to drive herself home! *Haven't you had this insatiable desire for sweets before? Remember the hours leading up to Ted's birth. That day, you inhaled Lilly's pumpkin pie.*

When I arrived home, my neighbor, Mae, suggested I have someone drive me to the doctor. "No thanks, I'm fine. I'll drive myself. I'll pick up my mother-in-law, and then you can go home."

The doctor's office was on West 130th Street and Pearl Road—a fifteen-minute drive from home. Walking, or—more accurately—waddling, from the parking lot into the building made me tired and breathless. Doctor Mayer's office was on the third floor. *Why are you even thinking of taking the stairs? You'll never make it up the steps. Take the elevator, silly!*

After the elevator door slid open, I walked in. The door closed with a loud *thud. Oh my God!* I was in total darkness! Evidently the elevator light bulb had burned out. Panicked, I began groping the wall in front of me for the control buttons. *How do the blind manage?*

After touching a row of three consecutive knobs, I pressed what I hoped was the correct button to take me to the third floor. Thankfully, the elevator rose. When it stopped, I prayed that the door would open. When it did, and I saw daylight, relief washed over me!

As I entered the doctor's office, a slow trickle of water began seeping through my panties and dripping down my legs. My water had broken. I knew that this was a sign that labor would begin soon. The receptionist took hold of my hand and helped me onto an exam table.

Doctor Mayer took one look at me and said, "Go directly to the hospital. I'll meet you there." Obviously, he assumed someone had accompanied me, otherwise he never would have let me leave alone.

Once again, I rode down to the first floor in a pitch-black elevator. Pulling out of the parking lot, I turned towards home. *I have plenty of time. My labor was at least two hours long for Ted's birth. I'll try to reach Chet, pick up my suitcase, and arrange for a neighbor to drive me to Southwest Community Hospital.* And that's exactly what I did. How naïve of me!

Roseanne, the neighbor who drove me to the hospital, was frantic. She was constantly asking if I felt contractions, and I responded in the same manner each time: "I don't know." I couldn't feel distinct contractions, just constant pain.

After parking the car, we entered the hospital through the emergency room. We were greeted by a frantic crew: the admissions clerk, a nurse, and an orderly pushing a gurney. Urging me to climb aboard, they transported me to the birthing room where my clothing was replaced with a hospital gown.

A quick examination revealed that the crown of the baby's head was exposed. I could hear them calling over the loudspeaker, "Paging Doctor Mayer, paging Doctor Mayer."

Steven Jeffrey Kowalski, our eight-pound, twenty-one-inch second baby boy, arrived at 2:32 p.m., on September 29, 1962. Steven had been born before Chet could reach the hospital. His little temples were black and blue and there were red bruises on his shoulders and arms, most likely from his rushed birth.

In spite of his quick delivery, Steven was a fair-skinned little bundle of joy. Pale yellow peach fuzz adorned his rounded little head. He reminded me of a newly hatched birdie; hence, he was nicknamed "Tweets."

Thinking myself an experienced mommy now, I had rejected Grandpa's offer of the assistance of a private nurse; there would be no Mrs. Myers to help me care for our newborn son. But when Auntie Julia—my mother's youngest sister who taught me how to play when I lived at Baba Rose Novak's house—called me the day after Steven's birth and volunteered to help me for a few days, I began second-guessing that decision. *Perhaps there are limits on what I can do now, since there are two.* I wholeheartedly agreed. She would arrive after our return home.

On October 4th, the five days of confinement required for a normal delivery were up. Steven and I were ready to leave the hospital. This time, I had no new-mommy jitters.

"Tweets" was a quiet little bundle of love. He slept peacefully throughout his entire ride home from the hospital and transitioned from my arms to his crib without a *peep*. More amazingly, he slept continuously—even throughout his brother's tantrum—until his six o'clock feeding.

When Ted saw Steven sleeping in the crib opposite his, he became agitated and would not nap. He stood, shook his crib's railing, and sobbed. At once, he became red-faced, squinty-eyed, and runny-nosed. Suddenly, the disturbed toddler bent and reached for his small rubber baseball, pulled back his left arm like a major league pitcher, and threw the object out of his crib. One by one, small plush toys and rubber balls sailed out of his hand and into the air. He appeared to be aiming at his brother whom he obviously felt was an intruder!

Ted definitely understood that his once-private kingdom was now being shared with this fair-haired little creature. Since there was no more than six feet between the cribs, Chet and I thought it best to move Steven's crib to the spare bedroom, away from his older brother. We were surprised by Ted's display of sibling rivalry for he was not yet fourteen months old. On the other hand, perhaps Ted's behavior wasn't unusual, since he was above average on the developmental scale. He could already drink from a sippy cup, feed himself finger foods, and use a baby spoon.

When confined to the playpen, Ted would pull himself up, stand, and bounce up and down. This was his way of letting us know that he wanted his freedom. He would squeal with delight when placed on the living room carpet, crawl all over, then abruptly stop, pick himself up from the floor, and take a step or two. Within a week of our homecoming, he was toddling about our home and his mis-chievous inquisitiveness needed constant attention—mine! Having assistance with a newborn was most welcomed.

Auntie Julia offered to take care of Steven's 2:00 a.m. feeding. "Why should you get up? I can't sleep anyway. When I do, it's on the floor. The disc in my lower back has herniated."

"Thank you, I am exhausted."

Julia, now in her forties, was divorced. Her two sons were grown and married. She had become a very lonesome, bitter divorcée. She once referred to Uncle Paul's remarriage so soon after the legal proceedings as an indication of his infidelity. "He betrayed me." *Perhaps this is the* real *reason for her sleepless nights.*

In the early morning, Auntie Julia delighted in bathing our new-born. Auntie loved how Steven's wispy blond hair curled. Taking a soft baby's hairbrush, she brushed his hair upward toward the center of his head to form a large curl and said, "He's got curly hair just like my sis. Angelina, he has your beautiful hair."

"Angelina." The mere mention of my mother's name would make my ears ring and reverberate. *Angelina, I love you. Angelina, I miss you. Angelina, you have another grandson.*

Visiting Mom over the past two years had been difficult. I tried my best to see her at least once a month. However, overwhelming personal responsibilities and my constant fear of running into my father made frequent visits impossible.

Three months have passed since you went there. Shame on you! How did you let that happen?

The last time I was there, the condition of the house depressed me. The windows were closed, shades were drawn, and dust was everywhere.

There's more to it. It's not just the dirty house that's disheartening. It's my mother's condition. It's Dad's unreasonableness. It's the whole damn situation! I feel guilty for not being there to help her, and for having a life of my own. But I must see her.

What if Carlo's there? I just can't take thinking about it anymore. No, no, no, no, no! Guess I've disowned him, too. *Carlo and I hadn't spoken since my wedding day, and I hadn't figured out yet how to piece our relationship back together.* Don't think about it. Blot it out of your mind!

When Auntie Julia left, two weeks later, Steven was almost sleeping through the night. He was the most well-behaved baby! Because he was so good, I often propped his bottle on a rolled-up towel which left me free to monitor Ted. My younger son missed out on the hugging and cuddling he may have needed—something I regretted later.

Childcare was now my full-time job. Ted was a happy, normally curious toddler who ruled the roost, while Steven followed his lead.

Chet, the children, and I settled into a peaceful groove: early dinner, playtime, evening bath, and watching a little television before bedtime. The routine agreed with me. Before long, I was expecting my third child.

As for Chet, he gradually reverted to his old habits. He began to bring home and consume a six-pack of beer nightly. Old habits are hard to break. Since there was no sudden change in his behavior, I remained in denial; I refused to acknowledge the problem growing before my eyes.

184

There was no dramatic local news to report from the Kowalski home front, since all appeared calm.

In preparation for the arrival of another little Kowalski in November, Chet and I purchased a set of trundle beds. Ted, being the oldest, would be the recipient of the new beds. His crib would be placed in Steven's room to await the arrival of the new infant—boy or girl.

Steven had formed an attachment to a darling little yellow stuffed lamb. Once "Lamb-chop" was placed in his crib, he would soon close his big blue-gray eyes and go to sleep. My little guy's lamb can be likened to the security blanket carried by the comic book character Linus, in *Charlie Brown*.

Chet and I felt secure in our decision to place our newborn in close proximity to Steven, since he was a quiet child who smiled in his sleep. What a delight! At bed or nap time, there would be none of older brother Ted's combativeness; a newborn would be safe in sharing a room with him.

My third pregnancy was completely unremarkable, as I was healthy and happy. Mindful of how rapidly I progressed through the stages of labor with my previous deliveries, Doctor Mayer felt I would be an excellent candidate for induced labor, once the baby's lungs were mature. The procedure would be scheduled after I reached the thirty-ninth week of my pregnancy.

On Monday, November 18th, I was told to prepare for the baby's birth on November 21, 1963. *Thank, God! I ache all over.* Again, as in the two previous pregnancies, I walked with a waddle, like a duck. My tummy, lower back, and legs were strained from the baby's position and weight.

The hand-me-downs were readied for our latest addition: crib, bottles, sterilizer, and layette were washed. For the first time, my overnight bag was packed with toiletries, PJs, robe, and slippers. *My, my, this is great! No need to race to the hospital. No fear of having the baby en route!*

The eventful day arrived. Ted and Steven were sleeping peacefully. Stella and my neighbor, Mae were there to care for the boys in my absence. If all went well, Chet planned on returning home shortly after the baby's birth, so Mae could return home to her children.

November 21st was a cold but sunny day. Chet and I did not talk as we drove to the hospital. His silence was okay with me, for I was anticipating the pain of childbirth, specifically the final excruciating backbreaking push to deliver the baby.

Ouch! No one likes pain! *At the end of Steven's delivery, didn't you vow never to have another child? You know you did.*

How soon I had forgotten the pain of bringing forth a child. Yet I wanted another child to love—even knowing full well the pain of giving birth.

We arrived at Southwest Community Hospital at 8:00 a.m. This time, I completed and signed admission papers. A hospital "candy-stripe" volunteer escorted me to the obstetric ward. I was given the traditional hospital garb and changed quickly. A nurse gathered up my possessions, walked me to the labor room, and helped me onto the examination table.

Doctor Mayer's assistant—a midwife—entered the cubical and conducted an examination. First, she placed the stethoscope on my belly to listen to the baby's heartbeat. "I think it's a boy. We'll know soon." Another nurse proceeded to connect me to an IV.

The monitors were beeping. Beep… beep…I drifted off to sleep until I heard Doctor Mayer. An hour had passed. No labor pains. After a quick exam, the doctor inserted a probe into the birth canal and broke my water. Almost instantaneously, the hard, intense labor began. No more dozing off for me. I was consumed by pain! My doctor asked me to lean forward as he administered, via a large needle, an epidural to help me endure the final contractions.

Martin Kowalski was born at 3:30 p.m. on a Thursday. He was twenty inches long and weighed eight pounds, nine ounces. My darling baby boy had the biggest brown eyes I'd ever seen and lots of hair! Martin resembled the baby in the ads for Gerber baby food.

That day, I was totally worn out from the birth process and stayed in bed. As with any stay in the hospital, your days are long and uneventful. Then, on Friday, November 22nd, I chose to spend my baby-free hours in the TV room watching "soaps," off and on. It was approximately three in the afternoon when CBS newsman Walter Cronkite broke into the programming of *As the World Turns* saying that an assassin had fired three shots at President John F. Kennedy.

Nurses and other hospital personnel within hearing range crammed into the small room. My eyes swept across the room, observing the shock and horror expressed on the surrounding faces. I felt a bit numb.

A few hours later, the news reported that the President was dead! *This is unbelievable!* Over the following days, like the entire nation, I was mesmerized by the live coverage of the funeral procession and the subsequent murder of Oswald, the President's assassin, by Jack Ruby.

We brought our darling son, Martin, home on Sunday. Between the demands made by the baby and two toddlers, all my free time was spent glued to the television set. However, while the Kennedy tragedy continued to dominate the news, our nation, including the Kowalski family, began to heal in anticipation of the approaching holiday.

Christmas in 1963 was especially festive. The joy of parenting three little boys gave Chet and me all the more reason to celebrate our favorite holiday. We had shopped for toys in October, before Martin's birth, since we knew a new baby would make gift hunting almost impossible.

Feeling like "Suzie Homemaker" the first week in December, I baked and baked, making cookies galore: chocolate chip, peanut butter, walnut, cherry nut, gingerbread men, candy canes, snow-men, and Santa Claus butter cookies. I boxed them in decorative tins and placed them out of sight until Christmas week.

Then, once the Christmas cards were signed, sealed, and ready for delivery, we had time to concentrate on decorating. Grandpa Vincenzo gave us his collection of trimmings. The fragile hand-painted ornaments were made in Japan, prior to the war — practically collectors' items.

Closing my eyes now, I can still see the decorations hanging from the limbs of a beautiful six-foot pine: a silver fish, a robust jolly Santa, crystal snowmen, and twelve miniature snow-suited cherub skiers who appeared to be skiing downhill, from the delicate angel tree-topper to the descending branches below. The tinsel-covered tree with glowing lights was centered in front of our large living room picture window.

The beauty of our home and the tree with all its decorations must have inspired Chet's creativity. The intermittent humming of the band saw announced his presence in his workshop. *What's he doing?* When the saw stopped running, I could hear he was humming "Jingle Bells." Being inquisitive, I ventured downstairs to see.

Nearby on the workbench sat several four-inch-wide arcs. The fourth piece was being cut from a piece of plywood as I watched. Next, he cut a groove and joint into both ends of each finished segment. Puzzled, but not wanting to interfere, I returned upstairs.

A little later in the day, Chet requested my help as he joined and glued each of the four quarter-circles together creating a perfectly circular five-by-five frame. "Voila!" The frame would become a Christmas wreath for our living room picture window. To my knowledge, he had had no pattern or instructions to follow, making his creation even more impressive to me.

Chet and I completely covered the bare plywood with green electrical tape. Next, we stapled multicolored outdoor lights, live pine roping, and a giant red bow to the frame. The wreath was hung outdoors in the center of our picture window. Our beautiful tree was displayed within the wreath's frame, inviting everyone outside to see our beautiful Christmas tree. The picture we created was a "Currier and Ives," postcard-perfect scene. For a brief time, we completed the picture by managing to recapture our innocent, youthful love.

18

CHOICES

It was now 1964. Having a third little darling around left me very little, if any, "me" time. Yet in spite of the demands my roles as a mother, wife, and housekeeper placed on my time, the role of dutiful granddaughter remained a priority.

Each Saturday morning, I would leave my boys with a babysitter and faithfully drive across town to my grandparents' home on Edgerton Road. Then I would take my grandfather to the Central Market to shop for produce—just as I had almost every Saturday since I had turned sixteen. I couldn't forget my promise to Grandpa Vincenzo when he purchased me the little red Studebaker.

At an hour each way, the trip there and back to my home was tiring in itself. Then add to it an hour roundtrip drive to downtown Cleveland, an hour to shop, an hour to visit after returning to Grandpa's house, and, on occasions, a trip to Guinta's Stop and Shop at Fairmount Circle for other necessities. Exhausting, yes! Grandpa Vincenzo suggested I move to the East Side to make our Saturdays together easier to manage. *Dare you suggest to Chet that we move? You'd better think about it!*

Chet had spent the past year completing work the builder had left undone on our house. The sliding glass patio doors had needed a deck or steps; otherwise, one would have to jump down five feet to access our backyard. Now, a beautiful brick and cement deck filled the previously vacant space. The steps from the deck descended to a twenty-by-thirty-foot cobblestone patio with a barbeque pit that housed an electric rotisserie. He had also installed gas lighting for evening entertainment, and we did entertain. Our previously unfinished basement now had a recreation room with a wet bar, thanks to Chet. *He loves this home! How can I convince him to move?*

On the weekends, Chet spent hours at a time in his workshop completing small woodworking projects. If I heard the hum of the band saw or router, I knew he was happy. *Can you take this away from him?*

Dummy, you're even forgetting about Chet's mother. Can we leave her living alone on the West Side? Now she's just minutes away from us.

How would he feel moving away from our family and friends? Most of our weekends were spent with Ted and Lee, who had become our best friends, and Steven's godparents, Richard and Ruth Frankowski. We would take turns visiting one another's homes, especially during the summer months. I'd make a dessert to bring with us, pick up bottles of vodka and soda, and dress for the occasion, which usually included conversation, word games, and cards. These gatherings were such fun! *How can we move away from his friends? Impossible!*

Ah, but perhaps we can move. My best friend—my Twinnie—Joyce and her husband Bill, live on the East Side. They're going to be Martin's godparents.

Darn, you forgot something! There's the Futura swimming pool we just installed in the backyard to think about. It was a beauty: the twenty-by-forty-foot swimming area with depths graduating from three to six feet in the plunge area. The pool provided hours of great summer fun for family and friends. Three mini life vests hung over the redwood fencing, one for each of our three sons. *How could we give up this summer luxury? There's no way we're going to do this! No, we can't!*

Yes, you can give it up! You can move to the East Side. You're not being fair to yourself to continue driving all day Saturday. You're worn out! You're not being fair to your family to continue having hot dogs and baked beans every Saturday!

Finally, my needs and rationale prevailed. Perhaps I was listening to my ego and not my more considerate and altruistic voice of reason. Looking back now, I realize I decided we should move without ever consulting Chet.

In the spring of 1964, while driving down Fairmount Boulevard, I noticed heavy excavation equipment digging what appeared to be a basement on one of the beautiful, empty lots on this older suburban street. Being a boulevard, the two-way traffic was divided by a grass- and ivy-covered median, enhanced with seasonal flowers and a succession of massive oak and maple trees.

The lot was between Eaton and Claridge Oval. A large play area separated the oval from the boulevard. The homes in the area were classic center hall Colonials or mini mansions built in the '20s and '30s. It was a picturesque semblance of affluence and class.

By the end of summer, a nine-room, three-and-a-half-bath, brick Colonial had been constructed on the site. Finally, the builder posted a sign in the front window which read: *Exclusive listing, shown by appointment only. Contact Merle Realty.*

Grandpa Vincenzo and I viewed the home. The interiors of the spacious rooms were flooded with sunlight from the unadorned windows. The smell of fresh paint, plaster, and mortar filled the air as we entered the foyer. To our left was a thirty-foot-long living room. On the right, the hall led to the powder room, utility room, and the attached garage. The rear section of the home contained the formal dining room, kitchen, and knotty pine family room.

The eat-in kitchen contained deluxe, copper-colored, built-in GE appliances; custom-made, cherry-stained, wood cupboards; granite-looking Formica countertops; and a butcher block island work-station. *Look, the oven has a rotisserie.*

Built-in bookcases and storage cabinets covered one wall in the family room. One outer wall of the room was overlaid with sand-stone with a wood-burning fireplace in the center. On the other outer wall of the room, there were sliding glass doors that led to a small but very private backyard. *Nice, we'll have less grass to cut!*

This new house would have been a dream come true for most people, but not for Chet. Our current home was his picket-fence dream home. Somehow, I convinced him to agree to the purchase. I didn't realize it until I was much older, but I put Chet in an impossible position: he had to choose between his happiness and my own. In my mind, there would be no compromise.

I don't really remember how I managed to convince Chet to move because, like so many painful scenes in my life, I've blocked it from my memory. There was probably a week of bickering before Chet agreed to the move. I can remember bits of our conversations and piece together Chet's objections.

"I've got everything I want and need here. It's going to be like starting all over again! How can we give up this life? We just put in the pool!

"You want to take me away from my mother and my only friends?! How selfish can you be? You're taking us away from the help that we have with Stella and Mae. How will you manage?

"Your grandfather convinced you to do this. You're picking Vincenzo over me."

Our sweet little ranch home became rental property.

Our tenants were a middle-aged C.E.O. of a major corporation, his stay-at-home wife, and their two standard-sized white poodles, whom they vowed were housebroken. *Ha-ha!* A later inspection of the home revealed stained carpeting and stinky piles in the dining room, and proved that we were gullible and naïve first-time landlords.

The process of moving from one home to another is stressful under the best of circumstances. These were *not* the best of circumstances! Tenant occupancy of our Ridge Road ranch was to commence on the first of November. Unfortunately, there was a snafu; we couldn't occupy our new residence until the first of December.

What will we do? Perhaps we can store our furniture and find a short-term housing arrangement.

Busying myself with the logistics of our move and managing the children helped keep me distracted from Chet's attitude. Although he went along with my plans, I knew that he was still salty about being forced into a no-win situation.

Fortunately, we were allowed to store our boxed items in our new home, saving us money. Our large furniture was kept by Parma Movers in their storage facility. Now that our belongings were safe,

192

where would we stay? The only short-term housing available to us at the time was a small efficiency in a motel off Pearl Road in Brooklyn.

Two adults and three healthy, energetic toddlers—a one-year-old, a two-year-old, and a three-year-old—had to squeeze into an eighteen-by-twenty efficiency. In addition to the furniture and mini appliances already supplied by the management, we added a crib, a fold-away bed, and luggage. Not much space was left on the floors.

Chet and I crowded the counters and cupboards with our daily living necessities: clothing, grooming essentials, and the bare basics needed for cooking—a toaster, a coffee pot, and disposable plastic anything and everything. *Stop! I need to catch my breath!*

Toddlers have necessities, too. The remaining space was crammed with a highchair, booster chair, bottles, cups, dishes, toys, diapers, diapers, and more diapers. In those days, there were no disposables. With three diaper-clad toddlers and no laundry facilities nearby, the only feasible solution to the problem was weekly diaper service. By solving one problem, another was created: a large smelly diaper pail was crammed into the corner of the room.

Our evening meal often consisted of carryout, or "carry in," as Chet and I jokingly named it. During meals, we sat on the edge of the bed and used the unpacked boxes as a makeshift kitchen table. The rest of the time, we were constantly tripping over toys and bumping into luggage, boxes, furniture, or little ones. The room was an unorganized, crowded, obstacle course; a mess, to say the least.

With Ted, Steven, and Martin eating, sleeping, and playing within the same area, we had no escape from them. Even our precious few moments of personal privacy in the small restroom were interrupted by the whacking of mini toy trucks, the invasion of tiny fingers in the gap under the door, and the sound of children crying for their mommy or daddy.

We were thankful when December arrived, and Christmas time was soon approaching. Traces of snow were on the ground as the movers brought our furniture to our new residence.

Within a week, Chet and I had unpacked all our belongings. The "comfort and joy" of being in our new home and the approaching holiday briefly defused any previous tensions we had felt from living in a motel.

Like enthusiastic children, we prepared for the holiday. This time, our decorations were even more luminous and beautiful than the previous year. A larger living room meant a larger tree, more ornaments, and more space to display decorations and gifts. Our new bubble lights made the scales of the silver fish ornament shimmer, and their light seemed to make the crystal snowman dance in place. Once again, the Christmas wreath was the focal point of our exterior decorating. Had Thomas Kinkade, the artist, seen our home, he would have chosen to paint it.

Now that our house was holiday-beautiful, buying gifts was the next item on our to-do list. The May Company, a major department store based in Cleveland, had a Height's branch at the Cedar-Center mall. Shopping there was convenient and the selection of merchandise was great, but something was definitely missing: the beautiful window displays that gave life to my favorite fairytale or story.

No matter whom I had lived with as a child, each Christmas, someone had taken me downtown to see the May Company or Higbee displays. I'd stand in front of the window, press my cheek against the cold pane of glass, and enter into the make-believe scene. The movement of the small animated figures totally mesmerized me.

Gazing at the displays each year is a tradition, like visiting Santa. We just have to go downtown! Besides, our new house is located just a short walk from the rapid transit stop.

"Chet, let's ride the rapid. You won't have to worry about parking. We can shop at Higbee's without leaving the Terminal complex. And May's and Bailey's department stores are directly across the street. I can use the trading stamps Grandma Caroline gave me to buy gifts from her for the boys."

Leaving our pajama-clad munchkins safely at home with Grandmama Stella, Chet and I rode downtown, via the rapid, early in the morning. Precise planning eliminated any wait for a train at the Courtland Road stop.

Once we boarded the train, the large panoramic windows allowed us to view the understated elegance and architectural beauty of the homes and apartment buildings that had been constructed along Shaker Boulevard. The ride was a memorable first for both of us. The cable car swayed slightly as it glided speedily over the steel tracks and squealed to a stop. We had reached our destination: the east concourse of Union Station. The downtown metropolis was practically humming with unquestionable excitement as the holiday shoppers purchased their gifts. And with that, I was swept up into the magic and euphoria of Christmas once more.

With our gift shopping completed, our focus shifted to holiday food. Christmas is not Christmas for a Pole without their dietary staples—pierogi and homemade kielbasa. Chet and I made a special trip to the Westside Market to purchase fresh pork and veal, casings, and garlic. The butcher was a Polish immigrant. Chet impressed him by speaking to him in Polish. "Music to my ears," the old man responded in heavily accented English.

Making homemade kielbasa was a Christmas tradition in the Kowalski family. Chet could make it without consulting Stella; still she sat at the head of the table to oversee our project. The meats were chopped into small pieces, seasoned with garlic and spices, and then the mixture was fed through the grinder into the casings. After the links were formed and tied, they were roasted. *Mm-mm—these are unbelievably great!* Everyone was pleased with the results.

The homemade sausage was the final task in our preparations for Christmas Day. The following days were filled with fun and food, and any conflict between me and Chet was forgotten.

On the evening of Christmas Eve, I felt like a child, hardly able to sleep. Chet and Stella had just left for Midnight Mass. Giant snowflakes were falling, covering the tire marks in the drive. *There'll be a white Christmas!*

I tiptoed down the hall and carefully cracked open the door to Ted's room, peeking in at him. It may have been my imagination, but it looked like my oldest boy had a smile of anticipation on his face.

The younger boys shared a room, and I couldn't help but take a look at them, too. I loved seeing them during their slumber, peaceful for a few hours.

Our home looks beautiful. The to-do list is complete. I couldn't be happier. Our family will have a merry Christmas, indeed!

19

AUGUST 12, 1965

Chet's brother, Ted, his sister-in-law, Lee, and their three children were invited to our home to celebrate our Ted's fourth birthday. Lee and Ted Kowalski had adopted a child each time I gave birth—Amy, Christy, and Jayson.

Like many a day in August, the sweltering heat and heavy humid air prevailed. With the noonday sun directly overhead, serving lunch, cake, and ice cream picnic-style in our yard was not inviting, so we lunched in the air-conditioned family room. Once party formalities were completed, the restless brood of children requested to go outside. Ted, the birthday boy, led the way.

One by one, in parade formation, everyone exited through the patio doors into the yard. Each child's hand clasped the string of a colorful balloon. The adults comfortably seated themselves in lawn chairs and proceeded to watch the children's playful performance.

With Ted in the lead, the line of children continued to move single file around the yard. Again and again, the giggling girls and boys circled the perimeter of the yard. Around and around they went, their swirling balloons blending into a kaleidoscope of colors. Then Ted stopped—parade, halt!

The small group of copycats stood still, but not for long. Amy marched ahead to lead the way. The pint-sized participants continued their skipping and jumping in circles with Ted in the rear, until the birthday boy fell, without shedding a tear. Before anyone could help him, he picked himself up from the ground to walk towards my extended arms.

Ted's eyes were wide open and his face was pale with a slight bluing of the lips. There were beads of perspiration on his forehead. As I hugged him, I could feel his small diaphragm pulsing, but he wasn't wheezing or coughing. *What's wrong?*

Before long, Ted seemed to recover, and he got back down from my lap. He wanted to play with his party guests, but every few minutes, he seemed to get worn out and would lag behind. I kept observing Ted to see if his condition got bad enough to warrant calling his doctor, but every time his symptoms would appear, they'd improve again after he took a break.

It had been a long day for everyone. By four in the afternoon, our guests had left. I asked Chet to help me bathe the boys, but he was oblivious to my request, as he was intoxicated from drinking beer all afternoon with his brother. *It has been a while since I've seen him behave like this—like a real alcoholic.*

As I placed Ted in the bathtub, he began making occasional wheezing sounds. His small diaphragm continued to heave back and forth. *What's wrong with him?* I was frightened for my son and mystified at the same time. *What's wrong?*

I had never seen anyone act like that, not even my cousin, Donna, who had seizures. *He needs a doctor!* Our pediatrician's answering services said the doctor would call back "shortly." The "shortly" seemed like an eternity, even though it was only ten minutes.

Dr. Lenard Frank said, "There's no doubt in my mind that you must immediately take Ted to Baby and Children's Hospital. It's located on Adelbert Road."

Leaving Steve and Martin home alone with Chet in his inebriated condition was concerning to me, but Ted and I had to get to the hospital. Without assistance, I carried my son to the car. *When did he get so heavy?*

As a child, I had lived near the University Circle area, but that was many years ago. Now, finding my way to the hospital was a challenge. While turning off East Boulevard onto Euclid Avenue and looking around, I finally recognized something. *There's Severance Hall and the Cleveland Museum of Art lagoon. Adelbert should be the next street on my right.*

What a relief. University Hospital's campus consisted of a series of buildings that stretched the length of the street before me. *Now where do I go?* The glare from the setting sun made it impossible for me to read the signs. There wasn't a pedestrian in sight, nor a car, for that matter.

Trying to get my bearings, I entered the first parking lot on the left side of the street and pulled into the only available space. It was Sunday, hospital visiting hours were over, and the parking attendant was no longer on duty. *Surely, someone inside can direct me.*

You'll have to take Ted with you. You can't leave him alone. As I wrapped my arms around Ted's torso, he wrapped his arms tightly around my neck and I lifted him out of the car. *My, he's heavy!* Carrying him up the flight of steps that led to the hospital entrance was no easy task.

An elderly lady sat behind the information desk. *She's probably a volunteer.*

The woman eyed us up and down. *Doesn't she recognize the urgency of our situation?*

I need immediate medical help for my child! I had better speak up.

"Perhaps there's a wheelchair I can use?"

"No. I'm sorry, there isn't." Then she looked sympathetic. "Do you realize that you're in the wrong hospital?"

"Where am I?"

"You're in Hanna House. Baby and Children's is further down the street."

"What shall I do? It is almost eight o'clock, and it's dark outside. I don't feel safe walking about in a strange neighborhood. And I'm exhausted."

Good; I've expressed my concerns. "Is there a guard or anyone else who can show me the way?"

She began shaking her head from side to side, "Sorry." Then her face lit up, "The buildings are connected by underground tunnels. Maybe you would feel more secure using the tunnel? The way is clearly marked."

"God, yes, I would!"

"Take the elevator to the basement level, turn to the right and follow the lines painted on the floor until you come to elevators you need."

Once more, I lifted Ted into my arms. As he clung to my neck, he began to cough. The strength of his rhythmic spasms had increased, making him feel heavier. He seemed to be slipping out of my arms as his seizure-like movements continued. Needing to rest my arms and back, I stopped frequently, pausing to put my son down.

I must continue. Does this corridor ever end? By the time I reached our destination, I had lost all track of time. Exhaustion and confusion had taken over my senses. *Thank God, an admissions desk!*

As soon as I said, "My son is Dr. Frank's patient," help arrived. Ted was gasping and crying, all within the same breath, while I tried to place him in the nurse's arms. "Mommy, Mommy!"

"Sweetie, everything's going to be all right."

The nurse took Ted into an examination room while an admissions clerk gathered information from me. In the background, I could hear my child's anguished cries. "May I go in there? If he knows I'm here, he'll feel better."

"The doctor will call for you when you can see him." All I could do was sit there, staring into space in a trance-like stupor for hours.

It was seven in the morning before a doctor asked me, "Are you all right?" Perhaps my blank look accounted for his question. Shrugging my shoulders undecidedly, I replied, "Not good, really!" He had the nurse bring me a cup of black coffee. It burned my lips and throat. "Can I see my son?"

"Yes. Follow me." *Finally!* Ted had been moved from the small examining room to the main ward. The doctor and I followed the hall until we reached a large set of double doors marked *Intensive Care Unit.* The doors opened into an enormous room filled with a nurse's station and row after row of cribs with IVs and oxygen tanks at their sides. Several of the beds, headboards, and railings were covered entirely by bandages to provide a cushion over the wood.

200

The small occupants of these beds were also bandaged. The doctor explained that the cushioning was done to prevent these dear little creatures from bruising themselves. They were hemophiliacs—bleeders—and the slightest bump or bruise could cause their death. The sight of the tiny, bandaged babies and the thought how vulnerable they were was more than I could fathom in my emotionally frayed state; my eyes began to tear.

We stopped at the third row of cribs. Now I began to feel weak; there was my darling four-year-old confined to an oxygen tent. The rhythmic sound of the air compressor was haunting.

Ted's frail, bruised arms were taped to wooden splints. Each arm was extended and stretched straight out at the side of his chest. An IV was inserted into each wrist. His head lay motionless with his eyes closed. His torso remained straight, while each leg was splinted and stretched out at the side of his body. IVs were also inserted at his ankles.

Instantly, my mind brought forth a picture of the Crucifixion. *Oh, dear God—he appears lifeless. He's an innocent child. Why must he suffer? Why?* My heart ached for my little one.

Ted's doctor told me that my darling son had bronchial asthma. An attack of this nature could last a few days to a week or longer and could result in death. This was not what a parent wanted to hear!

After our crib-side conversation—for my own sake—the doctor would not allow me to stay any longer. That I was able to remember where the car was parked and drive home safely in my condition was a bit of a miracle, considering my lack of sleep, food, and emotional stability.

Our little boy could be dying. How will I tell Chet? Upon arriving home, I expected a comforting, sympathetic husband; instead I found the evil Mr. Hyde. "You're the one responsible for this!" No matter how I tried to account for how this could have happened to our son, I always seemed to take the blame for it.

The entire week that followed, Ted remained in intensive care, fighting for his survival. My daily trips to the hospital, with or without Chet, wore me out. By the second week, our son began to respond to his treatments and was moved to a step-down unit.

Whenever Chet or I visited, Ted beamed with delight at our arrival. As much as it brought me joy to see his response to our visits, my heart was broken by his tears upon our departure. "Take me home! Please, take me home!" Having to reject his tearful requests as he clung to me during our goodbyes hurt the most!

Two months is a long time to be confined to a hospital, especially for a child, even with amusement. Playing with blocks and other building toys broke the monotony somewhat, but it was the television entertainers dressed in their storybook characters' costumes who visited the children on a daily basis that often cheered Ted the most.

"Raggedy Ann will be here this afternoon." Just the mention of her name and he beamed, but his mantra never changed. "I want to go home!" The month of October arrived and finally, on the 15th, he was released.

Somehow, someway, Chet had managed to control his alcoholism throughout the death of his father, Martin's birth, our move, and then Christmas; however, the stress of Ted's near-fatal bout with asthma became the straw that broke the camel's back.

He had resumed his excessive drinking—mind-altering drinking. When he was in his right mind, Chet would never dream of harming his boys. But the controlled and accommodating man whom I had loved was now showing his anger and frustration daily.

I knew that Chet loved all his boys. Steven, who especially took after his daddy, had a special place in his heart. But drinking changed Chet to his core, otherwise the incident that followed would have never taken place.

One chilly, rainy October day, Ted, Steven, and Martin were being served their evening meal early before Chet arrived home from work. The weather conditions made it a perfect day for serving soup for dinner.

Steven had just turned three years old on the 29th of September. He needed a booster seat to sit at the kitchen table. He typically fed himself quite well with the normal number of crumbs and spills for a child his age. But eating soup without creating a mess can be a challenge even for an adult, and chicken soup was not his favorite meal. While screaming and whining, Steven began rapidly hitting the warm broth with his spoon, causing it and bits of chicken to splash all over him.

At that moment, Chet walked in the room. Without saying a word, he stood behind our son and grabbed the back of his head, pushing the child's face downward, in and out of the soup bowl. The bowl fell to the floor—its contents splashed and splattered everywhere. "Now you have something to cry about!"

"What's the matter with you? Leave him alone!"

When Steven's face emerged from the soup, his eyes were shut and his cheeks, nose, and forehead were beet red. Before I could stop Chet, he picked up a paper napkin and stuffed it into Steven's open mouth, ceasing his screams, but causing the boy to choke and gasp.

My initial shock and fear quickly turned to anger towards Chet. I lifted Steven from his booster chair, holding him in my arms as I removed the napkin from his mouth. "You—you're a bastard!"

Chet's eyes were bloodshot and he reeked of alcohol. *Look at the bastard! He must have found a new watering hole—another Coral Reef. I wonder what this bar is called.*

If you know what's good for you, keep your mouth shut!

In that instant, Chet pulled the tablecloth off the table. A plate of boiled chicken, the tureen and its ladle, soup bowls, water glasses, silverware, and napkins went flying through the air. *Leave the mess on the floor. Get your boys and get out of his way.*

Once the assault on Steven began, Ted had immediately left his seat at the table to be at my side, protectively clinging to my blue jeans. With Steven now hanging on to my other leg, I had to remove Martin from his high chair. We had to get out of the kitchen. The four of us fled into the family room.

Sliding the entry door closed, I locked it, but I still didn't feel secure. Somehow, I disengaged the boys from my body and managed to barricade the door with the sofa. *Now we're safe.*

The little ones clung to me as we lay on the sofa. We were all frightened. Closing my eyes and catching my breath, I gave myself the freedom to tremble with fear. Not knowing what to anticipate, I silently prayed for our safety and the guidance on how to respond to the situation. Eventually, we all fell asleep.

Several hours had passed before I was abruptly awakened by the opening and closing of the front door and the sound of Chet's car driving away. Most likely, he had slept off his drunkenness. *He knew he was wrong. Now he is too embarrassed and depressed to face me. But it's four in the morning. Where is he going?*

One by one, I carried each sleeping child up the stairs to place them in their beds. *Now what? I'm not going to sleep. The kitchen needs to be cleaned. I may as well face the mess.*

The soup tureen had broken into five pieces. Piece by piece, I placed the broken pottery into the wastebasket. *Cry, if you must!*

Next, I filled the dishwasher and mopped the floor. *You'll survive! But will my little boys survive through this?* An hour passed.

Chet sheepishly returned. Not a word was said between us. There was no talking it out or talking it over. *What am I going to do? Chet is a time bomb that could explode at any moment!*

Fearing what Chet could do or say following this outburst, I tried an impossible task; not to say or do things that would displease him. Despite my best efforts to avoid doing anything to set him off, Chet and I still fought. Each new fight fueled the debate that raged within my inner thoughts day and night.

You're not addressing the real problem by acting phony like this. Aren't you in constant denial when you act out of fear? You can victimize yourself, if you want to, but you can't let one of your darling baby boys become a victim of his alcoholic abuse!

Taking heed of my gut feelings, I could no longer deny that the circumstances in which my tiny sons and I were living were unhealthy and intolerable. There was no way for me to control Chet, and trying to work out solutions in my brain was impossible. Our truce lasted only a short time before dissolving into an icy standoff.

With each confrontation, I became more and more depressed and disappointed in Chet and his behavior. The result was that I was caught in a downward spiral of feeling more drained, more stressed, and more depressed.

In addition to the upheaval in our home, Chet renewed his vendetta against my grandfather. Grandpa Vincenzo was responsible for everything negative and bad in his life; Grandpa Vincenzo was Chet's scapegoat. Each time Grandpa Vincenzo helped us, the good that was done by him was unappreciated.

"Can't you see your grandfather is controlling everything we do?" The truth of the matter was that much of what my grandfather did for us *was*, in reality, *my choice*.

How could I ever explain to Chet that Grandpa Vincenzo was "my rock"? He had been my only loving, supportive parent. We had a strong bond that could not be broken. Now that he was older, he needed my help, and I wanted to be the one to help him. He had earned my love, respect, and commitment long ago. And, because Grandma Caroline loved him and took care of him, I was also committed to her.

Why can't Chet understand why I made my choices? He should be able to understand. He saw my mother's bizarre behavior. Why, why can't he understand me?

Obviously, Chet's alcoholism was advancing and there is no way to talk things out with an alcoholic. An intervention was needed to stop him from drinking, but it never happened. In my usual enabling manner, I waited for an inevitable crisis to occur.

Squirrels, the dear little rodents, are delightful to watch as they scurry about, chasing one another's long, bushy tails. But the darling varmints are often destructive to homes—especially when using your patio door screen for their race track. We were concerned that if the screen broke while the sliding glass doors were open, it would allow our neighborhood squirrels entry to our home.

The preemptive solution to the problem, according to Chet, was to inflict pain upon the little rodents as they were climbing up and down the screen. He purchased a pellet gun. The gun would inflict pain but not kill. Little did I know the pellet gun would never be used on the squirrels.

One day, after a drinking bout, Chet came home from the bar in an enraged emotional state. Muttering obscenities as he rushed into the utility room, he removed the pellet gun from its hiding place high in the cupboards. Before our garage door slammed shut behind him, he was shouting, "I'll kill the bastard!" I knew he was referring to my grandfather.

This is insanity! Grandpa's home was less than ten minutes away from our home. Chet couldn't kill him with the pellet gun, but he could hurt him. Wanting to alert my grandparents, I frantically began to dial the phone. My fingers kept stumbling over the dial. Thank God, it's ringing.

No answer.

Call the police, dummy!

Meanwhile, Grandpa, hearing a car pull into the drive, looked out his kitchen window to see Chet emerge from his car and open the door to the three-family home's common hall.

Grandpa Vincenzo caught sight of the gun and was frantic! Fearing for his and Grandma Caroline's lives, he blocked the locked kitchen door with dining room chairs, creating an obstacle in the event Chet gained entry. Then he picked up the phone, dialed zero for the operator's assistance, and pleaded for help. This was long before cell phones were commonplace or we could dial 911 for emergencies.

Overhearing Grandpa's pleas, Chet had enough sense to return home before the police arrived. Once home, he began shouting obscenities. "Son of a bitch! The f—g bastard got away this time!"

Chet continued, "I'm going to murder him if he doesn't stop interfering in my life! And you—you're a whore! Quit fucking your grandfather!" The implication was horrid!

Does he actually think I could be in a relationship with my grandfather?
"F—you!"

My grandfather bore no responsibility for Chet's irrational response. He merely wanted and needed a son to help him with the management and repairs of his property. He had no sons of his own. Instead, he had a devoted granddaughter and, as my husband, Chet should have become his devoted grandson-in-law. No ill will was meant by my grandfather. *Why can't Chet understand him? How can he even think that way?!*

If he had wanted to shock me, he had done so! If he wanted to verbally abuse me, he had succeeded!

Meanwhile, the University Heights' Police Department had immediately dispatched a squad car when they had received my call. They spoke to my grandfather, but he refused to press charges against Chet.

Looking out our living room picture window, Chet could see a University Heights squad car turning left at the boulevard stop. When the police arrived at our door, Chet fled upstairs and locked himself in the bedroom. That left me with no choice but to answer the door. In a soft whisper I said, "I'm the lady who called. I'm his wife."

The officer wanted to speak to Chet. Tearfully, I explained that the situation was a family matter. "My husband's an alcoholic and needs help!"

Ted, Steven, and Martin, my darling, bewildered toddlers, were each sitting on different steps of the staircase that faced the front door. After a long pause in which the officer looked at me and the children, his face softened.

Then I continued. "Officer, please...he won't come to the door."

"Well then, make sure he understands that the next time he makes a scene and threatens Mr. Martinelli at his home, I will arrest him for disorderly conduct—with or without charges filed against him! And see that he gets help." After a long pause he said, "Ah— Alcoholics Anonymous." *Take heed Beverly, the officer has given you good advice.*

After closing the door behind the officer, I collapsed into a chair. *Who is this stranger?*

A sick alcoholic...Why have you tolerated his behavior for so long?

Quit kidding yourself; you've been enabling him for years!

Saturated with stress and pain from the previous day, despair and depression engulfed me. Even the antics of my boys could not dispel my feelings of grief. *If he speaks, I'll answer. Otherwise, it's best I stay quiet.*

The first thing Chet did after he slept off his drunkenness was to call my grandfather and quit his job. Did he apologize? I don't believe he did, but he knew his behavior was unacceptable; his sheepish looks said as much to me.

Next, he called Alcoholics Anonymous. He must have recognized at this time that he had hit rock bottom. If this was true, he was on his way to completing the first step in the twelve-step program.

Our neighbor, an older gentleman and an attorney who was a member of AA, agreed to sponsor him. The very next evening, Chet attended his first meeting. When he returned home, he was quiet and docile.

The next day, Chet's sponsor contacted me. He presented me with a small handbook that outlined the program's steps to sobriety. "Your husband will need your love and support more than ever as he gets sober. Can you be there for him?"

For years now, I had put up with the dark side of Chet's personality. Now his slanderous statements and violent behavior cast a shadow over every aspect of our life together. *Can I continue to love and support Chet as he goes through all twelve steps? He's changed so. He's just a hint of the man he used to be.* Feeling only numbness, I shrugged my shoulders and replied, "Maybe."

Then he suggested I join Al-Anon to meet other wives whose husbands were out of control. At that moment, I knew. *I won't!*

Chet's tirade of nastiness had gone too far. The culmination of his physical and emotional abuse, especially of Steven, was more than I could bear. How can this situation ever be repaired?

It can't be.

What can I do?

Get help!

This situation is beyond help.

After this incident, Chet appeared to be regretful, but his angry pride never allowed him to apologize to me. There was no conversation between us. I moved some of his clothing to the downstairs closet. The family room became his bedroom.

Now Chet was home twenty-four hours a day. I carried on with my normal activities as if he wasn't there. I couldn't trust him to be alone with the boys, so any time I left the house without them, I called the babysitter. Chet's behavior put me on the road to emotional and financial bankruptcy. *What am I going to do now?* We had bills to pay and, unlike Chet, I couldn't work for Grandpa.

While I was worrying about how we would pay our bills, Chet

passed his time building model airplanes and constructing puzzles. Seemingly oblivious to me as I secretly watched him, he would sit for hours, motionless, staring at the scattered pieces before him. His facial expressions frequently changed as they reflected the ruminations of his mind: resignation, despair, heart-wrenching sadness, and puzzling bewilderment. He felt my alienation. He had gone too far this time. The scattered cardboard pieces of the puzzle embodied us—Ted, Steven, Martin, and me—his sons, his wife, and our individual lives.

Will we ever live together in harmony? If we separate, can we find happiness? Or will there forever be a longing for what could have been…if only?

Even after his run-in with Chet, Grandpa Vincenzo never asked me to end my relationship with my husband—to divorce Chet. I was the one who asked him to move, saying, "We need time to see how we feel about each other."

A definitive request—let's get a divorce—will provoke him. Move slowly, one step at a time.

He'll adjust!

Isn't that being dishonest?

Of course, it is, but what choice do you have?

Knowing that Chet would not file for a divorce, I secretly filed. Doing so filled my heart with despair. *Beverly, you're a failure!* Again, I was acting out of fear. By not being forthright and then, by being self-deprecating, I clearly demonstrated my co-dependent characteristics!

In my mind, I was to blame for the failure of our marriage. Chet had struggled to cut the strings that tied him to economic dependence on my grandfather. But he didn't know how to, because I couldn't let him. How could I explain to any man the reasons for my adoration and loyalty to my grandfather? It couldn't be done, for the answers were impenetrable, even to me at the time. My life and finances had been intertwined with my grandfather's since my youth. *Why doesn't Chet understand this?*

I had also continued to harbor guilt over forcing Chet to move. I have wondered if I hadn't made Chet move, would we still have divorced.

In any case, Chet was served with the divorce papers and a restraining order at the end of the month. *Why couldn't I work things out with him for the sake of my three boys?*

I don't know. Was I worn-out from all the drama?

Yes. There was no other solution.

During our last week together, I was very sad. As sure as I was that divorcing Chet was the choice I had to make to protect myself and my boys, I was conflicted about what I had done. *I didn't give Chet the chance to heal. Could he have healed if I had just stood by him? As his wife, I should have.* Drained, but without remorse, I started to move on. I had to, for the sake of our boys.

20

GOING BACK IN TIME

Now that I was soon to be divorced from a volatile, angry alcoholic, I had to admit I feared what Chet would do. *Will he retaliate? Will my life be in jeopardy?* This precarious situation brought to mind thoughts about my dear maternal grandmother whose life had ended in tragedy.

Little snippets of information about her had been revealed to me on occasion, but I knew so little about her. I knew that her un-marked grave was somewhere in Calvary Catholic Cemetery. She had been laid to rest up on a hill under a large oak tree. Her grave lay beside that of a former mayor of Cleveland. Yet not once had anyone in the family taken me to the cemetery. *Had they mourned for her in the past? Why had she become a forgotten soul whom no one openly talked about?*

My mother never, ever mentioned her, not even uttering her name. And, surprisingly, Grandpa's lips were also sealed. Auntie Sue was the only one who talked about the past or my real grand-mother. She felt it was a disgrace that a tombstone had not been placed on her mother's grave after all these years. "It's Stepmother Caroline's doings," she said.

I wondered why my aunt spoke so harshly about her stepmother. *Why would Grandma Caroline object? Was she jealous of a dead person?* As I got older, I became more curious.

What secrets have been hidden from me? Had my natural grandmother been ill, like my mother?

Wanting to know more about my maternal grandmother, I decided to ask Grandpa.

On a spring day in April, bright sunlight was shining through the closed window. It had been a cold month. The daffodils and hyacinths were blooming, but only a few trees had begun to bud.

It was Saturday, a day for shopping or just visiting with my grandparents. Grandma Caroline was in the basement cooking. This left my grandfather and me alone in the kitchen of the Edgerton home. He was sitting in his chair, facing the door to the back entrance of their flat. I was seated next to him.

Our family had just celebrated Grandpa's birthday on the eighth of April. *Hopefully, our celebration has left him feeling nostalgic and willing to recall earlier events in his life. This may be the perfect time to ask him about my grandmother.*

The setting seems right, too. Why not ask here, in the kitchen? This room has been the hub of holiday activity and joy. While seated at this table, Grandpa Vincenzo had made decisions, had many conversations with family and friends, and signed numerous legal papers.

Grandpa Vincenzo and I were comfortable. The aroma of freshly perked coffee was in the air. I decided to ask.

At first, he was very reluctant to say anything. "*Mio caro*, my dear, that's so long ago. It's best we forget about it."

There was a long silence. I felt uncomfortable. *Why did I ask?*

Grandpa Vincenzo's face paled and I could tell he was struggling to contain his emotions. More silence.

His eyes filled with tears, as he began to speak. "Remembering *profondità*, deep feelings, and young *passione*, passion, is hard to do!

"Your grandmother and I lived in Colle Martino, Italy. We grew up there. From the first day I laid eyes upon her, I said to myself that I would marry her. She was eleven and I was fifteen." He laughed. "Of course, I was too young to understand love, but I

Grandpa Vincenzo, in his youth in Italy.

knew I liked her appearance—she was beautiful!

"My *bella, bella*, beautiful Adriana, creamy-white skin, *la faccia*, the face, of a Madonna, and long black hair that fell to her waist.

"The next summer, she was taller and my God, the breasts." Grandpa Vincenzo brought his right hand to his lips, kissed his fingers, extending them, and threw a kiss into the air. "Magnificent!"

I blushed.

He continued. "Her brown eyes were magnets. When she looked at me, I knew she liked me, too.

"Beauty gives a woman power over men. For her, only the best would do. To afford a beautiful wife like Adriana, I needed money. Having money would give me power! And, at that time, I was too poor, a farm boy, a common laborer for my father. I had seen the big city. I knew living in Colle Martino, I would never be rich.

"As a young man, my father and I would hike all day over rough stony hills to reach Napoli. In the market place, we would sell our produce and purchase supplies. I had been saving the few *lira*, dollars, I had earned to move to Napoli. There, I would have more opportunities.

"One evening my father, Dominico, and I were in a café, drinking wine and eating *scamorza*, cheese, when I heard the locals talking about the most opportune opportunity—the United States. What they said was not the truth; they were a little *pazzo*, crazy. Ha! They said, 'The streets were paved with gold.' Youth believes everything." He laughed. "From that day, I could think of nothing else—I would become rich in America.

"Fortunately, on one of the trips to Napoli, I found a sponsor. He would guarantee work for me once I arrived in New York City. Reluctantly, my father agreed to support my decision. I was only sixteen. I left Italy with the clothing on my back, an extra pair of trousers, two *lira* and a book given to me by my father—Italian words with the English translations.

"I was the first one from our family to travel outside Italy. As the ship pulled away from the dock and the mainland disappeared from sight, my heart ached from all that I was leaving. I had already begun to miss our village. I felt such an emptiness and longing inside of me. Perhaps going was a mistake?

"I solemnly promised myself that I would work night and day, if necessary, to accumulate enough money to provide well for my parents. I would send for them if they chose to follow me, or I would return a rich man and marry.

"The SS Madonna pulled into the dock at Manhattan on August 9, 1901. It had been an exhausting three weeks. When I wasn't seasick, I studied my book of translations. I had memorized the alphabet, could count to ten, and understood a few simple words: *hello, goodbye, yes,* and *no.*

"A small ferry carried me from the ship to Ellis Island. Once ashore on the Island, I spent hours waiting in lines for my medical examination and legal clearance. When the paperwork was stamped *approved*, another boat returned me to Manhattan where I met my

214

sponsor. He was there, as he had promised.

"The very next day, he had an assignment for me. I would work as a manual laborer. What else could I do? I had no schooling. But I did have youth, a strong healthy body, and a willingness to work. I joined the ground crew that laid the tracks for the railroad. The Atchison, Topeka & Santa Fe went all the way to Spokane, Washington.

"I traveled across the United States, working and learning many trades. By chance, on a job in Pittsburgh, Pennsylvania, I met a *compaesano*, fellow townsman, from Italy. His home was in Cleveland, Ohio. He was starting a new job in Cleveland the following week. He asked me to join him. This is how I came to make my home in Cleveland.

"Because of my know-how, I was made job foreman. The men came to me for directions and schooling. I was respected.

"My father's advice roared in my ears: 'Listen to me, Vincenzo, and remember: Be honest, do as you're told, do more work than the *datore di lavoro*, employer, expects, and do your best work. You will be respected for this—opportunities to make money come to a respected man!'

"My father was right; honest labor in the end produces success. More jobs were offered to me than I could handle. I was making more money than I could spend. To live, what did I need? Very little money.

"With the money I didn't send to Italy, I purchased a home. I remodeled it to house more than one family. Now I was a *proprietario*, owner. People paid me rent.

"I bought another and another *casa*, home. I didn't have to work for anyone any more. I could return to Italy now. I was a rich man. And, as you *Americanas* say, I could *woo* Adriana!

"Soon after my return to Colle Martino, Adriana accepted my proposal. We would leave Italy. We sailed on the SS Hamburg in June 1912.

"*La famiglia*, the family, Lombardi had been living in the United States, right here in Cleveland, for some time. Adriana was delighted to have her sister and brothers living close by. The house on Frank Avenue became our home. It was the same house where you lived as *un bambina*, a child.

"Your grandmother was happy, full of life. She would sing and dance all around the house while she cooked and cleaned. But if she didn't get her way—look out! Mamma Mia! She was as stubborn as a mule!

"The *bambini* arrived fast. Your Aunt Beatrice was born first, your mother next, and Assunta, two years later. Adriana took good care of our little ones, but she was disappointed that we had no friends. The neighbors were not friendly with her. They were from Abruzzi, another region of Italy, and had a problem understanding our dialect from Campobasso. But the real problem was not how she pronounced her words—it was the neighbors' jealousy! They didn't even try to be friendly. She was a beauty, and I, a propertied citizen.

"My third cousin from the Delfino side of the family, Cosmo Cutone, had recently arrived in Cleveland. You look out for blood relatives. The man was jobless. He had nowhere to live. We had an empty bedroom off the kitchen. I offered him the room on a temporary basis.

"Adriana had just given birth to your Aunt Julia. Now she seemed sad all the time. Sometimes women get that way after childbirth. Then she insisted that I tell Cosmo to move. That surprised me, because they appeared to get along. Anyhow, he moved.

"Weeks later, Adriana begged me to stay home from work. She said that she was having nightmares. In her dreams, Cosmo would appear at our door saying that she needed to be punished...he would kill her!

"Punished? Punished for what? Where would she get such an idea? She hadn't done anything wrong! Her worry didn't make sense. Why would she be afraid? Cosmo was my cousin. Why would he hurt my wife? Besides, I took him in when he had nowhere to go."

Grandpa's face grew red.

"A few times I caught him looking at Adriana just like other men did. Men liked to look at her body—those breasts! They would get this foolish grin on their faces. Men can be animals, but no one ever showed her disrespect.

"Cosmo was respectful in front of me. Adriana said nothing. So

216

why would I be suspicious?

"It was Friday morning, April 23rd, when your grandmother begged me not to go to work. I wouldn't listen. The outside of a two-family home about four blocks down the street needed painting. The men had already taken the extension ladders and scaffolding to the job. There was work to do. I had to go.

"As Adriana handed me the lunch that she had packed, she clung to me. I said to her, *'Non capisco cosa c'è di sbagliato!* I don't understand what's wrong! *Va bene!* It's okay! Nothing is going to happen.'" Tears filled his eyes.

"I loaded my tools into the wagon and began walking. The next-door neighbor, Mrs. Di Cillo, was in her front yard weeding a patch of daffodils. Most of the time, I had nothing to say to her. If we talked, it was about the weather. Today was different.

"That woman was always watching what was going on at our house. She was a nosey one. I asked her if she had seen Cosmo lately. 'Oh, yes I did. He's been at your home every day this week!'

"'*Grazie,* thank you.' I said to myself, 'That *bastardo*, bastard, is up to something.'

"My mind started working. That talk about dreams was bullshit! Why would he threaten her? He wanted something. *A Fanculo*, fuck! He wanted sex! Now, I could see. That son of a bitch! I had been a fool!"

A look of guilt, remorse, and pain crossed my grandfather's face as he continued, "He wanted her. The *bastardo* wanted her! Why didn't I comprehend this?

"It was eleven o'clock. Thinking, 'The hell with lunch,' I threw my tools into the wagon. I was going home. *Rapidamente*! Quickly! Adriana's words rang in my ears, 'Vincenzo, *non andare*! Don't go!'

"As I neared the house, I was taken aback. A rescue truck was in the driveway. There were *quattro*, four, or *cinque*, five, police cars along the curb. People were in the front yard."

A pathetic look of resignation crossed Grandpa's face. His shoulders sagged. Guilt is a heavy burden.

"I reached the walkway to the backdoor. Attempting to enter, I was abruptly stopped by two policemen. Why hadn't I stayed home? I could hear my children screaming and crying.

"The bastard's body was lying in the entrance to our flat. A gun remained clutched between his fingers. Skin! Blood! Everywhere! *Il pazzo*, the crazy one, had placed his pistol in his mouth and pulled the trigger. As disturbing as it was, seeing him dead gave me relief.

"The police grabbed me. 'Who are you? Why are you here?' Finally, they believed me. 'That must be your wife inside.' With a policeman on each side of me, we entered the kitchen.

"The room was still full of smoke. I could smell burnt sauce. The blackened pot sat on the stove.

"My God, nothing could have prepared me for this! Adriana had been shot twice in the forehead. *Il suo bel viso era scomparso!* Her beautiful face was gone!"

Tears splashed on to Grandpa's cheeks. He wiped his eyes. His voice cracked as he continued.

"A large puddle of urine was next to her. Two sets of tiny footprints left the puddle. They led from the kitchen, through the living room, and to the bedroom where they stopped. Your mother and Aunt Assunta had gone to the door with your grandmother.

"They saw it! Poor, poor *piccoli*, little ones! They saw what had happened and ran into the bedroom to hide.

"Your Aunt Beatrice had been sleeping. The commotion and cries woke her. Her screams were heard by a neighbor who was passing by. He saw the bodies, found the girls in the front bedroom, and called the police.

"A policeman was in the living room trying to rock baby Julia. She had been found screaming in her highchair. Angelina and Assunta had been wrapped in blankets. And poor Beatrice was so scared, she *non poteva parlare,* couldn't speak! She tried so hard to say, '*Papa,*' but no words would come.

"Good thing I came home when I did! The police were ready to take the girls to the police station.

"I immediately took the girls to their aunt's home. They couldn't return home—the horrible mess! And even then, with a clean house, who would take care of them?

"The police had all the information they needed. The murderer

Our flat in the Frank Avenue house can be seen on the top floor of the house on the left. I have always felt like an ominous shadow hovered over this house.

had committed suicide. They closed the case. I could return home.

"But the murder-suicide was news, big front-page news in *The Cleveland Press*. The Italian community had sympathy for me. The funeral was so big. Plenty volunteered to be pallbearers. When the hearse left St. Mary's Church on Petrarca and made its way down Frank Avenue to pass our house, the procession stretched all the way to 105th. Everybody and their brothers, too, came outside to look at us. They stood in groups along the curb. Our family couldn't even mourn in peace!

"Damn *giornalista*, journalists! For days after the funeral, our home attracted attention. Someone was always out front—looking for me.

"Damn the neighbors! Those gossips called your grandmother a *puttana*, whore! And the *il dannato*, the damned—Cosmo—was the victim. Ha! 'He's a lovesick man.' What did the *stupidi bastardi*, the stupid bastards, know?

"I never doubted Adriana. She loved me. She did no wrong. That's why she died. She refused him! The man was evil. Cosmo and *il Diavolo*, the Devil—they were one!

219

"Now that the funeral was over, I asked the church for advice. Who could take care of my little girls? St. Joseph's Church at East 23rd Street and Woodland operated an orphanage. I left my daughters with the nuns until I could make other arrangements.

"Soon I became very upset with them. I brought the girls new warm coats. A week later, they were gone. In their place were ragged and torn jackets. 'These are yours,' said the nuns. Liars!

"They had no right to call themselves 'Women of God.' How could I respect them? I had to get my girls out of there! I asked Adriana's family to help.

"Do you remember Aunt Josephine and Uncle Fred who lived on Petrarca?" He continued without giving me a chance to respond.

"When you were a child, you visited them often. They made their home in an apartment above Uncle Fred's upholstery shop, in that large brick building across the street from St. Mary's Church."

"Yes, Grandpa, how could I forget them? I loved visiting them with you. They had a swing in the backyard. It hung from the huge maple tree. When swinging, I would look up at the trains, and, as the engine passed over the trestle, motion to the conductor to blow the whistle. That was fun! And my sweet tooth won't let me forget Aunt Josephine's homemade oatmeal raisin cookies."

"Well, Josephine was your grandmother Adriana's older sister."

"I hadn't realized that at the time."

"Her husband was a good man. The Russos were happy people. They had two daughters, Marie and Enedina. They were a few years older than your mother.

"Aunt Josephine and Uncle Fred offered your mother a home. The family loved Angelina. She was so cute at five, with her tiny little face, big brown eyes, and lots and lots of curly hair. It was no surprise to me that your mother was the first to leave the orphanage.

"Next to leave was Assunta. Adriana's brother, Carl, and his wife, Julia, were childless. They would have kept your aunt forever, but I objected to this, for I wanted to raise the girls together. But I had no close family in the United States. There was no one else for me to turn to for help.

"Beatrice and baby Julia had to stay in the orphanage. They couldn't come home to live with me. How could I go to work? I wrote to my parents in Italy. I was looking for a full-time housekeeper. Perhaps they knew of a woman who would be willing to come to America in exchange for passage, room, and board.

"They did. I don't know why I never thought about Caroline Costa. She was the widow of my younger brother, Leonardo. He had died from influenza in the spring of 1918. My parents said I needed a wife. 'Marry her!'

"Trying to remember Caroline, after all these years, was hard. But we both agreed to follow tradition. Italian parents have been matchmaking for years.

"Now it was time to pay for Caroline's third-class passage. I agreed to go to Boston to meet her when she arrived on December 22, 1920. We were married two days later, on the 24th. After a small religious ceremony, I brought her home, to Cleveland."

"Grandpa, did you ever think that agreeing to an arranged marriage was risky?"

"Of course, I did. Perhaps you didn't understand what I said, that I had an obligation to accept the match made by my parents. But I also respected Caroline. She had more to risk than I. For her, everything would be foreign: the homeland, the language, family, friends, and me. I often wondered why *she* took a chance on *me.* I thought about that a lot.

"Caroline had been my brother's second choice, too. His first wife had died in childbirth. Caroline may have felt that if she remained in Italy she would die a widow. Or that being a housekeeper was the only way she would be able to find a husband. But she's a good woman."

I love Grandma Caroline. She's the only grandmother I have ever known. But according to Grandpa's description of Adriana, the two women were like night and day.

Grandma looks like a nun with her short, masculine haircut. She's definitely not a beauty. Grandma's someone who takes life very seriously. She's a no-nonsense person—all work and no play. She isn't anything like Grandpa's description of the happy, fun-loving, beautiful Adriana.

Grandpa Vincenzo continued, "After arriving in Cleveland, Caroline fell and broke her right hip. Doctors operated to mend it. She was exposed to tuberculosis, and a second operation was needed to remove the infected bone. Her right leg became four inches shorter. That's why her right shoe has a four-inch heel.

"After seven months in the hospital, Caroline returned home. Everyone told me that I had *sfortuna*, bad luck, being married to a sick woman. But she fooled me and everyone else; she managed to cook, clean, and sweep the floor while sitting in a wheelchair.

"Julia was almost two when I brought her home from St. Joseph's Orphanage. Caroline was learning to walk with a cane. Chasing after the *bambina*, the baby, wore her out. But at night she would pull the little one close and rock her to sleep. She treated her like her own flesh and blood.

"After a couple of months, Angelina and Assunta left their temporary homes. Aunt Beatrice had stayed in the orphanage all this time. You know how particular Grandma Caroline can be. Everything must be spotless. With just three girls home, Caroline felt overworked, and so she kept postponing Beatrice's return. Finally, at the nuns' insistence, I brought Beatrice home.

"Caroline expected everything to be *perfetto*, perfect. When the girls did something wrong, she'd scold them and give them a stern look. She could look very mean and her voice became irritating and shrill. That was just her way. With you it was different. But your mother and aunts, Beatrice and Assunta, thought she was a cruel stepmother!"

Grandpa's last statement wasn't news to me. I had already known that my aunts and mother weren't happy with Caroline. Grandpa Vincenzo was right; the girls did resent his wife. But it was not for her excessive cleanliness and scolding. She was receiving affection from their father that should have only been given to their real mother.

During a conversation with Auntie Sue, I learned how she and the girls really felt. "Papa was correct. Your grandmother was a pistol when it came to neatness. Everything had to be precisely in its place. She even starched the lace doilies! It was hard for us to get used to her demands.

"The four of us sisters shared a bedroom. At night we could hear

Caroline's giggles and their intimate sounds through the thin walls that separated the rooms. The knowledge that our father found satisfaction from this woman angered us.

"Our father and she had grown to genuinely love each other. How could he forget our mother? How could he love this mean, unreasonable woman? Except for Julia, we all resented your grandmother and gave her a hard time whenever we could.

"Now that I'm older, I understand. She was a good wife to Papa. I must admit that now I'm sorry for the difficulties I caused."

Grandpa Vincenzo continued, "Everything in my life was good—health, wife, daughters, and money. I had no worries until the girls grew up. The older girls were going to John Hay High School on East Boulevard. Beatrice, the oldest, was now sixteen and wanting to get married. Her suitor, Pasquale Gallo, was born in Bari, Italy. He was nearly twenty-five years older. Where she met him, I'll never know.

"Your grandmother and I didn't know it at the time, but Pasquale had abandoned a wife and child back in Italy. And there were too many rumors about the man. I didn't know what to *pensare*, think.

"I really didn't approve of Pasquale dating your aunt. For God's sake, he was my age! But the son of a gun had money! He could take good care of my girl.

"Pasquale spent lots of money on Beatrice. He bought her fancy dinners and took her to fine night clubs. Becoming Mrs. Gallo excited her. But she was a kid—*sedici*, sixteen! That's too young *per capire*, to understand, marriage.

"Grandma Caroline, on the other hand, approved of Pasquale. She was worried about herself; being a step-mother to four girls was a hard job. Having one less daughter to care for would make her job easier.

"In spite of my misgivings, with Pasquale's persistence, Beatrice's begging, and Caroline's nagging, I gave in. All of them made me crazy! She got married.

"When she was all grown-up, everyone knew and talked about my daughter—Angelina. Your mother was the most beautiful girl in the whole city. No one came close to her in looks.

"Angelina loved to sing, like her mother, but better. From the time she was a little one, she would sing, first in perfect Italian, then in English. She sang like an angel!

"Her voice and her beauty helped her win a pageant for Italian-American girls. The editor of *La Voce del Popolo*, Ohio's largest Italian newspaper, wrote a front-page article on her and the contest.

"Angelina loved the publicity, but all this attention wasn't helping her. She didn't know if she wanted to sing or find a job. She was going to parties with older rich people from Shaker Heights. It was rumored that she sang at an event for two very rich brothers. *Qual è il suo nome?* What's his name? I think they built the Terminal Tower.

"At the end of summer, Angelina told me that she had taken a job as a waitress. She left home early in the morning and returned late at night. A month later, she asked me for streetcar fare. *Perché?* Why? I questioned her. Why would she need money? After all, she was working. She said her boss did not pay her.

"The next morning, I left for work with your mother. We both boarded the streetcar and rode to the end of the line. Then your mother began to cry and finally admitted that she never had a job. *Povera figlia mia!* Poor daughter of mine! Something was wrong.

"Angelina *dormirebbe tutto il giorno*, would sleep all day, and *festa per tutta la notte*, party all night. I told her that she had to be home at ten o'clock—bedtime. Many a night I would open the door to the girls' room to check on her.

"One day, I discovered that Angelina had put pillows and clothing under her blankets to make it look like she was in bed. Instead, she had escaped through her bedroom window. Son of a bitch, she made a fool of me! I wondered how often I had been made a fool. Her sisters never told on her."

Perhaps this irrational behavior of hers was an early indicator that still greater emotional and mental breakdowns were to follow.

"Adriana and I named your aunt Assunta after the religious holiday celebrated on her birthday, August 15th. We felt Assunta was a beautiful name, but your aunt didn't. She hated her name. On her school papers, she wrote *Mary Ann. Pozzo!* Crazy!"

"I know, Grandpa. Remember how I couldn't pronounce Assunta, so I called her Aunt *Soondy?* Now I call her *Auntie Sue*. Even you and Grandma Caroline call her *Sue*."

224

"Sue is *bella*, beautiful, but she refuses to recognize it. She says her upper lip was scarred. It's a birth defect.

"Nobody looks at her lip. There are just a few little wrinkles there. She uses a magnifying glass to look! Her problem was Angelina. She was jealous because she was always in competition with your mother.

"Sue spent as little time as possible at home. She loved to play out-of-doors, roller skate, ice skate, swim, and go bicycle riding. Of all the girls, she was the most likable. I loved to joke with her because of her good nature. But she didn't recognize my teasing as being 'just for fun;' she felt 'picked on.'

"Julia was walking by the time she left the orphanage to join Caroline and me in the Frank Avenue home. Until the other girls returned home, she had her stepmother's undivided attention. The touch of her natural mother had been forgotten. This made it easy for her to truly love Stepmother.

"Julia was different from her sisters: black-black hair, sharp features, and black eyes. She was, what would you say, 'tomboy?' A rough-and-tumble girl. I had always wanted a son. That's why, when she was old enough to be my helper, she went with me when I decorated the suites I owned. She would mix paint, hand me tools, and spread the paste on the back of the wallpaper. She did a good job."

We heard the tap of Grandma Caroline's cane as she climbed the steps. The door opened and she entered the kitchen, and then stopped to catch her breath. Her advanced age had made the climb a challenge.

The warm kitchen air began to smell of the sweet aroma of sautéed vegetables. Grandma Caroline had used an antique Roper gas range in the basement to cook the onions and green and red peppers. It was lunch time.

Grandpa Vincenzo began slicing the loaf of Italian bread he had purchased from the Orlando Baking Company. He said, "It's the best, like homemade." I cut slices of prosciutto, Italian ham, and cheese and placed them on the table. Fresh-squeezed lemonade in Grandma's sparkling glass pitcher, with a mint leaf floating in the tart beverage, would complete our repast.

As we ate our lunch, I thought about my grandfather—an amazing man!

After our relaxing lunch, the kitchen table was cleaned, the dishes were washed and put away, and Grandma Caroline left the room. Her favorite television series, *The Three Stooges*, aired at two o'clock. She got lots of laughs from the show by watching the foolish antics of the characters, though she barely understood English.

"Mio caro, mi fanno una promessa. My dear one, make me a promise. Caroline will need your help if something happens to me. She's had a much protected life with me. I do everything: make the money, pay the bills, do the shopping, and make all the decisions. She can't read or write; her signature is a cross. Without me, she is a lost child. Promise me that you will take care of her when I am gone."

"Grandpa, I have loved Grandma Caroline my entire life. You have my promise. Let's not talk about it anymore. I can't bear to think about losing you!"

For the next five minutes, Grandpa Vincenzo and I sat in silence. Sharing his emotional adversities with me had left him vanquished. As for me, did knowing more about my grandmother's tragic death change anything? Yes, it did.

My steadfast love and respect for my dearest grandfather grew stronger. I simply marveled at how he managed to put his life and that of his children back together after Adriana's tragic death. He could have become a sad and bitter person. Instead, he chose to see his situation for what it was and took action in the best way he knew how.

Rising from my seat, I removed our empty water glasses and coffee cups from the table. Kissing Grandpa Vincenzo on the forehead, I silently left the kitchen to say goodbye and hug dear Grandma Caroline. I drove home, deep in thought.

After listening to Grandpa Vincenzo's story, I was in awe of him. He embodied everything I admire in a person. Hearing his story only made me love him more.

He was a mere youth, only sixteen, when he travelled over four thousand miles to a foreign land. He couldn't even speak the language and had no money. He had to have faith that his sponsor truly would be there with a job for him when he arrived.

I respected him so greatly for doing whatever he could to keep his family together after Adriana was murdered. He held his head up high, even though he still felt guilt and remorse. He had opened up his home to his cousin, and he took advantage of that generosity in the worst possible way imaginable.

I now realize that my mother's mental illness must have been part of the emotional fallout from her mother's tragic death. I, too, have been emotionally wounded by the legacy of Adriana's murder. Sadly, and unintentionally, I, in turn, have transferred my emotional damage to my children.

It was time to put the past aside and return to the present. I was once more at a life-changing crossroad—moving forward with the divorce, or staying and enduring the pain. I was forced to make a choice.

Will I ever find the unconditional love and peace I need? Maybe it's not meant to be for me!

21

MEETING ALLAN

I was at a turning point in my life. I was on my own and the decision of what to do next rested fully on my shoulders.

As fate would have it, the very first day I began my job search, the *Plain Dealer* featured an ad for a caseworker at Cleveland State Hospital. My interview was short and sweet, as I had the necessary education, but I had to pass a Civil Service exam prior to my employment.

Once I passed the test, I took the social service position at the psychiatric hospital. Gainful employment would solve my immediate problems, the first being money. I desperately needed a paycheck. While the divorce decree awarded me support for the boys, I doubted that Chet would be in a position to comply with the court order. Presently, he was unemployed. *Even if Chet does go back to work and can give me support for the boys, could I remain in contact with him without stepping back into the marital relationship? I don't know!*

What I knew for sure was that I didn't want to risk being at home when Chet came to remove his possessions. Being at work would relieve me of the pressure that would come with facing him.

I feared how I might respond if he expressed his undying love. Most likely I would forgive him, but only until his next drunken episode. I also was afraid of the possibility of him becoming violent. Being unsure of my true feelings, my constant indecision was maddening! Either way, this was a no-win situation for me. Knowing my weakness, I chose not to see him. I arranged for him to come to our home while I was at work.

Cleveland State Hospital was located in Garfield Heights off Turney Road. People jokingly called it "Turney Tech." It was a small city within itself, isolated on a hillside. The acreage set aside for the grounds had plenty of trees which added to the facility's seclusion.

The patients were provided with every service necessary for their care, including an infirmary to treat physical illness, a cafeteria, a commissary for purchases, and a laundry. The mentally ill residents were housed according to gender and the severity of their psychosis. A system of underground tunnels connected the buildings.

My office was on the lower level of the administration building. As a social worker, my job was to begin or end the paper trail for patients. Generally, I interviewed the family and completed an intake questionnaire for each prospective patient. I also made sure that the patients had housing and a treatment plan in place prior to discharge. I was a liaison between the doctor, family, and patient. I felt very comfortable with my new job and surroundings. Years earlier, my mother had been a patient at this facility. Sometimes I entertained the thought of reviewing her medical records.

As part of my daily routine I'd arrive early, enter the tunnel, and walk briskly to the commissary to purchase coffee and a bear claw, my newly discovered sweet maple-and-nut treat. As I savored my pastry, I would review patients' charts, flagging those that needed attention. My afternoons were spent visiting the wards.

One day in mid-July, the noonday sun was blistering hot as I entered the brick Tudor building that housed the male patients. I had hoped that once inside, I would find relief from the 90-degree temperature. Being removed from the direct rays of the sun was helpful, but relief from the heat could not be found within this structure. The open windows were protected by iron bars. Large, freestanding fans were used to circulate the stale air that was

230

permeated with the odors from residents in need of a bath.

At times I felt like Alice in Wonderland when I walked through the series of halls in order to reach the visitation area. Excluding the main entrance, every door had a lock on it. A key was needed to open the door, and, once on the other side of the door, a key was needed to lock you within.

Each time I locked a door behind me, my ears echoed from the unforgettably haunting clink-clank of the lock engaging. Locking the door to the visitation area, my mind's eye no longer perceived the here and now. A frightened little girl whose mommy had been confined within these walls stood before the door. *Why, Mommy? Why?* Jolting myself back to reality, I entered the room.

There were approximately thirty-five patients in this unit with two male attendants on duty per shift. Typically, the men who had limited privileges sat on hard wooden chairs or benches in a semi-circle around the room. Most of them were a sorrowful sight to see with their shoddy, soiled clothing and lack of grooming. Barbering services were given infrequently, and scissors and razors were not accessible for safety reasons.

Today, nine men were seated in the common area waiting to be groomed. A stack of once-white and frayed towels sat on the sink countertop, along with a white enamel basin filled with water, a straight razor, and two cans of shaving cream. I smiled as the Barbasol jingle from my youth came to mind.

Entering the room, ten sets of eyes stared directly at me. Being under such unexpected scrutiny caused me to blush. *Phew!*

Looking at the attendant for recognition, I felt the blood rushing into my cheeks. He could readily see my crimson cheeks. He smiled, nodded "Hello" and in the stylized manner of a barber, swirled the off-white ragged sheet in the air and swung it over the shoulders of the next patient in need of a shave.

In an attempt to regain my composure, I stared at the old man who was now seated in the makeshift barber's chair. The brilliant sunlight that flooded the room ridiculed the lines on the old man's bony face. He had deep-sunken, expressionless eyes. *Have those eyes ever sparkled with joy?* I pondered that thought for a brief moment.

Then a loud, shaky voice said, "Hey, pretty one!" Startled, I looked up. The compliment came from a disheveled, younger, kindly looking man. Without responding to or looking at him, I blushed again, went directly to the charts, completed my assignments, and left the ward. *Most embarrassing!*

A week later, I received a call from a patient's mother. Her son had been discharged and his glasses and leather jacket had been left behind. "Could you please find them?" I knew nothing about his discharge and needed time to investigate.

Another week passed before I located her son's possessions. When I contacted her, the poor woman was distressed and was unable to pick up her son's belongings. One of her other sons, Ray, was in the psychiatric hospital. At the time, she didn't mention the nature of his illness, but from her distress, I assumed that whatever it was, it was serious. Feeling compassion for her stressful situation, I offered to bring the items to her.

She lived in the Brooklyn area of Cleveland which, to me, was unfamiliar territory. Then she mentioned working at G & G Dry Cleaners located next to the Lincoln Inn at the corner of State Road and Lincoln Avenue in Parma. *Déjà vu. I've been there before.*

"Great! I'll see you on Saturday."

While driving to Parma that Saturday, I was filled with nostalgia. *What bitter-sweet memories!*

That was then, this is now. Please don't think about…your mother, your father, or Chet. Nevertheless, my ruminations continued. It was only when I arrived at my destination that my mind returned to the present.

Upon opening the door to the small establishment, I was greeted by three large fans; two were used to generate an interior breeze, while the third one, a window fan, let out the stale air. I could taste and smell the cleaning fluid as it saturated my nostrils.

The narrow counter and cash register were engulfed by hordes of clean garments that hung from the surrounding turnstiles. *Business must be good.*

A beautiful, oval-faced woman came to the counter and introduced herself as Mrs. Lazar, the woman I had spoken with on the phone. Wiping perspiration from her brow, she invited me into the rear pressing area. As I placed her son's glasses and jacket on a

232

counter, she picked up her purse, offering me money for my inconvenience. I just shook my head *no*. Replacing her purse, she smoothed back a few strands of golden-brown hair that had come loose from her neatly pinned bun. Following her to the front of the shop, I noticed that we were about the same height. As I began to say my goodbyes, she interrupted me to suggest I join her for Sunday brunch. She clearly needed to talk to someone.

"Thank you for the invitation, but I need to be with my three little boys on Sunday," I replied.

"You can bring the little ones," she said. I guess she felt grateful for my help. Anyway, I didn't say no!

That Sunday, after a few wrong turns, I found her small frame home. Rose Lazar lived off Memphis Avenue on West 38th Street, near the Cleveland Zoo. *Why are you doing this? This is not part of your job description!*

The home was the typical Cleveland frame Colonial. I noted that it was in need of paint, yet the abundance of summer flowers bordering the shrubs reflected that someone cared about the home.

The boys and I entered the house from the front porch which led directly into the living room. The large, comfortable furnishings were a muted brown. The end tables were covered with traditional velveteen-fringed scarves. Nondescript lamps sat on the tables. Old newspapers and magazines were neatly stacked in an unoccupied corner.

An arched opening separated the front room from the dining area. The massive walnut table and paper-cluttered buffet dwarfed the room. It was impossible to move around the area without bumping into a piece of furniture.

The small kitchen was cramped with a large white table. In fact, everything was white: walls, curtains, appliances, and flooring. To add to the antiseptic look, even the porcelain sink and side boards were white.

Perched in his cage on the breakfast table was the only splash of color in the room: a yellow-headed, green-bodied, black-and-white-plumed cockatiel.

The incessantly chirping little bird flitted about its cage as birdseed and feathers became airborne. Most of the debris conveniently

233

landed on the table's protective newspaper covering, but—unfortunately—the two-slice chrome toaster occasionally shared the litter.

How gross! It's very unsanitary to house a bird on the kitchen table, even if the table is covered with fresh newspaper.

Dismissing my thoughts about birds and sanitation, I let the boys stand nearby and goggle over the bird. While things were crowded and a bit cluttered, except for the bird, everything was spotlessly clean.

Did she clean all of this just for my visit?

Rose served all sorts of breakfast foods: little sausages, French toast, finger foods for the boys, scrambled eggs, stuffed cabbages, and the most delicious sliceable rice cake. I felt honored. *All this for my small favor!*

We were seated at the table when the front door opened and in walked her son. *Good looking! Tall! Wavy brown hair!* Rose introduced me to him. *I know that voice. But when and where did I hear it?*

As we finished eating, I realized where I had heard Allan's voice before. My ears echoed with the words, "Hey, pretty one." *Yes, that's him. He's the patient that embarrassed me.* The man who sat before me looked nothing like the pale, defeated-looking vagrant who had uttered, 'Hey, pretty one,' but I was sure it was him.

After our meal, Rose, Allan, the boys, and I walked up and down the street for air and exercise. There was a comfortable *déjà vu* feeling about the visit. She also had three sons and was a single, hardworking mother. We were invited back.

Before long, Sunday brunch at Rose's house became a happy part of our family's routine. Rose was born and raised in Hungary, where she met and married her husband. She loved to talk about her boys, Ronald, Ray, and Allan. She treated my little sons like her own grandchildren. I had extreme empathy for her because of the heavy burden we both bore, having mentally ill family members. I completely bonded with her.

According to Rose, her boys had grown up on a small farm in North Royalton. She acknowledged that she had been overprotective and shielded Allan from responsibilities from an early age. She had assigned him the fewest and easiest chores. Perhaps this was

234

because he was her youngest child. Then, when he was twelve, Allan's father died. She said she may have overcompensated her mothering even more in an attempt to shield him from the loss of his father.

Allan's father, Andrew Lazar, was a general foreman at Republic Steel. He was in charge of expediting production. His department relied on the use of an overhead crane. Many of the crane's malfunctions were the result of electrical problems. Andrew, being a certified electrician, often climbed a ladder mounted against the factory wall to walk onto the catwalk so he could make simple electrical repairs to the crane. He frequently took it upon himself to make the repairs without receiving clearance from his higher-ups or the safety expert.

One day, as Andrew climbed onto the catwalk, he slipped—falling twelve stories. His body was so shattered and mangled it could not be shown by the undertaker. His employer denied liability for Andrew's actions and refused to compensate Rose for the loss of her husband.

From then on, Rose supported her household by working long hours for a dry cleaner, tending the shop and standing for hours pressing clothing. She became tired and worn at an early age, but somehow, she managed to keep their family home in North Royalton until Allan graduated from high school.

Allan was not a scholar. He graduated from school with less than a C average, as he never took his studies seriously. He was also not a jock. Surprisingly, high school sports did not interest him, even though his older brother, Ray, was the football team's star player.

During Allan's junior and senior years, the need for spending money prompted him to learn the dry cleaning business from his mother. He could press a shirt like the professionals. Rose, who now owned the business, had hoped that he would take it over upon her retirement, but his interest in dry cleaning waned.

Upon his graduation, Allan enlisted in the Merchant Marine. He abruptly resigned after a short stint of sailing the seas. After a month of adjusting to civilian life, Ron, his oldest brother, suggested he find work in the trades. Allan followed his brother's advice and completed his masonry apprenticeship in November 1965. Unfortu-

235

nately, weather conditions made bricklaying impossible that winter. Living with his mother, he had too much free time on his hands. Consequently, he sat around the house smoking cigarettes and playing music so loudly it disturbed the neighbors.

After receiving repeated warnings by the police to tone down the ruckus, Allan was cited for disturbing the peace and taken to jail. During his incarceration, he became catatonic and was transported to Cleveland State Hospital for a psychiatric evaluation.

I didn't learn the details of Allan's first mental breakdown until much later, as he was not part of my caseload. Perhaps because of how removed I was from his case, his mental health history didn't concern me at that time.

Without his mother's phone call, we never would have connected. I believe that it was more than just chance that directed that call to my attention and that destiny brought us together.

Allan was handsome and, judging by his appearance and behavior, he was *normal!* Failing to acknowledge how I met him, I erased from my memory the textbook definition of a manic-depressive personality. I did not want to comprehend that, with my newly formed friendship, I was now venturing into uncharted, turbulent waters—ever so tumultuous! *No harm can come from such pleasant companionship, can it?*

Our courtship consisted of Sunday- and Wednesday-night meals at Rose's home, walks in the nearby parks, the zoo, the circus, and just anything and everything that was fun or amusement for my darling sons. Allan, too, was like an overgrown kid. He and his mother fit nicely into my life.

We found one another mutually attractive. Perhaps part of my attraction to Allan was that I thought he needed someone to look after him. And I became that someone. I now understand that, as a child, I believed that a lack of love is what caused my mother's mental illness. Subconsciously, I was most likely trying to prove my belief through my relationship with Allan. How naïve I was to believe that my love would cure him!

We decided to marry. Our ceremony was on a beautiful, sunshiny day in July 1967. A private service was held at the Methodist church on North Royalton, at one o'clock in the afternoon. The church's

236

pastor officiated. No family members were in attendance, nor were there any plans for a celebration in the evening. We planned to surprise everyone at a later date.

Allan and I wore street attire. I was dressed in a green knit, sleeveless, princess-cut, knee-length summer dress, and Allan wore a light gray suit with a white shirt and tie.

Our two witnesses were a strange, mismatched, newly married May-December couple. Clarence was Allan's high school friend. His wife, Annie, was Rose's widowed friend. She delighted in her young husband and followed him around like a puppy dog—his will was her will. Without his lead, she was lost and bewildered.

They had an idyllic life together without the stress of employment. Annie's widows' benefits and Clarence's disability check provided them with their necessities. Clarence was considered a slow learner. *Perhaps, not! After all, he did manage to attract a wife, and one with a steady income at that!*

I was never sure of their stability. At times they appeared to be living in their car as they stored personal belongings in the backseat. They often drove around town looking for something to do. Though they were less than my idea of ideal witnesses, they could attest to our character and love.

The service was short and sweet. We exchanged gold bands. I saw that Allan was perspiring profusely and trembling as he said his vows. *Is he questioning what he's doing?*

Do I know what I'm doing? I think I do. I'm making a commitment to Allan.

Thoughts of Chet were constantly entering my mind. *That's over. We divorced because it couldn't work out.*

All of a sudden, I started thinking about my father, and how Chet could never win his approval.

Whatever my father or anyone else thinks doesn't matter.

Suddenly, tears began to trickle down my cheeks. *Why am I crying? Why do I feel so sad and confused? I should be happy. I believe I love Allan. So why does what I'm doing not seem right? Why is it that I can never make a clear-cut decision? I need to get a grip on myself!*

A month after our marriage, Allan moved into my home. How

nice it was to have a man around the house, especially one with masonry skills. He manicured the lawn, planted shrubs and flowers, and made minor repairs. To enhance the front of the house, he built two tapestry-brick flower boxes beneath the front windows and skillfully placed several courses of brick around the light post next to the driveway, to create a spiral candlestick. In addition to all of this, he contributed a most-needed paycheck to the household funds. His job as a mason for a premier commercial builder paid well. Moreover, on weekends, he willingly worked for Grandpa Vincenzo. Miraculously, for the time being, our mutual love was holding the demons in Allan's head at bay. No crystal ball foretold me what was to come. I felt blessed!

Soon, a baby was on its way. My new doctor's office was located in Severance Center Shopping Mall in Cleveland Heights. It was just a ten-minute drive from our home.

I had an increased sense of well-being and energy for the usual household duties. The pregnancy was normal, free of complications, with no nausea, and only a twenty-pound weight gain. Throughout the nine months, Allan was charming—he couldn't do enough for me.

Due to my history of rapid deliveries, my new obstetrician, Lee Goldstein, recommended that labor be induced, as was done for Martin's birth. Our precious baby was considered full-term Wednesday, the fifth of June. With my delivery scheduled, there was no concern about getting to the hospital in time. Allan drove me leisurely to Mount Sinai Hospital.

As the car pulled out of our drive, I noted the time—6:50 a.m.—as he pushed the radio's on button. His hands were shaking. *He's nervous.* I smiled to myself, as we heard the Beatles singing the ballad, "Michelle, My Belle." *I have always loved that song.*

For the past year, I had told everyone that if I were blessed with a little girl, I would name her Michelle. *Wow, isn't that serendipitous?*

A brief period of silence followed: "We interrupt this program: Senator Robert Kennedy is dead!" There was another delay in the programming.

Allan and I listened intently to the chaotic madness recorded at the scene. Andrew West reported live from the Ambassador Hotel in Los Angeles, where Kennedy was celebrating his June primary victories.

While bodyguards and others wrestled with Sirhan, the assassin continuing to shoot wildly, Kennedy collapsed in a pool of blood. Kennedy had been shot multiple times and five others were wounded by gunfire. We heard the shots and the hysterical and fearful utterances. The people in the crowd had been eye witnesses to Kennedy's assassination.

The horror of it! Rose Kennedy has lost two sons! It's not right. No parent should ever have to bury one child, let alone two!

My thoughts returned to November 1963. My son Martin was born the day before John Fitzgerald Kennedy had been assassinated. I couldn't believe that another Kennedy had been assassinated while I was preparing to bring forth a new life.

Allan turned the radio off as he stopped for the red light at the intersection of Lee Road and Fairmount Boulevard. We drove on in silence.

What a turbulent world my child is inheriting! Just a few weeks ago, Martin Luther King, Jr. was assassinated. This was followed by racial unrest and riots. Now the United States is drafting thousands of our young men to fight a civil war in Vietnam and others are gathering for anti-war demonstrations.

What an unsettled, crazy world we live in. I've got to stop thinking about all of this!

Not wanting to dwell on misfortune, I concentrated on the beautiful scene before me: the brick Tudor mansions, the garden greenery, the mixed summer flowers, stately trees, long winding driveways, and the stillness of the morning. Taking deep breaths, I returned to feelings of peace, love, and joy.

Dr. Goldstein delivered our eight-pound, twenty-inch baby girl at 2:45 p.m. on June 5, 1968. We named her Michelle, with the French spelling, just as in the title of the 1965 Beatles' recording. For a middle name, I chose André, another French name, in honor of her grandfather, Andrew. *It's a very pretty name, Michelle André Lazar.*

When she was first brought to me, she was awake. Two big beautiful blue-gray eyes stared at me. *At last, a little girl. How wonderful! I'll dress her in ruffles and lace.*

Caressing her little round head, I noted her peaches and cream skin and her browless tiny forehead. I said, "Most likely, she'll be a blonde." Opening her clenched fists, I examined each perfectly formed finger.

Lifting her blanket, I smiled as I looked at the round little apple-shaped belly, her extra-long legs, and ten tiny toes. *She's perfect!*

While I was overjoyed with the birth of a girl, I missed my boys. My hospital stay couldn't end soon enough. In between baby feedings, I occupied myself by walking back and forth to the nursery to peek at my precious daughter.

Following Martin's birth, like 98 percent of all Americans, I stopped to watch the live televising of John Kennedy's assassination and funeral. This time, even though Robert Kennedy was a political icon, there was no desire on my part to follow the aftermath of the tragedy on television while at the hospital. At my insistence, I returned home on the fourth day.

Our homecoming weather was warm and sunny. As we pulled onto the asphalt drive of our home, tears of joy came to my eyes. Through the picture window I saw Ted, Steven, and Martin jumping with joy. Claudessa Mason, our babysitter, was at their side.

We entered the house and I sat on the piano bench to give the boys the opportunity to look at their new sister. Their eyes widened with amazement as they stared at Michelle. They grinned and giggled for at least five minutes until I took her upstairs to the nursery.

Allan was happy and his most charismatic self. He beamed from ear to ear as he distributed Cuban cigars to his guy friends. While I was in the hospital, he had planted row after row of geraniums and petunias in the front yard. At the end of my first week home from the hospital, he brought me a large white gift box. Wrapped around the box and fastened in a bow were yards of three-inch-wide white satin ribbon. The name *Laura Salkin's*—an exclusive dress shop located on Fairmount Circle—had been embossed in gold leaf on the cover.

Excitedly, I slipped the ribbon and lid off the package and lifted sheet upon sheet of tissue to reveal the most beautiful white dress I'd ever seen. It was an Oscar De La Renta original. With tears of joy, I hugged, kissed, and thanked my wonderful husband.

I was happy. Allan was happy. The boys were happy. Even Rose couldn't believe her son's good fortune—marrying well and now fathering this beautiful little creature!

Michelle's birth gave the entire extended Lazar family a reason to celebrate. Rose provided us with names, addresses, and phone numbers so we could invite all of the relatives on Allan's side of the family.

Our party would be held on the day of Michelle's christening. What fun we had planning the event! Over forty announcements and party invites were mailed to family, friends, and neighbors.

The menu was in place: ham, fried chicken, potato salad, and baked beans. Fresh fruits—watermelon, honeydew, cantaloupe, strawberries, blueberries, and apple chunks—were served in the empty watermelon shell that had been carved to resemble a basket. We also had sweet rolls, assorted cookies—including biscotti—and the christening cake. And let me not forget to add beer and liquor, of course. In our eyes, it was a feast for the gods!

Allan selected Michelle's godparents. His most enduring friendship was with Patrick Marino. They had met in elementary school in North Royalton. Pat was married to Rebecca, a golden-haired blonde, with big blue eyes, perfect Teutonic features, and a slender body. She turned heads when she walked down the street. They had met in Germany during Pat's tour of duty for the Armed Forces.

Pat wasn't too shabby either, with good looks and artistic talent. He owned, by virtue of his father's finances, a well-known restaurant in Parma. But, being a hardworking restaurateur was not his passion. Mural and oil painting were his preferred labors, but he couldn't support his beautiful wife or make mortgage payments on his new home as a starving artist.

Allan had introduced me to Pat and Rebecca at a party they held at their home. We had arrived late and most of the guests were "high on life." Beer kegs were everywhere. The thirty or more guests had clustered into small groups throughout the house, the screened-in porch, and on the lush grass lawn. Getting to know anyone, especially our host and hostess, in this situation was impossible.

Time didn't allow for me to develop a friendship with the couple. What I did know is Pat and Allan had been friends since kindergarten, and that Pat's father, Nick, was a good man. He owned the State Road Barbershop that Allan and the boys frequented on a monthly basis. Nick was always playful and gentle with my boys. He never charged us for trimming our little guys' hair. I liked and respected him.

Nick could have been cast by a director as the classic Italian barber. His image was picture perfect: olive complexion, just a hint of a mustache, precise razor-cut hair, and manicured nails. In addition, he was a very talkative individual. Anyway, because of my affection for Nick, I approved of the younger Marinos.

Allan and I never had an in-depth discussion regarding religion, nor do I ever remember asking about the Marinos' religion. The irony of it all is that they were most likely Catholic, and Michelle would be christened in a Protestant church.

I had declared myself a Catholic as a teen, but now that I was divorced and remarried, my marital status was in conflict with Church doctrine. Having "fallen out of grace," I was willing to look into other denominations.

As for Allan, his parents were God-fearing and had their sons baptized in the Lutheran faith, although their own church attendance was rare, limited to the occasional holiday. Perhaps selecting a new faith would be the answer.

One of our neighbors belonged to the congregation of the First Baptist Church. Located on the corner of Eaton Road and Fairmount Boulevard, the church was within walking distance of our home. There was a four-way stop at this corner which affords one traveling west the best position from which to view the church. I'd often stop and stare at its simple structural beauty. That beauty was enhanced by a tall, open bell tower, glistening gray limestone, a circular asphalt drive, a lush lawn, shrubs, flowering trees, and seasonal flowers.

The interior of the church was as beautiful as the exterior. Walking into the church, I was impressed: it had a towering ceiling, a panoramic view of the altar, stained-glass windows, row after row of seating, and a large baptismal pool for spiritual cleansing.

Allan and I were invited to attend the Sunday service. The minister delivered a direct straight-forward sermon in an expressively enthusiastic manner: If you sin, you'll experience the fires of Hell. We joined the congregation.

Michelle was introduced to God and the congregation in July 1968. She looked like a Dresden doll in her white organdy dress covered with white rosebuds made of lace and ribbon. Her tiny head was adorned with a matching bonnet that accentuated her milk-white skin, rosy cheeks, and rosebud lips.

Her godmother, Rebecca, handed Michelle to the minister who removed her booties and submerged her tiny bare feet quickly into the water. She kicked and squirmed as he returned her to her godmother.

After the ceremony, we returned home to celebrate. Over eighty family members, friends, and neighbors joined us. Thank goodness the weather was perfect—a sunshiny 75 degrees that allowed the overflowing guests to relax outdoors on the patio or in the yard. Even the garage was utilized for entertaining. With our vehicles parked elsewhere, it became a bar.

With the birth of Michelle, Allan felt we needed a larger vehicle and I agreed. We both drove two-door Chevy coupes. He was right about needing a new vehicle. The boys had joined Little League baseball, so on weekends we were driving to and from three different Shaker Heights school baseball fields. Fitting three squirming boys, baseball equipment, baby, stroller, chairs, and other paraphernalia into our cars was challenging.

Our neighbor, Clarence, who owned a car dealership, suggested we purchase a van because it could seat up to twelve riders. At his suggestion, we drove to his dealership where a super-duper salesman sold us a van. Now we could transport everyone and everything in one vehicle!

It seemed like we had it all together. Allan was doing his best to be a father to my three boys as well as Michelle. Our home life felt stable and safe. We were the picture of a happy, growing family.

22

WHAT'S THAT?

Not long after Michelle's christening, my oldest son, Ted, began to wet his bed. And his unfamiliar behavior didn't stop there. He began to sleepwalk, too. He would sleepwalk around the room and urinate wherever he stopped. After relieving himself, he would wake up. All of this was strange behavior for a child of any age, let alone a seven-year-old. *Perhaps he has a bladder infection. He's urinating frequently.* I took a urine sample to the pediatrician. The results were negative for any infection. *Now what?*

My next thought was that bed-wetting problems in older children often involve psychological factors. However, I believed Ted's self-image was good. He was good-looking, well-liked, and athletic. He had played first base for his Little League team. The Beavers had won the championship for the 1968 season. In addition, he was an All Star.

Could having a stepfather be the problem?

Maybe. Perhaps I should take him to a child psychologist. The night before I made the appointment, I took a good look at my son.

When it comes to height, Ted was always above average, but, for some reason, he appeared much taller. *Could he have had a recent growth spurt? Perhaps. He looks so tall and so very thin. Look at him!*

What's happened to his sturdy arms and legs? He must have lost weight! It's like he's changed overnight!

Concern over my child's health contributed to a long, sleepless night. The next morning dragged. The pediatrician's office didn't open until 10:00 a.m. "Ted has to be seen by a physician today." The receptionist must have heard the urgency in my voice. Dr. Frank would see him at 1:00 p.m.

Allan, Ted, and I went to the doctor's Fairmont Circle office. Once Dr. Frank completed his physical examination, including drawing blood and collecting another urine sample, he called Admitting at Mount Sinai Hospital. "Your son needs more tests. I'll see you at the hospital."

No young boy wants to go to the hospital. Ted's fear was clearly reflected in his eyes. They were large saucers as they filled with tears. But he agreed to go, without a whimper. Perhaps he was too fatigued to do anything else.

I called Mrs. Mason to take care of the other children. Once she arrived, we immediately left. Allan drove us to the hospital. On the way, Ted shared the front seat with me.

God, he's frail! I don't understand why. He eats constantly. I've found Twinkies and Ho Hos hidden under his bed. Why hasn't he gained weight?

Should I call Chet? No! Wait until you know for sure that there's a problem. Chet hasn't tried to see the boys. Why involve him? Besides, Ted hasn't asked about his father. Forget that idea.

Allan and I followed the orderly as he wheeled Ted onto the elevator and into the children's unit. The large, sterile room could accommodate more than one bed, but presently it contained only one. This concerned me. Ted would be alone.

We found two chairs and sat beside the bed while the nurse helped remove Ted's street clothes. His torso looked painfully frail. His thin arms were black and blue in several places. Hematomas had formed when the nurse had struggled to locate a vein. The nurse placed his arms through the openings in the hospital gown and securely tied it together at the neck and back.

Once he was situated in the center of the bed, a frightened, wide-eyed little boy sat before us. The picture was heartbreakingly familiar to me, as the memory of his near-death experience at

246

Rainbow Babies and Children's Hospital flashed before my eyes.

Before leaving the hospital, Allan and I were introduced to an endocrinologist, Dr. Saul Lenk. Since Allan wasn't Ted's biological father, the doctor questioned me. First, he reviewed Ted's medical history, then mine, my parents, and grandparents.

Looking back at his notes, he said, "Tell me about Ted's father's family—his parents and grandparents."

When it came to Chet and his family's history, I hadn't a clue. *Was I supposed to know this information? Why is he asking me these questions?* I shrugged my shoulders. God, I felt stupid!

Dr. Lenk looked into my eyes, paused, and said, "Your son has diabetes."

Then it was my turn to respond, but I couldn't speak. *What's that?* Still reeling in shock and feeling sick to my stomach, all I could recall was that diabetes was a serious disease that people feared getting.

Perhaps I asked Dr. Lenk for an explanation, but I don't remember doing so. I felt sick, as if I had to lie down, but I didn't. What I do remember is that the doctor asked me if I would like a beverage. The nurse brought me a can of ginger ale. The cool, effervescent liquid eased the dryness of my mouth and helped restore my speech.

"Mrs. Lazar, I would like to do some testing on your blood sugar levels tomorrow. The nurse will give you the information. Can you come in?"

"Yes, of course I will."

Ted looked painfully sad. Even though no one had yet told him, I think he intuitively knew that he would be staying in the hospital. Running my hand through his soft, light-brown hair and kissing his cheek, I said, "Love you, see you in the morning." Feeling as though I was leaving part of my heart behind, I returned home.

After everyone had settled in for the night, I went to the bookcase in the family room, took a medical book off the shelf, checked for the page number in the index, and turned to the section marked Diabetes. There was one paragraph with a grave prognosis...*difficult to treat...a high probability of death.*

Reading this book was a frightening mistake. It was old and out-dated. Treatment of the disease had come a long way since the early '40s when the book had been written, but I wasn't aware of that at the time of my reading.

A mother is never as helplessly unhappy as when her child has a grave illness. Sleep eluded me. Concerned that my tossing and turning would awaken Allan, I went to the family room and lay down upon the couch. With my eyes wide open, I continued to stare at the stars from the view through the sliding glass patio door. I prayed for my son's welfare. Morning couldn't arrive too soon!

Allan left for work, Mrs. Mason arrived, and I drove to the hospital on my own. After arriving there, my first priority was to see Ted. The staff had to have been incredibly attentive, for my son's spirits were high. "Mommy!" His smile extended from ear to ear. Tears filled my eyes. *Don't let him see you cry.* We hugged. After a short visit, the staff directed me to the lab for testing.

A nurse drew several samples of blood from my arm. Of course — they were testing my sugar levels. Perhaps they had told me earlier why they were testing me, but at the time, all I could think about was Ted's welfare. *Will my child be able to live and lead a normal life?* Fearing a negative response, I contained my questions while praying for my child.

After my extensive testing, the staff technicians ushered me into Dr. Lenk's office where my wait seemed like an eternity. He had reviewed my results and found that my blood sugar levels were normal. I had never doubted that fact. Distressed and not knowing if Ted could survive with diabetes, I broke down and cried before asking, "Can you help my son?"

"Of course, we can. Millions are afflicted with diabetes. Child-hood diabetes is the most difficult to treat, though; you'll have to help us. Ted will need a well-balanced diet and insulin injections. He received his first injection this morning. How did he appear to you?"

Hesitatingly, I said, "He did look much happier."

"It will take a while to stabilize his sugar levels. Once this is done, he will be able to return home only after you and your husband have met with the dietician and have learned how to give him injections. You may need to change your family's diet. Are you up to the challenge?"

"I'll do anything to cure my son."

"Beverly, a cure may not be possible in your or his lifetime. But the family and Ted will learn how to live with the disease! Keep your chin up. We're working hard to find a cure. Make arrangements for your classes on nutrition and how to give an injection."

Changing the family diet would be a difficult assignment. Allan, the children, and I enjoyed our pasta, bread, and cookies. *Oh Lord, how will we give up pasta?* Pasta is a carbohydrate and carbohydrates convert to sugar.

Ted's diet had to be consistent in nutritional value each day. To help with menu preparation, I was given a chart showing how different types of food would convert to grams of sugar. I had to be sure to stay within Ted's daily allotment.

My second assignment, learning to give injections, was more difficult and required more homework. My patient—an orange—sat on the table patiently waiting for me. Picking up the insulin syringe, I stabbed the plump orange with the needle, pushed the plunger down, and injected saline solution into my mock patient. *Good job!*

The following day, the scenario changed a bit. *Today, you're the patient.* I sat in the high-backed kitchen chair, placing the fatty part of my upper arm against the chair rail, desperately trying to flatten out the injection site. *Courage, Beverly, you can do it.* Picking up the insulin syringe, I fidgeted, squirmed in my chair, and placed the syringe back on the table. *Do it! Damn you!* Once again, I picked up the syringe. This time, the needle pierced my skin and I pushed the plunger down and injected the saline solution into my arm. *Thank God!*

The phone rang. Bubbling with pride, I answered the phone with the intent of telling my caller about my accomplishment—this was a first. I had no supervision!

To my surprise, it was Chet. *Mum's the word.* He sounded too good, almost flirty. *He must be drinking.* Once I told him the news about Ted, his tone abruptly changed. He would meet me at the hospital tomorrow.

What shall I do? Chet will be angry and argumentative. Fearing that an

249

argument would happen simply as a consequence of Allan and Chet being in the same room together, I chose to go the hospital alone.

Allan had taken on the role of a supportive father. He had attended classes with me to learn how to care for Ted. In fact, he was more at ease and accomplished at giving an injection than me. He wasn't happy with my request that he stay home. Consequently, I had another night made restless by guilt.

Finally, I drifted off. Then morning and Mrs. Mason arrived simultaneously, disrupting my troubled slumber. *What will Chet say to me?* He was always unpredictable. *All I can do is hope he will speak kindly to the staff, the doctor, and me.*

Chet had said he would meet me in the hospital lobby. It was 1:30 p.m. — and still no Chet. *Where was he? He's a half an hour late. Guess he stood me up.* Before leaving for Ted's room, I asked the gal at the information desk to tell Mr. Kowalski that Mrs. Lazar had gone to their son's room.

As the elevator rose to the fourth-floor children's ward, my thoughts were of Chet. I felt sad and sorry for him. He had returned to Parma and moved in with his mother in her one-room efficiency. Most likely, he was sleeping on the floor. His favorite watering hole, the Coral Reef, was a ten-minute ride away. My ex-sister-in-law said, "He is wasting himself away drinking."

He had returned to the house a few times to pick up the boys for an hour of feeding the ducklings at the Shaker Lakes. Of course, I made myself unavailable at the time. Facing him was just more than I could bear.

The elevator stopped and a buzzer sounded as the door opened. I was relieved that Chet hadn't kept his word. Breathing a sigh of relief, I sat down next to Ted in the playroom. A second later, my darling son made a beeline for the door as a familiar voice called out, "Teddy."

Standing in the doorway with outstretched arms, and looking better than he should, was Chet. "You're looking good, kid!" He scooped his son up into his arms and hugged him tightly. Next to his father's large frame, Ted's frailness was accentuated.

Then he turned to me. "What's going on here?" His eyes nar-

250

rowed as if he was beginning an inquisition. Trying my best to explain, I became tongue-tied at his barrage of questions. He didn't seem to understand what I was saying. I was under attack. I was responsible for Ted's illness. Chet refused to believe that his son was the unfortunate victim of the gene pool—heredity! I had fed him a diet of junk food. I was responsible—no one else!

He hasn't changed, has he?

Even though I knew Chet was being irrational, I had a feeling in the pit of my stomach that I really *was* responsible for Ted having diabetes. I have always questioned whether receiving a shot of gamma globulin to prevent contracting the mumps when I was pregnant with Ted had damaged my unborn child in some way.

Chet moved closer to me as he pointed his finger, "You're responsible!" I could smell mints on his breath. *What's he trying to conceal? Alcohol, naturally!*

Taking a closer look at him, I could see that his eyes were bloodshot. Ted began to cry and rushed into my arms in an effort to protect me as Chet moved into my space.

Meanwhile, the other children and parents had vacated the playroom. Somehow, Chet and I had totally forgotten that our drama was unfolding in front of an audience. Thankfully, a nurse interceded and asked us to leave. She returned our sobbing son to his room.

Chet left in a huff while I lingered in the hall praying that he would leave the premises before me.

Returning home, I agonized. *How could I have placed Teddy in that stressful situation?* I continued to blame myself, when in reality, Chet's addiction to alcohol had turned his personal problem into a public spectacle once again. This was a sure sign of my codependency.

The less Chet is involved with the children, the better it will be for them. He is too far gone to give his help and support to his sons—especially Ted.

Three weeks later, we had a homecoming celebration for Ted. He had adjusted to his new regimen, but there were times when I knew for sure he had cheated: Ho Ho wrappers would mysteriously appear in the strangest places, especially under his bed.

I wrapped up 1968 feeling grateful; my son's diabetes was manageable, my husband was functioning well, in spite of his illness, and now I had a daughter, in addition to my three sons, to love and cherish forever. *How fortunate you are, Beverly!*

23

ARRIVEDERCI, GRANDPA

I remember 1969 well. It was a significant year. Richard Nixon was our thirty-seventh President. Buzz Aldrin and Neal Armstrong landed on the moon. Golda Meir was the first female prime minister of Israel. Sharon Tate was murdered by the Manson family. The "flower children" attended Woodstock. Jane Fonda and others protested the Vietnam War. The Beatles were now singing, "Yellow Submarine."

And what about Beverly? What was the status quo in her small corner of the world?

My life at this time was happily revolving around my children, my husband, and my grandparents. The boys were attending grade school. Michelle was a year old and Allan was working. As for my loving grandparents, they were aging. Grandpa Vincenzo would be eighty-four years old this year. Despite his advanced age, he remained my rock.

We maintained the same routine on Saturdays—we shopped. His mind functioned well, although his body was showing signs of age. His long steps and fast stride had changed to a slow, deliberate gait. The once straight- and tall-standing man's shoulders had rounded a bit. *That's what happens when you carry the weight of the world on your back.*

Grandpa, the knowledgeable real estate tycoon, no longer repaired houses for resale or mentored anyone in the trades. He had stopped overseeing his workmen.

Collecting rent, banking, and the concentration required for bookkeeping and accounting had started to overwhelm him. To address his frustration, Grandpa Vincenzo assigned me more and more tasks.

The change in Grandpa Vincenzo started in 1960, as a result of the anxiety from his employee suing him for assault. This was when he had his first nosebleed. He pooh-poohed it, saying, "It's nothing, I just bumped my nose."

During the following year, he had more nosebleeds, but because he managed to stop the bleeding, he adamantly refused to consult a doctor. Each year that followed, he had more bleeds and greater blood loss. When the occurrences were alarmingly close together, Grandma Caroline and I finally convinced him to consult a physician. The doctor said to him, "Mr. Martinelli, you have hypertension. Cut down on your salt intake and stress."

By 1967, his hemorrhages increased significantly. On a few occasions, I observed how Grandpa Vincenzo stopped the bleeding. He stuffed his nostrils with tufts of absorbent cotton, pinched them tightly together, and lowered his head between his knees.

Then there was the day when the blood profusely flowed from his nose, and he couldn't stop the bleeding. He called me for help, panic in his voice. In turn, I called for an ambulance and immediately drove to his home to accompany him to the hospital.

Once again, his doctors advised Grandpa Vincenzo to eliminate stress. To help him, I had readily agreed to take on more responsibility for managing his real estate affairs. By 1968, although he was viewed as the administrator, I managed the property.

Now, with firsthand knowledge, I truly understood what caused his stress: on-going repairs, roaches, rent collections, evictions, lawsuits, large water bills, taxes, and more. The "more" is the real kicker. A "For Rent" sign on the door meant *Vandals Welcome!* It was their open invitation to strip all the copper plumbing from a house.

And then there was the challenge of dealing with eccentric tenants, like the little old lady who loved stray cats. She converted her living room into a sanctuary for the neighborhood's stray felines. She brought nine-foot-long tree branches into the room and jammed them between the floor and ceiling. Perhaps this was her idea of a scratching post! Soil and shredded newspaper covered the linoleum flooring. The flea-infested menagerie ran wild. All of this was guaranteed to stress even the calmest individual. Given Grandpa's age, dealing with tenants, especially this kind, was just more than he could handle.

The days and months passed quickly and, for now, all was well. Although money was far from plentiful, especially after having all kinds of rental strife; nevertheless, it was December, and I had to prepare for Christmas. The boys were older and really into Santa and the holiday. Michelle, now a year and a half, would also find it fun.

…Hmm…It's December 14th, only eleven days until Christmas. The weather forecast for the day was sunny and bitter cold. The window thermometer registered 17 degrees. It was nine o'clock on Sunday morning when the phone rang. The male caller spoke with a distinct accent, slowly pronouncing every word with authority, "Is this Beverly, Mr. Martinelli's granddaughter?" *That voice sounds familiar.* I became apprehensive. *Something's wrong.*

"This is Dr. Solomon." *I knew it!*

The doctor and his wife lived in the flat above my grandfather's suite. They were longtime tenants. Dr. Solomon was a heart specialist at the Cleveland Clinic.

"Do not be frightened. I have everything under control. I was in my kitchen when I heard a loud thump and your grandmother's screams. I rushed downstairs and found Mr. Martinelli on the kitchen floor.

"I examined him. From the contusion on his head, I believe he hit the table when he fell from his chair. I cannot assess what's wrong with him. An ambulance is on the way to transport him to the Cleveland Clinic. Please, come quickly! Your grandmother needs you."

"I'll be right there."

As the receiver clicked, I felt paralyzed. Grandpa Vincenzo had been well for months—nothing, not even a nosebleed. *How could this have happened?! This sounds so serious.*

Damn it, don't think that way. Just hurry! Fortunately, Allan was home, the children had been fed, and I was dressed.

Leaving in a frenzy, I pulled the car out of the garage onto the icy drive. Before turning onto the boulevard, I paused to look at our front door and the beautiful Christmas wreath that hung on it. *Hurry! You don't have time to think about Christmas now.*

I was numb. Somehow, I sensed that a life-changing event was about to happen. The fleeting—but all too familiar—choked-up, wrenching feeling in my gut was telling me that my heart would be torn apart again. *Dear God, what has happened? Please protect Grandpa!*

In less than ten minutes, I approached the top of the Edgerton Road hill. The EMS paramedics were closing the doors to their vehicle. Dr. Solomon was with them. He thanked me for arriving quickly and apologized. "I can do no more for him now. Later, while at the hospital, I will check on Mr. Martinelli."

Once I went inside the house, I found Grandma Caroline collapsed in a living room chair. She looked up at me and attempted to wipe the tears off of her face with her hands. Grandpa's handkerchief lay on her lap. She had shredded and knotted it in her wait for me.

The tears continued flowing from her eyes. I went to the kitchen and took a clean dishtowel from the towel bar, wet a corner, and wiped her face. It was then that I saw the tooth marks on her lower lip. She had bitten it so hard that she drew blood.

Grandma wanted to talk. She gasped and sobbed, as she tried to explain what had happened with her broken English. Between her words and gestures, I was able to piece together the sequence of events.

They were having breakfast, and had each eaten a slice of toasted Italian bread. Her Vincenzo peeled an orange for them to share. While sectioning it, he dropped the orange, put his hands behind his head and fell forward. His head hit the table as he slid off of the chair onto the floor, where Dr. Solomon found him. In her anguish,

256

she enacted the screams. When her exhaustion silenced her screams, she collected herself and addressed me.

"*Il mio caro uno*, my dear one, *il mio caro uno*...Your grandfather could speak no more."

Holding her in my arms I said, "I love you, Grandma. Everything will be all right." I picked up the dishcloth again, and wiped away her tears before helping her put on a coat and head scarf.

So many thoughts were jumbled in my mind. This emergency was not like the others—the nosebleeds. Grandpa Vincenzo was not responsive. I didn't want to wrap my mind around the improbability of his recovery. The thought devastated me! I couldn't bear to fathom the serious implications. For now, I chose denial and held back my tears.

Once in the car, I looked at Grandma Caroline. Her tears had dried and her eyes were red and swollen. *Dear, dear, Grandma, I hurt for you.* We drove to the hospital in silence.

When Grandma Caroline and I were finally allowed to see Grandpa, he had been placed in a private room. Monitors and intravenous lines were connected to him. We were told that Mr. Martinelli had had a cerebral hemorrhage. Now I knew I had to call Auntie Sue. Other than Grandma Caroline and me, she was his next closest loved one. Caught up in the seriousness of Grandpa's trauma and the whirlwind of events, I had overlooked calling her, or anyone else, for that matter.

Auntie Sue arrived and our vigil began. The three of us spent the night at his side. Every hour on the hour, a nurse arrived to check Grandpa's vital signs, swab his mouth, and change the position of his body. When she lifted and turned him, the light blanket moved to expose his feet. Each toe was perfectly formed, disfigurement free, like a newborn. There were no calluses or bunions—very unusual for a man who had spent his life laboring in the trades. Allan's feet had taught me this.

Each time the nurse entered the room, she encouraged us to go home. "Please go. We're doing everything that can be done. You need your rest." But we stayed.

When morning arrived, an entourage of doctors entered the room. Mr. Martinelli was brain dead. The main artery, located at the base of his skull, had burst. The blood flow to his brain had been cut off. We asked, "What can be done?"

"Nothing!"

One doctor was matter-of-fact when he gave us a simple analogy.

"The lights went out. His brain will not function again. We should disconnect the respirator." Once I was able to comprehend what he was saying, I was left physically weak and totally devastated. Auntie Sue and I understood that Grandpa Vincenzo was brain dead, but how could this be explained to Grandma Caroline?

The hospital staff brought in a doctor who spoke Italian. Now that Grandma Caroline understood that the doctors could not repair the damaged artery, we all agreed to remove the life-supporting equipment and let nature take its course. We were told that, even without medical support, he could survive for several days.

Grandma Caroline, Auntie Sue, and I silently watched as the nurse removed the breathing apparatus. While she proceeded with her task, the priest entered and administered last rites. Watching the anointing of Grandpa Vincenzo's motionless body reinforced the gravity of the situation. Grandpa Vincenzo was now in God's hands. My heart ached. My long-overdue tears flowed at last.

Auntie Sue was emotionless—understandably so. She had had no time to process the event. The sudden onset of her father's state had been a shock to her. "Why, I just spoke to him earlier in the morning!"

The Clinic insisted we hire a private-duty nurse in the evenings. Grandpa Vincenzo would require more care for his comfort than the night staff could provide. We employed a matronly woman with years of nursing experience, Nurse Rush.

Grandma Caroline began to weep as Auntie Sue and I gathered our belongings. Lacking the words to comfort her, I put my arms around her. *God, how I wish I could speak Italian well.* Reluctantly, the three of us left the hospital.

Grandma Caroline insisted that she return to her home. *Surprise!* Maybe she was emotionally stronger than Auntie Sue or I had anticipated, although familiar surroundings do provide for one's comfort.

The following day, at six in the morning, my aunt and I met at the

Edgerton home to get Grandma Caroline. I drove us to the Cleveland Clinic. We waited helplessly at Grandpa's bedside, praying for a response. When Nurse Rush arrived at 7:00 p.m., we left the hospital. Although this routine was exhausting, we persisted, hoping that the doctors were wrong.

On the fourth day, December 17th, we left early. Upon arriving home, I felt drawn and tired, so instead of eating, I drew myself a bath in the upstairs bathroom. Drained and exhausted, I slid into the tub until the warm water reached above my shoulders. Just as the stress of the day started to wash away, I was convinced I heard the phone ring.

I called out, "Answer the phone." The ringing seemed to continue, non-stop. "Allan, don't you hear the phone ringing?" The sound reverberated in my eardrums. It wouldn't stop! "Damn it! Where is everyone?"

Reaching for my terrycloth robe, I put on my slippers and abruptly descended the stairs. Bursting into the family room, I literally spat out in anger. "For God's sake, why didn't you pick up the phone?"

Allan looked dumbfounded and shook his head from side to side. "What are you talking about?"

"I heard the phone ring. Why didn't you answer it? It had to be the hospital calling. Grandpa died!"

"Calm yourself, Beverly. The phone didn't ring."

"I don't believe you!"

Walking away, I became teary eyed and very irritated with Allan. I mumbled under my breath as I climbed the stairs, "Damn it! He was sleeping!"

Shortly thereafter, just as I was about to crawl into bed, I heard the phone ringing again. This time, I picked up the receiver. It was the hospital. Grandpa Vincenzo had died at 7:35 p.m. *Had they called earlier?* I asked the caller if she had called the house fifteen minutes ago.

"No. I haven't, nor has anyone else! Nurse Rush has been at Mr. Martinelli's bedside until now and she just left the front desk after requesting that the family be notified."

Dear, dear Caroline, my grandmother—what will we do without him?

Putting on my street clothes, I literally ran downstairs to tell Allan the news. Meanwhile, my mind ruminated over and over again about the call.

Had the phone actually rung? According to Allan, it hadn't. But, God knows, I had heard a phone ringing!

Did I feel the transition of Grandpa's soul as he traveled to another dimension? From my experience, I believe I did. But my understanding of the spiritual world is limited by my mere human status.

What I did know was that Grandpa Vincenzo was my rock, my protector. He was always there for me. Separation and a loved one's absence were not new to me, but previously there had always been the possibility that my loved one would return. This time the circumstances were different: Grandpa Vincenzo would never return!

Putting on my winter coat, I hugged and kissed Allan and the children goodbye and ventured out into the cold. It was 19 degrees outside. The stars and the snow glistened. Feeling child-like, I wished upon a star: *Dear God, give me strength.* Deep in thought, I drove slowly to Edgerton Road.

How will I tell Grandma? Vincenzo was her Prince Charming. Since the day he met her in 1920 at the United States Port of Entry in Boston, Massachusetts, they had been together. He had married her, provided for her well, and sheltered her from all harm for forty-nine years. It's a terrible thing to learn that the one you love is gone— forever and ever!

The time interval—the days between Grandpa's stroke and the day of his passing—must have given Grandma Caroline the strength to accept her husband's death. We both remained stoic and quiet as I drove us to the Clinic. There was nothing that either of us could do to change what had happened.

Upon our arrival at the hospital, we went directly to Grandpa's room. Viewing his lifeless body intensified our grief. Then we were directed to a small meeting room to sign papers regarding payment for services rendered and authorization to release the body to the undertaker. The hospital staff expressed their condolences.

Grandma Caroline and I returned to the Edgerton Road residence in the wee hours of the morning. After notifying Allan that I wouldn't return home until early evening, I sat and waited with Grandma Caroline for Auntie Sue's arrival.

I had hoped to catch a short nap in the large, peach-colored sofa chair in the living room. Instead, I found myself studying the minute details of every object in the room. A large mirror with flowers etched around its border hung over the fireplace. Matching crystal hurricane lamps sat on each side of the mantel. Family pictures filled in the space between the lamps.

Two chairs were set in front of the fireplace: the dining room hostess chair used by Grandma Caroline and a large, blue sofa chair—Grandpa's favorite seat. I could easily picture them, sitting in these chairs as they watched television.

My eyes continued to scan the room, stopping at the small, four-drawer cherry wood desk and matching chair. Grandpa Vincenzo often sat at this desk completing paperwork, dressed in a blue vest that would bring out his kind, sky-blue eyes. Overcome with grief, my gaze quickly moved on to another mahogany table, this one in the middle of the oversized bay window. A porcelain lamp trimmed with a gold leaf design sat atop the table. In November, I had hand-stitched new trim and a ruffled maroon ribbon onto its silk shade.

A large, maroon sofa was positioned next to the interior wall. While seated there, one could view the passing pedestrians and traffic through the bay window on the opposite wall. Centered in front of the sofa was a mahogany coffee table. The table's top surface was covered with glass to protect the hand-carved Japanese scene. Tucked in the corner was an antique Philco radio. The cabinet was made from mahogany. Lastly, I concentrated on the flowery design of the plush, theater-grade carpeting.

Why am I doing this? Why am I trying to cement every detail of this room and its belongings into my consciousness?

Think about it. You know why! With death, everything changes. These are the things your grandfather left behind—a collection of souvenirs from his life. With the passage of time, this room will change. By memorizing this place and these things, his memory can live on even if time changes everything!

Grandma Caroline and I sat motionless in front of the bay window watching the drifting snow. An occasional car drove into view and then out of sight. Daylight hadn't arrived yet. Thankfully, Auntie Sue's car soon pulled into the driveway, and our silence was broken.

December 18th was an exhausting day. Grandma Caroline, Auntie Sue and I were worn out from the trying events and sudden loss of our loved one. We were grieving and naïve about what to do regarding funeral arrangements. We contacted Mario Gallo, a family friend and one-time suitor of my mother's. He had been providing funeral services for nineteen years. With his assistance, the funeral plans were finalized before nightfall.

In our grief, one of our decisions was very imprudent. We chose a copper casket which was a duplicate of the one used for President Kennedy. We reasoned that Grandpa Vincenzo was always replacing the old galvanized piping in his properties with copper. He often lectured his workmen about the value of copper plumbing. The funeral services and casket totaled over $7,000, close to $50,000 in today's dollars! Our decision was a very costly one.

Money was less of a concern to Grandma Caroline than spending eternity beside her beloved. We respected her wishes, as she was Grandpa's widow. She wanted the best funeral arrangements made for Vincenzo, and having her husband buried in the empty grave he already owned—next to his first wife—was not an option she considered for long. The thought of Adriana and Vincenzo embracing in death was just too much for her to endure! Grandma Caroline purchased two new lots.

Beautiful poinsettia plants surrounded the casket. A blanket of red and white carnations and roses lay at its foot. Grandpa Vincenzo was dressed in his finest blue suit, white, starched shirt, and blue tie that would have matched his now-closed eyes.

Calling hours were from two to four in the afternoon and seven to nine in the evening. For three days, from the 21st to the 23rd of December, friends and relatives paid their respects to our family.

Allan brought my sons and Michelle to the funeral home. Our housekeeper, Mrs. Mason, accompanied them. She found a seat in front of the casket and held Michelle, who was now a toddler, in her arms. I attended to my boys and received guests.

The boys, who were six, seven, and eight years old, viewed the body. Allan and I simply stated to them that their great-grandfather had died. They would no longer see him when they went to his home.

Whenever the boys went to visit, Grandpa Vincenzo had an unforgettable ritual. He had his great-grandsons hold each other's hands as he led them into the master bedroom. Then they stood in front of the large dresser as Grandpa Vincenzo opened the top drawer to remove a small box that contained his change. Each boy left the room with at least five precious copper pennies, a nickel, and a dime.

Also unforgettable to the boys, and anyone else who witnessed them, were Grandpa's innovative landscaping designs and gardening techniques. Fertile land was scarce in Italy. He lived on a hillside, at the foot of the Apennine Mountains. Every inch of tillable soil was precious to him.

Grandpa Vincenzo grew the best-producing tomato, cucumber, squash, and watermelon plants in the most unusual places. Vegetables were grown everywhere: in the front yard, between shrubs, trees, and flowers; in the flowerbed that separated his yard from the neighbors; and lastly, where they should have been, in the backyard garden. First, a small plant would appear, and—seemingly the next day—multiple vines would grow and wrap themselves around the pine trees like garlands on the Christmas tree. Grandpa's green thumb amazed everyone who saw his handiwork.

Grandpa proudly walked his young great-grandsons around the yard to view his new creations—a cucumber or perhaps a watermelon tree. One of these summers, he told the boys, he expected a bean stalk and a giant to appear before them! The boys would certainly miss him.

For me, I had lost a parent. I felt alone and in a new place in my life. There were many unanswered questions regarding what role I was expected to take, but Grandpa Vincenzo had given me a directive long ago: he asked me to promise him that I would look after Grandma Caroline if any harm fell upon him. I had made a promise and I would keep it.

Grandpa Vincenzo was a wise man who knew his wife well. He understood that she would be traumatized if something happened

Grandma Caroline, following the passing of her beloved Vincenzo

to him. With him at her side, she felt welcome in this strange land that was now her home. Without his presence, she would be a frightened immigrant who could barely speak the language or understand our customs and ways. But even without her husband's help, America was her home. She had to remain here. For her, there could be no return trip to Italy.

My grandfather had clearly recognized that I sincerely loved Grandma Caroline. Now she needed me more than ever. I had already been dealing with my grandfather's practical, legal, and financial issues, and I would continue to do so with Grandma Caroline's consent. He had willed everything that remained after his divesture—real or personal property—to his wife.

One might say that Grandpa Vincenzo was house rich, cash poor, as only $20,000 remained in his bank account at death. It was hard to say if he was even house rich, as the gross worth of the properties that he had previously transferred had depreciated, and it was almost impossible to ascertain their value, since the area was now considered a slum. Ownership of these properties was not profitable unless you could do your own repairs. In reality, inheritance of these structures also transferred money-draining problems, legal battles, and ulcers to the new owners.

I had been chosen as Grandpa's "golden girl" not just because he empathized with me because of my mother's illness, but also because I had proven to him that I was loyal and trustworthy. I was there whenever he needed someone. In many ways, when Grandpa Vincenzo entrusted me with his business responsibilities, he placed me in an uncomfortable, precarious situation with his four daughters and their families.

The relationship between Grandpa Vincenzo and his oldest daughter, Beatrice, had been fractured from the time of her teenage marriage. She had moved to Buffalo, then New York City, and later to Los Angeles. By making her home outside of Ohio, their broken father-daughter bond never had a chance to mend. How could I explain to her why Grandpa Vincenzo made no provisions for her in his will? I couldn't. I lacked the answer. And how could I carefully broach the subject of their broken forty-year-old bond? I couldn't. Naturally, when she discovered that she wasn't referenced in his will with any sort of remembrance, she was hurt.

Then there was my mentally challenged mother. I felt that telling her that her father had died was my father's responsibility. I knew that I didn't want to be the one to tell my mother, for regardless of age or how long they had lived apart, her father's death was a significant event in her life. *How will she react to his death?* The day Grandpa Vincenzo died, it was Auntie Sue who called my father. Carlo responded, "Angie isn't well. She can't cope with the death of her father. I'll tell her when she's able to deal with it."

In spite of our broken relationship, I had to talk to him, too. I needed to show him respect, especially considering the important role I had been assigned in taking care of my grandfather's estate. I had to work up the nerve to call him. Overwhelmed with a feeling of nausea, I dialed the phone. The ringing stopped. The receiver had been lifted. Without hesitation or a salutation, I blurted out, "I have something of major importance to tell you!"

The conversation was short and to the point, and he, too, was disgruntled because Angelina had not been provided for in the will. He said that he wasn't going to tell her anything at this time.

Auntie Sue understood, for she was ever-present and played an active role in Grandpa's daily life. He had already gifted her with financial assistance and a substantial amount of problematic property. She was thankful that Grandpa Vincenzo had requested my assistance and not hers in managing the property.

Then there was Auntie Julia. She was incredibly hurt that she had been left out of Grandpa Vincenzo's will. That pain prompted her to disconnect herself from the family in many ways. We never saw her during the holidays or any other family functions. She repeatedly said, "I want nothing from anyone." She became the family rebel, a self-described "black sheep."

To say that I was in a delicate situation is an understatement. It would be impossible for me to correct the misunderstandings of the past. I could only continue to do what needed to be done for all parties concerned. Up to this time, Grandma Caroline had continued to live in her home with my daily assistance. Our plans were to sell her home, after which she would live with Allan, the children and me. We had plenty of room. She would share Michelle's bedroom.

The Edgerton property had been placed for sale. After six months, a couple finally made an offer of $37,000. That was only $1,000 more than the original purchase price. I wanted Grandma Caroline to reject the offer. *At least she should present a counter-offer.* Grandma Caroline did neither. She felt anxious about living alone; consequently, she accepted the terms as they were written. Fortunately, title transfer wouldn't occur for ninety days after loan approval, because finding a home for a lifetime of belongings would take time.

Grandpa Vincenzo and Grandma Caroline's house on Edgerton Road held so many memories for me from the time I had lived there as a child. It is impossible to overstate the importance my grandfather had in my life. He was my rock, the only steady force in my life through so many turbulent changes. Saying goodbye to both the house and Grandpa Vincenzo was like bidding farewell to my very foundation. Once again, I had to find a way to move forward, but, this time, I would have to rely on my own counsel and be my own rock.

Arrivederci, Grandpa.

24

WHY, ALLAN, WHY?

Allan had been presenting himself with normality and congeniality, and then, just before celebrating our three-year anniversary, I noticed his habits were changing. He couldn't work, eat, or sleep. His hands constantly shook.

Something's wrong.

No, he just had a bad night. That's all!

I kept quieting my voice of reason by making excuses for his behavior. As I've said before, denial is easier, especially with my codependent thinking.

Finally, my reasoning side prevailed. I checked his medication bottles. The bottles of thorizine and cogentin were nearly empty. *He must be taking his meds.*

But he could be throwing his medication out. Remember, the patients in the hospital would hold meds in their cheeks or under their tongue only to spit them out when no one was looking.

Allan wouldn't do that. Forget that thought.

Two days later, to the best of my knowledge, he still hadn't eaten anything, had hardly spoken a word, had slept all day, and had remained fretfully awake at night. *Sounds familiar! Remember your mother? Why do you keep kidding yourself? He's showing all the classic symptoms of depression. He needs professional help!* I called his psychiatrist, Dr. James Fried.

Dr. Fried was an old-school, Freudian-trained psychiatrist. My first contact with him dated back to when I was in my late teens. I had consulted Dr. Fried when I had questions about my own stability.

During our sessions, Dr. Fried sat with his back to me, smoking offensive cigars like my paternal grandfather. While I spilled my guts out, he blew thick smoke rings that floated off into the air. He had been ineffective in helping me to understand my problems, partially because codependency was not recognized at that time. My indecisiveness and lack of confidence remained while Grandpa's bank account was drained at a rate of fifty dollars per week. My experience did not build my confidence in psychiatry, but at least it gave me an opportunity to talk to someone about my troubles.

Oh well, what the heck. Call him…he is Allan's doctor, after all.

Dr. Fried recommended immediate hospitalization. The severity of Allan's depression enabled the doctors to bypass the customary commitment procedure. He was admitted to Fairhill Hospital with ease, because if he didn't resume normal activities of eating, sleeping, and talking, his physical health would be in jeopardy.

During his time in the hospital, despite my love for Allan, that damn voice of reason kept interjecting negative thoughts into my mind about his stability and my relationship with him. At times I agonized over the fact that in spite of loving Allan, I felt that I should never have married him.

Deep down I knew what was best for me, but I quickly dismissed this thought.

Why must I continuously deal with mental illness?

Beverly, you had a choice in the matter—you married Allan for "better or worse," knowing that he had a psychiatric problem!

Ignoring what the textbooks said about mental illness, I had still been clinging to my childhood theory—that love was magical and could cure anything, even psychosis. Allan's recent breakdown gave me reason to doubt my premise. And the debate between my left-brain—the voice of reason—and my right-brain—my heart—began again!

But he loves me and needs me! And we have a daughter!

Shortly before his release, Allan left the hospital without permission, walking over three miles to reach home. As he jogged up Fairhill Road to reach Fairmount Boulevard, he passed the park at Shaker Lakes. He stopped to pick a bouquet of wildflowers for me—a boyish and charming gesture that captivated my heart.

He misses me!

Be cautious—take heed, gentle heart!

But my heart ruled. Any inclination to back away from my relationship dissolved. Had I known what the future would bring, I might have paid closer attention to my voice of reason.

During his six weeks in the hospital, Allan was given a series of electric shock treatments. His response to the treatment was favorable.

Upon Allan's return home, he functioned as if nothing had happened. He had returned to being his carefree, loving self, resumed working, and wholeheartedly helped with moving Grandpa's possessions.

For me, seeing my grandfather's possessions removed from his home only served to renew the emptiness and loss I had felt with his passing in December. And, as for dear Grandma Caroline, I couldn't even begin to guess how she felt. Signs of stress and heartbreak were clearly reflected on her face. Her black hair had become totally gray overnight and the faint frown lines on her forehead had become furrows.

Saying goodbye to her possessions had to be difficult for her, too. What wasn't sold was stored in our basement or given away. Grandma's traditional furnishings and antiques would have looked out of place in my home. The house had been designed for the more contemporary décor of the '60s. We had decorated our house with Mediterranean furnishings: large-scale furniture with chunky, turned up legs, distressed or carved tabletops, and tile or rough iron accents.

Regardless of how they suited our décor, there were two things that I had to have: the stainless-steel coffee urn that had sat on the buffet and the antique mahogany barometer that had hung on the outside wall of the dining room which Grandpa Vincenzo had consulted daily.

My cousin, Luigi, was given the building materials stored in the garage. Allan took possession of all the hand tools, stacking them in our basement without rhyme or reason. Anticipating a garage sale, I had already placed three antique sewing machines, several mahogany tables, Japanese painted porcelain, and Italian pottery where Allan decided to stash his tools. To my chagrin, he carelessly placed the shovels, picks, and other soil-covered garden tools on the exposed wood surfaces, marring them. The distress marks devalued the antiques. I was irritated with his carelessness, and his nonchalant attitude infuriated me—he just didn't give a damn!

My disgust at Allan's lack of respect for my grandfather's things turned into concern, as some of the stored items appeared to go missing, especially the porcelain and pottery. I suspected that Allan was to blame. I had an uneasy feeling that things weren't quite right with him. It was out of character for him to treat something of value with such disregard. But no one had taken an inventory, so there was no red flag to definitely indicate that trouble was brewing. I was preoccupied with the children, Grandma Caroline, the estate, and removing the contents from the Edgerton home, so I convinced myself that as long as Allan was working and bringing home a paycheck, he had to be all right.

In September 1970, my life became a bit easier since I was no longer maintaining two households. Grandma was now safely living with us. Adding her to our family had been the right decision. Grandma Caroline was a comfort to me and the children. And she loved to garden—my flowers thrived.

While on the job, Allan befriended another bricklayer, Al Levin, who lived nearby in University Heights. They became close friends and often drove together to and from their jobsites.

Al was a black-haired, short, wiry, shifty-looking man. Allan was a sandy-haired, tall, muscular, and good-looking man. On the job, the pair became known as "Little Al and Big Al." "Little Al" was ambitious and well-connected in the building trades. He also knew how to manipulate people. My Allan was impressionable and easily manipulated.

It wasn't long before the pair gave me jaw-dropping news, "We no longer work for a contractor." *Put on the brakes, what's happening?!*

There was no stopping what had happened for the task had been completed. As the French say, it was a *fait accompli!* They had had an attorney incorporate their joint business venture under the name of L & L Masonry. By the way, the third party to the corporation was Mrs. Levin, Al's wife.

...What about me? Al must have thought I could see through his deception. Perhaps I'm too smart for him.

Hold on; don't think so highly of yourself.

They presented me with their business card and announced that they had plenty of jobs lined up for they were now working as subcontractors for Pine City, Incorporated. L & L Masonry would design and build patios and fireplaces for luxury homes in Cleveland's eastern suburbs.

Allan appeared to be taking control of his life and making decisions without my input! Despite this outward appearance, I worried about his partner bilking him. Knowing his mental history, my instincts told me to be skeptical. My voice of reason was becoming too loud to ignore.

Money soon became our Achilles heel! Allan managed to pay his bills, buy groceries, and give me an allowance, but when I asked, "How much money do you draw from the business?" the query landed on deaf ears! And when I questioned him further, there was no fussing and fighting. Allan just left for the evening.

The marriage had now developed into a brother/sister relationship. There was no companionship and no passion. When I discovered that I was pregnant, I was in shock! At the same time, the thought of another child was soothing; I would have one more little person to love! Pregnancy number five was nondescript—textbook perfect, no special cravings, no problems, and the same doctor, Lee Goldstein.

For now, Allan seemed very driven to make his new business a success. He went to work every day and appeared to be aggressively quoting new work in the evening. He would come home at six in the evening, shower, shave, dress, and leave at seven without eating dinner. "Al and I have a job to estimate. See you later." The "later" was often after one in the morning.

Curb appeal is extremely important in an affluent neighborhood, especially if you desired acceptance. One must "keep up with the Joneses." Previously, Allan had done our interior and exterior maintenance. Now that he had a business partner and their work was plentiful, he told me he had no time to continue with his home projects. Our beautiful home was beginning to look neglected.

One Saturday, I was told by Allan that one of the men who worked for L & L Masonry needed extra work. I had met the man a few times when he came to our home to pick up his paycheck. He would be doing odds and ends around our home.

Somewhere in Al and Allan's travels, they had connected with this shady character. I have repressed his name, most likely due to the negative influence he had on Allan. At the time, I was totally unaware of this man's dark side. For the sake of convenience, I'll call him Eric.

Eric was a tall, good-looking black man. Anytime I observed him, he was immaculately dressed, well-groomed, with clean, manicured nails—very suave and mannerly. There was no discoloration on his hands from handling brick and mortar all day. In my opinion, he appeared too sharp to have labored very long as a bricklayer.

Almost every Saturday during the summer, Eric would appear at our home to wash the windows or do yard work. *I guess Allan wants the neighbors to know what a big shot businessman he is now!*

Now that Allan was bringing home a larger paycheck, he thought we could afford another car. He casually brought the topic to my attention. Perhaps I was humoring him, as I didn't express an objection to the idea, but adding another debt to our already full payment ledger didn't make sense to me.

A week later, Allan pulled into our drive in a lime green Mustang Boss 351 coupe with black detailing. It was the sharpest looking little hatch-back, two-seat sports car on the road! This pony had a fast V8 engine and a dual exhaust system that rumbled and echoed back as you drove. Possession of this attention-getter was a definite status symbol and an ego-booster for Allan.

Although I thought the car was nifty and I would have liked to cruise around in it, I failed to see his purchase in that light. I was furious! It was expensive and totally impractical. Unable to contain my anger, I blurted out, "How in the hell did you manage to close the deal?"

"I signed a contract. I'll make the payments."

"The car is useless. Only two can ride in it. What about the kids? And we don't need three cars! What a waste! All you were thinking about was yourself. You're a selfish bastard!"

How did Allan obtain financing without my signature? Baffling!

After he went to bed, I began searching his jacket pockets for the loan papers. All I could find was the salesman's business card. I jotted down the information and returned the card to his pocket.

When Allan left for work the next morning, I called the dealership. The salesman was one of Allan's high school buddies. Allan had signed my name to the contract. "Your husband said, 'I have her permission to sign for her.'" This information failed to surprise me. I already knew that the deal stunk! Allan was fraudulent, but what about the salesman? *Wasn't he at fault?*

Needing a legal opinion, I asked my attorney for advice. "Can a salesman allow my husband to sign documents for me without obtaining my verbal confirmation? I want to void the loan and return the car." My legal counselor called the manager.

The bottom line was that this could become a confrontation, my word against his, "She said," "He said." I could initiate legal action against my husband, the salesman, and the Ford Dealership at my monetary and emotional expense. The car could be returned and Allan could possibly end up in jail.

Do I want this? Of course not, for I would be the one hurting. The matter was dropped, but not without trepidation on my part, since I knew nothing about his business finances. *How can we afford another payment and another child?*

For the next two months, Allan pleasantly surprised me by earning more than enough money to make an extra car payment. The downside of his increased earning power was that he was never home! He would routinely leave our home at 5:00 a.m., return at

6:00 p.m., skip dinner, and leave again at 7:00 p.m. with his business partner. They had jobs to estimate.

My fifth child's birth, like my third and fourth, was scheduled by appointment—induced labor on Tuesday, September 21, 1971. Allan and I drove down the same boulevard, Fairmount, on our way to the same hospital, Mount Sinai, at approximately the same hour, seven in the morning. There was no conversation between us.

I had carried this child through an extremely hot summer and was welcoming the birth. Despite the 80-degree heat, it was a beautiful September day. A few wispy clouds appeared in the clear blue sky. A gentle breeze caused the trees to sway. Looking out the car window, I noticed that the orange daylilies, marigolds, and other summer flowers had lost their blossoms. The radio was playing John Lennon's new release "Imagine." Thankfully, this time there was no announcement of a tragedy involving the Kennedy family.

Throughout my pregnancy, I thought I would give birth to another little girl. Yet with so much to do and little time to think, I hadn't picked out a girl's name. *Amy, Becky, Carolyn*—I continued down the alphabet without a decision.

If we had a boy, the name Michael had been my suggestion. For a brief time, after the loss of my grandfather, I found myself reading at night. *The Godfather,* by Mario Puzo, was appealing because of my Italian heritage, and the family name, Corleone, was significant to me; it was my great-grandmother's maiden name.

Michael Corleone's persona attracted me to the name Michael. The beginning storyline depicts Michael as a good guy. He is the third—and only college-educated—son of the fictitious Corleone Mafia family. He's a World War II veteran whose young wife had been murdered by the Mafia. Yet his intentions were to steer away from the family business—illegal drugs.

Not having finished the book, I didn't learn that Michael Corleone became more ruthless than his father until I saw the movie in 1972. Nevertheless, learning the destiny of the fictional Michael didn't change my love for the name.

At 10:54 a.m., Dr. Goldstein delivered an eight-pound-one-ounce, twenty-one-inch long little boy who would be named Michael Ronald Lazar. He was perfect in every way, except he had an identifying birthmark—a two-inch, bright red port wine stain at the base of his skull.

Why? Is there a metaphysical connection between Grandpa Vincenzo and Michael? I believe it was logical to deem it so. My grandfather had a massive stroke before he died. The artery at the base of his skull had ruptured, and now Michael was born with a birthmark placed at the base of his skull. *Was the location of Michael's birthmark coincidental or preordained? Or is this twilight-zone thinking on my part?* Perhaps.

After a four-day hospital stay, Michael was brought home. The older boys had to attend school that morning. Grandma Caroline, Mrs. Mason, and little Michelle were sitting in the living room watching Allan and me as our car pulled into the drive. Mrs. Mason opened the door for us, removed Michael from my arms, placed him on Grandma Caroline's lap, and stated, "This is your baby!"

Grandma Caroline smiled from ear to ear—the infant had won her heart without even whimpering. Grandma Caroline began to sing an Italian lullaby:

Ninna nanna, mio Michael	Lullaby, my Michael
Questo bimbo a chi lo do?	To whom will I give this baby?
Se lo dò alla Befana	If I give him to the Christmas witch
Se lo tiene una settimana	She'll keep him for a week
Se lo dò al lupo nero	If I give him to the Black Wolf
Se lo tiene un anno intero	He'll keep him for a whole year
Ninna nanna, ninna oh	Lullaby, oh lullaby
Questo bimbo me lo terrò!	I will keep this baby for myself!

Childbirth had always agreed with my body, and I had always recovered long before the scheduled six-week checkup. But for some reason, this time there was no significant improvement. I was extremely tired, and instead of slowing down, my bleeding was increasing. I was constantly running to the restroom to change my pad.

My intuition told me that something was wrong. *My son is a month old today. I should be feeling much better by now.* Ignoring my feelings, I continued dressing for the occasion, as it was my birthday.

As I sat on the edge of the bed, pulling up my nylons, I had to stop and take deep breaths. Putting on my clothing was a chore. I felt weak and a bit nauseous.

Wanting to please Allan, I said nothing about my problem. This is another example of my codependent behavior. I heard the doorbell ring signaling the arrival of Mrs. Mason. My sixth sense said, *Stay home,* even as I quickly filled my purse with extra pads.

As Allan and I drove off in his sports car, I became nauseous from the heat in the car. *Now what? Take deep breaths.* Fortunately, we only had to travel a short distance to the Girves Brown Derby, located just west of our home.

The minute Allan and I were seated by the hostess, I knew that going out had been a mistake. Blood began trickling down my legs. Feeling faint and embarrassed by what was happening to my body, I became red-faced.

Allan was perplexed and unable to give the waiter an explanation. He helped me stand and supported me by my waist as we exited the restaurant. The dim lighting and dark carpeting provided cover for my medical dilemma. *Please, dear God, don't let there be a trail of blood following me.*

It definitely would have been best for me to have stayed home that evening. After consulting with my doctor, I was sent back to the hospital. I was experiencing postpartum hemorrhaging, and would require medical attention.

At the hospital, I received a transfusion and a dilation and curettage. Mrs. Mason's planned one-night stay turned into four. The experience left me totally drained, longing to see my children, and extremely worried about my newborn son.

Returning home lifted my spirits. Mrs. Mason had given the children the best care, and Grandma had begun to spoil Michael— rocking him and singing to him several times a day. As for Allan, he hadn't changed.

Night after night, the pair, Allan and Al, drove off in the Mustang, leaving me with only rumbling sounds in my memory. This routine continued for months. Christmas came and went without

276

the usual festive celebration. New Year's Eve was also uneventful, and then—in a flash—it was May.

One Friday afternoon, Allan and I dropped the back seat down on our 1969 Chevy station wagon to cover the floor with blankets and pillows. Our family-sized cooler was filled with bologna, cheese, peanut butter and jelly sandwiches, and cool drinks. A large suitcase contained a change of clothing for each family member. Other necessities were packed in two large, brown bags, one containing paper products, the other, Oreo cookies. The Lazar family—except for baby Michael, who would stay behind with Grandma Caroline and Mrs. Mason—was going to spend the weekend in Niagara Falls, New York.

Initially, I did the driving as we headed east on State Route 20 to Buffalo. It was a perfect day for a drive with clear skies and a balmy temperature of 70 degrees. The open front windows allowed the wind to blow through my long, black hair. The boys were entertaining themselves with their ETCH A SKETCH, and Michelle was coloring. We had left home at four in the afternoon, hoping to make only two stops to stretch our legs and visit the restroom. We had anticipated being settled in a hotel by midnight. My objective was to stay as close as we could to the Falls.

By the time we approached the Falls, Allan was driving and the children had fallen asleep on their makeshift bed. Touring the area, we drove from River Road to Whirlpool Street without finding a suitable place to stay. We ended up staying within walking distance of the Falls, at the Clifton Victoria Inn. Our accommodations consisted of two queen-sized beds and a crib for Michelle.

We spent the next day browsing in stores with souvenirs, cheap jewelry, gadgets, and soft drink concessions. The children found the sight of the Falls thrilling. It was a happy day for all.

We left the Falls early the next morning. Upon reaching Buffalo, Michelle began searching for her favorite baby doll, Suzie, whom she loved and wouldn't let her out of sight, especially at bedtime. Much to Michelle's distress, the doll had been left in our hotel room. Losing Suzie was the only event to mar an otherwise perfect mini-vacation.

Allan had been the perfect companion and father on our sight-seeing tour. During the time we spent together, his behavior revealed nothing abnormal. He was better than good. But things changed soon after he returned to his normal routine the following week. On Monday, Tuesday, and Wednesday, all was well. Then, one night, he left home without Al to estimate future jobs, and he failed to return home until the following morning.

Other than needing a shave, he looked good for a man who had been out all night—even his clothing had no telltale demarcations. *What the hell was he doing? Definitely not estimating a job!* Now, I was paranoid and angry—rightly so. *Beverly, look for lipstick.*

Listening to Allan's heavy breathing, I knew he had fallen asleep. Now I could safely check his pockets. All I found was his wallet, which I searched. Hidden between the children's pictures was a slip of paper with two phone numbers written on it. I called both numbers, but no one answered. *I'll call later.* I hid the paper between the pages of my personal phonebook and placed the wallet back into his pocket. Disliking confrontation and dissension, I said nothing.

The next morning, Allan spent an unusually long time getting ready to leave for work. He had showered, in his customary way, but extra care had been given to his grooming: although dressed in his typical business attire, his wavy hair had been combed off of his forehead, and he smelled of cologne. I remained silent. *Guess he's not planning to work today.* I listened to the cadence of the exhaust system as he drove down the drive onto the boulevard. He failed to return home that night. In the morning, I called his partner.

"Have you seen Allan?"

"No!"

"Thanks." *...for nothing.*

What did you expect him to say? He's been Allan's cover all along. He'll say nothing!

I busied myself with the children. The boys were on summer vacation—no school, but summer camp in the morning. The day seemed to creep by as I placed Michael in his stroller and walked around the block repeatedly. Allan hadn't returned. *Where is he?* By now, I was angry—damn angry!

Twilight—and still no Allan. *Not even a call. Where is he?* Hour by

278

hour, I would ask myself that question and the answer remained the same. *I don't know!*

After two days, I went to the Shaker Heights' Police Department and filed a missing person's report, giving his description and a description of the car. By now, my anger had dissipated and turned into fear. *Had someone hurt him?*

With each passing day, my wait for answers became more and more agonizing. The lamp on the sofa table stayed on all night, as Grandma and I sat on the sofa and watched the cars pass by until the wee hours of the morning. If it weren't for my darling children, my days would have been agonizing, too, but thankfully, they were there and they needed me.

Nearly two weeks later, I received news. The car had been located. It was near downtown Cleveland, on a side street near St. Clair. It had been vandalized. The hood had been battered, in fact, the entire body of the car appeared to have been punched. The front and side windows, steering wheel, and dashboard were all smashed. The back tires were missing.

"Who could have done this? And where is Allan?"

The Cleveland Police Department couldn't answer these questions. They had impounded the car. The damage was extensive. "Call your insurance agent. He'll advise you."

The car was a total loss, and there would be a deficiency balance after the insurance company paid the loan company. *Cars can be replaced, but a loved one can't. Allan is still missing!*

Later that evening, I received a very surprising call—it was Eric. "Miss Beverly, please come and get your husband. He's here with me and he refuses to leave."

"Where are you?"

"Home." He recited the address.

I was stunned! The address he gave me matched where the Mustang had been found.

"I guess the car was vandalized in front of your home. Let me talk to Allan."

Allan refused to talk to me, and he swore at Eric. "You're a son of a bitch! I told you not to call her. I'm not going anywhere."

279

Allan's loud, boisterous behavior led me to believe that he was experiencing a psychotic episode—he was manic.

"Eric, do you realize Allan isn't all right?

"I do now."

"I'll need your phone number in case I can't find your house. If Allan doesn't come with me of his own free will, I'll have to call the police for help. He'll need hospitalization!"

"Please, I can't have the police involved. I am truly sorry. I had no idea Allan had a mental problem. He seemed cool. He said that you were having a marital problem and he needed a place to stay.

"Last night was the first time that I knew he was sick. He had this large, plastic replica of a Coca-Cola bottle filled with change. He brought it here when he first arrived. He took the bottle outside with him as he went to the car.

"I was looking out the window, watching him. He was taking the back tires off the car. Once they were off, he took the Coca-Cola bottle and began beating the car. The bottle broke and the change flew in the air. Then he finished beating the car with a wrench. When he finished, he came inside. I asked him to go, but he refused.

"In the morning, the police towed the car away. It's not uncommon for vandalized cars to appear on this street. I couldn't talk to the police because they've harassed me in the past, so I waited to call you." And, with these words, our conversation ended.

It was after eight that night when I put my five children into the car and drove to pick up Mrs. Mason. The glare from the setting sun as I drove down Fairhill Road was blinding. *I hope I'll have enough time to get home before dark.* I had grave concerns about being alone in the inner city after dark.

Once Mrs. Mason and children were safely home, I immediately left my residence in search of Allan. Traveling west once more, the setting sun was no longer a problem as darkness had set in, leaving me apprehensive.

Carnegie was not my favorite thoroughfare, especially after crossing 105th Street. Both businesses and tenement houses lined each side of the street. Occasionally a portable barbeque pit could be seen on a front lawn or driveway.

Upon reaching 40th and Carnegie, I took the right fork in the road. The neighborhood's character changed to bars, strip joints, and prostitutes. Here the streetwalkers were brazen, parading their wares up and down the street.

I had traveled this way once before, when I had to detour due to a fire. That time, Grandpa Vincenzo had been with me as we drove cautiously down the street with doors locked and windows closed. We had been returning from the market.

This time, I was alone and darkness had set in. I feared for my safety, but I had to continue—Allan needed hospitalization.

The streets were dimly lit. As I drove up and down between East 30th and 36th Streets, I could see houses and apartment buildings. The houses on this street were mostly alike—large, old, front porch, frame construction. Looking at them, it was obvious that most of the property owners were absentee landlords; consequently, the area was now practically a slum. It was rare to see the fresh paint, cut grass, shrubs, and flowers that generally indicated that the home was owner-occupied.

Eric had a well-kept home, judging from the exterior. I chose not to go inside, tooting my car horn frantically upon my arrival. After several minutes, I became exasperated at Allan's outright defiant rejection of my presence outside. I got out of the car and began pounding on the front door. I could hear Eric.

"Man, go out there. Do you want to take me down? Go! All this noise will bring the police here. You know I can't have that."

The door swung open. Eric pushed Allan out onto the porch, slammed, and then locked the door. Allan snarled, "Man, what the hell are you doing to me? Let me in there. I don't know this woman!"

I had to take a good look at the man who stood under the shadowy porch light, for he was not my husband; a derelict stood before me. Surprisingly, he didn't have body odor, but he was in dire need of grooming with greasy, uncombed hair, unshaven face, and long fingernails. His shirt and slacks were soiled and torn. His shirt tails hung out, he had no belt or socks, and the backs of his shoes had been crushed from walking on them.

Shock and disgust filled my being. This had to have been some kind of macabre mistake! *This man can't be my handsome husband...*but he was!

When Allan left home two weeks ago, he had been dressed in an expensive sport shirt and slacks. His wavy, brown hair had been meticulously combed, he had been clean shaven, and his fingernails had been trimmed almost to the nail bed. His Italian leather shoes were brand new.

"Allan, you're sick. Let me take you to the hospital. Get in the car."

"Who in the hell are you? I don't know you, bitch! Take me to the bus station."

"You'll have to get in the car if you want me to take you there." I would tell him anything to get him to cooperate.

A disgruntled Allan reluctantly opened the passenger door and sat down. *I've got to get him to the hospital, but how?* St. Vincent's Charity Hospital on East 21st Street was close by. I headed west towards Carnegie. While waiting for a stoplight, the flashing light from a sleazy bar caught my eye and, unfortunately, Allan's, too.

In the split second that I took to look at the sign, Allan opened the car door, jumped out of his seat, and exited our vehicle leaving his door open. Before I could close the door to pull away and park, he had entered the bar. Now, I was truly frightened!

Cleveland's nightlife had never interested me. My experiences were limited to the more respectable businesses in town where they served good food and attracted a higher-class clientele: business-men, sports figures, and entertainers.

I'd never entered a bar unescorted. This neighborhood freaks me out! What shall I do? Call the police?

No, go inside the bar and convince him to leave with you.

With my forehead perspiring, my heart beating loudly and fast, and my stomach churning, I entered the dark, stuffy, long, narrow room. The smell of whiskey and stale beer permeated the air. Several men and women were seated at the bar.

Allan had found a seat next to a voluptuous blonde. *Well, if this shapely bar girl believes she can fleece Allan, she is sadly mistaken. The joke's on her. She'll be the one buying him drinks!*

Feeling as if everyone's eyes were focused on me, I started making my way to Allan. He had engaged the blonde in conversation. He had been served a short glass of Scotch. *I wonder who ordered that. I can't believe the bartender served him. After all, look at him!*

Glancing around the bar, I saw a grubby-looking old man, whose clothing wasn't much better than Allan's, slumped over the bar. *He's had a bit too much to drink.* His lady friend was a bit younger, slightly rotund, and overly made up. She turned to look at me and smiled, showing her lipstick-smudged, bucked front teeth. A big, muscular-looking guy in the corner appeared to be a bouncer.

"Allan, what are you doing?"

"I'm buying this beautiful lady a drink. Why do you care? Who are you anyway?"

I laughed to myself, embarrassed to say, "Don't jest, I'm your wife. Let's go home."

"Bartender, drinks for the bar, on my tab."

Allan had to be broke. *How is he going to pay for the drinks?* Before the bartender could start pouring, I caught his attention by saying, "You had better collect in advance for the drinks or they will be on the house. He has no money! Perhaps Blondie will pay for them."

"Why are you starting trouble, you bitch? I don't know you!"

"Ask him to pay for the drink he has in front of him." Allan began to search his pockets, pulling each one inside out. They were all empty.

The bartender responded, "Someone has to pay for the two drinks I've poured or I'll have to call the cops."

Allan began pounding his fists on the bar. The big guy in the corner, who now looked more like a thug than a bouncer, jumped up, threw a punch, and began trying to pin Allan's arms behind his back. He succeeded, and began dragging him towards the door. I threw a five-dollar bill on the bar, saying, "Stop this. I'll get him out of here. Please, he's not well."

The police were called, but miraculously, Allan voluntarily left the bar and returned to my car. I took off and continued driving towards downtown Cleveland. A series of one-way streets challenged my sense of direction. I seemed to turn every which way before arriving at East 22nd Street and St. Vincent Charity Hospital, my intended destination. *Thank God, I made it!*

It was then that I noticed that Allan had been hurt in the confrontation. His lip had swollen and was bleeding—a legitimate reason for a visit to the emergency ward. On the pretense of needing a doctor for his lip, Allan cooperated with me and agreed to be treated.

When Allan wasn't in my presence, I blurted out to the doctor that he needed a psychiatric evaluation. The doctor agreed and we were escorted to the Admissions department. The clerk, Sister Teresa was older and soft spoken. Her demeanor definitely eased the situation, as Allan had become verbally abusive. He was infuriated.

A split second later, he sounded astonishingly normal, "Sister, she's lying. She's a mental case—not me!" He tried to turn the tables on me, but it didn't work. He was admitted to the hospital ward. They could hold him for a period of assessment, but, after that, he would have to agree to treatment.

I chose not to look at Allan as two male attendants escorted him out of Admissions into the main hall. An elevator would take them to the fourth-floor hospital ward.

Leaving Allan there and walking out into the cool night, I took a deep breath of air and sighed. *Thank you, God!* There were no tears on my part.

Returning to the sanctuary of my home, the steady pace of childrearing consumed my days. During my nights, I had no sleep, as a constant debate raged in my brain: my children's welfare versus living with a mentally sick husband.

At first, Allan was angry at the world—especially me. He thought I had tricked him. And, in a way, I had. But it was out of necessity. He refused to see me, but that was okay with me. I needed the time away from him. I, too, needed healing.

Later, when Allan asked for me, I ran to his side. I could not escape my enabling behavior. *God, how I love to punish myself!*

Allan progressed to the point where he could wear his street clothes and receive the cigarettes and food treats I brought with me. After several visits, he asked to see the children. Perhaps because St. Vincent's was a general hospital, as opposed to a freestanding

284

psychiatric hospital, I never gave a thought as to the effect that having the children visit could have on their emotional health.

History was repeating itself, for I had inadvertently exposed my children to the same conditions I had experienced as a child. Only this time, the patient was not my mother, but their father.

The fact that the children were allowed to visit meant Allan had improved. A well-groomed, nicely dressed, soft-spoken man greeted us in the visitors' lounge. If you didn't notice his dry mouth, slightly glassy eyes, and slower speech, he appeared to be normal.

Allan had saved part of his allowance. He went to the snack machines to purchase small packages of Oreo cookies, pretzels, peanut butter crackers, and drinks. Without these goodies, the children would have been too restless to stay.

When it came time to visit again, Ted, Steve, and Martin begged to stay home. Michelle and I continued to visit until Allan had completed his six months of inpatient treatment. He was discharged from St. Vincent Hospital as improved.

Remembering all my experiences with my mother, I hated the ambiguity of that word.

Improved.

25

THE ENTREPRENEUR

It was now winter, and there would be no masonry work for months. Upon his return home, Allan accepted a job making pizza pies with the neighborhood pizzeria. His mother, Rose, was disappointed that he hadn't wanted to work in her dry cleaning business where we first met. She would have readily hired him.

Rose's business remained profitable only because she did her own pressing. The height of the press required her to stand. She had to use a foot pedal to activate the steam. Dear Rose had diabetes, and like most diabetics, she began to have problems with her feet. Even a press operator without diabetes can develop foot problems—blisters and corns—doing this daily.

A series of small blisters appeared on Rose's right foot. They were painless, so she ignored them—the wrong thing for a diabetic to do. Gangrene set in and her big toe had to be amputated. Rose could no longer press clothing, and she was forced to sell her business.

Rose was a dear person, always willing to help. She knew that Allan and I were having a difficult time financially, and suggested that I look into purchasing a business for the family to run. Jumping into an entrepreneurial endeavor excited me—after all, both of my grandfathers had owned businesses.

This is how it came about. Grandpa Vincenzo's property was older, and located in an area that was now labeled a slum. The insurance companies classified the homes as substandard. Fire and casualty insurance was expensive and difficult to find. Joy, my best high school friend, recommended an insurance agent who handled affordable insurance subsidized by the state of Ohio.

After several subsequent conversations with my insurance agent, I mentioned that I was seeking a business opportunity. One of his clients owned fourteen pizza stores. Due to his ill health, several of his stores were for sale.

The Maple Heights store was perhaps the best deal his client had to offer. The equipment was newer and paid for. And since the owner had constant problems maintaining help at that location, he was willing to sell the business at a loss: $4,000 for a quick sale.

This opportunity in the food industry made sense to me for all the right reasons. Allan definitely enjoyed his new job at the pizzeria. Customers watched him as he performed, hand-tossing the pies. As for Rose, she loved to cook. And, the price was most definitely right. Still, I needed more information, so I called the building owner, who referred me to her attorney.

After meeting with the building owner's representative, I learned that acquiring this particular business really wasn't as simple as it had been presented to me. There was one big hurdle: the lease was about to expire. Unless the new owner could successfully negotiate a new lease with the landlords, the equipment would have to be moved to another location. Now I understood why he was practically giving the business away.

Another major hurdle was the hired help. Upon the sale of the business, the former owner would terminate their employment. He advised me not to rehire them. To me, that wasn't a problem! Why, I already had three employees—Rose, Allan, and myself. I went to take a look at the store.

The store was situated in a small strip mall next to a Convenient Store and a bakery. The pizza shop was the largest unit. A large black and white sign hung over the door—Angelo's Pizzeria. Plate glass windows allowed one to see into the interior. There were no frills. The walls had been painted off-white. A large counter top separated the open work area from the patrons.

The area in front of the counter was open to the public. There were four black leather booths and six red Formica tables for the customers who chose to eat in. A jukebox stood against the side wall, and a payphone hung next to the door.

The area behind the counter was for employees only. Patrons could view the work area: a fully equipped kitchen, pizza ovens, refrigerators, and more. The storage area, office, and restrooms were enclosed. Everything appeared clean and workable. Allan and Rose liked it and left the final decision with me. I decided to go forward with the purchase, contingent on the success of obtaining a two-year lease with the owner of the building.

Armed with references and my financial statement, I met the attorney at his office in The Standard Building in downtown Cleveland. Mrs. Fitica's attorney was older, kind, and fair. Knowing that he was Italian, I made sure that he was aware of my heritage — second generation Italian — and my Grandfather Vincenzo's legacy. We had something in common. Perhaps his knowing this would make my job of negotiating a lease easier.

At the end of our meeting, we had agreed on a proposal to present to the owner. My trump card was a list of other available locations. After all, the store could remain empty for an indefinite period of time if I chose to move to another location. I totally ignored the fact that I felt as though I was jumping off a cliff when I presented this information.

The result was that our final agreement greatly exceeded my expectations. The deal was very attractive to me because the monthly rent for the first year was several hundred dollars less than the rent the previous owner had been paying. Businesses are seldom profitable in the first year. The second year contained an acceleration clause, but the figure still remained less than what the previous owner paid.

With the deal buttoned up on the rent, Allan's mother, Rose, and I contributed $2,000 each. Title transfer of the business would take place in April 1972. I was enthusiastic over our new opportunity. There was no looking back, only looking ahead.

Before the transaction closed, the Universe dealt all concerned a decided challenge: Rose had a severe heart attack and was hospitalized. Her work future was uncertain. And Allan, witnessing his mother's incapacity, simply lost it!

There is no "rhyme or reason" to explain how a manic person's mind works. It was Saturday. Allan was supposed to be working at Georgio's; instead, he drove to the rapid stop on Shaker Boulevard, parked the car, and rode downtown.

He must have had quite the day, for at three in the afternoon, I received a call from the Cleveland Police. Allan had been booked for trespassing and disturbing the peace.

Why had Allan gone to the Soldiers' and Sailors' Monument located in downtown Cleveland on Public Square and taken down the American Flag from the flag pole?

At his hearing, he was adjudicated incompetent. Following his incarceration, he was hospitalized at Hanna Pavilion where he would remain indefinitely.

While all of this was going on, money had exchanged hands and the keys to the pizza shop were in my possession. There was no going back! The minor repairs and painting had been completed. My job listing had run in the classified section of the Sunday *Plain Dealer*. Angelo's Pizza was scheduled to open at 4:00 p.m. today… *Now what?* I had no help—no employees. I was scared, but like I said, I had no choice; I had to go forward!

Thankfully, part of the sales agreement allowed for me to purchase supplies from the commissary located on 150th and Lorain Avenue in Lakewood, Ohio. My plan was to purchase pre-made dough and sauce to make the pies—a real timesaver. My number one priority, childcare, had been previously arranged with Grandmother and Mrs. Mason, but my to-do list remained overwhelming!

Being a morning person, leaving home at six was not a problem. It was a good weather day as I drove out of our drive onto the boulevard. My first stop was the commissary. By 10:00 a.m., I was turning the key to unlock the front door, and making several trips to and from the car to take my supplies inside.

Once the car was unloaded, I locked myself in. Opening wasn't until 4:00 p.m. According to Marty, the previous manager, Mondays were traditionally slow. He often ran the place with only one employee on a Monday.

With these supplies put away, I went into the office to try to plan my day, the likelihood of my plans working out being slim to none. Fortunately, I had purchased enough dough and sauce for at least two days. Projecting ahead, I began to worry about having to return to the commissary so soon.

Thank God, all the refrigeration units are working and we're well-stocked with beverages. Quit looking for trouble. Just get through the day.

My next priority was to recruit employees. The silence was getting to me. I kept praying for the phone to ring. Certainly someone has read our ad by now. Why isn't anyone calling? Doesn't anyone need a job?

Well, you might as well make good use of your time. Make yourself a pizza for lunch.

God, look at those ovens: one four-deck Blodgett and one single. Hopefully, these ovens will be filled soon.

What's this?

Um, a pressurized deep fryer.

God, I forgot that we have chicken and French fries on the menu. We won't serve any for a few days. That's a scary piece of equipment with its locking lid and steam vent. Oh, it clicks when locked.

Quit playing around!

Then, thank God, the phone rang. The silence was broken by a call from the jukebox company. Someone would be out to service it today. Within a few minutes, Ohio Bell called. They were sending a rep over to empty the coins from the payphone. I had a contract and papers to sign. *Well, I can cross these concerns off my list.*

At the commissary that morning, I had learned how to press out the pizza dough. The pizza pans were neatly stacked according to size on a shelf over the work area. I picked up a ten-inch pan. Putting on my white apron, I went to the sink to wash my hands and scrub my nails. After drying my hands, I placed a ball of dough onto the pan, pressed it flat to fit the pan, and fluted the crust, as if I were making an apple pie. Next, I spooned the sauce on the dough, sprinkled on cheese, mushrooms, and onions. The oven completed the job. *Voila!* My lunch.

The phone remained silent until two in the afternoon when a customer called to place an order. He would pick up a large plain pizza at 4:15 p.m. *Get prepared, Beverly. Press the dough out ahead of time and place it in the cooler. Make a few pies in each size: ten-inch small, fourteen-inch medium, and sixteen-inch large.*

As I was working, there was a knock on the door. It was a young high school student. He was looking for a job. Customers were calling and coming in at the same time. Conducting an interview pursuant to a three-ring circus was difficult. *What can I do?*

"Robert, you've helped your mother making bread. Let me see how you handle dough. First, you'll have to wash your hands."

I proceeded to demonstrate the proper way to wash after which I placed the dough on a fourteen-inch pan. Then I asked him to press or stretch it out to cover the pan.

Robert failed terribly. The dough fell apart. He didn't get the job.

Three other young men applied, with two failing the demo. The third looked like an auto mechanic; his clothing and hands were stained. He didn't have to demonstrate his skills to be told, "No, thank you!"

It was dinnertime and the phone seemed to ring every five minutes. My frustration level was high. *Perhaps you had better close early. Tomorrow's another day.*

Then in walked this confident, chubby, freckle-faced, redheaded teenager, Aaron Wright, and, thankfully, he was the right one! He pressed the pie dough with skill and ease. His mother had taught him well.

"Aaron, call your mother. Ask her if you can stay until eleven tonight." He stayed. In a short time, he proved to be my right hand.

Allan's indefinite stay at Hanna Pavilion ended six months later. Upon his return home, he occasionally joined me at the pizzeria, where he demonstrated for the customers his knack for hand-tossing the dough. The business was beginning to thrive.

Many months before Allan's release, his mother Rose had been discharged from the step-down unit of Cleveland Clinic. Her heartbeat had been stabilized and follow up with an internist was a must. She refused outside help and chose to keep to herself.

Rose had been plagued with an irregular heartbeat. A month after Allan came home, unknown to family members, Rose returned to the Clinic where she suffered a massive heart attack, never regaining consciousness.

Rose deserved the finest of burials. Sadly, there was no formal mourning for her. Allan's older brother, Ray, had a mental condition, and Ronald Lazar, the oldest sibling, was in charge of her affairs. Concerned for the feelings of his mentally ill brothers, he chose not to have a religious service or showing of the body. Rose was unceremoniously buried beside her husband in a cemetery in North Royalton, Ohio.

Following Rose's burial, Ron had to file the estate in Probate Court. Filing meant that he would need his brother's signatures. Allan and Ray had to be told.

Once Allan knew the hurtful news, he was unable to cope with his grief. Depending on him for any help at all was out of the question—especially at the pizzeria. I was facing another roadblock. *Now what? Help!*

Beverly, reevaluate the situation. I had to admit that I was not superwoman.

You're managing a business, five children, elderly Grandma Caroline, and a mentally ill husband. I surrendered!

Angelo's was sold in August 1973. The sale of the pizzeria left me unemployed.

ON MY OWN

26

NOT AGAIN...

Where would I earn additional income? While drinking my morning coffee and reading the classified section of *The Cleveland Plain Dealer*, one ad caught my eye. "Wanted: Real Estate Agents...Will train the right individuals...Must obtain professional licensing...Flexible hours." *Now you're talking—flexible hours—exactly what I need. After all, I managed property for Grandpa and I've been a pseudo building contractor for the City of Cleveland. Why not?*

The real estate brokerage was led by a husband and wife team. My interview went well and they agreed to sponsor me. Equipped with study materials, a reading list, and samples of elementary math, I prepared for my new career.

My broker offered evening classes, twice weekly. The math proved to be my most challenging subject—reducing fractions to lowest terms, decimals, finding missing dimensions, geometry, finding square footage, and more. But my determination prevailed—nothing could or would stop me from succeeding. This was my big opportunity. My exam was scheduled for August, in Columbus, at the Ohio Division of Real Estate.

Teaming up with another prospective agent to tackle the exam made sense. Wilma and I studied and made the trip to Columbus together. We left home on Thursday, spent that night at a Holiday Inn near the testing site, took the exam on Friday, and returned home after the testing.

A hundred or more applicants sat for the test. It was a formal and judicious procedure: seating was alphabetical, proof of your identity had to remain on your desk, and restroom breaks were limited and timed.

The test consisted of three sections. The true or false questions were tricky, the multiple-choice section could be confusing, and the math? Proration of taxes was simply maddening. But I passed!

Meanwhile, in spite of being moderately depressed, Allan returned to work as a mason. When he came home from work, he would forego changing his soiled clothing and showering. He would barely nod "Hello" to me before he descended the stairs to the recreation room. His depression was blatantly apparent to me.

One night, after Allan returned home from work, the silence in our house was suddenly broken; the high-fidelity equipment began to play "I Got You Babe," and the knock of a pool cue hitting billiard balls into the pockets of the pool table could be heard. He was running a rack of billiard balls on the slate Brunswick pool table he had purchased for his own entertainment—a purchase I knew we couldn't afford.

"I Got You Babe," by Sonny and Cher, was our song. Allan and I often mimicked the couple, karaoke style. This song was for the good times—fun stuff and loving.

Although hearing our song out of context was frustrating, when the song "Vincent" became the only record left on the turntable, playing over and over again, I wanted to scream. *He's driving me mad!* He wasn't disturbing anyone but me. Grandma and the children were outside.

The ballad was depressing. "Vincent" was written about the impressionist artist, Van Gogh, a man—like Allan—who spent many years in an asylum.

Does Allan know that Vincent Van Gogh ended his life with a self-inflected gunshot wound? *Perhaps he had read his bio, but I doubt it.*

The song's haunting lyrics compelled me to listen, conjuring up images of all the mentally afflicted people I had ever known, the

298

abandoned who were left in institutions by their families—unloved, lonely, solitary souls. *Was this how my mother felt? Is Allan feeling unloved?*

I became melancholy myself. Perhaps I understood only too well the meaning of the words of the song. *Why are you doing this to yourself? Stop lamenting your past. You had better look at your future—you have children.*

For months, Allan continued to teeter on the brink of a full-blown depression. And then, just as the wind changes direction, he became manic.

One day, Allan called work and said, "I won't be in today." He left our home early in the morning on foot and rode the Rapid to downtown Cleveland. Later that day, his behavior made front page news. Thankfully, his name was omitted. The shame would have been impossible to ignore.

Allan entered the Third District police station at East 21st and Payne Avenue in Cleveland in the afternoon saying he had been robbed. Then he changed his story, saying that he had lost his money and needed a ride home to Parma, even though we lived in Shaker Heights. He was ignored by the officers.

When Allan left the station, he decided to help himself to a cruiser. Although no one knows for sure how he got them, the keys had probably been left in the ignition. The police contended that he removed them from a clipboard without their seeing him.

Regardless of how he got the keys to the police vehicle, Allan drove off in it. When he arrived at Pleasant Valley and Ridge Road in Parma, he stopped a motorist. The motorist happened to be a Parma policeman's son, and found it most peculiar that this "officer" was shirtless. Once Allan allowed the motorist to drive off, the young man called the Parma police.

Cleveland and Parma police spotted the cruiser and forced Allan to stop on Fulton Parkway near the Cleveland Zoo. He could give the police no explanation—only a big smile. And, by this point, not only had he lost his shirt, but his shoes had disappeared too.

Allan was prosecuted in both cities, but once I explained to the authorities that he suffered from mental illness, he was transferred from jail to St. Vincent Charity Hospital. This was his second admission to this facility.

After a two-month hospital stay, he returned to apparent normalcy, came home, and thankfully resumed his masonry work.

Allan's repeated hospitalizations had become a financial burden. He never seemed to work enough months to qualify for health insurance from the bricklayers' local union, and my present job selling real estate provided no benefits.

Beverly, you need a job with benefits pretty damn quick! Going back to teaching isn't practical; you'd need recertification. Perhaps you should talk to Auntie Sue. She may have some suggestions.

27

ROTOR BLADES AND REAL ESTATE

During World War II, Auntie Sue had joined the multitude of women who worked in factories. Auntie Sue could have been the poster girl for Rosie the Riveter. After the war, she helped make jet aircraft parts in the Compressor Components Division of TRW in Euclid, Ohio. She now had almost thirty years seniority with the company. She praised her job at the Tapco plant.

"You can't beat the pay, and the benefits package is the best. Why, Travelers Insurance is what you need with Allan and the kids! I'll bring you applications for the Tapco and Valve plants." TRW had four manufacturing facilities in the Cleveland area. "You can't go wrong working for TRW—so you get a little dirty. What's wrong with that?!"

I whole-heartedly agreed with her. "No, I can't go wrong with TRW!"

Auntie Sue picked up the applications and brought them to me. With my brief work history, completing the forms was fairly simple. But waiting two months for an interview was distressing. *Have they refused to consider your application? After all, you have no experience.*

Finally, I received calls from each facility and had my interviews. Then the waiting began again.

Three months passed. Auntie Sue told me, "I see new hires every day."

Critiquing the situation in my usual manner, I commented, "Perhaps they're hiring only people who have previously worked in a factory."

In response, Auntie Sue decided to look into the situation at Tapco. She went to the personnel office to check on the status of my application. "My niece has an application on file. She had her interview months ago. Why hasn't she been employed yet? It's definitely not because of her lack of experience. I've trained a few of your new hires. They weren't the sharpest tacks. Are you discriminating against her because she's college-educated?" The human relations manager said that he would look into it.

Auntie Sue's persuasive manner helped move things along. The following week, I received a letter from each plant requesting that I report to work. I chose the Tapco plant to be closer to Auntie Sue.

I do not believe anyone in the personnel department would have intentionally placed me in the inspection department with my aunt. Perhaps it was the luck of the draw, but that's exactly what happened. When I reported to work at 6:30 a.m. in November 1973, more good fortune followed me—Auntie Sue, being the lead inspector, was responsible for my training. This was just too good!

The plant ran around the clock, with three shifts per day. With job assignments, seniority overruled merit. Senior employees were allowed to displace or "bump" the less senior from their assignment. In a work shortage, you could even find yourself laid off. Auntie Sue was certain that I would be bumped the month after I started work. She was right; I was assigned to the manufacturing department—on third shift. *Here I come, ready or not.*

My new job was to remove burrs from the stator blades found in the engine of a jet plane. The blades varied in length, from several inches to approximately three feet. The larger the blade, the more of a challenge it was to remove the burrs, as you held the part under the small grinding wheel to edge and remove them. It was a dirty and dusty job.

Being a newcomer, it was likely I would remain in that department—and on third shift—for several months, until hiring resumed and I was able to "bump" someone else. Good Lord, now what will I do? Allan had just returned to work.

Somehow, I'll make this work. We need the benefits.

How are you going to adjust to working 11:00 p.m. to 7:00 a.m.?

I'll sleep once I'm tired enough.

Who's going to take care of Michael during the day?

After Ted, Steve, Martin, and Michelle go to school, Mrs. Mason and Grandma can take care of Michael. Then, I'll sleep. Mrs. Mason won't let me down — she'll work.

And, she did. So did I, until September 1975, when prevailing economic conditions resulted in me being laid-off. Then, I became eligible for unemployment.

Other than the normal everyday challenges one faces, our lives were—thankfully—drama-free. Allan remained employed. While he was back at work, his firm was one of the many contractors used to build the Coliseum, a sports arena in Richfield, Ohio. Having such a long drive to work, he left before daylight and returned home long after darkness set in.

When the phone rang one afternoon, I had a premonition that all was not well with Allan. A clerk from Suburban Community Hospital called, saying, "Your husband has been admitted to the hospital for a back injury."

"What happened?"

"He can tell you himself." Admitting connected me to his room.

According to Allan, he had been holding a concrete block when he slipped and fell from a six-foot-high scaffold. Amazingly, he said he had landed on his feet with the cement block still in his hands. All I could say was, "Wow!" *Allan sounds like Superman!*

Although his story sounded a bit fictitious to me, Allan had no broken bones. *Thank God!* However, by landing feet-first on the ground, he had jarred his spine and herniated a disc in his back. He couldn't stand or walk without assistance, and he was in excruciating pain. His long, drawn-out, slurred words—and intermittent pauses to catch his breath—only served to confirm that he was suffering!

After determining that his injuries were not life-threatening, the emergency crew had transported him to Suburban Community

Hospital in Warrensville Heights, close to our home. Allan was placed in traction for a week and fitted with a back brace. Upon returning home, he had recovered to the point that he could walk with a walker.

After several weeks, Allan progressed to using a cane to walk, but the ongoing, radiating pain in his lower back remained. The pain intensified when he bent down, tried to lift anything heavy, or had to stand or sit for prolonged periods. Using prescription pain medication while working was prohibited. *Without a strong, healthy back, how can Allan continue working as a bricklayer?*

The accident significantly altered Allan's emotional well-being. He withdrew into a catatonic state of depression, failing to speak or eat. This resulted in his seventh hospitalization for psychiatric reasons. He returned for the third time to St. Vincent Charity Hospital.

Beverly, don't you deserve moral support? You are always there for every-one, but who is there for you?

No one. Isn't that the role of a husband?

Of course, it is, but he's mentally ill. You already knew that. Are you having second thoughts about marriage again?

The strain of being supportive to so many was starting to wear heavily on me. The last thing I wanted to do was to feel sorry for myself, but that's what I was doing. Our debts were mounting once more, and now my unemploy-ment benefit was running out. With my layoff from TRW, my insurance benefits had been terminated. Fortunately, Workman's Compensation would be responsible for Allan's recent medical bills, but Grandma, the children, and I were in jeopardy.

What shall I do?

Real estate. After all, your license is still active. Find a new broker.

I was drinking my morning coffee and browsing through the classified ads in the Plain Dealer when I came across one that read, "Hilltop's residential offices are open seven days a week, from 9:00 a.m. to 9:00 p.m., for your convenience."

Working for a company that's open twelve hours a day will give me lots of flexibility. I'll call them.

Once Hilltop received a copy of my license, I began my sales training. This would become my chosen career. I loved to mingle with the other sales associates—especially the successful ones who became my mentors.

Aren't you selfish! You're not spending enough time at home. The children need you!

It's all right—Mrs. Mason's there and I'm paying the bills.

I was driven to succeed! I busied myself with learning to be a better real estate agent, working hard, and positively reframing all the negative happenings in my life.

At this time, Allan was working in Cleveland. How he decided to become a parking lot attendant was beyond me. The parking lot owner had a series of lots scattered throughout downtown from Prospect Avenue to Ontario. As long as Allan wasn't idle, sitting around at home and becoming depressed, I was happy.

28

OUT OF CONTROL

Perhaps there were signs of his impending mania. If there were, I chose to overlook them because I was too busy climbing my ladder to success. I ignored the fact that Allan had purchased new clothing, shoes, and expensive aftershave. He was dressing too well for a parking lot attendant, and, unbeknownst to me, returning home from work later and later each night.

No one—Grandma, Mrs. Mason, or the children—said anything to me. Perhaps they thought I knew his hours, but I didn't. I was showing homes seven days a week, even on holidays.

All my mentoring had paid off. I began my rise to the top of my profession in 1977. It was taxing working all those hours, managing a family, and attempting to be a wife, but I was fueled by my success.

My professional lifestyle gave Allan a free ticket to do as he pleased with his wages and time. As my income grew, my concern over his need to contribute to the bills ceased to exist.

And I was enjoying myself, too, having occasional lunches with admiring colleagues. The attention was flattering and helped me start to build a new, more outgoing image of myself. I started to let go of some of my insecurities. Building your own ego is second nature for sales associates. The lunches were an opportunity to pick their brains and learn things about the industry that weren't taught in class.

One day, chauffeuring couples around the city to look at homes—normally a very rewarding task—became the cause of a great deal of stress. A group of people had positioned themselves on the corner of the street to watch as I showed a home to my clients—a cultured, charming, black married couple. *I'm a bundle of nerves.* The racist group gestured and shouted obscenities at my clients as we pulled onto the driveway. I apologized to the couple for the crude crowd's behavior and showed the home anyway. The potentially volatile situation left me fearing for my safety and that of my clients.

If I experience this again, I'll quit!

On my drive home from the office, I felt troubled and sad. My thoughts moved from real estate to Allan's recent behavior. *What's with Allan? He's listening to those songs and lyrics over and over again. He must be depressed.*

A couple of days ago, Allan had come home from work, nodded "Hello," and had gone directly to the basement. Within seconds, the stereo could be heard playing, followed by the sound of a pool stick hitting the cue ball and then the click-click-click of the billiard balls as they fell into position on the pool table.

Paul McCartney and Wings' song, "Let 'Em In," a tribute to the assassinated heroes of the '60s, spun around and around on the Pioneer turntable. Granted, the tune was on the Billboard Top 100 List, so thousands had shown an appreciation for the song, but hearing it once was enough for me.

Then it was the Hollies' turn to tell a story about a "long cool woman in a black dress." Listening to these lyrics over and over again was *not* cool to me.

On this particular day, Allan's choice of music affected me like chalk screeching on a blackboard. Even our older boys made a smart-alecky comment about the nonsensical repetition. Grandma put cotton in her ears and Mrs. Mason hummed along—a sad, but amusing, scene. I left for work. *Beverly, stop ruminating about yesterday! Return to the present!*

The day had been nerve-racking. *I don't think I can keep working under these volatile conditions. That crowd today was frightening! I've got enough to stress me out at home.* I felt burned out. Skipping dinner, kissing the children, and saying my "Goodnight," I lay down upon our king-sized bed, closed my eyes, and slept soundly until six in the morning, my normal wakeup time.

Stretching and squirming about the bed, I sat up. Squinting for lack of sunlight while looking around the room, my gaze fixed on the smooth, untouched sheets on Allan's side of the bed. *Where is he? Perhaps he's downstairs?*

Rising, I gazed out the window. The driveway was empty—no car. *Where is he?* I've written this storyline before. Déjà vu!

Allan finally arrived home, less than twenty-four hours later, looking clean but tired. Without any explanation, he removed his clothes and immediately fell asleep. And what did Beverly do? She did what she had done in the past: she searched his clothing and wallet for clues.

Where has he been? There was a Cleveland phone number on a folded slip of paper in his wallet. *Call it.*

This time, a young lady answered. Her voice was melodic, and her accent and choice of words led me to believe she was Southern and possibly black. Yes, she knew Allan and had seen him last night. "He had a lot to drink last night, so he stayed with me."

"Really?! Why didn't he call me if he was at a bar? I would have picked him up."

"Look, Beverly, it's not what you're thinking—I like him. He's clean-cut and handsome, but I need the money he gives me." *She even knows my name! What else does she know?* I had heard enough!

Before I could hang up the receiver, I began to shake with rage. Now I understood what was meant by the phrase, "Hell hath no fury like a woman scorned!"

How could the son of a bitch do this to me?! I wanted to kill him! Was she the "long cool woman in a black dress?"

Instantly, an inner voice attempted to control my primitive instincts and interjected reason into my thoughts. *There is no denying that Allan has been depressed. But you've been too stressed and busy to look at his behavior. Why didn't you talk to Allan the night his music was driving you crazy?*

Work! Work! That's all you think about. Had he been hospitalized back then, perhaps he would have behaved himself.

Quit blaming yourself! You can't excuse his infidelity, even if he was psychotic at the time.

Many times, I had suppressed my anger towards Allan. I had wanted to kick, beat, and throw things, but I hadn't. I had stuffed my feelings inside for such a long time that now my emotional state was unmanageable. Now, trying to take control of my behavior was like having to grasp the very air we breathe.

Returning to a primitive state of mind, I found myself standing in front of the cutlery drawer, picking up a knife, and wanting to plunge it into him! Mayhem and destruction were all that I could think of. I began stabbing the kitchen cutting board. With the loud throbbing of my heart sounding in my ears, I barely heard the soft, gentle voice of Grandma Caroline, "Beverlena, what's wrong?"

Wiping perspiration from my brow with my shirt sleeve, I dropped the knife. *You're out of control. You're a psychology major. Shame on you! Violence is an unhealthy way to express your anger.* I returned the knife to its place in the drawer and sat down. My own behavior astonished me, never before having experienced such fury!

Grandma Caroline and I talked. She had overheard my side of the conversation with Allan's lady. She knew Allan had betrayed me, and she understood my anger. Even her dear Vincenzo had strayed, and the temptress was her own sister. Grandma Caroline told me that her husband and her sister had gone to downtown Cleveland together one morning and failed to return until early evening. Upon their return, Grandma Caroline's sister was sporting a Longines 28 carat gold watch.

Grandma Caroline had managed to turn the other cheek. Without Vincenzo, she would have become a homeless bag lady. After all, Grandpa Vincenzo provided everything for her. She had it all because of him.

My situation was different. My standard of living would not take a nosedive. I had become the breadwinner and could not stand the thought of my man having sex with another woman, even though Allan and I had a celibate lifestyle at the time. Learning of his

310

infidelity triggered feelings of inadequacy and humiliation.

Grandma Caroline and I concluded that men were easily seduced—driven by the desire for sexual adventure. And some men feel no guilt; for them, infidelity was acceptable—a part of their values.

I had studied all the psychobabble and knew that, for Allan, seeing a prostitute could be symptomatic of his illness, part of his reckless pursuit of gratification. He was in control of the relationship. It was his escape from responsibility.

For now, I had to say nothing, and keep my emotions in check. When the time was right, Allan and I would talk. Meanwhile, I would figure out how to get him the psychological help he needed, and initiate divorce proceedings.

I left for work the next morning to cover my floor time. While driving, the tears began to flow. In the solitude of the drive, I came to realize that I had created the same sad scenario for myself and children that I had grown up with: an absent mother and a cheating father. Again, my childish notion that love could heal everything—even mental illness—was proven false.

Reaching the office, I desperately tried not to think about my life, but the other sales associates were gone by the time I arrived, and the phone failed to ring, leaving me alone with my thoughts.

Like my father, I married a psychotic. The reality was that no amount of love from my father could have prevented my mother's dysfunctional and scandalous behavior. Likewise, no amount of love or actions on my part could have stopped Allan from the embarrassing and scandalous actions he chose. How naïve and narcissistic it had been of me to think that my love could change Allan's behavior.

And again, like my father, I was delivered a final knockout punch by my own psychotic spouse, who acted out because of his mental instability. Having a spouse I can't trust is the antithesis of what my heart desired for us.

To cope with my situation, I chose to become a workaholic and like my father, I was seldom home. Grandma Caroline and Mrs. Mason are there for my children.

Didn't your experience teach you anything? You're rationalizing again. Children need their mother!

That evening, coming from work, traffic was light on Mayfield and Warrensville Center. I pulled into our drive at 9:15 p.m. Stressed to the bone, my aching body sought the comfort that only sleep could provide.

The school year had commenced and the children went to bed early. They were in their rooms. The bedroom doors were open, welcoming me to walk in. Ted and Steve were awake. Glancing at the large aquarium that sat on the first shelf of the bookcase, I couldn't help but notice that the water was cloudy and the rocks were covered with moss. In a whisper I said, "Have Mrs. Mason help you clean the fish tank tomorrow or you'll soon find another betta or angelfish dead. Lunch money's on the kitchen table. I love you. Goodnight."

Entering Martin and Michael's room, I found them asleep in spite of the noise from the gerbils scampering around and around on their exercise wheel. Martin's grease-covered clothing was scattered on the floor in front of his bed. *Guess he was playing mechanic on the dirt bike in the garage today. We'll talk tomorrow.*

Lastly, I observed Grandma Caroline and Michelle. My darling daughter was sleeping peacefully. Grandma Caroline was propped up in her usual manner on two fluffy pillows, wide awake. She nodded "Hello," and whispered in her broken English, "Allan goes to work."

Relieved, I responded, "That's good." I was just too tired to deal with him. I kissed my sleeping child and Grandma Caroline. "Goodnight."

Now it's my turn to sleep. But the voices in my head were at it again. *When and what will you say to Allan?* Tossing and turning from one side of the bed to the other, the mock rehearsal of our conversation began. First, Beverly asked a question, trying hard not to be confrontational. Then, Allan responded defiantly.

Good Lord, how does someone discuss infidelity? Playing out this situation in my head and putting myself in Allan's shoes was not easy, but it was my attempt to work through the delicate subject without confrontation. Becoming enraged and releasing pent-up fury was not the answer.

We need to act like grown-ups.

God, you're unrealistic—after all—he's a mental case! Sleep finally put a stop to the chatter in my head.

Being a creature of habit, most of my day would begin before dawn. A feeling of peace and joy permeates my heart in the tranquility of the morning. This was my time to slowly sip coffee, plan my day, and—most of all—savor the silence before the children woke up. But tomorrow would have to be different! I'd have to confront Allan.

The next morning, I woke up at my usual early time. I discovered the top sheets and coverlet on my side of the bed had been pulled from beneath the mattress and a pillow had been placed in the middle of the bed. *Did I do that?* With the tug-of-war taking place in my brain, I certainly could have. After my fretful slumber, every nerve in my body was on edge. Even my hands seemed to tremble. *For God's sake, calm down!*

As usual, I gazed out the window. Allan was home. Taking a deep breath, I sighed. *You've got to be honest. Talk to him. Tell him what you know. Tell him you want what's best for him and that you suspect he's not well.*

As I dressed for the day, my inner monologue continued. Looking out the window again, I noted that the morning haze was clearing. I thought to myself, *I'd better get on with it. If I don't, it'll be time for the children to get ready for school.*

The early morning air cooled my skin as I approached the stairs to the first floor. The front door had been left open. *Who did this?*

Allan, who else?

Then I noticed that our collection of prints, watercolors, and miniature oil paintings was missing from the front hallway. Someone had removed the artwork. *Were we robbed?*

All thoughts about Allan's indiscretion ceased. The overriding thought of having my home robbed made me feel unsafe, fearful, and violated. We're lucky the thieves hadn't come upstairs.

Beverly, you're wrong. Something's not right. Surely, Allan would have confronted the thieves or alerted you if he had come home and discovered the theft.

Then I entered the kitchen. *God, what a mess!* The double-sided sink was completely filled. On one side, clean and dirty dishes were carelessly stacked together. Some had been broken. The other side was filled with pots, pans, and the percolator. Used coffee grounds, bacon grease, and the remains of fried eggs were intermingled among the dishes and flatware.

Then I looked at the oak trestle table. A portion of my art collection had been placed upon the top of it in a surrealistic manner. Some pieces were facing up, others down. Several larger pictures were standing up, others resting flat on the chairs and the bench. A self-portrait of Salvador Dali was upside-down. A half-eaten bowl of Kellogg's Raisin Bran occupied a place at the table.

It was impossible to hold back my tears. I knew that the eye cannot perceive balance or symmetry when one is experiencing the visual distortions of a manic episode. The abstract becomes the norm. *Only Allan could have done this! No other person could have done something so bizarre.*

There was more. The cabinetry in the family room had been emptied and the contents randomly strewn around the room. The liquor bottles were now lined up on the fireplace mantle. Books were placed like children's blocks in towering stacks throughout the room. Another group of pictures from over the sofa bed had been removed from the wall and placed haphazardly on the shelves of the open cupboards. Allan's work shirt had been tossed on the game table.

The screen door to the patio was wide open. I stepped outside. The ivy and fern plants that had previously adorned the family room were now on the patio deck. *Obviously, Allan has been here, but where is he now?*

Chilled by the morning breeze, I considered getting a sweater as I scanned the backyard looking for Allan. *Weather-wise, the day will be perfect. There's not a cloud in the sky.*

I looked at the children's seven-foot round sandbox that had become my flower garden. *How beautiful!* Now, red geraniums, and white, yellow, and burnt orange mums grew in the space that once contained sand. The flowers surrounded a five-foot-tall statue of Saint Francis holding a tiny bird in his hand.

Just the day before, Grandma Caroline had sat on the sandstone ledge overlooking the flowers, the sun shining brightly upon her

314

back. Her eyes were fixed on the flowers as she removed the dead petals, stems, and leaves. Her lips were closed, yet they turned upward as if she was about to smile—an expression artists reserve for a Madonna. Her normally plain face appeared radiant and beautiful.

Staring at her from inside the kitchen window, I had tried to decipher her thoughts. She had looked so happy and serene—like she had just received a gift that connected her to Godlike energy. It was the same look she had had when she cradled newborn Michael in her arms and sang him an Italian lullaby. But that was yesterday.

My eyes continued scanning our yard for Allan. Then I saw him. He was lying in the far corner next to the shrubs and bushes that formed a natural fence. He was shirtless and oblivious to my stare. Surprisingly, he was also oblivious to the dew and chilly morning air.

All I could feel for him was empathy and compassion. *He's sick. Perhaps I can convince him to go to the hospital. Get him to come inside.*

I could hear chatter and running water. Soon Grandma Caroline and the children would come down for breakfast. *Tell them what's happening. They should get dressed and remain upstairs until the school bus arrives. Shield them from this, if you can. You can't do this alone. You need help. Call Betty White.* Mrs. White was my beautiful, blue-eyed neighbor. Her son John John was a change-of-life baby. *She has wisdom way beyond her years. She'll understand. I can count on her. She can take the children to her home. They can wait with her son, John John, for the school bus.*

My next call was to the Shaker Heights Police Department. After explaining the situation, the dispatcher said he would send out a squad car.

Before I could replace the receiver on the phone, there was a soft knock on the door. It was Betty. She had come for the children. "I'll give them breakfast and they can catch the bus in front of my house." The children scrambled down the stairs and out the door.

Once they were safely gone, I checked on Allan. *He must be sleeping.* He hadn't moved. I was about to open the screen door to the patio when I heard another knock at the door.

Two uniformed policemen were attempting to see through the

screen door into the house. After greeting them and explaining that Allan was sleeping in the back yard, they entered the house to have access to our fenced yard.

Just as I felt I had control over the situation, my slumbering tomcat unexpectedly turned into a jungle beast. With the agility of a lion, Allan sprang up from the ground and picked up the bench from the picnic table to shield himself from the policeman. "You son of a bitch, there's nothing wrong with me. Since when is it illegal for a man to sleep in his own back yard? Get your asses out of here!"

It was as if the words of Gilles Delouze had come to life: "The shadow escapes from the body like an animal we had been sheltering." From that point on, I became terrified and helpless. Trying to reason with Allan or control his behavior was impossible. His system flooded with adrenaline and he suddenly had abnormal strength. Still holding the bench from the picnic table, he threw it down to obstruct the policemen. Then, using his bare hands, he pried the top of the picnic table apart, freeing one of the boards. He swung the plank as if it was a baseball bat. Then he began taunting them saying, "What are you going to do? Shoot me!" Throwing the plank at his assailants, he shouted defiantly, "Go ahead and shoot me!"

Trampling over my beautiful flowers, Allan picked up Saint Francis with ease and hurled the statue at the startled men. The two hundred-pound statue broke into several pieces. Awed by his brute strength, they fled to their squad car for backup, for Allan was too much of a challenge—someone would get hurt.

Next, Allan entered the family room. To my horror, he pulled the top from a liquor bottle and poured the contents over his bare chest. The air filled with the harsh and overwhelming smell of bitters as it splashed onto his trousers, the floor, and sandstone mantel. Then he proceeded to empty the contents of each bottle from the mantel. One by one, our liquor—Jack Daniels, Black Velvet, and Jim Beam—bathed his body.

The two patrolmen entered the front door and made their way to the family room, while another twosome scaled the fence and stood on the patio, observing the chaotic scene. Allan's flashing eyes filled with terror. He knew he was trapped as he shouted menacingly,

"Back off!" His face became sinister—the personification of evil. With a box of matches in hand, he began striking them and throwing the lit matches at his perceived aggressors. Luckily the flames went out before they could hit their intended targets.

When this offense proved inadequate, Allan started throwing the lit matches into the pool of liquor that surrounded him. Again, they didn't ignite anything. His arsenals of both might and ingenuity had failed him. Defeated at last, he was a man resigned to his fate. His captors easily handcuffed him and escorted him to the ambulance that had arrived sometime during the helter-skelter.

Meanwhile, I was feeling as if I was experiencing the sudden onset of an infectious disease. My body was worn-out, clammy, and nauseous. I had to sit down. The policemen asked me to accompany them to the hospital, but I simply couldn't go. I sat motionless on the staircase, staring into space, not seeing the ambulance and five squad cars that drove off without me.

Stunned by these events, the broken child within me took control of my senses. I was transported to an earlier place in time.

Three-dimensional images from my past appeared before me. Now I was the naïve youngster who had returned home from school to find the outdoor shrubbery hacked down. I followed the trail of branches and greenery into our home. Trembling, I began to cough. Smoke filled my nostrils. I smelled sulfur from burnt matches. There was Angelina, my beautiful mother. She knelt on the fireplace hearth, feverishly striking matches. Sweat poured down her forehead as she cursed and threw broken matches into the air.

The similarity between what had occurred in the past with my mother, and now, in the present with Allan, was chilling. My mind had been on overload for far too long. Horrified by my revelation, I shouted, "God, help me! Give me a break. I can't handle the bizarre anymore."

Later, Grandma Caroline told me that I had sat on the steps in a stupor for several hours. She had wanted to come downstairs and had repeatedly asked me to move. In my existing mental state, I was noncompliant. Being a cripple and using a cane, she could not navigate around me.

The recent events had rendered me out of touch with reality, but being the survivor that I am, once the afternoon sunshine shone brightly into the foyer, it awakened my senses and returned me to the present once more. I arose from the steps and called to Grandma Caroline to come downstairs. We hugged tightly as tears spilled from our eyes.

It was now three in the afternoon. The school bus stopped at the corner of Claridge Oval and turned back onto Fairmount Boulevard. Michelle and Michael were now home. When they walked through the door, I hugged them tighter and kissed them more than I ever had before. *They're beautiful. I've been blessed.*

"Mommy's got a big job. Go upstairs. I'll bring you a snack. Do your homework and then you can play." It was best that the children didn't see how their father had attempted to destroy his home and himself.

Dear sweet Grandma Caroline had begun to clear the sink. The broken dishes had been placed in the trash can and the others were rinsed and neatly stacked in the dishwasher. *What would I do without her?*

My job was cut out for me. The first floor had been so completely trashed that I didn't know where to begin. *Where shall I start? The family room.* A chair from the game table had toppled over when the policeman moved to handcuff Allan. It had broken in two in the fall. The doors to all the cabinetry in the room were wide open. Bottles— broken and unbroken—matches, and pieces of glass lay in the puddles of liquor covering the tile floor and sandstone hearth. Stench from grain alcohol permeated the air throughout the house.

I'll start cleaning in here. As I began to clean, my thoughts returned to my children. *I must look after them and shield them from this insanity.*

It was Michelle who looked out for her baby brother Michael. At ten years old, she was mature beyond her years. Earlier in the day, as soon as she became aware of her father's frenzied behavior, she was the one who had helped ready Michael for school. She had taken hold of his hand and led him out the door as Mrs. White waited for the children.

Michelle was sensitive to criticism and peer pressure. The youngster agonized over the fact that she was chubby. Shopping for school clothes was not fun as she became irritated when nothing seemed to fit right, except "Pretty Plus" clothing from the Sears department store. Then she would become touchy over the labels. They provoked her so that she would burst into tears until I had taken scissors and cut them from the collar. Struggling over one's self-image as an adolescent is never easy, and trying to convince Michelle that one day she would grow out of this awkward stage was difficult.

Trying to explain Allan's recent behavior to Michelle would be even more difficult. This time, her father's bizarre actions were out in the open for the neighbors and her friends to see. Once she was on the bus, her classmates asked her, "Why are there so many police cars and an ambulance in front of your house?" To avoid embarrassment she answered, "My grandmother fell."

My innocent daughter lied to hide the actions of her parent, as I had done at her age. Michelle was becoming a replica of the young Beverly. The thought that she might have a life anything like mine broke my heart.

Allan's frequent hospitalizations had prevented Michael from having a true father-son connection. Yet he appeared to be an uncomplicated little boy with a good self-image and an incredible intellect and maturity for his age. His teachers frequently applauded his reading and language skills.

Ted, Steve, and Martin were often oblivious to what was happening to Allan, as long as their dinner was on the table. The boys were typical teenagers who loved the outdoors and sports. When not at school, they could be found wherever there was a basketball hoop, a ball diamond, or an open field where they could play football. The outdoors beckoned them to play even in the most torturous winter weather.

Whatever the season, the boys were always playing with water. Consequently, Grandma Caroline hid the handles to the faucets on the outside of the house. Much to her chagrin, they always managed to find one. They would use the spigot in the garage, connect the garden hose to it, and flood the drive with water, creating a make-shift hockey rink. The bottom line was that Allan's step-children didn't seem to care much about what he did, unless his behavior threatened to harm them or me.

One such incident occurred while Allan was incessantly playing one of his senseless songs as he had done so many times in the past. It got to me and I lost my cool. "Shut that damn music off!" I screamed as I fled down the stairs to the rec room.

Picking up a pool cue, I continued yelling at Allan as I slammed it against the pool table until it broke in two. In response, Allan threw the cue ball at me. I ducked and it just missed my head. Our shock at the force with which Allan threw the ball at me diverted a physical confrontation, but a hole remained embedded in the basement paneling as a permanent reminder of the incident. Ted, the oldest, was home at the time. Fearing for my safety, he called the police.

Another vexing situation involved Martin. He was the only Kowalski boy subjected to Allan's physical abuse.

Martin had taken a *Plain Dealer* paper route to earn spending money—an admirable undertaking. But, after a few weeks, the paper dispatcher presented Allan with a bill. The papers hadn't been paid for. The question was: did Martin pocket the money? He hadn't. He simply hadn't collected it.

Allan reasoned, "That boy needs discipline!" In Allan's mind, this was just cause for beating him.

Why hadn't Martin collected the money? Blue jays had nested in the tree next to the walkway to the apartment building where Martin had customers. To protect their newly hatched chicks, the parents would swarm around the nest. When Martin attempted to deliver the morning paper, the birds proceeded to attack him, pecking at his head. Consequently, he never delivered the papers. The obligation to pay became ours.

Allan took it upon himself to discipline Martin by beating him with his belt. The large buckle left welts and bruises on his bottom, but, at thirteen years old, my son wasn't about to show and tell on his step-dad.

Being a parent can be difficult for even an emotionally secure individual. When considering Allan's psychosis, the children were fortunate—circumstances could have been worse.

Taking stock of the accumulation of traumatic events, I came to realize that too much of my energy and attention had been diverted from my children's needs. My husband's mental illness was the

320

culprit that monopolized my time. The trauma and drama of living with him had taken a toll on all of us.

Why didn't you see this before? What pleasure could your children possibly derive living in an environment filled with constant upheaval?

None! You simply cannot continue to let them live like this. God, we all need relief!

I had believed that I was a good, kind, and understanding person, but I was shocked at the realization that Allan's behavior had been enough to make me snap. Living with someone who was out of control had brought much of the same out of me. It was frightening to realize that even-tempered Beverly could be driven to seriously contemplate homicide by butcher knife.

What's happening to me? I feel like I'm the one going crazy. Is this how my father felt with my mother?

When my mother's disgraceful behavior had pushed my father past his breaking point, I had been there. But there was nothing I could do to stop him from beating her black and blue. Perhaps next time, there will be no voice of reason or Grandma Caroline to stop you from going berserk.

What will happen to you if you continue on this path? If you continue living like this, your sanity will be jeopardized. Then who will be left to provide a supportive environment for your children? No one.

My already-damaged psyche would never heal if I continued experiencing ongoing emotional trauma. I had to separate myself and the children from Allan. We all had been too scarred to give him the emotional support he needed. We had become needy ourselves. Our parting would be in the best interest of everyone — including Allan.

With understanding and help from the doctors and staff at St. Vincent Charity Hospital, I summoned the courage to divorce Allan. Initiating a divorce while Allan and I each had a support group was the kindest way for us to part. After all we had been through, I had to take some time to process through my conflicting emotions. I ultimately came to acknowledge that there had been love between us. Although separating from Allan was the best decision, it still brought pain.

What lessons had I learned? I had followed my heart when marrying Allan. My heart had been in control. I knew he had a mental illness, yet I married him. And now I had to finally accept that he,

321

like my mother, had lost the game of genetic roulette. This fact was a reality. There was no way I could control his psychosis by loving him.

Once more, my life's history had repeated itself. I had an ongoing attraction to unhealthy relationships that took me from one crisis to another. Now I was capable of seeing the theme upon which I had structured my life. I had to stop recycling my emotional inheritance—pain—to save my children.

Just as I had enabled Chet, I had also enabled Allan. Allan would have to learn to exist without me. And he could! Family responsibilities were all mine because he was unable to provide for us. Schizophrenia prevented him from working, making sound decisions, and parenting. He was a victim of his disease.

Even though I knew that Allan's promiscuous behavior was symptomatic of his illness, I still felt violated. Although I had forgiven him for his actions, my self-esteem was not high enough to keep his behavior from triggering feelings of inadequacy and humiliation. My ego had been badly bruised during the course of our marriage. Instead of recognizing that our problem arose because of Allan's illness, I had placed the blame on myself. I had continually asked myself, "What's wrong with me? Why wasn't I good enough?" I knew now that I simply couldn't remain his wife.

I hoped to rediscover myself and my children. What seemed like an ending could really be a new beginning. Once more, I continued to seek my freedom and make a fresh start.

I'm going to make it after all!

29

BEGINNING AGAIN

I desperately wanted this new beginning. My marriage to Allan was over. The divorce was final in November 1978. TRW called me back to work in the inspection department shortly thereafter.

Allan's illness, coupled with living on unemployment from TRW for two years, and my inability to find a job with the necessary income to support my children, had placed a heavy financial burden on my shoulders.

Continuing to own a home in Shaker Heights was totally irrational. An executive's income was needed to support the maintenance and taxes. While my factory job—with good wages and benefits—was an asset, there wasn't enough money from my wages to meet all my obligations: a first and second mortgage on our residence, mortgaged rental property, charge cards, doctors' bills, groceries, clothing, and much more. I didn't want to sell our home, but I had no choice.

I placed the home for sale and after three months, I received an acceptable offer. I quickly took it. With the proceeds from the sale, I was able to pay off $60,000 in outstanding debts. The remaining money covered the down payment on a new condo in Willoughby, plus moving expenses. We would now be closer to Auntie Sue, who was living in Concord.

Buying another property at this time was a bold move. The monthly payment for a new condo, including taxes, insurance, and condominium fee, was over half my income. I had learned to work hard for my living, and I chose not to settle for less for my family. I would do whatever had to be done, including work two jobs, to take care of the children and Grandma Caroline.

I wonder now what I would have done if something bad had happened; a medical emergency or something that would keep me from working. Thankfully, being young and healthy, I never gave any thought to the possibility of negative happenings. Undoubtedly, that was a Pollyanna approach to my situation, but miraculously, it worked out. Perhaps the universe aligned the stars in my favor to change my economics. Or, perhaps, my determination and hard work brought a higher-paying job to me. I do believe that divine intervention played a part in the dramatic financial change soon to occur in my life.

In May, I started preparing for the move. For the three months, I brought discarded cardboard boxes home from TRW to pack our belongings. I spent every spare moment packing boxes. Fairmount Boulevard had been our home for fifteen years. There were now ten rooms of furnishings, a garage filled with tools—some of which had belonged to my grandfather—antiques that I had hoped to sell, a pool table, and other items in the basement. All these items needed to be packed or find a new home—an overwhelming project! My mind swarmed with details.

This wasn't the time for me to feel helpless or overcome with emotions. However, as I lay in bed in the evening, I couldn't keep from thinking about how a change of residence would affect everyone.

No one could dislike moving any more than me. As a youngster, the thought of having to readjust to a new neighborhood, school, and friends had always saddened and stressed me. Nevertheless, this move was an economic necessity. My resistance to change couldn't stop the move. *Being an adult sometimes forces you to make the hard decisions.*

324

The decision to change our residence was never a topic for discussion with my children. I alone initiated the change. Did they feel uprooted like I had, when I was a child? *Yes, what about them? What's your rationale?*

For my oldest son, Ted, this was the opportune time to move, as he was about to graduate from Shaker Heights High School. Graduation meant new experiences and change were on the horizon even if we didn't move. If the funds were available, he planned to attend Ohio University in Athens.

Martin would be a junior—an eleventh grader. Two more years of school would give him plenty of time to make friends. His easygoing nature allowed him to roll with the punches. At this time in his life, he had two passions: riding his dirt bike and taking it apart. Our garage virtually looked like a bike repair shop. My hope was that, once he transferred to the new school, his hobby would help him if he experienced the melancholies.

Darling Michelle had already experienced a change of schools within the Shaker Heights school system. The Malvern district had lacked the equipment needed to school her in reading, so she had been bused to Moreland School. She had proven that she had the fortitude to accept another change. She would be enrolled in the fifth grade.

My youngest son, Michael, was the little star in the family. He would enter the second grade. His teacher was very disappointed that we were moving. Michael excelled in his use of the English language. "He's a gifted child. You may have another Hemmingway," she told me.

Then there was my Steven. Of all my children, he would be affected the most by moving. This was the most inopportune time for him to leave the Shaker Heights schools as he had just completed 11th grade. Teens can be fragile when faced with transition.

Remembering my move from the Heights schools and my difficulties adjusting to the ninth grade at Parma Senior High, my heart ached for him. Hopefully he'll adjust.

But can he? It's his year to graduate. You should feel guilty. You're forcing him from his home. You've been there. You know how it feels. Talk to him.

"I'm sorry, Stevie. How I wish things were different for you." He understood that it was economically unfeasible for us to continue living in Shaker, and he, too, felt that attending a new school in his senior year would be a challenge.

"It's no fun being the odd man out—outside of the clique. The school year will be over before your classmates can get to know you. Perhaps we can arrange for you to live in Shaker Heights with one of your classmates. Or I could contact school, arrange to pay tuition for the year, and you can commute. You can drive."

"Mom, forget about me driving to school every day. I don't want to live with any of my friends. I'll move with you and go to Willoughby South."

Naïvely, after my conversation with Steven, I believed that everyone was emotionally ready for the change.

My strategic plan to relocate was recorded on a large calendar that hung on the inside of a kitchen cupboard door. Each day, I had to consult it to stay on track because I was so tired and frazzled from all the hours I spent working.

On weekends, Auntie Sue devoted hours to our project. No one could pack as neatly or efficiently as my aunt. She had been taught well by TRW, packing jet aircraft blades for shipment. All the items within each box were listed on labels in the finest bold black print— permanent Magic Marker, of course. Once the box was transported to the new location, the mover simply looked at the box for placement directions. Somehow, someway, and with lots of help—paid and voluntary—we managed to ready ourselves for relocating.

Moving day arrived. My older sons had procrastinated boxing their possessions—typical behavior for teens. Their rooms were a chaotic obstacle course. There were boxes everywhere. The shelves of their bookcases still needed packing, and the aquarium needed to be disassembled. I was standing in the vestibule, looking out the front door, when I heard loud thumping from the room above me. *Could someone be pushing and shoving someone or something else?*

Why or how it happened, I don't know, but Ted and Martin began fighting just when the moving truck drove onto the drive. I ran up the stairs, two at a time. *This has got to stop! And fast!*

Ted had punched Martin. They were wrestling when I entered the room. Blood began to pour from Martin's nose and smeared all over his face. His shirt was torn. It was obvious he had taken a fall. Steven was trying to separate them.

Steven was the voice of reason. "Mom needs your help. Why are you fighting?"

There was no response from either recalcitrant. The doorbell rang. It was the movers. Ted and Martin separated, but scowled at each other. I left the room to answer the door. Tears filled my eyes.

Three burly men entered. They looked into each room, after which their supervisor said that they would begin loading the upstairs first. All I could do was nod, "Okay," for my voice wouldn't have been audible. I was choking back my tears. There was no more withholding of my pent-up emotions. *We are really moving! Where did I go wrong?*

I felt as if a large weight had been placed on my shoulders. The "would have, could have, and should have" feelings flooded my mind. *You're guilty! You are the one who has failed.*

Yes, I was disappointed in myself for not being able to maintain our present lifestyle. Swallowing my pride, I said, "Goodbye," and moved on once more.

Our new location was convenient and beautiful. The Interstate 90 and Route 271 interchange, Pine Ridge Golf Course, the Metropolitan Park, Lake West Hospital, schools, and shopping were all within ten minutes of our home. The townhouse was newly built. Our unit was at the rear of the complex which gave us space and privacy.

The scents of fresh paint, wallpaper, grouting, glue, and carpeting still lingered in the air. The appliances sparkled and glistened. The newness and attractiveness of our surroundings was joyful, yet having to downsize diminished our joy. We all felt like someone was always in our space—after all, there were seven of us. And someone was always running up or down the steps.

The entrance level consisted of a small living room and an extra-large kitchen with a dining area and a powder room. Sliding glass doors in the dining area led to a small, enclosed patio. We had been accustomed to spacious living quarters. In Shaker, we had a banquet-sized dining room and a dine-in kitchen. Now, the drop-leaf oak kitchen table that seated eight would be used for our breakfast, lunch, and dinner.

The steps to the basement were off of the kitchen. Half of the basement had been paneled and carpeted. The other half housed a full bath, utility room, and heating and plumbing fixtures.

Carpeted steps off of the living room led to the second floor. There were three bedrooms upstairs. The master bedroom had its very own dressing room with a built-in, multi-draw vanity, mirror, and sink, and a large walk-in closet. This was my new domicile.

Michelle and Grandma Caroline roomed together in the next largest room, and Ted and Michael shared the smallest room. Bathing did cause us some stress, as the five of us shared one bathroom.

Steven and Martin had plenty of privacy, for their hideaway was the large, aforementioned, paneled area in the basement, furnished with twin beds, desks, bookcases, and the slate pool table from our home in Shaker. They even had their own stall shower, sink, and toilet. The downside of the room was that other members of the family often intruded to use the washer and dryer or retrieve items from the storage area. Lacking cupboard space in the kitchen, small appliances—a mixer, a roaster, cast-iron frying pans, large spaghetti pots, and other pans—were neatly stored there.

Ted, Steven, and Martin longed for our home in Shaker. They missed their friends and found excuses, almost on a daily basis, to drive to Shaker. Thank goodness fuel was plentiful and cheap with two cars traveling back and forth daily.

Auntie Sue had given Ted her canary-yellow Cutlass Supreme when she purchased a newer model. Steven inherited my bright yellow stick shift Fiat. I had leased a new '78 Bonneville sedan to comfortably accommodate four passengers. After all, my real estate career had taken off; I was now a member of the Million Dollar Club with an annual income of $27,500 or more.

Now that I had returned to work for TRW, a company that provided benefits, real estate sales became less of a priority. Starting work at 6:30 a.m. left me unable to supervise the children before they left for school. Grandma Caroline was there for them, but each child pretty much kept his own counsel and arrived at school on time.

My shift ended at 2:30 p.m., at which time I went home to make dinner. Then there were the days when I had floor time at the real estate office. On these days, I brought take-out, since Grandma Caroline had only ever cooked in her very own kitchen. Upon moving, her cooking days ended.

At first, food from Arby's, McDonalds, and all the other fast-food joints were considered a treat and fun to eat, but the party was over when it became a steady diet. Luckily, despite the kind of food they were eating, all the children were healthy and active, which accounted for their hardy appetites. This high-carb, unbalanced diet isn't the best for Ted and his diabetes.

Beverly, what are you doing? You know what it feels like not to have home-cooking. Again, this was a replication of my childhood.

Martin was the first child to take the initiative of learning how to cook. He longed for home-cooked meals, especially my Sunday sauce. To him, pasta and meat sauce was an epicurean delight—he craved spaghetti, and developed his own culinary skills, thanks to prepared foods. With two bottles of Ragu, meat sauce was a cinch, but cooking the San Giorgio linguine *al dente*, firm to the bite, was a challenge. Still, with enough practice, he mastered it.

Unpacking and settling into our new surroundings was not an easy task, but somehow, we did it. Starting school would be the real challenge. Steve and Martin were enrolled at Willoughby South, while Michelle and Michael attended Edison Elementary.

Once school started, Martin lacked interest in his academic studies. Even his dirt bike didn't seem to hold his interest anymore. He secretly longed to return to Shaker, yet he never complained to me. But each time Steven left for Shaker, he tagged along. They were becoming inseparable.

Ted, knowing that I was in a financial bind after paying off debts and relocating, decided to postpone college for a semester. He took a job at a discount store, Zayres, to save money for his schooling. Meanwhile, I began to complete financial aid papers to help with paying his tuition.

The school year started without incident and then, two months later—out of the blue—our world turned upside-down. It was about one o'clock when my supervisor told me to report to human resources. They informed me that Steven had been taken to Lake West

Hospital. My immediate thought was that he had been in an accident. Returning to my work station, I immediately packed up my belongings and locked my toolbox. Fortunately, it was a short drive to the hospital.

When informed that there was no accident, I sighed with relief. Then, a second later, I felt as if someone had punched me in the gut. "Your son is being held for admission to the psychiatric facility in the rear. Just follow the signs. Social Services is waiting for you." *They're wrong. It can't be!* Yet I instinctively knew that it could be. I took a deep breath and proceeded to Ridgecliff Hospital.

The admissions director told me that Steven had gone to the school guidance counselor complaining of hearing loud, menacing voices chattering in his head. The voices had been saying offensive things to him...taunting him...swearing, and calling him filthy names. He kept slapping his hands against his temples while screaming, "Stop it!" He expressed his pain with long and loud disturbing cries. He told his counselor, "You've got to stop it. I can't. Please turn off the radio that's playing in my head. Stop it! Please, please, stop it!" School authorities had an ambulance transport Steven to the hospital.

Our family history had just repeated itself. Again, I found myself robbed of my precious tranquility and my dream to live a happy life without mental illness—and there was nothing I could do to prevent it.

Social services presented me with a comprehensive questionnaire regarding Steven and our family's medical and social history. The doctors wanted to know more about my mother's mental illness and Chet's alcoholic behavior.

Although questions about my second marriage never entered into the equation, they should have. Our family had been in a dysfunctional state for six of the past ten years, due to Allan's psychosis.

I reviewed the brief life inventory I had completed regarding my son. His physical development was normal. His intelligence quotient was above normal and his temperament—good. Why, he was the family mediator!

Steven had participated in Cub Scouts, Boy Scouts, Little League baseball, and summer camp, where he learned to swim like a fish.

And, when his school offered skiing lessons, he proved to be a fearless skier, tackling the difficult black diamond paths. *What has happened to my child? It's not fair!*

As soon as I saw Steven, I knew he was psychotic. That look in his eyes and his changed speech patterns both indicated an obvious breakdown. There was no denying it—Steven had inherited my mother's genes.

Oh God, this is not a new beginning! Will we ever heal? The episode in the yard with Allan had made me painfully conscious of the hidden scars my mother's illness had left in my subconscious. Now I was clearly able to see that I had recreated the dynamics of my child-hood for my family. Would this pain ever end...for me...for my children? And what about Steven? There could only be more scar tissue.

Why, dear God? Why have you inflicted my son with this incomprehensible disease? I silently prayed for answers, even as the ground beneath me appeared to yield under my feet.

I'm caught in a quagmire. It's hopeless. I can't escape! I'm visiting a psych ward. And this time it's my child who's the patient. This was *not* where I wanted to be.

Giving in to the feeling of my world crashing around me and losing my sanity wouldn't help anyone, especially Steven. I had to believe that his illness would be short term—a mild case of schizophrenia. I arranged for him to have a temporary leave of absence from school, telling myself that his hospital stay would be for only a brief duration.

Then Steven's doctor informed me that this was not to be—he was a very sick young man. In fact, he had a dual diagnosis. I was asked about Steven's use of alcohol and drugs.

"What?" A long silence followed. I felt as though I had been hit in the gut by a bolt of lightning. *It can't be true!*

"Ms. Lazar, your son has admitted to drinking, and, on occasion, using marijuana and other drugs with his friends."

I could understand the alcohol. His friends' home liquor cabinets were unmonitored and easily accessible, as was ours. Most likely, Steven and a group of his friends from Shaker Heights had sought solace from family dysfunction in alcohol.

As for the use of drugs, I couldn't fathom that happening at all. *Where did he get the money? And how did he purchase drugs?*

In shock, I responded to the doctor with disbelief, "You mean to tell me that he has a problem with alcohol and drugs, too?"

I've had enough! This is just too much! I have to block it out—no more talk about dual diagnosis—alcohol and drugs! Without waiting for the doctor's response, I terminated our conversation.

Nevertheless, walking out the door, I knew I had to face the truth. Chet's addiction had been passed on, and I had been so consumed with Allan's behavior that there had been no room in my mind to even recognize more problems.

The conversation with Steven's psychiatrist was a harsh awakening! The only excuse I had for my ignorance of my son's alcohol and drug use was that it wasn't on my radar screen. In my presence, Steven revealed no physical or mental evidence of using either substance. His breath, body odor, and clothing were clean and untainted. He never exhibited tremors, slurred speech, or impaired coordination. I hoped that Steven had had a limited use of these drugs, and he had not built up a tolerance to them to the extent that he would have developed any physical changes.

Being unable to wrap my head around Steven's use of drugs, my ruminating continued. I had never seen his eyes glassy and red, as is symptomatic of using marijuana. Nor did he show the other symptoms of talking loudly and laughing inappropriately, followed by sleepiness.

What a naïve mother I had been! *Wake up, Beverly, things are different now. Why, smoking cigarettes is even allowed on school grounds.*

Who knew how easy it was for teens to acquire drugs—especially marijuana? It was plentiful and cheap, easily purchased at school or from the kid down the street—quite the contrast from my school days when alcohol was the prevalent problem.

As appalling as it was for me to acknowledge my son's deception, Steven had hidden his actions from me on numerous occasions. He often spent the night in Shaker Heights with his best buddy. *Maybe it happened then?*

My eyes were now opened to the possibility that the other boys may have been involved with drugs or alcohol. Previously, nothing in their behavior had waved a red flag. They had attended school as required and never sneaked around or requested more money from me.

Once Steven was confined to the mental hospital, Martin's trips to Shaker stopped. I asked myself why, and as I thought about his behavior, the red flags began to fly: he was apathetic towards school, his grades had plummeted, and he had lost interest in his hobby, his dirt bike.

Perhaps Martin, like Steven, was keeping secrets from me. So far, he had been lucky. No one had caught onto him yet. And, at this point in time, he wasn't ready to confess his involvement to anyone, especially me. For now, he just continued bringing Steven's weekly assignments home, and I, in turn, delivered them to the hospital.

Graduating from school this year was of utmost importance to Steven, and missing too many school days would prevent it. Without a definitive discharge date, other arrangements had to be made for Steven's schooling. Fortunately, the Willoughby-Eastlake school district had established a program in conjunction with Ridgecliff Hospital that allowed for inpatient schooling. This would allow Steven to complete the courses he required for graduation.

The staff's social service representative invited me to attend a family support group that was held in the evening. I had already sacrificed doing my motherly chores, like cooking and cleaning, because of my work schedule. Attending a group meeting meant giving up overtime. The time-and-a-half and double-time pay made a significant difference in my paycheck. Reluctantly, I agreed to attend their meetings even though I feared the impact of loss of additional income.

Work had to be my first priority, for it provided medical insurance for me and my children. Otherwise, how could I afford to pay for Steven's hospital bills? Psychiatric care was expensive.

The idea of losing my job or my ability to work for any reason really frightened me. It was my boogey man. There was so much at risk if I lost my job. After all, I had to support seven—the children, Grandma Caroline, and myself. How would I make the mortgage payment? We were living from paycheck to paycheck. *It won't take very long for the bank to be knocking at our door.* Everything was on the line.

The tug of war between my desire to be a good mother and the need to provide for my family left me in turmoil once again.

Will I ever have the opportunity to give my children the emotional support they need?

30

1980

Work became my savior. While receiving on-the-job-training and attending classes on shop math, instrumentation, and blueprint reading, I had to concentrate on the task at hand. There was no time to ruminate over Steven's misfortune. Work was my escape from the sad reality of my life. Once again, I couldn't break free of the damnable random selection of genes. My son had been victimized and I had been robbed of my dreams—my new beginning!

At TRW no one asked me personal questions, for which I was grateful. No one knew about my lifelong entanglement with mental illness. That was my secret. There, I had a genuine camaraderie with my co-workers and supervisor based on being a capable and efficient inspector.

The lead inspector of Department 639-91 was Emma May Yardley. She was a tall, good-looking, black gal—a bit of a no-nonsense person who worked hard and efficiently. She was responsible for my training which gave me the good fortune of sitting next to her.

The loud stamping of presses and hum of machinery called for earplugs, making conversation difficult even in close proximity. Most of the time, Emma May and I only talked about our work. Our relationship was that of an instructor and trainee.

After three months on the job, when I had become proficient, we began to make idle chit-chat about the weather and other pleasantries. Then one day, our conversation became more personal. We shared facts about our lives: backgrounds, family history, dreams, and aspirations. Opening up, I revealed to her that I had taught school before coming to work at TRW.

"Girl, you've got to be kidding. You're working in a factory with that background?!"

"Emma, what's wrong with that? You're working here."

"But I don't have a degree. You do!"

Then I proceeded to lament my sad song. "Teaching doesn't pay well and benefits are nonexistent. My children's medical bills have been astronomical—one son is a diabetic and another has a mental illness."

"What about their fathers? Don't they help with the bills?"

Shaking my head "No" from side to side, I replied, "They have more problems than me and my children combined. To depend on them would be ludicrous."

Emma May took hold of my hand and literally led me like a dog on a leash. "Lazar, follow me." We stopped in front of the bulletin board. She pointed to a posting from the Aircraft Worker's Alliance, the union that represented TRW employees in the Cleveland area. "Read it."

"On April 1, 1980, the union membership will select a new slate of Officers and Chief Stewards via a general election…" I stopped reading and turned to Emma. "So, what? That means nothing to me!"

"Hey, kid, that means a pay raise if you're lucky enough to win. Now do you understand? Get with it! Your teaching background more than qualifies you for a position with the union. As far as I know, none of our representatives has a degree."

"Good God, Emma, I don't have the foggiest idea about what a union is or does, let alone know what's required of an official."

"You can learn, can't you?"

"Of course, silly. Do you want to get rid of me?"

336

"You're damned right I do! The sooner the better. You're getting too smart. Two lead inspectors in the 639-91 Department is one too many." We both laughed.

When the levity of our kidding wore off, I knew that winning was not going to be easy. There were seven thousand members in the union. Who do you think you are? Girl, you're not a politician! Remember, you're just a nobody, and this is a pretty gutsy undertaking for a nobody. Goodbye, steady paycheck!

Oh well, sometimes you have to be willing to roll the dice.

I had three days to declare my intent to become a candidate. During my fifteen-minute break, I wrote my first campaign letter. It basically stated that as a former teacher, I possessed the necessary qualifications needed to handle the union's communications, and that I sought the position of Executive Secretary. Also, I openly admitted that there was a lot for me to learn regarding union protocol, but that I was willing to do so.

Emma May became my campaign manager, and, true to her word, she obtained signatures from several hundred union members in support of my candidacy. A tall, lanky, slightly handsome machine repairman who also happened to be an amateur photographer, stopped at the inspection bench daily to talk to me. Once he heard I was running for office, he offered to take my picture in his home studio for my campaign posters. Although he was a bit of a flirt, I felt reassured when he said his wife would be there. Hoping beyond hope that he was sincere, I decided to accept his offer. It was worth the risk—pictures were expensive, and I didn't need any more debts. Losing three weeks of pay in order to campaign would be a whopping loss in itself. Winning was a necessity.

Thankfully, the photographer was sincere and the pictures were good. The printer designed my posters and literature for a nominal fee. Now the big challenge was distributing the literature and becoming known to the membership.

Emma May and I sat down to strategize. Being unknown and unfamiliar with three of TRW's facilities was a decided disadvantage. But 50 percent of the membership worked at my home plant, a definite advantage. Emma May advised, "Concentrate on getting known at Tapco. Generally, you'll get a majority of your votes from your home plant. To win, you'll need this plant's votes."

TRW had four plants in the Cleveland area: Tapco, Valves, Main Plant, and the Replacement Division. Management gave each candidate clearance to enter any of the facilities, day and night, to campaign. The only stipulation was that we were not to interfere with production or safety. Non-employees were permitted to pass out literature for a candidate at the entrance of each plant between shifts. With me at their side, Ted and Martin manned the door at the Tapco plant. My goal was to meet and be seen by as many members as possible. That was the only way an unknown dark horse like me could win.

Campaigning took stamina. The Tapco plant alone covered eighty-four acres. Walking through each facility was exhausting and challenging. In some areas, special gear—steel-toed shoes and hard hats—were required. I put aside my vanity and dressed appropriately. This allowed me to stand with the other workers even alongside a blast furnace as molten steel was being pressed into bars.

Soot covered my hair and filled my nostrils. The oppressive heat felt as if it scorched my fair skin. But I stood there long enough to say, "Hello, I'm Bev Lazar. Please vote for me. Thank you." And I left my literature at their work station.

My car and I zigzagged back and forth from Euclid Avenue to East 185th Street. Then we traveled across town from East 55th and Cedar Road to the Replacement Plant in Independence. At each stop, I smiled, passing out literature and smiley buttons that said, "Elect Bev Lazar."

April 1—election day—arrived. Voting would take place in each plant's cafeteria. The results from Valves, Main Plant, and Replacement would be brought to Tapco by each plant's respective chairman. There, the tallies would be combined and the election results certified.

I voted before my shift. Then it was back to work on the inspection bench. Emma May welcomed me, saying, "Girl, don't look so sad. You've won." Everyone she had talked to assured her that they had voted for me. I wasn't so sure.

The past three-week sabbatical from working on the factory floor had ended. I had been on an emotional high from all the new places

338

and faces. There had been absolutely no time to think. My days had been filled with movement and action. Now I had come down from my high, and I was certainly feeling down. On top of it all, Steven and I had had too little time together. Now all I could do was wait for the election results. At the end of my shift, I stopped at the hospital to check on Steven. After a brief visit with him, I stopped at the grocery store for a pot roast, a dinner favorite.

Arriving home, I began prepping for dinner. Being there felt so good. How I had missed Grandma Caroline and the children over the past three weeks!

At eight in the evening, I received a call from election headquarters. The election chairmen had arrived. I had to hurry if I wanted to be present when the results were posted. I returned to Tapco just in time.

To my dismay, I learned that neither the incumbent nor I had received enough votes for a clear majority, and a runoff election would be necessary. *Oh God, another week of campaigning chaos!*

Suddenly, I was feeling guilt-ridden. *I may be squandering another week's pay for nothing! The condo needs cleaning and my meals have been eaten on the run, while the children made do with fast food. And what happens if I don't win? Will this sacrifice be worth it?*

The runoff election was held on April 8. For me, it was a most favorable date, since it was Grandpa Vincenzo's birthday. Again, I voted before my shift.

Exiting the voting booth, somehow the curtain closed when it shouldn't have, and my ballot flew into the air. Looking up to catch it, the edge of the paper hit me in the eye, scratching my cornea.

My eye became inflamed—red, irritated, and tearing. Inspecting jet aircraft parts would be impossible with my limited sight. The plant nurse placed a healing ointment on my eye, covered it with a patch, and sent me home.

As I passed well-wishers walking down the factory aisles, they said, "Don't worry, Bev. You're going to win!" Wishing I felt that confident myself, I left work. This time I would not return to the plant for the results.

Friends' predictions proved accurate. The election secured my job and financial future for the next three years. I was elected to a three-year term beginning on June 1, 1980.

Living in gratitude, I was, and would be forever, grateful to Emma May for the gift of her friendship and direction. Amidst hugs and tears, I said my goodbyes to the inspection bench and the girls in the department. On my last day working on the floor, they gifted me with a gold-plated Cross pen and pencil set.

The zeal I felt from campaigning continued. Once again, there were new places to go and new people to meet. There was a reception to introduce all the new officials to management—all the corporate bigwigs, including the Chief Operating Officer. Time moved on much too quickly.

Success lifted my spirits. How I savored each exhilarating moment after experiencing such profound sadness and many losses. I had triumphed! All the struggles I had fought to survive had only strengthened my resolve to succeed. And I had! I had tapped into my reservoir of resilience.

31

FROM "GRADUATION" TO THANKSGIVING

It was the end of June. Such a beautiful day! Standing alongside our mailbox, I tore open the plastic bubble mailer. Inside was Steven's diploma in a padded black leather cover with the words, "Willoughby South High School," engraved in gold letters. I found myself overcome with regret for what should have been, and my eyes filled with tears as I imagined my tall, handsome, brown-eyed, curly haired blond son wearing a black robe and mortarboard.

But Steven was deprived of the proud, happy moments it took to walk across the auditorium stage and to hear the school's orchestra playing the melodic stanzas of "Pomp and Circumstance," as he received his diploma. There was no family gathering to celebrate the event. This was not what I had anticipated for my son!

In September, Steven was finally released from the hospital. Now that he was home, he slept away his mornings and idled away his afternoons. Sleeping excessively was most likely a side effect from his psychiatric medication. He appeared to have lost his ability to concentrate. That meant that all of his former academic aspirations had to be set aside.

As a baby, if you would let him, Steven would take his tiny fingers and place them in your mouth, examining every pearly white within his reach. "Ah, he will be a dentist." Our family had laughed about the cute jester. The occupation of dentist had resonated with Steven, but that dream was in the past. How my heart ached for what would never be. For now, if Steven just managed to attend his evening group therapy sessions, I had to be content.

On Thanksgiving morning in 1980, around five thirty that morning, I was about to prepare our holiday turkey. I needed the large roasting pan which was stored in the utility room on the lower level of our home. To enter the storage area, I had to walk through the bedroom Steven shared with his older brother.

At first, I thought Steven had rolled off his twin bed. *I'll wake him. He'll be more comfortable if he gets back in bed.* "Stevie, get up! Wake up!" I rolled him over. Kneeling at his side, I began shaking him. NO RESPONSE. "Stevie, what's wrong?" *Oh, my God—he's unconscious!*

Placing my ear next to his mouth, I listened for his breath. *Is he breathing?* I wasn't sure. Yet I felt his warmth. *Get a cold washcloth. Perhaps that will revive him.*

Walking into his bathroom, I saw five empty prescription bottles lying in the sink. Just yesterday I had picked up his weekly refill of psychiatric drugs—thorizine, copizine, cogentin—and sleep meds. *Oh, God! No!*

Vomit and saliva oozed over the toilet seat. There were three pills in the toilet water. *Oh, God! How many could he have taken?* It was impossible to know how much of the medication he still had in his stomach.

Picking up the empty bottles, I searched the labels for quantity. Frightened for my son, I couldn't think, let alone calculate the numbers. I only knew I needed help to get him to the hospital.

My hands shook as I picked up the rotary phone to dial the emergency squad. I cried out to the operator, "Quickly, please, I need an ambulance. My son isn't breathing! Please come quickly."

Panic stricken, I waited. Looking out the window, I expected to see the flashing lights of the ambulance. Instead, I was startled by the ringing of the phone.

342

"Hello." It was the ambulance driver. "I can't find your unit!" He had been driving in circles around our condominium complex, but couldn't find our address. Our unit was at the back of the complex and difficult to locate.

I became tongue-tied and unable to explain how to find us.

Again, loud and distinctly, "I can't find you. How do I get to you?"

Once more, I couldn't respond.

"Can you come to the front of the complex and direct us?"

"Yes. Yes." I hung up the phone.

Jumping up from my seat next to the kitchen phone, I frantically dumped my purse out on the kitchen table. *Car keys, where are you? Thank you, thank you, God!*

Bolting into the car, I drove recklessly—ignoring the twenty-mile-an-hour limit and the strategically placed speed bumps—to the front of the complex to escort the EMS to our home. We were losing precious time. Steven needed immediate help!

The yellow, orange, and red lights flashed as the driver followed me to the back of our complex. Gurney in tow, the paramedics went directly to Steven. The first thing I did was give them the medication bottles.

Then I ran up the stairs, two at a time, to tell Grandma Caroline where I was going. "Grandma! Grandma! Wake up!" She flinched as her eyes opened wide, alarmed by the urgency in my voice.

Meanwhile, my daughter, Michelle, who shared a room with Grandma Caroline, immediately jumped out of her bed. She, too, recognized my urgent tone. Sensing my distress, she came to the side of Grandma Caroline's bed to hug me.

"I'll take care of Michael and Grandma. Don't worry. I can fix us toast and jelly for breakfast."

Taking a coat from the entrance closet, I just made it in time to follow the ambulance to Lake West Hospital. The vehicle pulled into the unloading zone in the emergency pavilion as I sought a parking place. Steven was rushed inside and into a room while I completed his admissions paperwork.

Then I was sent to a waiting room. As I waited for what seemed an eternity, my mind raced. *Most likely they're pumping his stomach by now.*

Then I prayed…desperately, I prayed that he had received medical help in time. *So often, help doesn't arrive soon enough. He'll pull through. He's got to pull through.*

Why would he ingest all his medication? Suicide?

No! There were no warning signs. He never threatened to kill himself. He never wrote about killing himself. Yet I've often heard psychologists say when someone attempts suicide it is a cry for love and a call for help, pleading, "Save me!"

Then what could have triggered his actions?

The voices, the unseen voices that kept shouting relentlessly at him. They had returned. They triggered his intense anxiety. Feeling trapped, he had no other way out. The pills were his only hope to quiet the voices. I had to believe that the most significant cause of his suicide attempt was his mental disorder. Surely, this was his reason for overmedicating himself.

Why did this happen? I didn't know that Stevie couldn't be trusted with his medication.

I don't remember the doctors saying anything about having to dispense the medication to him, but I had taken some precautionary measures. I had filled two shot glasses each day with his morning and evening medication.

God, I feel so responsible! Perhaps I should have been more cautious and personally dispensed his meds to him. It's my fault this happened.

No, you're not.

My only concern had been keeping his meds safe from both the younger children and Grandma Caroline, who took her own pills daily. That's why I had kept Steven's meds in his bathroom. I believed that keeping them away from the rest of the family would prevent any mix-ups. I was naïve to think that I didn't need to worry about keeping Steven safe from his meds.

The contents of Steven's stomach had been pumped. Much of the medication had entered his blood stream, rendering him unconscious. It was too soon to know if he had any residual brain damage. Only time could tell us.

After three days in intensive care, Steven no longer had the need for life-sustaining equipment. *Thank God, he's alive!* I finally had the courage to call Chet and tell him about Steven's suicide attempt, but there would be no scene this time. He completely dismissed me. He was too busy with his new family.

Steven was transferred to the psychiatric facility that adjoined Lake West Hospital—Ridgecliff.

Oh, God, we're right back where we started!

32

OFF THEY GO

While I was in my own private hell, admonishing myself with guilt, my youngest Kowalski boy, Martin, was doing the same. He did have a God-awful secret that he was keeping from me. He had been drinking beer with his brother and friends while sitting in the jungle gym in the school playground. This same group had gotten high, becoming glassy-eyed and talkative, from smoking pot on a few occasions.

"Mom! Listen to me! I've got to get out of here. I'm going to join the armed forces."

What brought this on? Stunned and speechless for the moment, all I could say was, "Seventeen is too young to join!"

"I can join, if you and Dad sign papers giving me permission." He had done his homework—a recruiter had advised him.

"More than likely, I'm going to fail in school anyhow. That will eliminate my shot at going to college."

"Martin, there is still time to turn your grades around. I'll talk to your teacher. We'll get you a tutor."

"Mom, you don't get it. I have to go! I have to man-up. It's my way out of this mess! You must understand. It's for my own preservation! Going is my only hope."

Martin finally opened up to me. He was worried that he, too, might become mentally ill or addicted to drugs or alcohol like Steven. Recent events had served to intensify his fears. His friend, Billy, had been sent away to a rehabilitation center in New York City by his parents, and Steven's breakdown and suicide attempt had really freaked him out.

My son had felt as though his world was crashing down on him when he heard the news. "First Steve and now Billy! Are we all destined to become an addict or a psycho? Who's next?"

Martin knew his present path—flirting with drug and alcohol addiction—was wrong, and, if he continued this behavior, he would become an addict. Martin wasn't aware of the degree to which Steven's genetics had predisposed him to psychiatric issues, and that his drug and alcohol abuse had merely been the trigger for his breakdown. He thought that if he continued down his current path it was inevitable that he would lose it all and walk in his brother's and friend's shoes. He reasoned that it was better to act now and remove himself from his present environment before he got into trouble.

There was no dissuading Martin. He wasn't trying to prove anything. He was simply running away from a bad situation. Being intelligent and analytical, he had even reasoned out which branch of the service was best to join.

"I thought about life on a ship. The Navy tour of duty is easy, because they are more protected. But the enemy will most definitely bomb a ship.

"If there's a war, the Marines are the first line of defense. If reinforcements are needed, the Army, the foot soldiers and artillery, are dispatched next. If the Marines and Army need assistance, they send in the Flyboys with the bombs. I'm going to join the U.S. Air Force."

While the decision to leave home and join any division of the armed forces didn't make sense to me, I agreed with the logic of Martin's decision to join the Air Force. His childhood best friend's father owned a plane. On Saturdays, the three of them would spend the day at Cuyahoga County Airport waxing it. That was the beginning of Martin's love affair with flying.

When he was a little older, Martin would request that I purchase a remote control plane for him when he had done me a favor or an odd job. When I sold real estate, he would often accompany me to an open house, as having a large, fifteen-year-old youngster with me gave me a feeling of security. If the house sold, the plane was his.

Our conversation left me feeling very frightened for my son. *He's a kid, for God's sake! He knows nothing about the world! The military is not the panacea he thinks it is.* I knew from his father's stint in the service that alcohol use and abuse were rampant among the recruits. The military was anything but a refuge from alcohol!

Although the service wouldn't take Martin away from the temptation of alcohol, it did have a lot to offer: discipline and respect for an authority figure, exercise, good health, three square meals, a chance to complete school, and a paycheck. A young man without direction could possibly find his way there. I simply wasn't ready to let go of my son. He was just too young.

I hoped his father would have the wisdom not to sign. His refusal would have given me the opportunity to get help for our misdirected son. But the timing wasn't right. Chet had recently remarried. His wife was a widow who supported her nine children by dancing in a bar. His plate was full as he had just purchased a farm for his new family. He didn't give his son's welfare a second thought, dismissing Martin just as he had Steven.

"Beverly, you don't know how to raise those kids. You let them run wild. Sure, the military's good for Martin. It will make him a man!" Chet had most likely said these words with a belly full of beer. But I didn't need to hear them. I had already convinced myself that I was to blame for Martin's desire to join the military.

With Chet's signature given, I reluctantly added mine. Martin would leave on April 28, 1981.

On the eve of Martin's departure, I was seated on his bedroom floor watching him remove his belongings from the dresser drawers. We were alone. Feeling weighed down, I remained silent as I intently observed my son. As he moved about, he kept brushing aside his thick, straight, raven-black hair from his forehead. The hair had grown long enough to hide his beautiful deep-set brown eyes.

Soon he'll sport a brush cut, like his dad. Then I'll be able to see his almond-shaped eyes and those thick, long, black lashes. Those eyes belong to Carlo, my father.

Martin reached over and handed me his jackets, T-shirts, and faded, torn blue jeans. I placed them in a plastic bag for Goodwill.

He's big and tall, like Chet. But look at that baby face—he's just a kid. He's my baby, and he's leaving home tomorrow!

There was little conversation between us. I was desperately trying to be brave and not cry. He was packing his belongings, his running shoes, a shaving kit, forty dollars, and a Bible into a gym bag.

"Martin, you're really packing light." *That's a silly comment, Beverly.* Taking clothing wasn't necessary as he would be issued uniforms.

"Mom, I don't need anything else."

Saying, "Goodnight," I held back my tears as I left Martin's room. That night, sleep eluded me.

At 4:00 a.m., the recruiter pulled the van into our driveway. Martin and I were the only ones awake in the house as he had said his goodbyes to Grandma Caroline, Ted, Michelle, and Michael at our evening meal.

Picking up his bag, he refused to look me in the eyes as he said, "Later, Mom." And with those words, he left. My silence as he walked out belied my churning emotions. I couldn't let myself speak, as I knew that even one word would cause me to break the promise I had made to myself that I wouldn't cry when he left.

My baby's really leaving.

At Martin's first stop, he would have an entrance exam, a physical, and shots. After all the preliminaries were completed, he would be sworn in. Then it was off to Cleveland Hopkins Airport for a direct flight to San Antonio, Texas.

At 9:00 a.m., I was waiting at the departure gate to see my son one more time. Ten young men approached the gate. At the rear of the group was my overgrown kid. Tears filled my eyes at my first glimpse of Martin.

The gate had been open for some time, and the third class passengers were boarding when the young inductees arrived. We barely had time for a kiss and a long hug.

At this point, it was impossible to contain my emotions. Tears splashed down my cheeks. My nose ran. Reaching up to embrace him, I pressed my wet cheek against his. I didn't want to let go of him. Breaking free from my embrace, Martin exited the double doors and disappeared from sight. At that moment, I felt as though I couldn't move forward. Inner peace had escaped me again.

As the doors shut behind Martin, I felt the full force of a one-two punch. One, Steven was confined to a psychiatric ward. He was schizophrenic like his grandmother. Two, Martin had departed for the military because he felt that by continuing to live at home, he was destined for drug addiction or the psych ward. As a mother, I believed myself a failure.

Feeling like I had lost two of my children, I hurt from the very center of my being. My heart had been broken. It ached more than it ever had before, not as it had when I was a child, an adolescent, or an adult, but more. The personal bond between mother and son made my pain more intense. Pangs of regret reverberated throughout my body.

Feeling vanquished, I was barely able to contain my emotions enough to leave the airport, to drive home, to think, and to feel. Somehow, later in the day, my misery miraculously lifted and I managed to raise my emotional energy. There was no other choice; I had to accept the reality of what was and persevere as I had done so many times before.

While his younger brothers were struggling with mental health and drug challenges, my reliable and conscientious firstborn was preparing to leave for his freshman year at Ohio University in Athens. Ted had worked and saved most of his earnings the previous year, and was fortunate enough to receive several grants, as well as the opportunity to participate in a work-study program.

Athens, Ohio is a small college town located in the southern part of the state. The day Ted moved on campus was beautiful—the clear blue sky had hardly a cloud, and it was a bit breezy and temperate, at 72 degrees.

351

The car had been packed with all the essentials needed for a college dormitory, clothing, and toiletries. Ted also brought a mini refrigerator which made it convenient to store snacks and his insulin.

Our drive took us along Route 77 for about three hours. Scenic farm land on either side of the road made for a smooth, traffic-light-free drive over the hilly terrain.

We left the highway and turned southwest toward Marietta on Route 550, following the shore of a river. The land along the river bank appeared free of man's intervention. The trees and aquatic plants—oaks, maples, chestnuts, and hundreds of other rare species—had grown wild.

The sunlight reflected on the water. *How beautiful!*

Distracted by the dazzling view, I had to jam on the brakes when I saw that a large turtle, at least ten inches in diameter, had positioned itself in the middle of the road—a dangerous place for the slow-moving creature. The car stopped within inches of the poky critter.

After pulling over to the side of the road, Ted and I got out, at first to gawk, then to assist. With a tree-branch in hand, Ted nudged and pushed the rotund traveler back onto the river embankment. Hopefully he stayed put and remained safe.

Returning to the car, I looked at Ted. *He'll do well in college. He has certainly matured.* The once-tall, willowy teen had spent many an afternoon in the gym, working out with weights, to develop his tall muscular frame. All the neighborhood cuties thought of him as quite the hunk!

Turning the ignition key, I looked over to study my son's face. He, like Martin, had inherited his grandfather's deep-set dark brown eyes and thick eyelashes.

He's handsome and likeable, too, with his fun-loving humor and antics. He's quite a catch for some young lady!

It was 5:00 p.m. before I drove home, alone and lonely for my son. But this was how things should be. It was the normal progression of a child moving on with his life, becoming an adult and leaving home, which is how I had hoped it would be for all my children.

352

33

GOODBYES

It was a new year—1982. The lighthearted joy everyone else had seemed to feel at Christmas had passed me by. *Bah, humbug!* My life felt totally out of control once more. In spite of my emotional turmoil, I had made a resolution to be courageous instead of fearful, and I was hopeful that my life-long goal for a new beginning would finally materialize this year. My top priority was to help Steven regain his sanity.

Despite my resolve, a conversation with Steven's doctor left me paralyzed with fear. I still needed a beacon of hope.

Dr. Allen Monnley, the head of psychiatry at Ridgecliff, and I had a lengthy discussion regarding my fear that Steven's behavior would be just like his grandmother's—bizarre and psychotic for his entire life.

"Be hopeful, Mrs. Lazar. I have a young male patient who is very much like Steven. He's a little older than your son, but their diagnoses are the same. He just returned from a year stay at an exclusive hospital in Baltimore, Maryland. He's been home for the past six months. The parents were astounded by his psychological transformation."

HOPE. Dr. Monnley had given me hope: hope that Steven could lead a happy and productive life, even though he had schizophrenia. "Yes!" I would take the doctor's advice. Now I was infused with a bit of optimism. *Perhaps this will be a good year after all.*

More good news arrived. This time it was regarding Martin. During the second week of February, I received a letter from the Department of the Air Force. It read, "Your son, Martin, was selected as the 355th Tactical Training Wing Airman of the Month for January 1982."

A week later, Steven was discharged from Ridgecliff. Upon his release, he was lost and without direction. His thought processes remained illogical and disorganized, prohibiting employment or advanced schooling.

Isolating himself from everyone, he chose to remain within the confines of his room, only to venture outside when escorted to the hospital outpatient program and AA meetings. It was obvious that his recent hospital stay hadn't provided the results I had hoped for. This was discouraging. My last resort was to seek treatment for Steven from another facility, one with a different approach to treating schizophrenia. *This will make my son whole once more.*

In the meantime, Dr. Monnley submitted a preliminary request for Steven's admission to the facility in Baltimore. Now I did my part by providing the hospital with a financial statement, health records, completed questionnaires, and proof of medical coverage.

My benefit package from work included medical insurance for the children. The personnel department contacted Travelers Insurance Company on my behalf, requesting pre-approval for Steven's stay in the facility. Now, all I could do was wait and worry. Coping with an uncontrollable situation filled me with fear. My child's future was dependent on an affirmative answer and I wanted more than anything in the world to have a "normal" son.

The week dragged. On Friday, I was called into the personnel office. *Yes!* My medical coverage provided up to an astonishing $1 million for his illness. And, what made it even better, as my sponsored dependent, Steven would be covered until he reached age twenty-two. Gladdened and relieved by this information, I literally danced out of the office with the biggest smile on my face, wanting to kiss the very ground beneath my feet. Working at TRW was my good fortune!

Having had Travelers certify Steven's coverage, I called an airline to book tickets; a one-way ticket for him and a round-trip ticket for me. We would depart Cleveland on Wednesday, March 3, 1982, for Towson, Maryland. With the travel arrangements completed, the ticket agent hung up.

Trapped within the confines of my mind, I sat frozen with the receiver still held to my ear. Even when the brief silence was broken...beep...beep...the annoying dial tone failed to move me. *This is really going to happen!*

The mere thought of leaving my son at a mental facility in a distant city, six to eight hours away by car, catapulted me into sadness. What an emotional rollercoaster!

Wednesday morning, the day Steven and I would travel to Towson to admit him to Sheppard and Enoch Pratt Hospital, arrived cold and snowy. Nine inches of snow had fallen while we slept. Steven had packed his meager belongings before bedtime and slept soundly while I desperately tried to get organized and maintain my composure. Tears kept trickling down my cheeks. My mind was swimming with details. What must I take? I reviewed the contents of my briefcase: medical records and insurance papers. What an array of papers. Check your purse. You can't afford to forget anything. Glancing at the clock, I noted it was five o'clock. We must leave soon. Do I have everything?

Steven and I will already be on our way to Baltimore when the alarm clock rings at 7:00 a.m. to awaken the other children. They will be entirely on their own today. Have you spent enough time with them lately?

I had to have faith that the youngest—Michelle and Michael—were trustworthy and self-sufficient. Working with the union was demanding, requiring twelve hours per day, six or seven days a week. Having quality time with my children was impossible.

As far as I knew, Michelle had adapted well to my schedule. Michael—my good-looking, brown-haired, brown-eyed boy, with the warm and friendly smile that lit up a room—was my concern. There was no question in my mind that because he was brilliant, he marched to the beat of a different drum. Trying to predict what he would think or do was a challenge. Making his nature more complex was the fact that he was the youngest and had been a bit spoiled, especially by Grandma Caroline. And because he was the youngest and fifth child, he received less attention, less time, and less mothering from me.

My dear youngest child would sit in front of the closed bathroom door as I readied myself for work, and jumped at the silences between surges of running water to ask me this or that. Every morning I could be heard saying to him, "I can't hear you, honey. The water's running."

I had so much vying for my time that Michael had to find this sad—but creative—way to get attention. Thank God, he found a way to make himself heard; otherwise, meeting his needs could have been left on my emotional to-do list. But these closed-door sessions made for poor communication.

The child needs more time to talk to me.

Hey, kid, you're guilty as charged.

On weekdays, Michael often needed to be coaxed to get out of bed because he found school boring. The curriculum failed to challenge and excite him. If he could, he would find a way to skip school. Being a genius, he often got away with it, too! The attendance officer and I were often unaware of his rash decision to skip a class, but frequency and probability worked against him and he eventually got caught.

In an attempt to make up for the lack of quality time I had to spend with Michael, Michelle did her best to be the ideal big sister. She tried to mother her younger brother, and provide a little discipline when she could. However, once she moved up to the junior high and no longer walked to school with him, Michael had the freedom to do as he pleased.

Michelle transferred from our public junior high to Immaculate Conception, the local Catholic school. Her best friend, Kara, a very pretty girl who lived in our development, had influenced her choice of religion and schooling, just as Helen had influenced me when I transferred to Parma Senior High. In May of her eighth-grade year, Michelle made her confirmation.

The girls were inseparable. Kara's mother drove them to school, and after school, she drove them to Huron Road Hospital where she worked in the gift shop. The two girls volunteered as candy stripers, passing out reading materials and various sundries to the patients.

The morning of my departure with Steven to Towson, I entered Michelle's room. Looking at her pretty face as she slept, I couldn't help but think about how she had changed now that she was fourteen years old. *No more "Pretty Plus" dresses for her.* She was a long-legged slender beauty with long, straight, strawberry-blonde hair that swung from side to side as she walked. Her darling nose crinkled and her eyelids lowered—like her dad's—when she smiled.

Sweet, dependable Michelle will fix breakfast for Michael and see him off to school today. I kissed her on the forehead and whispered, "Goodbye. I love you."

Will he skip school today? Will he miss me this morning? Not wanting to wake Michael, I walked past his bedroom.

Before leaving Michelle's room, I had glanced at the empty twin bed that had belonged to Grandma Caroline. My eyes filled with tears, remembering…my dear grandmother had departed earlier in the year. She had entrusted me with her well-being and care since my grandfather's death thirteen years prior. *Where did the time go?* Twelve of those years, she had lived with me and the children. She had been the most innately good person I had ever known—loving and helpful.

Her ending story was bittersweet. Age and infirmity had made living at home impossible. She had been crippled since her hip operation in 1920. At ninety years old, she had no longer been able to use the stairs, bathe herself, or take care of her toilet needs. Placing her in a nursing home broke our hearts, but it was what we had to do.

Grandma Caroline, lacking an income, soon had used up all her personal funds. Thankfully, she was granted Medicaid and placed in a facility in Geneva, Ohio. The distance from home prohibited us from visiting as often as I wished we could have. My goal had been to see her once a week. This didn't happen, giving me another reason to feel guilty.

The first week in April had found Caroline struggling from congestive heart failure. On April 8th, a staff member called me early in the morning. "Your grandmother is conscious, but she's failing. I recommend that you come here as soon as possible." Dropping everything—even work—I went directly to her side.

The eighth was her beloved Vincenzo's birthday. When I told Grandma Caroline what day it was, she smiled at me with the most beautiful face-transforming expression. Why, her eyes even twinkled! She closed them, but her smile remained. Perhaps once more, she was a twenty-nine-year-old who had just arrived in Boston to meet the love of her life.

I sat with her late into the evening, but—for the sake of my children—had to return home that night. Caroline died the next day, April 9th, Good Friday. *How fitting!* I had always said she was a saint!

Sadly, Grandma Caroline had faced death alone. Again, it was not what I had wanted. When I had viewed her body, she appeared ravaged from her fight to cling to life. Apparently, she had struggled valiantly to remain alive until I returned to her side. Her beautiful sweet smile had disappeared.

I wiped my tears. *No more reminiscing. I need to focus on the present and get Steven to the hospital.*

34

WHERE DO WE GO FROM HERE?

The Helmsley Hotel was a five-minute drive from our condo. It provided limo service to and from Cleveland Hopkins Airport. Fortunately, I was able to reserve the last two remaining seats on the 5:30 a.m. airport run. The plan was to park my car in the hotel's lot until I returned later in the evening.

The snow was deep and heavy as I pulled my car out of the garage onto the unplowed street within the condominium development. Slowly, I navigated my Chrysler Shadow through the snow until reaching the main street. Driving was obviously a challenge, but fearing the uncontrollable situation I was facing—getting Steven situated—flooded my mind with "What if's."

Steven's behavior had continued to be very unpredictable, especially since his first psychotic breakdown. Trying to foresee how he would behave during the trip filled me with fearful uncertainty. *What will he do? Will he embarrass me? Will he rebel? Will he become combative? Or will he co-operate?*

Only God knows! He has to cooperate and board the plane! He'll do it. I mustn't doubt.

I tried to convince myself. *Whatever will be, will be. I'll do what I must. Somehow, someway, I'll see that he gets there.*

My distress didn't stop here. There was an internal tug-of-war going on inside my mind over the conflicting no-win situation I found myself in.

Hospitalizing Steven was not easy, even if it was for his own good. I didn't want to hospitalize him at all, let alone place him in an out-of-state psychiatric facility. Yet it would be totally unbearable for me to see him end up like his grandmother.

There's no turning back. We must go on.

Outwardly, I appeared composed, but inwardly, I was a mess. My stomach churned as we climbed the steps and sat behind the limo driver. Actually, the Helmsley Limo was a small, ten-seat jitney. Steven placed his suitcase in the luggage carrier and sat down next to the window. *All is well. Thank God!*

The snowplows had had little opportunity to clear State Route 2 in Euclid. Our driver had no choice but to follow in the previously made tracks, making for a rough ride. Several times, the small bus swayed from side to side as it skidded across patches of ice. Then, we reached the interstate and found that road almost as forbidding; still, we arrived safely at the airport.

Once inside, Steven and I had breakfast at the restaurant in the main terminal. *You'd best eat something, Beverly.* "Two eggs over medium, wheat toast, a small orange juice, and coffee, please."

As for Steven, he was hungry. He stuttered, "Scrambled eggs, saus…sausage and pancakes." His order brought a smile to my face, as I recalled him as a child, begging Mrs. Mason to make pancakes for breakfast.

Before Mrs. Mason began cooking, she would wrap a red and white polka-dotted scarf around her head, tie it in a bow, then place her hands on her hips and proclaim that she was the original pancake lady, Aunt Jemima.

Steven used to brag to his playmates, "Aunt Jemima cooks my pancakes. It's true. Come on over and see for yourself."

Why had I decided to eat? I felt like I was choking on every bite of food. After three or four bites of toast and a bit of eggs, I pushed it all aside. I sat there, slowing sipping juice and coffee as I watched Steven eat.

360

Steven turned the small container upside down and poured the syrup, nonstop, until the server was nearly empty. Oh God! The syrup oozed off his plate and onto the table. Looking up at me, he apologetically said, "Sorry." Then he leaned over his plate and gulped down a huge slice of pancake, as the syrup continued to drip and dribble about.

God, what's happened to his manners? I reached for a napkin. Stay calm, Beverly. Be patient. He's behaving all right.

The hum of people chattering and moving about made it difficult to hear the public address system. Straining to hear each announcement, my heart skipped a beat when I heard, "Freedom Air now boarding Flight 450 for Baltimore, Maryland, at Gate A." Not knowing exactly where to find Gate A or how far we were from the gate, I quickly paid the bill.

Luck was with us. The door to the gate hadn't opened yet.

Once Steven and I were checked in, we were allowed to pass through the gate to aluminum steps that took us onto the tarmac where the plane awaited its passengers. Instinctively, I took hold of my son's hand. To my chagrin, he pulled away. My feelings were hurt by the rejection. I looked around to see if anyone had noticed but no one was behind us.

Looking up at the sky, I could see that daylight was failing to penetrate the black snow clouds. Strong gusts of wind came from behind us, shoving Steven and me forward, commanding us to get aboard. The cold penetrated my body. I was shivering. I pulled the collar of my coat up, gathering the cloth tightly together, covering my neck.

Looking at Steven, who was now walking ahead of me, he, too, had to be feeling the biting, frigid air. He was wearing a waist-length winter jacket without a hood.

When climbing the steps to enter the plane, both his shirt and jacket rose above his waistline, exposing his backside. He had worn a summer T-shirt beneath his jacket—one that he could no longer tuck in. His stomach protruded beneath his shirt. His tall, lean, muscular body now sported a bloated stomach, one of the side-effects from taking psychiatric drugs.

Why hadn't I checked his clothing? He needs new shirts.

We boarded the plane and fastened our seatbelts. As the plane jetted into the air, I closed my eyes and transported myself to an earlier time when Allan, the boys, Michelle, and I had flown to Washington, D.C. to see the historic sites.

Steven was eight years old. Blond curls covered his forehead, and his big brown eyes were wide open, filled with excitement. It was his first plane ride. He was leaning over his big brother, Ted, to look out the window. He was a happy, well-behaved youngster.

What if we could go back in time and do things differently? Would we, could we change the outcome? If he had experienced fewer traumas, would he still have become schizophrenic?

Stop it! Be real. You must accept what is.

Opening my eyes and looking at my son, I wondered if he was as distressed as I.

Steven had the seat next to the window. He was intently looking down, appearing devoid of emotion. Even the shortcomings of the jet failed to stir him.

The plane was a small, very old turbo-prop. The seats were worn and uncomfortable. With the slightest bit of turbulence, the plane emitted loud creaking noises as it bounced about. The cold air that circulated throughout the cabin appeared to enter the plane from the seams around the windows and doors. My imagination ran wild.

This plane is defying all the laws of physics! Are we flying in an unpressurized cabin?!

It could have been true, based on our altitude and the age of the plane. I wasn't sure, being unknowledgeable about aviation. I simply had to dismiss my fears.

Steven appeared to be oblivious to the noises, taking everything in stride. Meanwhile, if I had been a nail biter, I would have chewed my nails down to the quick. I was a nervous wreck!

Our forty-minute flight finally ended as the plane taxied to the gate. As we exited, the baggage handlers were already removing the luggage stowed away under the belly of the plane and placing it in a row.

When Steven grabbed the handle of his large rectangular bag, the case fell away from the handle and hit the ground. It opened upon impact. His clothing fell in a pile at his feet.

A look of bewilderment crossed his face. He stood there holding the handle until the older—but spry—gentleman who had been seated in front of me kneeled down to help. Together, they tossed the clothing back into the case which had obviously been broken by one of the baggage handlers.

Steven was not the least bit phased. He walked away with the case cradled in his arms, his shirt hoisted up above his belly. Somehow, he managed to carry his cumbersome package.

We exited the Baltimore airport from baggage claim. The sky was cloudy. The air was cold and brisk, if a bit warmer than Cleveland. The street was a hubbub of activity with moving vehicles, pedestrians, and luggage everywhere. Empty taxis and limos were parked along the curb, waiting for riders. One at a time, the taxis moved forward, stopping to load a passenger or two.

Finally, we were first in line. The driver rolled down the front window and asked, "Where to?"

"Towson, please." The driver shook his head, "No! Sorry."

This was followed by several more negative responses from other drivers. *Why? What's wrong with Towson? Hmm!*

At last, I found an agreeable driver. He was a kindly faced, older gentleman. *Perhaps he's retired.* Steven placed his broken suitcase between us and I closed the door. The driver lifted the lever on the meter.

As we drove through the city, I kept listening and looking at the ticking meter. I asked, "How long a ride is it to Sheppard Pratt Hospital?"

The driver cleared his throat, "Um, maybe forty minutes to an hour. It'll depend on traffic."

"Approximately how much will the trip cost?" There was sixty-eight dollars plus a credit card in my wallet. Cab fare was a cash-only transaction, and I had no way of knowing if the driver was taking the shortest route possible.

He thought awhile. "Maybe twenty dollars."

To and from will cost me forty dollars.

With five children to house, feed, and clothe, I was always one paycheck away from being broke—credit cards were my salvation. But, today, money wasn't my only concern.

There was too much to do in so little time. I hadn't factored in the travel time to and from the airport. Nor had I considered the possibility of delays.

It was now 11:30 a.m. *Please, God, keep me on schedule.*

Social services had recommended that I meet with the entire team assigned to Steven's care: his psychiatrist, his medical doctor, social services, the occupational and vocational therapists, and his nutritionist. This would allow for an exchange of information and could take untold hours. I had hoped for a tour of the facility along with seeing his room and meeting his roommate, if that was possible. All this, plus time for parting and my return trip to the airport, had to be accomplished before 6:30 p.m.

Hoping to avoid any snags in my return to the Baltimore Washington International Airport, I asked him, "Sir, is there any possibility you could return later?"

"No way. I quit work at noon. After you, I'm off the clock." He pulled a business card out of his pocket, "Call the dispatcher about two hours before you're ready to leave the hospital."

Now I had reason for concern. My estimated time of departure from the hospital was during rush hour. Cabs are known for being notoriously late—something I couldn't afford to be today.

If I miss my plane, will I end up sleeping on a bench in the terminal?

Better erase that thought!

Our cab had traveled north from the airport. The lack of conversation between Steven and me made the hum of the engine sound like a roar. He hadn't spoken a word since climbing into the car. At least this was acceptable behavior.

Our driver broke the silence. He pointed as he spoke, "Look over there. That's Towson Market Place, the largest indoor shopping mall in the surrounding area." Like a travel guide, he continued to tell us that Towson was the county seat—we were in suburban Baltimore.

Soon, the business district transitioned into a residential section. Large stone and brick homes dotted the landscape. The area reminded me of our previous home in Shaker Heights.

Looking at my reflection in the rearview mirror, my face appeared worn and worried. The cabbie saw it, too. Recognizing my stress, he said, "Miss, don't be so worried.

"Sheppard Pratt is topnotch. I'm from Baltimore and I know the hospital is ranked among the best in the country for psychiatric treatment. Like you and your boy, people travel long distances for treatment here. You'll see. Your son will do well!

"Why, you'd think it was a spa. Many chauffeur-driven limousines have been parked alongside my cab. The people I've taxied there are educated and refined. It's often difficult for me to decide who the patient is. The talkative individuals tell me the same story. They're being treated for exhaustion. They need rest and relaxation."

Silently, I reflected on his comment. *So, Sheppard Pratt caters to the rich and famous!* That thought gave me a little comfort. Leaving Steven at an out-of-state facility for months or years troubled me. At that time, Sheppard Pratt utilized Dr. Karl Menninger's treatment plan which meant long-term hospitalization.

Am I making the best decisions for him? According to his doctor, I was.

Or am I? Damn it! There's that God-awful indecision again.

Deep in thought, I had become momentarily oblivious of my surroundings until the cab slowed as the driver negotiated a turn. Our vehicle was about to pass through the central archway of a gatehouse—a structure I would expect to see at the entrance to a rich man's estate.

It looked magnificent! The exterior's decorative stone walls were composed of three triangular peaks. The gables enclosed the sloping ends of a ridged roof. Each gable was trimmed with scalloped lattice work. The Late Gothic Revival architecture was characteristic of French and English churches and castles that were built in the 1800s. As the cab continued on its way, I turned around to look back at the gatehouse, a National Historic Landmark.

In the foreground, on each side of the thoroughfare, tall stately woods and pines grew freely as nature intended. To shed light along the way, there stood an occasional, gothic-style lamppost. The cab gently swayed as the road twisted and turned until we reached the facility, a series of red brick buildings with towers and gables. *Tucked away in this secluded and serene setting, it doesn't even look like a hospital. What a harmonious setting!*

Sheppard Pratt Hospital's conditions were ground-breaking when it finally opened in 1891. Elsewhere, the norm was to have patients hidden away in dark, dungeon-like facilities. Patients at Sheppard Pratt were guaranteed sunlight and fresh air. Its founders were Moses Sheppard—who was inspired by the work of social reformer Dorothea Dix—and Enoch Pratt. Although Dix envisioned a state-run institution, Sheppard felt strongly that such a facility should be private. As a result of the financial stipulations he put in place to ensure its autonomy, The Sheppard Asylum—as it was originally to be named—didn't open until more than three decades after Sheppard's death, with its financial stability still uncertain. The hospital saw its name and future prospects change dramatically when, in 1896, it was bequeathed $2 million by Pratt.

While placing the meter's on-off lever in the off position our driver said, "We're here, miss. Good luck!"

Without responding, I continued to stare at the buildings. I had been totally captivated with the surroundings. Everywhere I looked, there appeared to be an entrance. There were doors galore: double doors, single doors, wooden doors, and glass doors. Immediately, I felt confused. *Where do we enter?*

Scanning the doors once more, in search of a directional sign, I exited the vehicle. As I rose from my seat in the cab, I continued to look up at the lovely three-and-one-half story structure. Instantaneously, I became paralyzed with fear and taken back in time. I was once more a five-year-old helpless child tightly holding Daddy's hand as I looked up at the towering hospital building.

"Mom! Pay the driver." Steven's loud voice startled me!

Pulling 3 ten-dollar bills from my purse, I gave them to the driver. "Thank you." Blood rushed to my face. "Keep the change."

Beverly, get a hold of yourself! You're an adult, Steven's mother, and he needs your help. Steven and I followed the walkway before us and entered the facility.

Like the architecture and grounds, everything inside the building was impressive. This included the staff. An elegantly dressed receptionist sat at a large mahogany desk.

"Who are you here to see?" She had a decided accent that I couldn't quite place—perhaps she was a Brit or maybe a New Englander.

"We have an appointment with social services and Dr. Hill. My son's being admitted today."

The chic lady picked up the receiver to her phone to announce our arrival. After a short wait, a young fortyish, stunning black woman walked towards us. Dr. Hill gave me a cordial, "Hello," and ushered Steven into a nearby office.

The social worker, a petite older woman, led me to her office. Mrs. Ward's desk was strategically placed in front of an elongated window with a view of the grounds. Had the sun been shining, it would have been a cheerful office. Remembering how dungeon-like my windowless cubbyhole of an office had been at Cleveland State Hospital, I smiled to myself taking pleasure in the knowledge that Steven would make his home for the foreseeable future in a place that was so vastly different from my former workplace.

First, there was a portfolio of papers regarding admissions for me to sign. Afterwards, Mrs. Ward proceeded to ask me a barrage of questions regarding Steven's birth, childhood, schooling, health— medical and psychiatric—and the family—father, grandparents, aunts, uncles, and siblings. At last, she stopped talking.

My God! I thought all that information was on the papers I already gave her.

Finally, she asked, "Do you have any questions?'

"No!" I felt brain dead. I looked at my watch. *It's already 4:00 p.m.*

"Could you please call a taxi for me?"

As it turned out, there was no time to meet with the rest of Steven's treatment team. Steven was waiting for me in the lobby, looking like a misfit in these formal surroundings. His shirt was hiked up, exposing his tummy. And the suitcase that he should have been carrying in his arms was now being held by the rope that had been used to fasten it shut when the handle broke.

Being apprehensive that at any moment the contents could spill to the floor, I began to stammer, "Steven." Fortunately, he became aware of the impending predicament, lifted the case with both hands, and resumed carrying it within his arms. A short, pudgy young man approached us and introduced himself. He would escort us to Steven's room.

Again, I was impressed by what I saw. The bedroom was large and the window had *no bars!* The furnishings—twin beds, dressers, and nightstands—were made of highly polished walnut. The beds had comfortable-looking mattresses, box springs, fluffy pillows, and cotton bedding. Adjoining the room was a full bathroom with a stall shower—hotel-like, I'd say!

Other mental facilities of the same vintage were cold and austere, almost prison-like, with rooms typically small, nine feet by six feet in size. Windows were often peepholes, and always barred. The bed frames and springs were made of steel and covered with thin mats. If the patient was fortunate, he had a flat pillow, a coarse sheet, a wool blanket, and a metal nightstand. And the bath and toilet facilities were communal.

Steven's roommate was seated on his bed, apparently studying. He, too, was in his teens. He was a healthy-looking, well-groomed young man who appeared alert and energetic—free from the side effects of psychiatric drugs. From my brief conversation with him, he spoke intelligently. In fact, he had no faulty speech patterns and, in every way, seemed like a perfectly *normal* individual. I wondered how long he had been a patient at the hospital. I knew he was schizophrenic, like Steven, because housing patients with similar afflictions was the applied treatment technique at Sheppard Pratt.

My tour and brief introduction to his roommate were over. It was time to leave. An attendant accompanied Steven and me to the lobby. I studied the doors—no locks. Even Ridgecliff Hospital had locked wards, and it was a newer treatment center.

Saying goodbye to Steven would not be easy. Feeling stiff and awkward, I walked towards my son with my arms extended, in an attempt to embrace him. He turned away. I desperately wanted to hug my son, but I knew from the past that he was not capable of showing his affection to anyone—he didn't like physical contact. There were no hugs, no kisses or emotion expressed, just, "Goodbye, Mom."

How can he be unmoved by my departure? He's totally detached emotionally from the experience. Unlike me, he's devoid of feelings because he's ill.

As I walked away, I kept turning around in hopes that Steven would throw me a kiss or wave goodbye. I expected some reaction—rational or irrational—from him. When there was none, I felt rejected!

I slowly walked down the path to the waiting cab, stopping on occasion to retrieve a clean tissue from my handbag. The walk seemed unending. The pounding of my heart echoed in my ears. *How can I leave him there?*

The loneliness I felt was incomprehensible! My heart quivered with the same separation anxiety I had felt as a child. *Mommy!*

There was no denying my wound had opened once more. Only this time *I* was "the mommy."

Dear God, why did this have to happen again?

The taxi driver leaned over and rolled down the window, snapping me out of my thoughts. "BWI, miss?"

35

STEVEN'S NEXT CHAPTER

While he was hospitalized in Maryland, I would look at Steven's empty chair on holidays or other celebrations and my heart would ache. A part of me felt detached and lost without Steven. *Dear God, please bring Steven, his siblings, and me back together once more.*

Steven turned twenty-one during his stay at Sheppard Pratt. His siblings and I couldn't be with him on his birthday, since it fell on a weekday. So I planned for the delivery of a cake on his special day, and celebrated the occasion with him the following weekend. It still fell far short of what I longed for in my heart. Only time would tell if my prayer would come true.

Steven's stay at Sheppard Pratt was long and drawn out. I had not anticipated how taxing it would be for him to be institutionalized so far away. For over two years, every other weekend, I made the long, lonesome journey to Maryland.

Very quickly, I began to accumulate debts. Michelle and Michael were too young to be left at home alone. Providing them with a caregiver around the clock was costly. I would usually fly out and back on the same day, but on occasion, I stayed overnight at a nearby hotel to have more one-on-one time with Steven. Although round-trip plane tickets were expensive, driving to Maryland was just as costly, if not more so, because of the extra travel day. But I had made a commitment from the first day of Steven's admittance to Sheppard Pratt that I would beg, borrow, or sacrifice, whatever the cost, to be there for Steven and help him regain his sanity.

My heart swelled with joy as I smiled at Steven. A handsome, tall young man with curly blond hair strolled down the hall to greet me. His skin was clear and his brown eyes sparkled as he smiled and said, "Hello." He radiated health, vitality, and confidence. He was dressed in black slacks, a long-sleeved white dress shirt, and new brown leather shoes. His clothing fit on his trim, muscular body—no sign of a tummy—as if they were made for him.

Steven was completing his second year of treatment. He could hold a conversation on sports or politics or just chitchat with you. He had a job at the school nearby as a playground instructor for disabled children. He had a bank account into which he deposited his wages and he was learning how to manage his money.

I was elated. *He can have a normal life!* Dr. Monnley had been right; Steven's stay at Shepard Pratt had returned him to the young man I had known before schizophrenia. I had high hopes for his future.

It was now May 1984, and preparations were being made for Steven's discharge and return to Cleveland. The treatment team's goal was for Steven to be as independent as possible. The team recommended that he be transferred directly from the hospital into a halfway house.

In June, he flew from Baltimore to Cleveland and back, without a chaperone, for an interview with the administrator of the halfway house. We found out the next day that he had been accepted. I was beside myself with happiness over his progress.

To afford the cost of living in the halfway house, Steven needed an income. His social worker had helped him apply for Supplemental Security Income. His first check, which included back payments, was directly deposited in his account in Towson. But when the time came to transfer his funds to a bank account in

Cleveland and pay the deposit for his room, over seventy-five percent of the money had been withdrawn.

My gut instinct told me that something was wrong. Steven was the only one who had access to the account in Towson. I had been paying for his clothing and any expenditures over and above his inpatient care. *How did he spend the money? Did someone take advantage of him? Was it spent foolishly?*

I couldn't figure out what had happened with Steven's money. I didn't know his friends and it was impossible to investigate from several states away. Allowing myself to get swept up in my euphoria over his good behavior and pending discharge, I ignored my gut. But the missing money was a red flag that I should have paid better attention to.

July came and Steven was discharged from Sheppard Pratt. He flew back to Cleveland on his own. I met him at the airport and spent the remainder of the day with him at the halfway house. We met with the director, unpacked Steven's clothing, personalized his room, and had dinner at a local restaurant. He was well-mannered and compliant, but uncharacteristically quiet. *He's just overwhelmed by the travel and change.*

After two nights in his new surroundings, Steven began calling home three and four times a day, each time asking to come home. After several days, it was more of the same. "I don't like it here. Can I come home?"

"Steven, living in a halfway house is part of your treatment plan. How about spending Saturday with us?"

"Sure, that'll be good." The words echoed in my ear.

I replaced the handset on its base. I didn't sleep well that night.

The next day, Steven left the group home without permission, and walked five miles to Shaker Heights where he knocked on the door of our previous home. When he was told, "You no longer live here," he lay down on the grass and began crying hysterically. He bit his lips until they bled and thrashed about as if he was having a seizure.

My friend and former neighbor saw Steven and called me. She had tried to calm him down and suggested that he stay at her home until I could get there. He refused to leave the lawn. Before I arrived, the home's new owner had notified the police. They transported Steven, by now totally incoherent, to Cleveland Psychiatric Institute.

In less than a week after his discharge, Steven was actively psychotic. Despite more than two years of treatment in a leading psychiatric hospital, the attention of the best psychiatrists, and access to the newest and most effective medications, Steven still couldn't function outside of a hospital. He had the best possible treatment and support at Shepard Pratt.

There was no way to escape my feelings. I was devastated. I had failed. His doctors had failed. His treatment team had failed. The whole universe had failed my son, even God!

Why?! What do you want from me?! What more could we have done for Steven?

After I shared my distress with Steven's psychiatrist, she advised me not to give myself too hard a time over his need for further hospitalization. In her words, "many times, a short hospitalization following some traumatic event can redirect the patient and help him to continue working on existing issues." Her advice gave me a sorely needed sliver of hope.

Three months later, Steven was discharged from Cleveland Psychiatric Institute. Making the halfway house his home was no longer an option, so his siblings and I welcomed him home.

He planned to find a job and eventually leave the nest. But having been challenged with mental health issues in his teens, finding his niche in life was a challenge. He scanned the help wanted ads and called on several fast food restaurants but the gap in his employment history was hard to explain away. He became a discouraged young man as he looked for work.

At twenty-two, Steven could no longer be covered under my health insurance. With such a low income from Supplemental Security Income, I took him to Job and Family Services to apply for Medicaid. While waiting for approval, Steven had to use the free clinic for his psychiatric care. The nearest one was in Cleveland's inner city. Back then, public transportation from Lake County to Cleveland didn't exist so I had to drive him. Once there, long lines made for an extended wait to see a psychiatrist, and while we waited, much to my chagrin, Steven would talk to himself, fidget, and smoke like a chimney. I expected him to flee the waiting room at any second.

Despite facing these challenges to receive treatment, Steven managed to stay out of the hospital until mid-February 1985. One day, his behavior suddenly became shockingly bizarre.

Steven had finished eating breakfast. He left the table and went into the bathroom, leaving the door ajar. Several minutes passed. I heard no water running or toilet flushing. *Why is it so quiet in there?* Concerned, I walked over and looked in through the open door.

Steven was standing in front of the washbasin, glaring at the mirror. I looked on in shock. He leaned closer to his reflection and repeatedly dug his fingernails into his skin, pinching the tissue together, leaving angry red marks. Blood trickled from spots on his nose, cheeks, and chin. He was mumbling under his breath in a strange voice saying, "You're an ugly son-of-a-bitch," and contorting his features into a series of evil-looking grimaces expressing hate, contempt, and disgust in turn. He clearly disliked the man in the mirror.

In a loud, stern voice, I called out, "Steven, stop it! You'll scar your face!"

He didn't seem to hear me, and continued with his self-mutilation and also began pulling out chunks of his hair. He clearly needed to be admitted to a hospital as soon as possible.

Even though I managed to get him to the nearest hospital, Steven adamantly refused to sign any papers! There was no reasoning with him. Hospital staff informed me that now that he was an adult, Steven had to voluntarily give his consent for admission and treatment. We returned home.

The next day, I valiantly tried to convince my angry son to get help. I begged him saying, "Please come with me."

The same evil look of dislike that he had given himself was now directed at me. He was behaving exactly like his grandmother, Angelina. In a deafening voice he hollered, "No! I'm not going anywhere!" Then he cursed me and pounded his fist against the wall. I called the police.

In spite of the obvious property damage that Steven had caused, the officers first tried to coax him to come along with them peacefully. He truly didn't understand that he was ill or why he had to leave his home and became combative.

When one of the officers moved as if to grab his arm, Steven threw a punch, knocked a chair over, and tried to escape. But he was outnumbered, and the three officers managed to restrain him in handcuffs.

It broke my heart to see Steven treated like a criminal. History was repeating itself, as he was dragged out of his home with an officer on each arm, just like his grandmother had been. Seeing the parallels between my son and my mother brought a feeling of dread to my heart. *What if Steven is never truly well again? Are we destined to repeat this scene over and over?* I couldn't bear the thought of having to call the police every time my child refused to get the care he needed. *There has to be a better, kinder way than this.*

This time Steven was taken to Western Reserve Psychiatric Hospital. The state-run facility was really more of a mini-city, located in a secluded section of the City of Northfield. Chronic patients were either sent here or transferred to this location from private hospitals when they found themselves without insurance or funds. Unfortunately, this was my son's situation.

Steven was housed in a cottage, a three-story brick building with over a dozen seven-by-eight private bedrooms housing only male patients. The cottage also had communal dining, indoor recreation, visitation, bathroom, and bathing facilities. The hospital had at least twenty of these cottages for male and female mentally ill patients. Each cottage had a separate fenced-in outdoor recreation area, and maintained its own security system, with bars on all the doors and windows.

From the road, high, barbed-wire fencing and a vacant guardhouse gave this hospital the appearance of a prison. As I drove onto the grounds to visit Steven, I noted that the condition of the hospital's sign, gated fence, large electric generators, gravel drive, and even its landscaping indicated years of neglect. An old familiar knot began to form in the pit of my stomach. I had also come here as a youngster, decades earlier, to visit my mother.

Why? What did I do wrong? Why Steven? Did someone cast a Maloik, the evil eye, on us?

376

The longer I thought about my lot in life, the angrier I became. *God, why have you abandoned me?! Why are you punishing me?! I don't deserve this! Steven doesn't deserve this!*

After parking my car near Steven's cottage, I slowly climbed the eight concrete steps to its front door and was surprised to find it unlocked. Inside the vestibule there was a second door with a sign posted next to it that read *Ring for Attendant*. I rang the bell, and within seconds, a head appeared in the small window in the steel security door. Several men took turns peeping at me. There was disheveled-looking, foggy-eyed young man, a plump, moonfaced fellow who looked to be in his fifties, and a bald, round-shouldered gent who gave me a big, toothless grin.

Finally, a tall, muscular, broad-shouldered man dressed in a lab coat appeared and opened the door. Without any pleasantries or introductions, he stated, "Visitors are few and far between at this facility. You've stirred up a bit of excitement for the patients. They're just looking for a familiar face, their social worker or a family member."

The attendant left to get Steven from his bedroom while I sat alone in a small visitation room. The area was sparsely furnished with a few worn, brown-padded chrome chairs and a small wooden table strewn with outdated magazines.

Steven walked in and sat in one of the chairs. His movements were awkward and stiff. He was like a walking zombie.

What's happened to my boy? Steven's sweat suit was wrinkled and his curly hair was tousled from sleep. His eyes were glazed over and his lips looked cracked and dry. White patches of dried saliva had accumulated in the corners of his mouth.

For several minutes, I attempted to have a conversation with Steven, but he had a flat affect—a complete lack of emotional expression—and appeared not to comprehend a word of what I was saying. I finally gave up and called for the attendant. He returned Steven to his room and then escorted me to the door.

After I asked Steven's doctor about his behavior and explained what I had seen, he was prescribed a lower dose of his psychiatric medications. He rebounded quickly and was discharged within a few months. But I believe that despite his progress, he returned home too soon. Within a month, he had another relapse, yelling, screaming, and threatening all of us. He set fire to the carpeting and punched the walls in his bedroom.

Getting Steven committed again was another emotionally crippling experience. This was his sixth hospitalization. Like it or not, I had to accept the truth that my son was chronically ill.

Steven's doctor recommended that I seek to have him declared mentally incompetent by reason of chronic schizophrenia. I consulted an attorney to complete the necessary paperwork. Probate court appointed me guardian over Steven's person and finances in August 1985.

This time, Steven remained at Western Reserve until June 1987. His story becomes repetitive between 1987 and 1990. During this period, Steven was caught again in the revolving door of hospitalization, as he had three stretches at Western Reserve Psychiatric Hospital. I was eaten up by worry and stress, longing for relief from the pain I felt.

By 1990, Steven was receiving assistance from Lake County Mental Health Services. Upon his discharge from Western Reserve, he received a respite bed at North Coast House, a transitional short-term housing unit in Painesville for the mentally ill. He was expected to live there until he qualified for independent living quarters.

From the very first day, he didn't want to be there. He told the manager of the facility in no uncertain terms that there was nothing wrong with him, saying, "I don't need to be in a halfway house, and I don't need medication. I can live on my own." He dismissed any logical explanation for why he should stay and left after a three-day stay.

I wasn't aware of Steven's actions until he showed up at my door. Within minutes of his arrival, his attending psychiatrist called to inform me that he had left North Coast House.

"I know. He's here with me. Who gave him the authority to leave? I didn't! I'm his guardian, for God's sake! He had no right to leave!"

The doctor responded saying, "He followed the established procedure. He gave a three-day notice regarding his intent to leave the facility. There's no way to justify keeping him in the transitional house with his lack of willingness to participate in the program, in spite of your guardianship. The staff has given up on him. They have a lot of people to care for. He's an adult now and can choose for himself. And, no, he can't be reinstated to Western Reserve unless you have him probated."

The doctor's last statement jarred me. *What good is my guardianship?! It's worthless if I still have to go through probate court! For God's sake, he's adjudicated incompetent! He was discharged too soon. If they'd kept him longer, he would have been co-operative.*

After my indignation and anger subsided, I found myself conflicted over my son's options. Should he be probated and return to the hospital, or temporarily live at home, where I could see for myself how he was behaving? Having him at home would give me additional time to look into my other options. Because he was mostly compliant and pleasant, I decided to keep him home for the short-term, while I sought out some advice.

My first call was to my attorney. She confirmed what the doctor had said. I would have to use probate court to return Steven to Western Reserve.

She suggested that I look for a nursing home that provided care for the mentally ill—one that would take assignment of his Supplemental Security Income. *Why would I want to place him in a facility with old people with dementia?! He's still so young and vital! There's got to be another way for him to make a life for himself.*

She also suggested that I transfer Steven out of state to a long-term, publicly funded hospital. *No! He already went to another state and it didn't work. He needs interaction with his family.*

Next, I consulted several mental health experts. Their responses were less than satisfactory.

A social services worker at the local mental hospital told me, "Sorry, the community is not set up for assisting the mentally ill with housing."

A mental health service provider showed me sympathy, but offered no viable suggestions.

Steven's Pathways case manager said, "All is not lost. He can return to North Coast again after he's hospitalized, and stay there while he's waiting to be placed in more permanent housing. But for the time being, I have found an opening for him in a homeless shelter in Cleveland!" *No! There's a hole in this system. Where's the safety net?! I'll keep him home with me before I see him begging in the street!*

Instead, I found Steven a room at the downtown Cleveland YMCA. The front desk clerks at the Y offered to keep an eye on him for me, but they didn't realize what a handful someone like Steven could be. Although they kept Steven's valuables—his medicine, money, and cigarettes—protected in the YMCA's safe, before his first week was out, Steven had gone through all of his money and two cartons of cigarettes. The fellows at the front desk couldn't protect Steven from himself.

There's got to be a place for him to live! God knows I can't continue being torn between Steven's needs and those of my other children.

Before long, Steven had another breakdown and returned to Western Reserve. Several months later, he again left the hospital for a respite bed at North Coast House. The second time was the charm, as he followed the rules and qualified for his own apartment. But once he was alone, without twenty-four-hour-a-day supervision, the apartment quickly became unfit to live in.

Even though I cleaned it for him three times a week, in between my visits, it was the same old story. Steven scattered ashes and cigarette butts everywhere. Soda, chips, cereal, and all types of crumbs were spilled over the kitchen table and chairs, sofa, and end table. Worst of all, because Steven was smoking so much, he would cough to the point of gagging, and vomit on top of dirty dishes in the kitchen sink, on his clothing, carpeting, and just about everywhere and anywhere. And he never cleaned up after himself.

Steven's lack of cleanliness was his nasty little secret. Although he probably could have been evicted for creating unsanitary conditions, his loud laughter and piano playing is what got him in trouble. In November 1992, after less than six months, he was evicted for causing a disturbance.

His case manager suggested looking into the Lake County Home for Steven's next residence. The building was constructed in 1876–7 and formerly was known as the County Infirmary, or "poor house." It now houses the Lake County Historical Society,

380

and is located on several acres of land on the outskirts of down-town Painesville. The home is a large, impressive-looking, brick building. It had separate facilities for men and women, and fulfilled its mission to provide residential care for those unable to provide care for themselves by housing the city's indigent. This described my Steven. I was hopeful.

I immediately went to talk to the superintendent, who lived on the property with his wife and children. He shared with me that he and his family ate meals and celebrated holidays together with the residents. I thought this would be a great place for Steven to live, and was relieved when he was accepted and assigned his own room.

The superintendent and I came to an agreement. Each week, I would fill Steven's pillbox and bring it to the home, along with his weekly allowance and cigarettes. Steven's medication, money, and cigarettes would be stowed safely away in the office. The superintendent would monitor Steven's usage.

Seeing that he was an able-bodied young man, the superintendent assigned Steven daily chores of mopping the hall floors and cleaning the tables after meals. But other than these chores, Steven's days were largely unstructured. He'd often walk away from the home and roam the streets of downtown Painesville. He frequently missed lunch or dinner and his work had to be done by someone else.

All was well for a couple of weeks, and then Steven's complaints began. "The building's old and I can't see. It's too dark inside. It's too cold. It's spooky. There's a ghost in my room."

And he was partially right. His room was painted dark brown and had brown woodwork. One forty-watt lightbulb in a ceiling fixture struggled to illuminate the rectangular, six-by-eight bedroom. And the architectural style of the building and dim lighting would lead even an individual less apt to delusions than my son to envision a ghost emerging from the shadows on the walls.

About six months into his stay at the Lake County Home, things went downhill again. Steven, alone in his room at night paced, pounded on the door, or lay on his bed screaming, disrupting the other residents. Despite my efforts and that of the superintendent to monitor his medication, he hadn't taken it. Most likely, Steven pretended to swallow his pills, and spit them out when the superintendent was out of sight. The plan had failed. Being actively psychotic once more, he returned to the hospital.

From 1992 to 1994, Steven was in and out of three different hospitals. During the "out" periods, he lived in his own apartment. But each time, the results were the same; he would become psychotic and be asked to move for disrupting the tenants.

In 1994, Steven returned to Western Reserve Psychiatric Hospital. He was a very sick young man and was restricted to his cottage.

One day in November, the doorbell rang in the cottage where Steven lived. Several visitors were waiting together to enter the building. As usual, the presence of callers excited the patients, who soon gathered in front of the door, taking turns to quickly glance at who was there. When the attendant opened the door to let the visitors in, two of the patients stopped them to beg for cigarettes or change. The attendant failed to notice Steven as he darted past and exited the building.

That evening, the staff informed me of the incident. A patient returning from the commissary had reported seeing Steven race down the steps and head for the woods. I was told that no one had been able catch up with him.

I cried. I worried. I called the police. Everyone said nothing could be done for forty-eight hours. For now, no reports could be made, no search party could be organized, and I felt like I had no one to talk to. I sat and agonized over Steven's disappearance. It was maddening!

My thoughts ran wild as I envisioned Steven, running through the woods, all smiles and happy. I imagined him darting to and fro, swept away in the elation of newfound freedom. I knew hunting season had begun and he had been dressed in a brown shirt, brown trousers, and black tennis shoes. *Will Steven be mistaken for a young white-tailed deer?*

Sleep eluded me as I pictured my hungry son, venturing far into the forest, stumbling over rocks, walking between the brush and thickets in the darkness of the night, without the faintest idea of where he was going. Steven was out in the cold without a hat, coat, or gloves. The longer he remained missing, the more mishaps and fears my mind created.

Miraculously, Steven found his way out of the woods. He had been missing for almost two days. The soles of his tennis shoes had fallen apart. His clothing was now tattered and torn. His exposed knees and elbows were cut and scraped. He had frostbite and an infection in his foot. He was exhausted and more delusional than ever when the Northfield police found him wandering the streets and brought him back to the hospital.

Prior to his release from Western Reserve in 1995, I gave my consent for Steven's participation in a pilot program. He would have a case manager to assist him with integrating back into the community.

That same year, Steven started receiving a new long-acting injectable medication. Just as with any of his medications, Steven was initially resistant to the shots, and it took six years for him to freely comply with the administration of the injections. Because he was noncompliant on occasion, the drug was not as effective as it might have been.

From 1995 to 1997, Steven found himself once again in the revolving door phenomenon: four stays in the hospital alternating with five failed independent living stints. Like the frustrated TV weatherman in the movie Groundhog Day, Steven and I were damned to the same fate with each recurrence.

Living by himself isolated Steven. Without the basic living skills of meal planning, shopping, cooking, and cleaning, he created an unsanitary mess in his apartment. Living alone meant he had no one to hold him accountable for taking his medication. Without consistent medication, he became psychotic and his disruptive behavior led to eviction.

Steven never truly lived independently. I helped him by allocating his money and taking him to dinner and many other activities. I always had to help him with cleaning, grocery shopping, and washing his clothes. He couldn't begin to do these jobs without direction. He couldn't fend for himself. Wrapping his brain around the task at hand was not possible.

While Steven was bouncing in and out of hospitals and housing,

I felt like I was losing my sanity. I was struggling to walk a tight-rope, balancing my time between helping Steven and caring for my other children. I was a doing a poor job, because providing Steven's basic needs outweighed everyone else's, including my own.

I found myself caught up in a catch-22: bringing Steven home with me wouldn't last in the long run because I couldn't always be there for him, and he didn't have the skills to successfully live independently. Trying to make the best of this situation, I was caught in an exhausting vicious cycle. This was my worst night-mare. There had to be a way to resolve this problem. *Without a home, what kind of future does my son have?! None! All the psychiatrists and psychiatric drugs in the world won't heal a person unless their basic needs of food, shelter, and love are met!*

One of the few things that kept me sane was knowing that I wasn't alone. I met parents, siblings, and other family members who faced a similar challenge—providing a home for a loved one with mental illness. Together, we found the strength and hope to contin-ue on this journey. We never gave up on finding a permanent home for our loved ones. We met weekly, sitting around the kitchen table, drinking coffee, and discussing our options. Our coffee klatch grew and later became part of the National Alliance on Mental Illness.

Our group educated others about the need for a residential treatment facility, or group home, in Lake County. We lobbied our government representatives for support and funding. From 1993–6, I was a member of an ad hoc housing committee that established two group homes for the mentally ill of Lake County.

Steven's next move, in December 1997, was to one of those group homes. He had trouble adjusting to a group situation and abiding by the house rules. I was devastated when I was told that Steven wanted to move out of the group home. He returned to the inde-pendent living program in February 1999.

His new residence was a small efficiency apartment in a stately century home in Painesville. In August, he received a warning for causing flooding in the boiler room directly below his apartment. In November, he received a second notice when the basement flooded again. Fortunately, there was no structural damage at that time. But, adding to my distress, I knew that if he had received a third warning, he would be forced to move.

In Steven's defense, he wasn't entirely responsible for the water damage. I discovered a hole under the cabinet in his bathroom. The floor in the room sloped towards the hole and water from Steven's shower found its way into the basement.

Once the floor was repaired, there were no more floods in the basement, but I still found wet and mildewed rugs beside the tub. Steven had always taken to water like a seal. Now, sometimes he showered twice a day, probably without pulling the curtain closed.

I was back on my tightrope, balancing Steven's needs and everything else in my life. This time, the demands of his care threatened to topple me. I was constantly replacing rugs and mopping up Steven's bathroom in addition to all the other duties I had assumed. Even spending three evenings a week with him wasn't enough. I was getting really stressed out.

The plumbing continued to be Steven's nemesis. He managed to plug up the toilet next. It turned out that when he didn't finish his cereal or soup, he would flush it down the commode. Several times, I found a clogged, overflowing toilet on my visits.

I talked at Steven about not treating his toilet like a garbage disposal until I was blue in the face. He must have tuned me out because his behavior didn't change. As a last resort, I bought a plunger and instructed him on its use.

Eventually, the toilet gasket leaked. The combination of a wobbly potty and water leaking through the seal damaged the flooring. In order to avoid having Steven evicted, I paid to have the flooring repaired, the apartment cleaned, and the walls painted.

In September 2004, Steven was still residing at the efficiency. His new archenemy was the lock on the door. It could be locked with a key from both the inside and outside. He kept misplacing or losing his key and would find himself locked in or out. My solution was to place his key on a long chain around his neck. That didn't help, as now he lost the chain *and* the key.

Steven lost his key one time too many, and tried to circumvent my wrath over his negligence by leaving his front window slightly open when he went out. He didn't see anything wrong with entering and exiting his apartment through the window, but the police did. They contacted me, saying, "For his own protection, this behavior has got to stop. He'll be mistaken for a robber and get shot!"

I was constantly on edge waiting for the other shoe to drop as Steven went from one predicament to another. It was an exhausting way for me to live.

By December, Steven was showing signs of decompensation. He seemed to play a game with his medication. Getting him to co-operate was hit or miss. When he would adamantly refuse his injections, he'd say, "I don't need meds. I'm okay." But, of course, he wasn't.

That month, Steven was hospitalized for the twenty-first time. The brevity of this psychotic episode allowed him to maintain living at the efficiency.

Then in March, I ran into the third-floor tenant in the entryway to Steven's house. She told me, "I hear Stevie sobbing and pounding on the walls at night. The couple on the second floor said they were going to report him. But I like Stevie. I didn't want to see him in trouble, so I went downstairs and knocked on his door. I thought he needed someone to talk to and would quiet down if I talked to him, but he wouldn't listen to me."

I thanked her for her concern and then paused before slowly opening the door to Steven's efficiency. I began coughing as the smell of cigarette smoke practically knocked me over as opened the door.

I looked inside and cringed. Cherry soda and potato chips were spilled all over the furniture and floor. Clothing that I had neatly stacked on the shelves of the built-in storage unit two days before was strewn about the room.

The smell of sour milk along with the pungent odor of rancid meat gagged me. The door to the refrigerator had been left wide open. *I wonder how long he left it like that?* An empty carton lay on its side on the top shelf. Milk had spilled and collected in a puddle on the bottom. Steven had taken out several frozen dinners, opened them, and then tossed the untouched food into the trash can. *What a waste!*

The stench of human waste halted me at the bathroom door. The toilet had overflowed, the plunger still remaining in the bowl.

As I looked around at the work I had cut out for me, I felt nauseated and even the marrow in my bones seemed to ache. *I can't keep doing this. I can't! I can't keep picking up and cleaning up after Steven. I've got to be crazy.* I wanted to scream and cry at the same time. Then I looked at the bed.

Steven laid in a fetal position. His body was encased in a large brown blanket. I knew that he was sick again and my heart broke. *Living alone like this isn't good for you. Will you ever have a good life? Where will you go from here?*

By then it was April, the month that always vexed me. I knew Steven's days in independent living were now numbered. He had exhausted all but one of his housing options. My heart ached for my child as I signed the papers to have Steven admitted to a nearby nursing home in their locked psychiatric unit.

Steven had long had problems with coughing, gagging, and vomiting, especially at mealtime. I had begged him to see a doctor, but my pleas fell on deaf ears. Now that he was being observed by the nursing staff on a daily basis, it became apparent these symptoms were more serious than I had suspected.

By July 2005, Steven was admitted to University Hospital and diagnosed with pericarditis, or inflammation of the membrane surrounding the heart, and a life-threatening abscess in his lungs. The doctors explained to him that he was gravely ill, and his smoking was prohibited. He was a cooperative patient while he was in the hospital.

At this time, Steven's siblings were living out of state. I had recently been diagnosed with breast cancer and was undergoing chemo. As much as it pained me, I followed my doctor's advice not to visit my son. Steven fought a valiant battle alone, and won!

After a month in the hospital, Steven was transferred back to the nursing home. He had a PICC line for several months for intravenous medication, and required skilled nursing as well as psychiatric care.

My memory of the following period is not very clear because I was going through chemotherapy and radiation at the time. I do remember that Steven and I talked on the phone occasionally and his caseworker consulted me regarding his discharge plans. Steven, of course, wanted to return to independent living. I was adamant when I expressed my objections to Steven's caseworker. I knew I couldn't let that happen. Steven would recreate the same unsanitary living conditions. I also knew that placing him in an unstructured environment would lead to a relapse. *He needs more structure and supervision, not less!*

In 2006, Steven was discharged from nursing home care to a group home. After all those years of dashed hopes, Steven finally found a place to live that provided a safe, stable environment. It is a place that gave him a fighting chance to thrive.

Since moving to the group home, Steven has remained out of the hospital. He gets his injection of anti-psychotic drugs regularly. The staff at the group home makes sure that he takes his other drugs. With twenty-four-seven supervision, we can nip any psychosis in the bud before it has a chance to become full-blown.

Today, Steven's life has some quality. He has a healthier diet. He has assigned chores and someone supervises his work. With reminders, he can arrange transportation to and from doctors' appointments and the clinic where he receives his injection. He meets with his disabled peers weekly to eat out, for mall walks, to go bowling, for parties, and to receive education.

As much as his life has improved, Steven hasn't been able to shed certain parts of his previous lifestyle, such as his grooming habits. Typically, his curly hair is disheveled, he's in need of a shave, and his standard gray sweatpants are bleach stained. He's usually dressed inappropriately for the occasion or weather even with prompts from the staff. He's had behavioral problems, but they've been few and far between and far less serious than before.

Steven still can't be expected to cook on his own, handle his money responsibly, or limit his smoking. Whenever someone suggests moving Steven to a less restrictive environment, my greatest concern is about his inability to dispense his own daily medication. He needs more than custodial care in order to be successful.

My visits with my son are enjoyable now. There's no more deep cleaning and much less stress. We will usually share a meal together and I will sometimes bring along a friend. Steven says things like "please," "thank you," and, "I appreciate that." When our visit ends, he says to me, "I love you, Mom." Things are as "normal" as they're going to get for Steven.

I have finally found a bit of a respite from the heartache. But a shadow is closing in on me.

It seems like our approach to people with severe mental illness has shifted from one of locking them out of sight in institutions in my mother's day to now trying to integrate all of them into the community through independent living. I call it the one-size-fits-all approach. However, the reality is that, in every era, there have been and always will be individuals with mental illness who will need to live in supported housing units. To be clear, I do not view nursing homes as appropriate long-term housing options for individuals with mental illness whose physical health does not necessitate that level of care.

I live with the fear that Steven could lose his home and that I won't be able to intervene on his behalf. Individuals who are like Steven but lack a supportive family member often end up homeless or land in jail. There is a dire need for more permanent supportive housing for these most vulnerable members of our communities. But we haven't devoted the necessary funding to build and staff enough facilities to satisfy the growing demand.

I shudder at the thought of my son becoming a panhandler, dressed in soiled and tattered clothing, begging for his meals, and sleeping under a bridge in a cardboard box. This could easily happen to him once I'm gone.

THE LAST ACT

36

CHET KOWALSKI

The gods smiled on Chet after he married his second wife; he finally saw his life-long wish to own a farm become a reality. He bought a black pickup truck and seven-acres with two barns in Seville. He was like Old McDonald, with a couple of pigs, a couple of cows, a horse, chickens, and a goat or two.

While Chet ran the farm, he continued working for the Higbee Company as a maintenance manager at their warehouse in downtown Cleveland. He had made the most of his time as an apprentice for Grandpa Vincenzo. He would never have the humility to admit it, but Grandpa Vincenzo had taught him well.

After his marriage to Cynthia, Chet had no time for phone calls or visits and provided me with no financial support. He used the farm, his job, his new wife, and her nine children all as reasons why he was "too busy" to be part of our sons' lives. *He's taking care of someone else's children but neglecting his own flesh and blood!* Unless I reached out to Chet or Chet's brother and his wife invited him to their home for the holidays, the boys didn't see their father. Understandably, this fostered great resentment in Ted and Martin. Steven didn't have the capacity to understand.

When a Kowalski niece got married in October of 1986, she graciously invited me and all five of my children to the wedding. Only Ted could accompany me to the hall on that rainy evening for the reception. Neither of us had seen Chet in years, nor had we ever met Cynthia. When I had heard that Chet had married a stripper, I had pictured an exotic, sexy, buxom woman. Contrary to my expectations, she was thin and very leggy with light brown curly hair, and her look was surprisingly conservative.

I was dancing with my ex-brother-in-law when I noticed that Cynthia and Ted were engaged in a serious conversation. Later, I asked my son, "What were you and Cynthia talking about?" Ted replied, "Dad, of course. I asked her what the hell she sees in him. She said he was a lonely man who needed somebody." *Perhaps I misjudged her. Maybe she was attracted to him for the right reasons and didn't just see him as a meal ticket for her family.*

A year later, I saw Chet and Cynthia again when they made an appearance at Ted's wedding. I had been seated just before the processional. Turning to look back at the flower girls, I watched as the couple walked hastily down a side aisle and slid into a pew at the rear of the church. After the ceremony, they made their presence known to me, congratulated the newlyweds, and left. That was the last time I saw them together.

My impression is that Chet managed to stay sober for the first six years of his new marriage. But he had lots of stress between his nine step-kids, money, and work. He began calling me regarding our boys, and from the sound of his voice, I could tell that he had started drinking again. One day he phoned me and said, "I'm moving tomorrow. I want you to have my new address and phone number." From the tone of his voice, I could feel Chet's pain. I responded, "What happened?"

Chet had come home from work earlier in the week, and found an empty house. Cynthia had packed up and left with all her kids. The only item she had left behind was a cardboard box in a kitchen cupboard stuffed with unpaid bills and foreclosure statements.

Many an alcoholic has shared Chet's fate. His behavior had shattered his dreams once more. I felt compassion for Chet, yet I knew better than most how living with an alcoholic can push a woman to her breaking point.

For more than two years, Cynthia had been taking the money Chet had been giving her to pay off the mortgage, and saved it in a secret bank account. Obviously, she had been planning her exit for some time.

Cynthia's deception had ruined Chet's credit and the mortgage was in serious default. The bank repossessed the farm. Chet's dream came to an end. They divorced in the fall of 1990.

Chet must have been shocked back into sobriety after his second divorce, because he was able to work for the Higbee Company, attend college at night, and sell real estate on the weekends. Chet had a newfound ambition to leave the past behind and start over. He finally started showing some affection by calling to talk with the boys and sending us birthday and holiday cards.

One weekend, Chet was showing houses in a gated community called Cinnamon Lake, in West Salem. He turned down a cul-de-sac and knocked on the door of a small three-bedroom ranch. The man who greeted them was the current tenant and told them he was moving out. Chet and his buyer were surprised to learn that they had gone to the wrong address and the house was not for sale.

Making that wrong turn ended up being Chet's fortunate stroke of serendipity. He had been searching for a place to live and this house seemed to fit his present needs. He met with the property's owner, and agreed to purchase the lot and the two adjoining lots on a land contract.

The "lonely man" had a gift for attracting girls. His choice this time was a woman with a round babyface and button nose that gave her the appearance of a teenager. She was twenty years his junior and had a two-year-old daughter. For a while, Chet's calls and cards stopped. Then, just shy of two years after they married, the pair divorced. It had been a turbulent marriage from the start, and I suspect that alcohol played a part in their breakup.

Chet was now middle-aged, three times divorced, unemployed, and financially strapped. He had mortgaged his house to pay off his third wife's debts. As his marriage had been falling apart, he had lost his job with the Higbee Company and his enthusiasm for selling real estate.

Somehow, Chet managed to pick up the pieces of his life and find sobriety and another job. His position this time was a maintenance position at a country club in Rittman, Ohio. Now he could make ends meet.

We started speaking on the phone again regularly. We rediscovered a genuine concern and affection for each other. Chet wasn't drinking now and he seemed like himself again—like he was when we first met. But too much had happened to each of us and between us to ever again be romantic.

I came to understand that his alcoholism, much like the schizophrenia that victimized my mother, Allan, and Steven, was a disease. If Chet's sons could understand this, perhaps they could find a way to forgive their father for shutting them out of his life. Martin tried to be forgiving and made the hour-and-a-half drive to Chet's home with me on several occasions.

Hard work and the long-term use of alcohol had taken a toll on Chet's body. He had his hip replaced in 2004. Following the surgery, Chet wasn't the best patient. He had a black Labrador retriever named Dakota that he had left at home, chained to the deck outside of his house, with a three-day supply of food, a bed of straw, and a doghouse to fend off the frigid December air. Worried about Dakota, Chet left the hospital without his doctor's permission after only one night. Because he pushed his body too soon after his surgery, his hip never healed right, but Chet was willing to risk anything for Dakota. He was always at Chet's side, riding around in his truck, and showing him unconditional love—the kind of love he couldn't seem to hold on to.

A year later, Chet was diagnosed with cirrhosis of the liver. The disease would cause a buildup of fluid, necessitating increasingly frequent abdominal taps. When he was bloated, he couldn't fit in his clothes or shoes. His hands swelled to twice their normal size. Eventually, Chet was unable to leave his home on his own. The black pickup truck didn't move from its spot on the drive.

Although we were miles apart, I did my best to help Chet. He didn't have anyone else. I couldn't assist him in person because I was ill, but I called Chet every day. When he was unable to do his own grocery shopping, I would call a grocery store near him and have food delivered to him. I also arranged to have someone take him to the doctor.

When I couldn't get a hold of Chet on the phone, I would follow the advice I received from the Council on Aging, and asked the sheriff to look in on him. When the sheriff discovered Chet's physical condition and the appalling state of his home, he was taken to a local hospital and then air-flighted to Akron General Hospital.

When the sheriff reported back to me on Chet's grave condition, Ted, Martin, and I made the trip to Akron to be at his bedside. I tried to brace myself for what was to come. Although I've seen people close to death before, I was not prepared for the scene in Chet's room.

In my experience, the lights in the rooms in a hospital's ICU are usually dimmed. The light in Chet's room was harsh and bright and drew my eyes to a multitude of gallon jugs that were lined up on the counter. Thankfully, Chet's gurney was facing away from the door and he was spared the look of shock that came over my face as I realized that the jugs were filled with fluid that had been drained from his body.

Though he was alert and smiling, Chet was a pitiful sight. His body had remained bloated despite the medical treatment. I looked up at my boys' faces and could tell that they were trying to be brave and hold back their tears. My heart ached as the realization hit me that the man I had once loved so deeply, my first love, was dying.

Tears filled Chet's eyes as he looked at his sons. "You've gotten so grown up." I couldn't speak, so I began stroking his bloated arm to show him some comfort and affection. He smiled at me as he said, "I'd forgotten how good your touch makes me feel." I smiled back at him, and as our eyes connected, it was like he was really seeing me for the first time.

It felt like Chet was finally at peace. In the end, he knew by our presence that we had forgiven him for all the pain he had caused us, and I knew that he had forgiven me for any pain that I had caused him.

Before we left, we asked Chet if there was anything we could do for him or if he needed anything from his house. His only concern was that we check on Dakota. Someone needed to feed him. We assured him that we would take care of the dog and return to the hospital the next day.

We could hear Dakota barking as we pulled in front of Chet's home. The house had, at one point, been an idyllic retreat, but was now anything but inviting. The grass and hedges were overgrown. The yellow, orange, and red chrysanthemums and asters that bordered the driveway had died. The window frames needed putty and paint. The screen door was broken and torn. It hung by one hinge.

The door had been left unlocked. Martin was the first to enter and when he realized the condition of the interior of the house, he told Ted and me to stay out. We should have heeded his advice, but we entered anyway.

The condition of Chet's house was staggering. He had always been meticulous about cleanliness and grooming, and it was hard to imagine that he had spent his days wallowing in filth. The stench of human waste and rotten garbage permeated the air and made me want to gag. There was rubbish in every room, making it difficult to walk. Red ants crawled over the kitchen counters and floor. Flies swarmed over an open can of soup and the dirty dishes in the sink. In the bathroom, the porcelain sink, tub, and toilet were covered with brown and red stains. Empty bottles of pain killers filled the shelves of the medicine cabinet. Towels littered the floor.

In the living room, Chet's lounge chair was covered with vomit and feces. The TV and books had collected an inch of dust. I picked up the CD from the turntable. It was a recording of Handel's *Messiah*.

I felt a lump rise in my throat. As I held the disc in my hands, the notes began to play in my mind. Simply imagining the music was a visceral experience. The melody imparts to the listener such a sense of pain and suffering in death and release and celebration that follows. I believe that Chet spent the last few days stuck in that chair, refusing to answer the phone when I called and unable get up to relieve himself, listening to the emotional music, waiting for death to come and take him away.

When the phone rang early the next morning, I sensed that it was about Chet. A nurse from the hospital told me that he had passed away, and we needed to claim his body.

Following Chet's death in September 2008, Ted and Martin asked that I arrange his funeral and burial. He had a military funeral at the Ohio Western Reserve National Cemetery in Rittman.

Steven didn't attend the funeral, but Ted, Martin, and I were there. Over twenty-five people sat on the benches under the pavilion where the memorial was held. Chet's friends expressed their sympathy to the boys and me. They said, "He will be missed."

I made it a point to be present when Chet's belongings were removed from his home. One thing that I went through personally was Chet's small security box. When I opened it, I was touched to find it contained his parent's wedding rings, the ring I had given him on our wedding day, and several pictures of me and our boys that he had carried in his wallet. They were worn and dirty, bearing evidence of the many years that he had kept us close, even after we had parted ways.

I was incredibly moved to find that he had saved pieces of the puzzle I had seen him working on more than four decades prior. I recalled watching him from the living room doorway, unobserved, as he moved them around, trying to find a way to put the pieces together. I have no way of knowing what the pieces meant to him, but I think that perhaps, despite how broken he was and how much hurt he had caused, Chet was still trying to figure out a way to put us back together again.

In the end, I think we did find a way back to each other. We were both there for each other, but at different times in our lives. I was a troubled teen when he rescued me. I longed to escape from the hell of living with a schizophrenic mother. Some of my happiest memories are from when I was a teenager, riding around town with him in the red Studebaker, windows down, my hair blowing in the wind.

I rescued Chet right back at the end of his life, when he needed someone to help him. I like to think that he's driving down the highway in his black pickup truck with Dakota sitting in the back, the wind blowing through his hair, finally happy and free.

37

ALLAN LAZAR

Upon his release from the hospital following the incident with the police cruiser and our divorce, finding a new residence was Allan's first and biggest challenge. Although he had income from Social Security Disability Insurance, the potential of becoming homeless because of his mental instability lurked like a shadow overhead. Fortunately, his older brother, Ron, Ron's wife, and their three daughters welcomed him to their home in Hinckley.

Ron's home was an eleven-room brick mini replica of a castle and sat on three acres of land. Ron had recently built the home and was in the process of completing three fireplaces and intricately patterned exterior brickwork. Allan earned his keep by helping Ron finish the masonry work. In turn, he regained his self-confidence. For two years, this living arrangement benefited everyone concerned. Once the work was completed, Allan moved to his own apartment in Brunswick.

Allan managed well living alone over the next several years. Ultimately, however, he was plagued by a series of breakdowns during which he would trash his apartment and disrupt the other tenants. This repeated behavior led to his being declared incompetent by the court. Probate court appointed an attorney as guardian of his personal and financial affairs.

Incapable of living in an unsupervised environment, he spent the last five years of his life at Wayside Farms Nursing and Rehabilitation Center in Peninsula. The owners, administrators, and the staff gave Allan plenty of tender loving care.

After all those years, Allan was still handsome and continued to charm the women—including me. We exchanged phone calls, letters, and cards, and, on occasion, I visited him with the children. Our marriage lasted only ten years, but our friendship endured until Allan's death from heart failure in 2009.

38

AUNTIE SUE

There is so much more I wanted to share about Auntie Sue that I couldn't fit into the preceding story. She was my substitute mommy and my teacher. This fun-loving extrovert had lots of friends, roller skated, bowled, played gin rummy, and on occasion drank Jack Daniels over ice.

I can't remember her ever being sick. She was incredibly disciplined when it came to her health—she prepared nutritious meals, ate on schedule, and walked five miles a day. Her good looks and positive qualities attracted many suitors. But when faced with the challenge of choosing between two men— an attractive womanizer she worked with and an appealing, upstanding man who adored her—she chose the womanizer.

True to his nature, he flaunted his affairs and left Auntie Sue humiliated and profoundly hurt. She filed for divorce. He begged for forgiveness but when she didn't relent, he brought another woman to a TRW picnic, possibly to try and make my aunt jealous. On the way home from the picnic, still feeling the effects of an afternoon of alcohol consumption, he swerved off the road and his car crashed into a tree. The steering wheel crushed his chest and he was killed instantly.

Still recovering from her marriage to a man who had complete disregard for her feelings, she began dating a good-looking Italian who possessed old-world charm. This man could never commit, however, because he was still married. Although he was legally separated from his wife, they had wed in the Catholic Church, which doesn't sanction divorce.

My aunt and her partner maintained separate residences, yet his truck spent many a night in her driveway. After fifteen years, she got fed up with performing the wifely chores of cooking, cleaning, and laundry for him without the benefits of marriage. She once told me, "I'm sick and tired of washing his dirty shorts and socks!" He wasn't ready for a second marriage, and they eventually parted.

Auntie Sue was madly in love with the next beau, Joe—a lean and lanky postal worker who resembled Gregory Peck. She wanted to marry him in the worst way because he was a steady worker and his government job meant great health and retirement benefits.

Like her previous suitor, Joe, too, was unattainable. He was a confirmed bachelor who lived with his widowed mother. Joe was not only a momma's boy, but an alcoholic, and—you've guessed it— a womanizer.

They dated for several years. Auntie Sue put up with a lot of shenanigans. He was late for dates and, on a few occasions, he didn't show up at all. The last straw for her was when he stood her up on New Year's Eve.

Her first telephone call to me was placed around seven o'clock that evening. "I can't believe Joe would do this to me. He's over an hour late. I skipped lunch and I'm starving. I've opened a can of black olives to snack on." Her calls to me continued every hour on the hour. By ten o'clock, she had finished the can of olives and a bottle of wine. After midnight, she finally came to grips with the fact that he wasn't showing up and said, "How will I ever fall asleep, knowing that Joe's out on the town without me. I'm going to take a sleeping pill." I advised her not to mix prescription drugs with alcohol. She assured me, saying, "I won't." How could I believe her in her present emotional state of mind? Very concerned that she might overdose in her condition, I began calling her every half hour. By two in the morning, her speech was nearly incoherent,

404

so I drove to her home and took her to the ER. Her stomach was pumped and fortunately she fully recovered. As for Joe, Auntie Sue put two thousand miles between them and moved to Florida.

I had moved to Willoughby to be closer to my aunt, but not long after the New Year's Eve incident, she packed up and left! She said her reason for moving away from the family was that, "Ohio winters were harsh." And that statement was partly true. She hated the challenge of driving on ice-covered roads. The November before she moved, she accessorized her canary-yellow Oldsmobile Cutlass with giant steel-belted snow tires and chains. Watching her pull onto our driveway was a hoot. The car looked like a Sherman tank.

Auntie Sue had a few mild flirtations after she moved away — some fun in the sun — but nothing serious. Her early days in Florida were spent bowling, swing dancing, and night clubbing with other fashionable divorced or widowed retirees. Her life was a series of lunches and parties.

When it inevitably got too hard for her to do some of her favorite activities, she turned to crafting. She was a whiz at crocheting, knitting, and needlepoint, and filled her home and everyone else's with hand-made items: holiday dolls, needlepoint patterns and pictures, macramé…She sent out so many boxes of her handiwork to family members in Ohio and California that her best friends became her mail carrier and UPS driver.

Family and friends always had a place to visit once my aunt was settled in Florida. She welcomed us all. Her condo was perfect for entertaining company. I visited Auntie Sue in Florida several times over the last twenty-five years of her life. As she approached her seventy-eighth birthday, she was still the petite, fiery dynamo, but age had forced her to shorten her daily five-mile jaunt to one mile. By eighty-three, her osteoarthritis became debilitating and so painful that she couldn't handle her affairs. When she seemed to really be struggling, I went again to try and convince her to move to an assisted living facility. She refused. Instead, she had a neighbor assist her with paying bills and buying groceries. In the end, consumed by pain, she refused to eat for several days, and passed away in deep, drug-induced sleep. My aunt was eighty-eight when she died in March 2006.

Michelle and her husband brought Auntie Sue's ashes home to rest the following August. A priest, my children and their spouses, my father, and I watched as the gravedigger placed the small marble vault in the hole above her mother's grave, in Calvary Cemetery. Once the vault was in place, we prayed together, and then each of us placed a shovel of earth on top of the vault. I hesitated as I picked up the shovel. Tears of joy welled up in my eyes. *Auntie Sue was finally able to bring herself happiness. She had learned how to enjoy life!*

39

ANGELINA

As my mother grew older, her behavior changed. Whether it was because of her advancing age, shifting hormones, or her new medication, she became docile and compliant. She no longer ventured outside while scantily clad or destroyed her belongings and home. She had a newfound awareness of things other than the voices in her head. And, most remarkably, she agreed to see a psychiatrist.

The stepstool still remained in the kitchen next to the electric range, but she no longer sat on it chain smoking, gesturing, or talking to herself.

Now, when I stopped by, she was either resting on the couch, napping or watching television, or preparing food in the kitchen. If she heard the breezeway door open, she'd call out, "Is that you, Carlo?"

I'd answer, "No, it's me."

I would be greeted with a faint smile and a softly spoken, "Hello," as she wrapped her arms around me. I would bend down and hug her back, pulling her close, careful not to squeeze her fragile frame too hard.

As I held her near, there was just a hint of tobacco on her breath. She had cut back to only five cigarettes a day. And the muumuu she wore was clean and free of ashes or stains. Her brown eyes looked even darker and lovelier than before, enhanced somehow by the shadows that surrounded them. Neither age nor mental suffering had erased her beauty, although her face was now lined and her dark black hair was streaked with grey.

It was a hot, humid day in October 1985 when I entered my parents' house and practically tripped over a large, fluffy, white ball of fur. The critter had been sitting in front of the closed door. It streaked down the hall and hid under the couch in the living room. As I followed it, my mother greeted me, saying, "I knew it was you. Fearless never hides when your dad comes home."

My mother continued. "Lipstick is in the basement. The cats don't get along and have to be separated. To be fair to them, at noon each day, I open the door to the basement and they zip past each other, hissing as they come close."

Mom chuckled as she added, "Your father calls it the 'changing of the guard.'"

I joined in the laughter, inquiring, "How did you end up with two cats?!"

"Your father's friend died. He promised that he would take care of the cats."

My parents were now the caretakers of Fearless Fosdick, an angora, and Lipstick, a red, black, and white calico. After their arrival, my father made a change in his behavior. He began coming home for lunch and dinner, which encouraged my mother to start putting easy-to-fix meals together again. My mother was finally able to recapture a bit of domestic bliss. Although her sheltered existence continued, she now had a devoted caretaker in my father and I was happy for her.

I never confirmed it with my father, but I instinctively knew that the friend who had died was Mary, the beautiful, fashionable saleslady with the pageboy hairdo from the bridal shop. My guess is that while Mary was living, he had developed a close attachment to her two cats. He couldn't give them away.

My father had retired and, without Mary in his life, he had to establish a new routine. Now, he went to the YMCA to exercise in the morning, came home for lunch, spent the afternoon at the library, came home for dinner, and then watched television until he went to bed. He no longer had a reason to spend nights away from his home and started sleeping again in the twin bed in my old room.

I often visited my mother in the late morning, and now that my father was spending more time at home, the odds favored a run-in with him. We had a close call one day when I passed his blue Dodge as I drove down West 54th Street. I was relieved that he didn't appear to see me.

Mom hadn't had a chance to put away the carton of cigarettes I had purchased for her yet when my father arrived at home. He spotted the carton and questioned her about them asking, "Where did these come from?"

She answered, "Beverly was here and gave them to me." He responded, "Next time she's here at noon, ask her to stay a while longer. I'm not the 'terrible Mr. Bang.' I'm her father!"

The next time I visited my mother, she told me what my father had said. I couldn't believe it! The change in my father's attitude towards me was nothing short of astonishing. He wanted to see me!

My father had finally taken a step towards letting go of the hurt and pain he felt when I defied him and married Chet. Now I could visit my parents without fear. At least once a month, I dropped in on them and shared a simple, tasty meal with them. Mom served Campbell's soup, crackers, and either a delicious array of veggies or a chopped salad for lunch. She was quiet during our meals, but always had a wistful smile on her face as she ate, listening to my father and I as we talked.

For the next three years, Angelina led a very peaceful, solitary life. She spent much of her time napping and could often be found on the couch with either Fearless or Lipstick curled up nearby. Just like bodyguards, one or the other was always at her side.

I was my mother's only visitor. Her friends had ceased to come around early on in her illness. Her sisters telephoned and sent cards but never came to see her. She had no extended family to turn to. My children hardly knew their grandmother. The world outside of her home didn't exist for her except as she viewed it through the windows or on television. And the rest of the world had forgotten about her.

The only time she ventured outside of the confines of her home was to consult her psychiatrist. Otherwise, she had no checkups or medical treatments. Doctors were taboo. And the dentist was off limits, too. When she had problems with one of her molars, she would literally push and wiggle the tooth until it loosened and then pull it out herself. This happened several times. But luck favored her front teeth, and she retained her smile.

My mother's life had been mostly free of responsibilities. But the dark, dense pool of madness that had enveloped her for so long brought with it a great deal of stress that inevitably revealed itself. Angelina never said a word about having chest pains or shortness of breath, but in the spring of 1988, her symptoms became apparent to my father and were severe enough to warrant admitting her to the hospital.

It was an early Saturday morning when my father first called me to let me know my mother had been hospitalized the night before. He was distraught. He asked if I could pick him up after lunch and take him to the hospital.

I tooted the horn and watched him exit the side door and enter the car. This was the first time in years we had been alone together. As I caught sight of the look on his face, he suddenly seemed like a hurt little child, reminding me of my own sons when they were boys. Compassion welled up in my chest and I involuntarily leaned over to give him a hug, surprising myself. This was another first in many, many years.

A teary-eyed father and daughter found their way together to the sterile intensive care unit. We made a dramatic picture as we sat closely together at my mother's bedside. No one would have guessed from our appearance that our family had endured so many decades of pain and separation.

My mother's bed was tilted upward and two large pillows propped up her torso. Her long, salt-and-pepper hair was drawn away from her face, accentuating her dilated pupils. Her eyes darted all over the room but when her gaze fell upon me and my father, the fear that had been reflected in them began to fade away.

410

By the bewildered look on her face I could tell that she didn't really comprehend what was happening to her. She said she would do what was being asked of her, but despite warnings from her nurses, she still occasionally tried to get out of her bed or tug at the IV lines connected to her tiny wrist.

Every day, Carlo could be found at Angelina's bedside. He genuinely felt pain for what she was going through. He made sure that she was given the care she needed and didn't have to experience the fear that might come from finding herself alone in her hospital room.

Once my mother was discharged from the hospital, she returned home with my father. Her life continued in its solitary fashion, revolving around Carlo, her beloved cats, and an occasional visit from me. I could tell that she loved him. If he wasn't around, she would always ask, "Where's Carlo?" When he walked into a room, a gentle smile would brighten her face and crinkle the corners of her eyes. He had become Angelina's hero, idol, and caregiver. She needed him now more than ever.

And Carlo needed her just as much as she needed him. Caring for Angelina filled the void created by Mary's death. I believe that, at least initially, he devoted himself to caring for Angelina out of remorse for his infidelity. But my instincts told me that his motives became less self-serving as he began to understand her illness, eventually acknowledging that she was an innocent, helpless victim of schizophrenia.

Despite her actions during my adolescence, Angelina's love and admiration for Carlo had never faltered. She had never abandoned her feelings for him. Her illness had been the source of her shameful behavior. Carlo knew this now and accepted it. He had looked into her deep brown eyes with caring and compassion. He saw his own vulnerabilities and needs reflected in her. He ultimately honored his wedding vows to her and cared for her until death parted them.

The morning of Monday, April 23, 1990, my job with TRW officially ended. That afternoon, my father called. Choking on his words, he said, "Your mother died this morning. We need to talk." I was speechless.

My father had returned from the library and discovered my mother's body sprawled across the bathroom floor. I suppose it provided some relief to learn that she didn't know what hit her when she passed, as doctors found at autopsy that she had suffered a massive heart attack. But the experience of finding her lifeless body took a massive toll on my father.

Grief-stricken, he requested my assistance in making the funeral arrangements. His voice was trembling as he said, "I need someone I can rely on." I was pleasantly surprised that he had turned to me for help.

We held a private service at the funeral home. Angelina was buried in Calvary Cemetery beside her mother, Adriana.

After several weeks, I returned to the cemetery to check the engraving on the marker, a flat headstone that covered the graves of mother and daughter. I read and reread the dates. A chill traveled down my spine as it struck me that my mother had died on the anniversary of her mother's death. *This is no coincidence.* Recalling Grandpa Vincenzo's story, I began to cry as I pictured the hellish scene of Adriana's murder.

The beautiful curly haired four-and-a-half-year-old child clung to her mommy's legs as her mother stood in front of the open door, pleading with her assailant. Then the crack of gunshots rang out, filling the air with the strong smell of sulfur. Adriana fell backwards to the kitchen floor, knocking down her little girl. Terrified, Angelina picked herself up from the puddle of urine that had collected beneath her, leaving a trail of tiny footprints as she ran and hid in the bedroom with her sisters.

The murder had done more than end my grandmother's life. It had far-reaching repercussions and caused a tsunami of destruction; a series of waves that impacted four generations of my family.

Adriana's murder had planted a time bomb in my mother's brain. That time bomb remained dormant until I was four and a half years old and we were living in that same house where my grandmother met her tragic demise. Whether it was my age or the shadowy past of the house or something no one could foresee, on that fateful day,

412

the environmental factors must have been just right and triggered its detonation.

It's no wonder I dislike the month of April. The opening lines from *The Burial of the Dead*, the opening section of T. S. Eliot's poem, *The Waste Land*, have always resonated with me:

> April is the cruelest month, breeding
> Lilacs out of the dead land, mixing
> Memory and desire, stirring
> Dull roots with spring rain.

After my mother passed away, the responsibility to pack up her things fell on me. Her little blue slippers still sat just inside her bedroom door. The knot in my stomach tightened as I looked at them. *What did it feel like to walk in my mother's shoes?* I wanted so badly to understand her pain, to see things from her point of view, to understand exactly what it was like to be mentally ill. I didn't have the heart to include my mother's slippers in the bag of items I would donate to charity. They sat in her room for the next ten years.

My mother's possessions were few. It took me less than two hours to sort through them. While emptying her dresser drawer, I found spools of thread and needles carefully stored in a glass container. Next to it was a glass jar that once held grape jelly. She had used it to cut out biscuits when I was a little girl. To my surprise, it held the jacks I had played with as a child. Suddenly, I felt overcome by emotion as I realized that she must have saved this memento from my childhood out of a love for me that her mental illness had made it impossible for her to show.

I was so grateful that my father remained committed to my mother even to the end. He had made a promise to her when they were young that he would make a home for her forever and he stayed true to his promise.

413

My mother's life after the onset of her illness wasn't ever "normal," but having a consistent home with my father granted her life greater stability. His support saved her from the fates suffered by so many other people suffering from severe mental illness, like schizophrenia: being abandoned by their families, permanent institutionalization, long-term homelessness, or dying without the love and compassion they deserve. Although she was cloistered from the outside world, in the end, she was safe and secure. She had a home.

I now celebrate this beautiful woman, my mother. She gave me life. She gave me an appreciation for the arts. She taught me acceptance, because there are some things that will never change. She taught me that people with mental illness need love and affection. She taught me how to love someone unconditionally. In the end, she taught me how to cast light on the shadows from the past.

40

Carlos De Angelis, My Shadow

After my mother's sudden death in 1990, my father turned to me as a source of solace in his grief. From then on, every Sunday morning, I'd pick up the phone and call him to chitchat about the prior week's events. On holidays, I'd invite him to my home to celebrate with me and his grandchildren. We spent more time together and started to function like a family.

Over the next ten years, my father kept himself busy just as he had when my mother was living. In the morning, he went to the YMCA to swim. At one o'clock, he visited the library. In the late afternoon, he would discuss politics and local news over coffee at McDonald's with a few other older men who met there for a bit of camaraderie.

Carlo looked at least ten years younger than his peers. His face was smooth and wrinkle free, a thick crop of grayish-black hair covered his head, and his body was well toned from years of swimming. He stood straight and moved with ease. Because of his looks and his vitality, I took his health for granted. And I believe he did, too.

This is the only explanation I can come up with for why he thought it was a good idea to drive himself to the hospital in

February of 2000. He must have thought that the pains in his chest were indigestion, and not, as was in fact the case, a sign that he was experiencing a heart attack.

The admitting clerk didn't call me until the next day. My father had been incapable of providing her with any information until he had been stabilized. I was stunned when I heard what had happened! I cancelled my plans for the day and went directly to Parma General Hospital.

As I drove past the emergency parking area, I spotted my father's little blue Dodge hatchback. It was parked perfectly straight and within the yellow lines. I shook my head in disbelief. *How could he have driven himself here while he was having a heart attack?! My God! And he even parked it straight?!*

I had a feeling of déjà vu as I entered the cardiac unit. I had walked hand in hand with my father into the same room when my mother had been a patient in the unit.

My father looked up at me from the bed, smiled, and said, "Thank God you're here. The doctors tell me I've been bleeding internally for some time. They say I had a heart attack from the loss of blood. I don't understand how this could have happened to me because my heart is strong! I swim every day!" He was receiving a blood transfusion as we spoke.

The doctors took a week to be sure that Carlo's heart had stabilized. Then he was sent home. Per his discharge instructions, my father was to take slow-release iron tablets, have his internist schedule a series of out-patient tests, and not drive. *How's he going to get all these tests if he can't drive himself? I'm going to have to help him. Who else has he got?*

I arranged for time off from my new sales job. For the next three months, two days a week, I drove across town to take him for blood work, scans, x-rays, and appointments with specialists.

His first appointment was with his internist. When the doctor told my father he had scheduled him for a stress test, Carlo said, "What are you talking about? My heart's fine. I don't need a stress test." After an hour of pleading with him, he relented and agreed to an EKG. Then, when the results of the test proved him wrong, he refused to believe them.

416

After getting a second and third opinion from the best cardiologists in town, my father finally acknowledged that he had a heart problem and agreed to have open heart surgery. But repairing his heart would be useless if his internal bleeding wasn't stopped. He needed a CT scan with contrast to pinpoint where the blood was coming from.

We were driving to a clinic in Strongsville for the scan when my father began to slur his words. As his utterances became incomprehensible, he slowly slid off of the front seat, and ended up hanging from his seatbelt. *Oh God, he passed out!* I pressed harder on the accelerator. We were now traveling at least twenty miles per hour over the speed limit.

I pulled up to the front entrance of the clinic and parked in a fire zone. *How will I get him out of the car?* I was all thumbs, fumbling as I removed my seat belt, throwing the car door open, and tripping over my feet as I rushed into the building. Looking around frantically, I ran up to the information clerk stationed in the center of the lobby. "Can you call someone to help me? I need assistance getting my father out of the car." She indifferently motioned to a row of folded wheelchairs near the door and turned away to answer her ringing phone.

I need help! What's wrong with her?! Tears stung my red cheeks as I flew over to the wheelchairs. *Damn it! How do you unfold this contraption?!* Once I got the wheelchair open, one of the small levers that released the rear wheels wouldn't budge. *You're wasting time.* I forcefully pressed on the lever again. This time the chair began to roll.

Why isn't the exit door opening? Where's the automatic door opener?

I started pushing and pulling on different buttons and handles. Bells began to ring. *You fool! You pulled the fire alarm!* I had finally gotten everyone's attention and a good Samaritan opened the door for me. I burst through with the wheelchair and rushed to the car. By then, the fire fighters had arrived and one of them helped me get my father into the wheelchair and wheeled him into the building.

At least the receptionist had to acknowledge me now. She called a doctor who checked my father's vital signs and revived him with smelling salts. Carlo opened his eyes, saying, "Where am I?" *Oh, thank God!* He had fainted because of fasting in preparation for the CT scan. Once he regained his composure, the CT scan was completed and he was given a snack.

I could feel a slow burn rising from my neck to my face. I looked around the lobby. *Everyone's staring at me.* How I wished I could disappear from sight! I heard myself say out loud, "I'm so sorry," as I shrugged my shoulders and scanned the room for a sympathetic soul. The entire time we were in the facility, I felt embarrassed and humiliated for the scene I had caused.

We had been at the clinic for hours. The sun had lowered in the sky and exhaustion washed over me as we left the building. Normally, I would take my father to his home on the West Side and then return to my home on the East Side. I glanced over at him.

It suddenly struck me how my father's physical problems had affected his body and his mind. *He looks drained.* The man I still thought of as take-charge and energetic had needed to hold on to me when we walked back to my car. That day, he had slumped while sitting, and needed directions and assistance in everything he did. I had written off his behavior as a symptom of low blood sugar from fasting for the scan, but the more I thought about it, the clearer it became that my father needed help.

He shouldn't be alone. It's too risky. What if he passes out again or falls? There's no way he'd be able to drive himself to the hospital this time.

I decided that my father should come with me, and he agreed.

Dad and I went to pick up some of his belongings. This was the first time I had entered the house in over a year. Every time we went somewhere together, he would be ready and on his way out of the house as soon as I arrived.

Today, I pulled onto the drive and parked my car. As we entered his house, I noticed how soiled, dingy, and threadbare the center hall carpeting had gotten. Dad's long-departed feline companions, Fearless and Lipstick, had left behind some prominent stains as permanent mementos.

"Bev, my medications are on the kitchen table. Please get them for me. Take everything that's there. And don't forget my eye drops in the refrigerator."

418

A lazy Susan holding several medications sat in the center of the table. I spun it around and checked the bottles. *Empty…expired.* I tossed them all into a plastic grocery bag. *I'll sort them later.* The vinyl tablecloth hadn't been wiped in a while. It was covered with bread-crumbs and coffee stains. I looked around the room. *The kitchen could use a lot work.* Handles were missing from the cupboards. Floor tiles were broken or missing, exposing the bare wooden boards beneath. *This is a trip hazard.* And the floor needed to be swept and mopped.

I opened the refrigerator to look for Dad's eye drops. The mold growing on an open can of peaches caught my eye. I began to check the "Best Used By" dates on other containers of food and bottles of juice that were stored on the shelves. *Expired…they're all expired.*

Looking at the electric range, I could see that the drip pans underneath the coils were covered with crud and coffee stains. I opened the door to look at the broiler. It was caked with grease.

My father was quietly packing his suitcase while I went into the bathroom. *What a mess!* The handles on the hot water spigots for the sink and tub were missing. *No hot water! How does he bathe?!* Later I learned that he had been showering at the YMCA, and using the laundry tubs in the basement to wash his face and to take sponge baths.

That evening, my dad slept on my couch. Hearing his steady breathing as he slept gave me a sense of security. *I won't worry about him tonight.*

Several days later, we received the results from the scan. They revealed a small tumor on one of my father's renal arteries. His left kidney would have to be removed. However, without repairing his heart first, it was unlikely my father would survive the removal of his kidney. We immediately set a date for surgery.

My father's first procedure, a quintuple heart bypass, would be followed a few months later by a left nephrectomy. My father's recovery from both operations would take several months. We decided that he would continue living with me in my one-bedroom apartment. He would sleep on the living room sofa during the months leading up to his first procedure.

July arrived and with it, my father's surgery date. He stood straight and tall—chin up, chest out, shoulders back, stomach in—

as we walked into the hospital admitting room. *He looks like a guard at Buckingham Palace.*

With a relaxed look on his face, he announced to the clerk who he was. His hand was steady as he signed the consent papers. *How can he be so calm?* I had a queasy feeling in the pit of my stomach. The seriousness and enormity of his operation hit me. *They're repairing five arteries. He could die.*

The surgery began at six in the morning. I sat in the family waiting room on a brown leather sofa but couldn't get comfortable. I picked up a magazine but couldn't focus enough to read or watch anything on the large television set. I tried to strike up a conversation with the other family members in the waiting room, but we had little to say to each other.

A nurse called the waiting room each hour to update me on my father's progress. At noon, she said the doctors had removed his heart and were lowering his body temperature. A machine was doing the work of his heart and lungs.

While I waited for the operation to end, I toyed with the idea of having my father move in with me on a permanent basis. *Even though the past few months have gone pretty well, are you sure that you want to do this?*

I picked up one of the waiting room phones and called the rental agent for my apartment complex. *A two-bedroom suite could work. You've got some thinking to do.* My wait continued.

It was now five thirty in the evening and the nurse was on the phone for me again. The operation had been a success and I would be able to see my father in an hour. Martin arrived at the hospital in time to join me.

We entered the large, sterile-looking recovery room together. Patient beds and hospital equipment lined the wall, spaced about twenty feet apart and separated with curtains.

I grasped Martin's hand tightly as we approached my father's bed. The sheets were pulled up to his neck, exposing just his head. His eyes were closed. There were wires and tubes everywhere. Liquids were being pumped in and out of his body. He looked like he was part of a giant machine. I was in shock and Martin was in disbelief.

420

In less than twelve hours, my father's appearance had completely changed. I hadn't been prepared for what I saw in that recovery room. His strong, muscled frame had transformed and a small and fragile old man lay on that hospital bed. *That's not Carlo!*

I left the hospital in a fog. I returned home to my little one-bedroom apartment and got ready for bed, but I couldn't sleep. My mind was racing with scenes from the recovery room. My father's altered appearance had sealed the deal for me; he would move in with me permanently.

I expected my father to leave the hospital in about ten days. I had plans to make, and so much to do in such a short time. *Ten days!*

The next morning, I signed the lease for a two-bedroom apartment. I went to the furniture store to buy a single bed, a mattress set, and a large lounge chair. I had learned that having his chest cracked open for heart surgery would make sleeping in a bed uncomfortable for my father for weeks.

Then I went to visit my father. *Wow!* After removing some of his tubes, the hospital staff had been able to get him out of bed. It was amazing how rapidly his condition improved.

The days passed quickly for me as the move consumed every spare hour of my day. I had to complete a change of address form at the post office, contact the utility companies, arrange for movers, and take care of countless other details. Having a cell phone helped, but a secretary would have been better!

On Wednesday evening, I was exhausted but dutifully went to visit my father. He looked good and was very happy for he had just been told that he would go home on Friday.

Dad left the hospital with all kinds of instructions, many of which he found irksome. It would be six months or longer before he would be back to normal—if that was possible—and he had another operation on the horizon.

While Carlo convalesced in our new apartment, my days were filled with caring for him, work, and housework. My father was not a good patient. Even with the help of a neighbor and a visiting nurse, my days were long and my father often seemed ungrateful and was combative. We argued regularly and I struggled to keep from getting angry and feeling unappreciated.

This routine continued for three months. With his repaired heart, Carlo was ready for the removal of his kidney.

The second operation was also a success. Within a couple of months, his visiting nurse and physical therapist were discharged. I no longer needed our neighbor to prepare Carlo's lunches while I was at work. It was marvelous to see how strong he was again.

When we left the apartment, I would always lead the way. He would follow right behind me, holding on to the banister, as we walked down the six flights of stairs. On days when the bright sun shone through the window, Dad's frame would cast a shadow on the stairs below. We'd laugh over the image and sing the words to "Me and My Shadow" together.

Actually, Dad became my shadow even when we weren't on the stairs of our apartment building. Everywhere I went, he followed.

Every Sunday at eight in the morning, Dad and I attended mass together. We always sat in the last row of the first section—close enough to clearly see the altar but far enough back to have a few rows of parishioners in front of us for guidance in the rituals.

Dad's commitment to church attendance puzzled me. He had received a Catholic education as a youth, but in his adult years, he proclaimed himself an agnostic. Perhaps his devotion meant that he had finally found a reason to believe in God, or maybe it just meant that he wanted to be with me.

We began to have a bit of a social life together. We often shared dinner with friends. During the summer, I played bocce while Dad watched. My friends really liked him. They found him interesting, handsome, and an adroit conversationalist.

We frequently attended Sunday matinee performances by the Cleveland Opera. One of the best performances we ever attended was a delightful romantic comedy. The sweet, tender innocence of the couple's love brought me to tears during the wedding scene. Living happily ever after with my own Prince Charming was always my unattainable dream. *All I'd ever wanted was to be a wife and mother. Why didn't I get to have a normal life?*

On our drive home, Dad picked up on my melancholy mood. He asked me what was on my mind, and I hesitantly shared my thoughts with him.

422

In the past, I never would have risked talking to Dad about the men in my life. I was sure he would have responded in anger. We had finally arrived at a point in our relationship where we could openly share our feelings. Dad admitted that he had been disappointed in my choice of husbands. He hadn't recognized how badly I had been struggling to know my own heart. "You were so pretty and intelligent. You appeared to have it all together." That was the first time I remembered him ever complimenting me.

Even though my dad had softened a bit after his surgeries, he still could be testy. He was mostly bothered by nonsensical things, like having to eat leftovers or being asked to change out of his favorite pair of slacks when they were dirty. But despite his crotchety behavior, I was glad for his company and liked looking after him. I had no idea that the tables would soon be turning. I would need him to care for me!

In 2005, I discovered a lump in my breast. *Cancer.* My diagnosis was serious. My ears rang with the words "lymph nodes," "metastasized," "biopsies," and "surgery." I was confronted with my own mortality and the possibility of becoming disfigured, disabled, and dependent on other people. I was forced onto an emotional rollercoaster that carried me through denial, fear, anger, despair, depression, hope, and finally, acceptance and resolve.

The cancer treatment was a living nightmare. I went through twelve weeks of chemo, fourteen radiation treatments, and countless injections and blood tests. I lost my hair and about ten percent of my body weight. Life was a fog of days on end of weakness, nausea, gagging, and vomiting. I had trouble enough taking care of my own needs, let alone those of my father or Steven.

The day of my operation, I was dressed and ready to leave for the hospital at five in the morning. Dad wasn't going to accompany me to the hospital, yet he had dressed for the day and was sitting in his favorite chair in the living room, waiting for me. One glance at him brought tears to my eyes. He looked worn-out. I bent down to hug him and tears filled his eyes as he wished me luck and said good-bye. I tried hard to smile. My voice cracked as I told him, "Don't worry, I'll be alright. See you soon." The lump in my throat prevented me from saying more. As I stepped away, it struck me just how much I loved him and how glad I was to have him living with me.

The operation was a success. The three days I spent in the hospital were filled with visits from family and friends. They showered me with love, flowers, and gifts.

Once my chemo and radiation treatments began, Dad's presence and support brought me great comfort. I'd lay on the recliner in our living room for hours, feeling nauseated and weak, depleted of strength, unable to move. Day after day, he sat in the large yellow chair across from me. He would silently watch me rest and then bring me tea and graham crackers when I stirred. I had someone to be with me, something I really needed.

Dad took on more responsibility during this time. He knew how much Steven's well-being meant to me. He did the best he could to have lunch with Steven on his own, while I was home recuperating. Dad hired someone to drive him to Madison. His actions demonstrated his love for me and his grandson.

By October 2007, a year and a half had passed since I had completed my cancer treatments. Dad hadn't had any significant health setbacks for several years, but he wasn't behaving like his usual feisty self, so I scheduled a doctor's appointment for him. The scheduler reminded me to bring his medical cards and his driver's license for identification, but Dad's driver's license had expired. Since he wasn't driving any more, this meant that he needed to get a state ID. This would prove to be quite a challenge.

Dad would need two forms of identification proving his birthdate to obtain a state ID. Before we left for the Bureau of Motor Vehicles, I helped him sort through the strongbox where he kept his important papers. Inside, we found a birth certificate with birthdates made illegible by suspiciously precise ink spills, a Social Security award letter with a birthdate of September 13, 1914, an army draft card that gave September 23, 1923 as Dad's date of birth, and an expired driver's license with a birthdate of September 5, 1928. We took all these documents with us, and, unsurprisingly, Dad was not issued a state ID. I certainly understood the examiner's decision! Dad was to return with a letter from Social Security verifying his birthdate.

On the way home, Dad was not his usual talkative self. He kept dabbing at his eyes, wiping away his freely flowing tears. I suspected that my father's pride had prompted him to fudge his birthdate a few times. Now, he was being humbled into revealing his true age.

When we arrived at home, I held Dad's hand as I led him into the building. Up on our floor, I held out my hand to Dad as I stepped off the elevator, offering to lead him again. He waved me off and told me to walk on ahead of him, just like usual. As I moved several paces ahead of him, I looked back to see Dad, swinging his arms and walking straight and tall. *He's okay.* I continued walking on ahead.

Our apartment was at the end of a long hall. About halfway down, I moved to the right to avoid a large maintenance vacuum cleaner that had been left unattended in the center of the hall. Just as I turned around to warn Dad to watch for the vacuum, I froze. Feeling completely helpless, I watched him trip on the vacuum and fall, face-first, over the handle and tangled cord, landing in a heap on his left side.

Dropping my purse, I ran to Dad's side. Tears streaming down my face, I cried out, "Daddy, Daddy, are you alright?! Don't move! I'll call for help!" Glaucoma had impaired Dad's peripheral vision. He hadn't even seen the vacuum.

Dad insisted he was all right, yet he couldn't get up without help. He grasped my arms and somehow, I got him up, down the rest of the hallway, and into a chair in our apartment.

As I started checking Dad over, I noticed a large, round lump, dotted with small drops of blood, that had grown on his left temple. I examined his shoulders, arms, and legs but, miraculously, he didn't seem to have broken any bones. I wanted to call the emergency squad to transport him to the hospital, but he refused treatment. As I wiped the blood from his forehead with a cold washcloth, he maintained his composure and insisted he was fine.

This wasn't Dad's first fall. He had fallen down the steps at my friend's aunt's house about six months before. That time, I had taken him to the emergency room. He had had no broken bones and his MRI results had been normal. Afterwards, he had been his old feisty self. We had lightheartedly referred to him as the "cat with nine lives." This time, he was responding differently. The rest of the day, he was docile, quiet, and withdrawn. I felt uneasy. His atypical behavior worried me.

The next day, we called Social Security. *What a fiasco!* Again, even with the 1978 letter that acknowledged his entitlement to Social Security, there was confusion about his date of birth. I didn't know what to think. Social Security would investigate the situation and get back to us with a determination.

Two days later, Dad's odd behavior grabbed my attention again. We were sitting at the table eating breakfast when he started making odd motions with his right arm. It looked like he was having trouble holding on to his spoon. He tried to speak to me, but his voice was unrecognizable. His words came out as deep, throaty sounds. I could barely understand him.

I was terrified that his strange behavior meant that his condition was more serious than it had originally appeared. It reminded me of my frantic drive to the clinic in Strongsville. "Dad, you're going to the hospital. I'm calling for an ambulance."

Even in his altered state, Dad's determination prevailed. He insisted that he could get to the hospital without help from the emergency squad. He demanded that we take the six flights of stairs down from the apartment to the parking garage. He must have called upon all his strength and willpower to navigate those steps, trying to prove to me he was all right and in control.

We were greeted by a friendly face when we arrived at our local hospital. Luckily, the volunteer working at the admitting desk was a lady Dad and I knew from church. Not only was her presence reassuring, but she vouched for Dad, helping us avoid any potential issues with his insurance cards and expired driver's license and before long, Dad and I were directed to an exam room.

A resident soon came to Dad's room, took his medical history, and completed Dad's preliminary workup. When he was done, he ordered an MRI of Dad's head. Once this test was completed, our wait began.

After what felt like hours, a doctor finally entered the exam room. "Mr. De Angelis, you have a bleed on the brain. Your records have been reviewed by a specialist from University Hospital's main campus. They are holding a room for you. I've arranged an ambulance to transport you there." *What?! How can his condition be so serious?! Is Dad going to be okay?*

Upon our arrival at the UH main campus, we experienced the same problematic situation with Dad's identification and his birthdate discrepancy. However, the severity of Dad's injury preempted the necessity for verification of all his documents. *Thank you, God!*

Dad was taken directly to the neurology ward, where he was placed in a private room and immediately connected to monitors.

By six in the evening, exhaustion had set in. My head and body ached. Ten long hours had passed without an opportunity to eat or even have a cup of coffee.

The neurosurgeon entered the room and unceremoniously announced, "Mr. De Angelis, I've arranged for immediate surgery."

"What?!" Less than five minutes earlier, a resident had told me that there was a possibility the bleeding on Dad's brain would stop on its own. The plan was to keep him under observation until morning, and then decide whether to perform surgery.

"Hey, let's back up a little! Why the rush?"

"A bleed on the brain can destroy brain cells. Your father's a relatively young man, his heart is strong from the bypass, and we feel we can correct the problem."

Dad sat upright on the examination table. I looked into his eyes. They were so wide, his pupils looked like small black dots. *He's scared.*

"Has he told you how old he actually is?" I continued, whispering, "We're not sure of his age, but he may be over ninety." *There's no way Dad should have this surgery!* "Besides the bypass, he's had one kidney removed. We need some time to discuss this. We'll give you a decision in the morning."

Dear God, will he be able to survive a major operation on his brain after what he's already endured?

"Daddy, please, please, don't make a decision now. Wait until the morning. That'll give Ted time to check your records when he gets off his shift tonight in the ER."

Dad and the doctors agreed and shortly thereafter, I left the hospital.

At eight-thirty that night, as I pulled into my parking spot in the garage, my cell phone began to ring. After frantically searching through my purse, I managed to answer it before the call was sent to voicemail. It was a nurse from University Hospital. The nurse and an orderly were transporting Dad into surgery and Dad had wanted me to know. *How can this be happening?! Two hours ago, we all agreed that a decision wouldn't be made until the morning. Now they're operating?!*

My chest started to pound as I questioned the nurse. "Did something happen after I left? What changed? I was told a decision on operating would be made in the morning. Who signed off on the operation?"

She answered simply, "Your father."

My throat tightened with fear and anger. My voice cracked as I demanded, "Let me speak to him."

I could hear the gurney's casters turning as the nurse put Dad on the phone. *They've got to wait!* "Daddy, are you sure this is what you want to do?"

His response was barely audible. "No."

"Then stop them! I love you, Daddy!"

I could hear other voices in the background as Dad cried out, his words unintelligible. He was already in the operating room.

Pounding my fist against the steering wheel, I pitched my phone onto the passenger seat. I felt as if I had let Daddy down. Tears burned my eyes as I sat there, feeling completely helpless as I heard a quiet voice coming from the seat next to me. In my frustration, I hadn't even hung up the phone.

The nurse was back on the line. She informed me the operation would take approximately five hours and Dad would be in the recovery room for another three to four hours. *No use rushing now. I'll go back to the hospital with Ted in the morning.*

Ted and I arrived early enough to see Dad as he opened his eyes for the first time. As he spoke his first words, his voice was loud, strong, and clear. His voice had always sounded youthful, but today it sounded exceptionally young and jubilant.

Dad lifted his hand from the bed and I took hold of it. Looking at me, his eyes sparkling, he spoke to me with words I had longed to hear since I was a little girl. "You're my angel. You saved my life. I love you."

"I love you, too, Dad." The corners of his mouth turned up as his eyelids closed. His peaceful, rhythmic breathing was all that we heard as he dozed off. I left the hospital hopeful and happy with no idea about what was about to come.

The following day, my hope slowly began fading, and my happiness eventually turned into an emotional hell. It started when Dad lost his ability to speak. The doctors were hopeful that his speech would return after the swelling subsided, but it brought me little comfort to know that his condition was fairly common after brain surgery.

My days were long as Dad spent his hours lying silently in bed, recuperating. During my bedside vigil, I was caught up in my memories of who my father had been in my childhood and thoughts about the father I had gotten to know over the past seven years.

I now knew that beneath his proud, angry shell, Dad was a vulnerable and hurt man. Dad's dreams had been shattered by schizophrenia, too. He had needed my mother's love as much as I had. But Angelina had been incapable of being a mother, wife, or homemaker. His life had been turned upside down by my mother's illness.

The last few years had helped me see beyond my own pain and see in him a loving father and husband. He had done the best he could with me, and despite my mother's illness, Dad had done right by her and saved her from permanent institutionalization by keeping her at home with him until the day she died. *I love him. I don't want to lose him.*

In many ways, the last few years had been the happiest years of my life. We had spent so little time together in my childhood, but now, I finally had a father to love. I smiled as tears started to well up in my eyes, making my vision blurry. *Dad, my friend. Dad, my best guy. Dad, my beloved father.*

Every morning, I made my daily pilgrimage to the hospital. Thankfully, my children came with me on occasion or visited him in the evening. The visits wore on me. Somehow, I managed to smile through my tears. The hospital staff treated me so kindly. I would often be asked, "Is your father that darling little older fellow in room 404?" They would proceed to tell me how he had fared during the evening. Somehow, even without speaking, Dad charmed the nurses. He was the favorite patient on the ward.

Dad's condition grew worse. He started to have trouble eating.

Dad never regained his ability to speak. He couldn't even communicate using his arms or hands, as they seemed not to follow the directions his brain was giving. Being next of kin, the doctors would call me for permission to administer life-saving care. I was always conflicted over the decisions, since Dad had left no health directive for us to follow.

On October 24, I received an early call. "Will you approve the insertion of a filter in Carlo's groin to prevent blood clots?

The next morning, another call. "Will you approve placing Carlo on a respirator?"

Dear God, be kind. I do not know your plans for me or Dad but please, be kind to him!

Now they wanted permission to perform a tracheotomy. I asked the doctors for time. *God, please give Dad new breath!*

Before I could make a decision, Dad contracted a virus. The surgeons could not operate. The tracheotomy was off the table for now. Then the doctors requested the insertion of a G-tube in his stomach for feeding. *God, why are you letting Dad suffer? How can he endure this? Shall I say yes, to preserve his life? Or shall I say no to the doctors and let him come home to you? Are you calling him home?*

The days passed quickly. By November 1, Dad's infection had been cured and I decided to allow the doctors to move forward with the tracheotomy and G-tube.

Two days later, I was concluding my daily visit to the hospital. It had been a long day and I was very, very tired. I was getting ready to say goodbye to Dad when a little voice in my head said, "God will decide Dad's circumstances. Stay at his side, close to his side, my girl." I felt a pull in my heart to stay, but my exhausted body

430

begged for sleep. I kissed Dad on his forehead and said goodbye.

Back at my house, I drifted off to sleep while the worrisome thoughts that played in my mind night and day continued on repeat. *Will Dad be ok? Is he going to make it through this? What kind of life will he have? What kind of shape will he be in?* Then a phone started ringing in my dream.

I awoke with a start and realized that I hadn't been dreaming. The living room phone was ringing. It was the hospital. "Your father had a heart attack. He asked for you. He's still alive." I frantically called my children but couldn't reach any of them. I didn't feel comfortable with night driving and the area around Dad's hospital had earned a reputation as a high crime area. *Oh God, I'm too scared to go to the hospital alone! But I must hurry!*

I finally called a family friend, Jim, who lived in Aurora. It took him at least a half-hour to pick me up in Willoughby and an additional half-hour to reach the hospital, a regretfully long time.

When we arrived at the hospital, we found Dad with his eyes closed. A heating blanket covered his small, frail frame. An IV line was inserted in his right arm. A ventilator was helping him breathe. A heart monitor beside the bed showed his heartbeat.

A senior nurse was at Dad's side. The hospital staff had done their best to bring Dad back to consciousness. They had administered Levophed, a cardiac stimulant that narrows blood vessels to treat dangerously low blood pressure, and kept his body warm with heating pads.

Thankfully, Ted and his wife arrived before Jim and I entered the room. I hugged and kissed them and took hold of Ted's hand as we entered the room and walked to the bed. I wanted to hug Dad but couldn't reach around him. I kissed him several times on the forehead and whispered, "I love you."

The nurse took a needle and placed it in the quick of Dad's nail. No response. She shrugged her shoulders and shook her head then looked at me, silently asking me what to do.

"Please let me sit here for a bit."

After a few minutes, the nurse placed the needle in the quick of Dad's nail. No response.

"What shall I do?" the nurse asked.

Ted spoke up. "Mom, it's time."

With a heavy heart, I murmured to the nurse, "Go ahead."

Ted's words provided me little comfort. "Mom, you're doing the right thing."

I began to sob. The nurse methodically removed the IV line and then the ventilator. We silently watched the heart monitor as the little peaks and valleys became a straight line. The leads from the heart monitor were removed. There was no response from Dad. He had slipped away.

Dad's time had come. The nurse pronounced him dead at 11:32 p.m., November 3, 2007. To this day, I regret letting my fears prevent me from being at Dad's side before he became unconscious. I pray that he knew how much I loved him.

Having Dad around for the past seven years had given me a sense of security. With his passing, I was left alone again. But I think of my father whenever I look up at the sky at night and see a bright star. That's my dad, my protector, sitting up there and looking down on me.

A Message to My Readers

From chapter to chapter, you have been an observer of a recurring series of events—multiple circles that begin and end without a satisfying resolution. The peace, love, and new beginnings I sought throughout my life eluded me.

I have played various roles within the family constellation: the child battered by her schizophrenic mother, the arrogantly naïve wife who thinks love can cure mental illness, and lastly, the disparaged mother who clings to the hope that her child can find a future in spite of his schizophrenia. Each role I've assumed has been emotionally painful and each one has tested my resilience and strength of spirit.

Following my mother's breakdown during my childhood, I had no control over what happened to me. My life was painful, difficult, and frightening. To feel safe once more, I tried to find ways to control my response to my unwanted circumstances. But from childhood until well into adulthood, I allowed myself to be controlled by my emotions, feeling victimized by the situations life presented, repeatedly crying out, "Why me?"

On occasion, the negative voices in my head still begin their chatter...*Why? Why? Why?* In those moments, I must gather emotional strength to remember that there are some conditions and events I cannot change; I can only accept. The Serenity Prayer says it best:

God, grant me the serenity to accept the things I cannot change,

the courage to change the things I can,

and the wisdom to know the difference.

Once I accepted that I cannot change anyone's behavior but my own, the opportunity to heal the hurts began. Now I understand that I have the power to choose how to react when painful events occur. I can "cry out" or take positive action to make my life better. For me, it's a continuous process.

Writing this story has given me another chance to get to know the little girl who felt unlovable and abandoned, to study the choices she made, and to love her unconditionally. She's quite nice, after all.

If this has been difficult to read, it is likely that you have been shielded from the realities of mental illness. I am compelled to pull back the curtain so that more people can understand the reality of life in the vortex that is created when you live with and love family members who suffer from mental illness.

I have shared this story of the lives of Steven, my mother, my father, and my other loved ones to help my readers experience what life is like for individuals who are mentally ill and for the family members who love them.

I have experienced so much more than what is recorded on these pages, especially now that I am living in my golden years. The person I am today has been shaped by my changing family relationships, health crises, and the devotion I have had over the past several decades to improving the quality of life of my Steven, in spite of his illness.

I do not want the reader to think for one moment that I would trade my life for someone else's. I have had a well-lived life. I wouldn't want to be anyone else.

To those who share my plight, I would like to believe that reading this book has made a difference in your life. My desire for you is to realize that others are dealing with the same problems you face, and that this knowledge provides you with hope and strength to meet the challenges your life presents.

As disturbing and shocking as some of the events in my life have been, I have found peace. Over the years, I have evolved into a happier and more positive person who continues to move forward and grow. Although my life has had the lowest of lows, I have also soared to the highest of highs. In fact, I believe that the deepest lows, or perhaps my response to them, have helped me achieve the greatest highs.

434

I've come to the realization that my childhood theory and misguided notion that love could fix my mother and my husbands wasn't so far off after all. I've learned that although it's not reasonable to expect love to be a cure, love is exactly what someone with mental illness needs, just like the rest of us. By opening your heart and connecting with someone's humanness, you can harness the incredible power of love to change their life.

Everyone has a story. I've told mine. Now go and tell yours.
Love and best wishes,
–BEVERLY DE ANGELIS

AFTERWORD

An attentive reader might wonder why Beverly chose to marry a man with a severe mental illness and virtually no substantial future while she was well settled in her career. Her behavior seems to be particularly counterintuitive given the traumatic experiences she suffered while growing up with a mother hobbled by schizophrenia.

The answer to this complex question lies in understanding the shearing nature of psychological conflict Beverly had to endure, both as a child and a grown-up. On one hand, she was searching for an ever-elusive explanation for her mother's plight. On the other, she was probing for a solution for her mother's woes.

As Beverly describes herself, she was tormented by questions such as, "Did I do anything wrong to cause Mother harm? Do I need to love her more? Does my father need to show her more love? Do my grandparents need to offer her greater affection?"

It was a subconscious desire to "undo" or "right" the painful events from her childhood that rendered Beverly attracted to Allan. "He would do better if I just loved him enough."

Sometimes, people even have fantasies of "curing" a mentally ill person with love. Beverly said she had "this childhood theory that love was magical and could cure anything." This once again is a subconscious attempt to "undo" a severe and unresolved psychological conflict emanating from one's past.

There is a myriad of lessons to be learned from this heart-wrenching story:

- The importance of early detection and treatment of a mental illness. Children with mental illness are at a greater risk because of diminished abilities to express their difficulties and sufferings. Therefore, a higher index of suspicion, on the part of both families and mental health professionals, is warranted.
- The need for utilizing a bio-psycho-social approach to treatment, whereby attention to social and family support is emphasized in addition to rational pharmacotherapy.
- The necessary involvement of family members in treatment. They are an important collaborative source of information and a resource in implementing a treatment plan.
- The need to pay attention to the emotional fallout in family members. They should be provided support, assessment and treatment as and if needed.
- The necessity for educating law enforcement agencies on mental illness.

Schizophrenia is a brain disorder in which the affected person loses touch with reality, may have problems with perception, may have beliefs which at times are overwhelmingly absent of supporting facts, and has significant difficulties in social interactions and overall day-to-day functions.

I have had both the privilege and responsibility of treating Beverly's schizophrenic son, Steven. Beverly and I worked closely together to formulate a sensible treatment plan for him. Consequently, he was placed on a long-acting injectable anti-psychotic. The treatment approach has resulted in more than a semblance of stability in Steven.

–RAKESH RANJAN, M.D., president and CEO, Charak Center for Health and Wellness, executive medical director, Charak Clinical Research Center

438

BEVERLY DE ANGELIS

Beverly De Angelis is a mental health advocate in Lake County, Ohio. She is motivated by her deep love for Steven, her schizo-phrenic son, who receives residential care and treatment from the network of service providers for the Lake County Alcohol, Drug Addiction and Mental Health Services (ADAMHS) Board. Estab-lished by Ohio statute, the ADAMHS Board is responsible for planning, funding, and evaluating Lake County's mental health and recovery services.

In 1988, she joined the Families Do Care Foundation (FDC)—a group of families with mentally ill loved ones. They organized for the express purpose of addressing the housing needs of the mentally ill, and were the pioneers of mental health advocacy in Lake County. In 1991, FDC officially changed its name to the Alliance for the Mentally Ill of Lake County, later affiliating with the National Alliance of Mental Illness (NAMI).

In 1991, Beverly represented Lake County at a national confer-ence held by NAMI in San Francisco, California. At the conference, she attended seminars that addressed the challenges of homeless-ness and explored the possibilities of fundraising.

In 1992, Beverly chaired the fundraising committee that arranged for television and movie celebrity, Patty Duke, to travel to Mentor, Ohio for a speaking engagement and luncheon. There was extensive statewide media coverage of the event, and approximately nine hundred people were in attendance.

From 1993 to 1996, she was a member of the ad hoc housing

committee that established two residential treatment facilities for the mentally disabled of Lake County.

Beverly twice served (1992–2001, 2002–2011) on the board of directors for Pathways. The primary function of the Mentor, Ohio non-profit agency, which later merged with Beacon Health, was case management. In 2010, as chair of the agency's fundraising committee, she hosted their first community walkathon, held at the Great Lakes Mall in Mentor, Ohio.

Beverly currently serves as a volunteer on the resource and development committee of Extended Housing, Inc. in Painesville, Ohio. This non-profit strives to prevent and end homelessness for individuals battling serious mental illness.

One can often hear Beverly repeat the following quote from an unknown source, saying, "Although psychiatric disorders are conditions modern psychiatry can treat, without a home or a place for recovery, the future for a person with persistent mental illness is nevertheless bleak."

THANK YOU!

Turn your face to the sun

and the shadows fall behind you.

—MAORI PROVERB

Made in the USA
Monee, IL
13 July 2020